The Consumer, Credit and Neoliberalism

> This book provides a fresh and persuasive approach to the development of Thatcherism and neo-liberalism in Britain, and in doing so illuminates a great deal about how the British economy was driven towards the crisis which unfolded after 2008.
>
> Jim Tomlinson, *Bonar Professor of Modern History, University of Dundee, UK*

This book is an investigation into the economic policy formulation and practice of neoliberalism in Britain from the 1950s through to the financial crisis and economic downturn that began in 2007–08. It demonstrates that influential economists, such as F. A. Hayek and Milton Friedman, authors at key British think tanks such as the Institute of Economic Affairs and the Centre for Policy Studies, and important political figures of the Thatcher and New Labour governments shared a similar conception of the consumer.

For neoliberals, the idea that consumers were weak in the face of businesses and large corporations was almost offensive. Instead, consumers were imagined to be sovereign agents in the economy, whose consumption decisions played a central role in the construction of their human capital and in the enabling of their aspirations. Consumption, just like production, came to be viewed as an enterprising and entrepreneurial activity. Consequently, from the early 1980s until the present day, it was felt necessary that banks should have the freedom to meet the borrowing needs of consumers. Credit rationing would be a thing of the past. Just like businesses, consumers and households could use debt to expand their stock of personal assets.

By utilizing the method of French philosopher Michel Foucault this book provides an original analysis of the policy ideas and political speeches of key figures in the New Right, in government and at the Bank of England. And it addresses the key question as to why policy-makers both in Britain and the United States did little or nothing to stem rising consumer and household indebtedness, instead always choosing to see increasing house prices and home ownership as a positive to be encouraged.

Christopher Payne is currently a senior economist at Bloomberg Government in Washington, DC, USA.

Routledge frontiers of political economy

1 **Equilibrium Versus Understanding**
Towards the rehumanization of economics within social theory
Mark Addleson

2 **Evolution, Order and Complexity**
Edited by Elias L. Khalil and Kenneth E. Boulding

3 **Interactions in Political Economy**
Malvern after ten years
Edited by Steven Pressman

4 **The End of Economics**
Michael Perelman

5 **Probability in Economics**
Omar F. Hamouda and Robin Rowley

6 **Capital Controversy, Post Keynesian Economics and the History of Economics**
Essays in honour of Geoff Harcourt, volume one
Edited by Philip Arestis, Gabriel Palma and Malcolm Sawyer

7 **Markets, Unemployment and Economic Policy**
Essays in honour of Geoff Harcourt, volume two
Edited by Philip Arestis, Gabriel Palma and Malcolm Sawyer

8 **Social Economy**
The logic of capitalist development
Clark Everling

9 **New Keynesian Economics/Post Keynesian Alternatives**
Edited by Roy J. Rotheim

10 **The Representative Agent in Macroeconomics**
James E. Hartley

11 **Borderlands of Economics**
Essays in honour of Daniel R. Fusfeld
Edited by Nahid Aslanbeigui and Young Back Choi

12 **Value, Distribution and Capital**
Essays in honour of Pierangelo Garegnani
Edited by Gary Mongiovi and Fabio Petri

13 **The Economics of Science**
Methodology and epistemology as if economics really mattered
James R. Wible

14 **Competitiveness, Localised Learning and Regional Development**
Specialisation and prosperity in small open economies
Peter Maskell, Heikki Eskelinen, Ingjaldur Hannibalsson, Anders Malmberg and Eirik Vatne

15 **Labour Market Theory**
A constructive reassessment
Ben J. Fine

16 **Women and European Employment**
Jill Rubery, Mark Smith, Colette Fagan and Damian Grimshaw

17 **Explorations in Economic Methodology**
From Lakatos to empirical philosophy of science
Roger Backhouse

18 **Subjectivity in Political Economy**
Essays on wanting and choosing
David P. Levine

19 **The Political Economy of Middle East Peace**
The impact of competing trade agendas
Edited by J. W. Wright, Jnr

20 **The Active Consumer**
Novelty and surprise in consumer choice
Edited by Marina Bianchi

21 **Subjectivism and Economic Analysis**
Essays in memory of Ludwig Lachmann
Edited by Roger Koppl and Gary Mongiovi

22 **Themes in Post-Keynesian Economics**
Essays in honour of Geoff Harcourt, volume three
Edited by Claudio Sardoni and Peter Kriesler

23 **The Dynamics of Technological Knowledge**
Cristiano Antonelli

24 **The Political Economy of Diet, Health and Food Policy**
Ben J. Fine

25 **The End of Finance**
Capital market inflation, financial derivatives and pension fund capitalism
Jan Toporowski

26 **Political Economy and the New Capitalism**
Edited by Jan Toporowski

27 **Growth Theory**
A philosophical perspective
Patricia Northover

28 **The Political Economy of the Small Firm**
Edited by Charlie Dannreuther

29 **Hahn and Economic Methodology**
Edited by Thomas Boylan and Paschal F. O'Gorman

30 **Gender, Growth and Trade**
The miracle economies of the postwar years
David Kucera

31 **Normative Political Economy**
Subjective freedom, the market and the state
David Levine

32 **Economist with a Public Purpose**
Essays in honour of John Kenneth Galbraith
Edited by Michael Keaney

33 **Involuntary Unemployment**
The elusive quest for a theory
Michel De Vroey

34 **The Fundamental Institutions of Capitalism**
Ernesto Screpanti

35 **Transcending Transaction**
The search for self-generating markets
Alan Shipman

36 **Power in Business and the State**
An historical analysis of its concentration
Frank Bealey

37 **Editing Economics**
Essays in honour of Mark Perlman
Edited by Hank Lim, Ungsuh K. Park and Geoff Harcourt

38 **Money, Macroeconomics and Keynes**
Essays in honour of Victoria Chick, volume one
Edited by Philip Arestis, Meghnad Desai and Sheila Dow

39 **Methodology, Microeconomics and Keynes**
Essays in honour of Victoria Chick, volume two
Edited by Philip Arestis, Meghnad Desai and Sheila Dow

40 **Market Drive and Governance**
Reexamining the rules for economic and commercial contest
Ralf Boscheck

41 **The Value of Marx**
Political economy for contemporary capitalism
Alfredo Saad-Filho

42 **Issues in Positive Political Economy**
S. Mansoob Murshed

43 **The Enigma of Globalisation**
A journey to a new stage of capitalism
Robert Went

44 **The Market**
Equilibrium, stability, mythology
S. N. Afriat

45 **The Political Economy of Rule Evasion and Policy Reform**
Jim Leitzel

46 **Unpaid Work and the Economy**
Edited by Antonella Picchio

47 **Distributional Justice**
Theory and measurement
Hilde Bojer

48 **Cognitive Developments in Economics**
Edited by Salvatore Rizzello

49 **Social Foundations of Markets, Money and Credit**
Costas Lapavitsas

50 **Rethinking Capitalist Development**
Essays on the economics of Josef Steindl
Edited by Tracy Mott and Nina Shapiro

51 **An Evolutionary Approach to Social Welfare**
Christian Sartorius

52 **Kalecki's Economics Today**
Edited by Zdzislaw L. Sadowski and Adam Szeworski

53 **Fiscal Policy from Reagan to Blair**
The left veers right
Ravi K. Roy and Arthur T. Denzau

54 **The Cognitive Mechanics of Economic Development and Institutional Change**
Bertin Martens

55 **Individualism and the Social Order**
The social element in liberal thought
Charles R. McCann Jnr

56 **Affirmative Action in the United States and India**
A comparative perspective
Thomas E. Weisskopf

57 **Global Political Economy and the Wealth of Nations**
Performance, institutions, problems and policies
Edited by Phillip Anthony O'Hara

58 **Structural Economics**
Thijs ten Raa

59 **Macroeconomic Theory and Economic Policy**
Essays in honour of Jean-Paul Fitoussi
Edited by K. Vela Velupillai

60 **The Struggle over Work**
The "end of work" and employment alternatives in post-industrial societies
Shaun Wilson

61 **The Political Economy of Global Sporting Organisations**
John Forster and Nigel Pope

62 **The Flawed Foundations of General Equilibrium Theory**
Critical essays on economic theory
Frank Ackerman and Alejandro Nadal

63 **Uncertainty in Economic Theory**
Essays in honor of David Schmeidler's 65th birthday
Edited by Itzhak Gilboa

64 **The New Institutional Economics of Corruption**
Edited by Johann Graf Lambsdorff, Markus Taube and Matthias Schramm

65 **The Price Index and its Extension**
A chapter in economic measurement
S. N. Afriat

66 **Reduction, Rationality and Game Theory in Marxian Economics**
Bruce Philp

67 Culture and Politics in Economic Development
Volker Bornschier

68 Modern Applications of Austrian Thought
Edited by Jürgen G. Backhaus

69 Ordinary Choices
Individuals, incommensurability, and democracy
Robert Urquhart

70 Labour Theory of Value
Peter C. Dooley

71 Capitalism
Victor D. Lippit

72 Macroeconomic Foundations of Macroeconomics
Alvaro Cencini

73 Marx for the 21st Century
Edited by Hiroshi Uchida

74 Growth and Development in the Global Political Economy
Social structures of accumulation and modes of regulation
Phillip Anthony O'Hara

75 The New Economy and Macroeconomic Stability
A neo-modern perspective drawing on the complexity approach and Keynesian economics
Teodoro Dario Togati

76 The Future of Social Security Policy
Women, work and a citizen's basic income
Ailsa McKay

77 Clinton and Blair
The political economy of the third way
Flavio Romano

78 Marxian Reproduction Schema
Money and aggregate demand in a capitalist economy
A. B. Trigg

79 The Core Theory in Economics
Problems and solutions
Lester G. Telser

80 Economics, Ethics and the Market
Introduction and applications
Johan J. Graafland

81 Social Costs and Public Action in Modern Capitalism
Essays inspired by Karl William Kapp's theory of social costs
Edited by Wolfram Elsner, Pietro Frigato and Paolo Ramazzotti

82 Globalization and the Myths of Free Trade
History, theory and empirical evidence
Edited by Anwar Shaikh

83 Equilibrium in Economics
Scope and limits
Edited by Valeria Mosini

84 Globalization
State of the art and perspectives
Edited by Stefan A. Schirm

85 Neoliberalism
National and regional experiments with global ideas
Edited by Ravi K. Roy, Arthur T. Denzau and Thomas D. Willett

86 **Post-Keynesian Macroeconomics**
Essays in honour of Ingrid Rima
Edited by Mathew Forstater, Gary Mongiovi and Steven Pressman

87 **Consumer Capitalism**
Anastasios S. Korkotsides

88 **Remapping Gender in the New Global Order**
Edited by Marjorie Griffin Cohen and Janine Brodie

89 **Hayek and Natural Law**
Eric Angner

90 **Race and Economic Opportunity in the Twenty-First Century**
Edited by Marlene Kim

91 **Renaissance in Behavioural Economics**
Harvey Leibenstein's impact on contemporary economic analysis
Edited by Roger Frantz

92 **Human Ecology Economics**
A new framework for global sustainability
Edited by Roy E. Allen

93 **Imagining Economics Otherwise**
Encounters with identity/difference
Nitasha Kaul

94 **Reigniting the Labor Movement**
Restoring means to ends in a democratic labor movement
Gerald Friedman

95 **The Spatial Model of Politics**
Norman Schofield

96 **The Economics of American Judaism**
Carmel Ullman Chiswick

97 **Critical Political Economy**
Christian Arnsperger

98 **Culture and Economic Explanation**
Economics in the US and Japan
Donald W. Katzner

99 **Feminism, Economics and Utopia**
Time travelling through paradigms
Karin Schönpflug

100 **Risk in International Finance**
Vikash Yadav

101 **Economic Policy and Performance in Industrial Democracies**
Party governments, central banks and the fiscal–monetary policy mix
Takayuki Sakamoto

102 **Advances on Income Inequality and Concentration Measures**
Edited by Gianni Betti and Achille Lemmi

103 **Economic Representations**
Academic and everyday
Edited by David F. Ruccio

104 **Mathematical Economics and the Dynamics of Capitalism**
Goodwin's legacy continued
Edited by Peter Flaschel and Michael Landesmann

105 **The Keynesian Multiplier**
Edited by Claude Gnos and Louis-Philippe Rochon

106 **Money, Enterprise and Income Distribution**
Towards a macroeconomic theory of capitalism
John Smithin

107 **Fiscal Decentralization and Local Public Finance in Japan**
Nobuki Mochida

108 **The 'Uncertain' Foundations of Post-Keynesian Economics**
Essays in exploration
Stephen P. Dunn

109 **Karl Marx's *Grundrisse***
Foundations of the critique of political economy 150 years later
Edited by Marcello Musto

110 **Economics and the Price Index**
S. N. Afriat and Carlo Milana

111 **Sublime Economy**
On the intersection of art and economics
Edited by Jack Amariglio, Joseph W. Childers and Stephen E. Cullenberg

112 **Popper, Hayek and the Open Society**
Calvin Hayes

113 **The Political Economy of Work**
David Spencer

114 **Institutional Economics**
Bernard Chavance

115 **Religion, Economics and Demography**
The effects of religion on education, work, and the family
Evelyn L. Lehrer

116 **Economics, Rational Choice and Normative Philosophy**
Edited by Thomas A. Boylan and Ruvin Gekker

117 **Economics Versus Human Rights**
Manuel Couret Branco

118 **Hayek Versus Marx and Today's Challenges**
Eric Aarons

119 **Work Time Regulation as Sustainable Full Employment Policy**
Robert LaJeunesse

120 **Equilibrium, Welfare and Uncertainty**
Mukul Majumdar

121 **Capitalism, Institutions and Economic Development**
Michael Heller

122 **Economic Pluralism**
Robert Garnett, Erik Olsen and Martha Starr

123 **Dialectics of Class Struggle in the Global Economy**
Clark Everling

124 **Political Economy and Globalization**
Richard Westra

125 **Full-Spectrum Economics**
Toward an inclusive and emancipatory social science
Christian Arnsperger

126 **Computable, Constructive and Behavioural Economic Dynamics**
Essays in honour of Kumaraswamy (Vela) Velupillai
Stefano Zambelli

127 **Monetary Macrodynamics**
Toichiro Asada, Carl Chiarella, Peter Flaschel and Reiner Franke

128 **Rationality and Explanation in Economics**
Maurice Lagueux

129 **The Market, Happiness, and Solidarity**
A Christian perspective
Johan J. Graafland

130 **Economic Complexity and Equilibrium Illusion**
Essays on market instability and macro vitality
Ping Chen

131 **Economic Theory and Social Change**
Problems and revisions
Hasse Ekstedt and Angelo Fusari

132 **The Practices of Happiness**
Political economy, religion and wellbeing
Edited by John Atherton, Elaine Graham and Ian Steedman

133 **The Measurement of Individual Well-Being and Group Inequalities**
Essays in memory of Z. M. Berrebi
Edited by Joseph Deutsch and Jacques Silber

134 **Wage Policy, Income Distribution, and Democratic Theory**
Oren M. Levin-Waldman

135 **The Political Economy of Bureaucracy**
Steven O. Richardson

136 **The Moral Rhetoric of Political Economy**
Justice and modern economic thought
Paul Turpin

137 **Macroeconomic Regimes in Western Industrial Countries**
Hansjörg Herr and Milka Kazandziska

138 **The Political Economy of the Environment**
Edited by Simon Dietz, Jonathan Michie and Christine Oughton

139 **Business Ethics and the Austrian Tradition in Economics**
Hardy Bouillon

140 **Inequality and Power**
The economics of class
Eric A. Schutz

141 Capital as a Social Kind
Definitions and transformations in the critique of political economy
Howard Engelskirchen

142 Happiness, Ethics and Economics
Johannes Hirata

143 Capital, Exploitation and Economic Crisis
John Weeks

144 The Global Economic Crisis
New perspectives on the critique of economic theory and policy
Edited by Emiliano Brancaccio and Giuseppe Fontana

145 Economics and Diversity
Carlo D'Ippoliti

146 Political Economy of Human Rights
Rights, realities and realization
Bas de Gaay Fortman

146 Robinson Crusoe's Economic Man
A construction and deconstruction
Edited by Ulla Grapard and Gillian Hewitson

147 Freedom and Happiness in Economic Thought and Philosophy
From clash to reconciliation
Edited by Ragip Ege and Herrade Igersheim

148 Political Economy After Economics
David Laibman

149 Reconstructing Keynesian Macroeconomics Volume 1
Partial perspectives
Carl Chiarella, Peter Flaschel and Willi Semmler

150 Institutional Economics and National Competitiveness
Edited by Young Back Choi

151 Capitalist Diversity and Diversity within Capitalism
Edited by Geoffrey T. Wood and Christel Lane

152 The Consumer, Credit and Neoliberalism
Governing the modern economy
Christopher Payne

The Consumer, Credit and Neoliberalism

Governing the modern economy

Christopher Payne

Routledge
Taylor & Francis Group
LONDON AND NEW YORK

First published 2012
by Routledge
2 Park Square, Milton Park, Abingdon, Oxon OX14 4RN

Simultaneously published in the USA and Canada
by Routledge
711 Third Avenue, New York, NY 10017

Routledge is an imprint of the Taylor & Francis Group, an informa business

British Library Cataloguing in Publication Data
A catalogue record for this book is available from the British Library

Library of Congress Cataloging in Publication Data
Payne, Christopher.
The consumer, credit and neoliberalism: governing the modern economy/by Christopher Payne.
p. cm. – (Routledge frontiers of political economy; 152)
Includes bibliographical references and index.
1. Great Britain–Economic policy–1997– 2. Great Britain–Economic conditions–1997– 3. Neoliberalism–Great Britain. I. Title.
HC256.7.P39 2012
330.941–dc23

2011028142

ISBN: 978-0-415-68011-0 (hbk)
ISBN: 978-0-203-13906-6 (ebk)

Typeset in Times
by Wearset Ltd, Boldon, Tyne and Wear

MIX
Paper from responsible sources
FSC® C004839
FSC www.fsc.org

Printed and bound in Great Britain by
TJI Digital, Padstow, Cornwall

To Nadia and my parents, Ian and Pauline,
with love and gratitude

Contents

Figures and table

Figures

Table

Preface and acknowledgements

Like most people who grew up in the 1980s, I inherited a fairly basic historical picture of Britain and the world after 1945. In this narrative, after thirty years of Keynesianism and the experience of high inflation and high unemployment in the 1970s, there had been a return to free market ideas and values in the 1980s under Margaret Thatcher in the UK and Ronald Reagan in the US. But while working in the financial district of London in the 1990s and early 2000s, I saw that there was a more complex narrative to tell.

One such incident struck me as particularly noteworthy. In the midst of the Asian crisis in August 1998 the central bank of Hong Kong bought over 7 per cent of the stock market in a last-ditch stand against speculators. For some of my colleagues at the time this intervention in markets represented the end of capitalism. But clearly no such thing occurred, in fact, this government action marked a turning point in the crisis. It was another example of the interventionist and active role that monetary authorities and government were taking in monitoring, preserving and maintaining a competitive market order. It was, for instance, similar in motivation to the emergency interest rate cuts enacted by many central banks around the world after stock markets crashed in October 1987.

It seemed as if governments viewed orderly and rising stock markets and other markets, such as residential property, as a barometer of confidence and a sign of a functioning market order. No one seemed to worry particularly about the extent to which markets were rising, certainly not enough to do anything about it. But rapidly falling stock markets and house prices was a different matter; so long as inflation was within acceptable bounds, cutting interests rates was, in appropriate circumstances, regarded as the right and necessary response. And certainly no government in the UK or US acted to slow the accumulation of debt by consumers who were borrowing to buy houses and other goods and services. Consumers, so it seemed, could do no wrong and banks were given the freedom to increase their mortgage and consumer lending.

These kinds of market interventions did not appear to conform to the image of laissez-faire and the free market taught in the classroom. But neither was this old-fashioned Keynesianism. Back before Thatcherism and Reaganomics, government intervention in the economy had revolved around direct attempts, some successful, some not, to put people to work. Economic policy had definitely not been about encouraging individuals to actively participate in the housing, stock or any other markets. Apart from anything else, in the post-Keynesian era, notwithstanding their interventions, central bankers continued to be avid supporters of free markets in their own country and around the world. Hong Kong, for instance, remained committed to a monetary system, the currency board, which acted like the gold standard of the nineteenth century, only replacing gold with US dollars. And Alan Greenspan, the Chairman of the US Federal Reserve from 1987 to 2006, had made his sympathies with libertarianism clear. He was a keen reader of the American libertarian author Ayn Rand and the Austrian school economist Ludwig von Mises.

This book represents my attempt to understand and explain what happened to economic policy, as neoliberalism replaced the Keynesian and progressive liberal consensus. Essentially it began as a challenge: to take seriously the idea that government and policy-makers were both proponents of free markets and yet also believed strongly in the need for government action to maintain market order and, if need be, to control markets as they fell. In this regard, neoliberal economic policies have to be understood as something different in nature both from Keynesianism and classical laissez-faire.

It became clear that the history of neoliberalism was both long and complicated and revolved around the way policy-makers have come to view human behaviour and conduct, especially in relation to the consumer. Much of my research was conducted as part of my doctoral studies at the London School of Economics, having returned to academia after ten years of working in financial services. It was here that I re-read the work of Michel Foucault and some of his 'Foucauldian' followers. Foucault (before his death in 1984) and governmentality scholars since had long been thinking about neoliberalism in connection to the way the economy is governed. I was able to utilize many of these insights in writing this historical account of neoliberalism in the British context.

My research has led me to thinking about one of the most pressing questions of recent economic history: why nothing was done in Britain (and for that matter the United States) to address the problem of rising consumer and household indebtedness; and why concurrently, rising house prices were invariably taken as a sign of economic health. Not only is so much economic history replete with examples of booms and busts in property and other asset markets, but, contrary to conventional wisdom, there were no shortage of people in the early 2000s warning of the dangers to come and predicting, with some accuracy, the approaching crisis. Perhaps ironically, much concern could be heard from analysts working in the financial markets, including the most famous of them all, Warren Buffett, fretting over ever-widening global trade imbalances, derivatives markets that, in size, dwarfed the economy of the United States, and booming asset markets, including residential property. It is simply not true to say that no one saw the crisis and ensuing 'Great Recession' coming. While I was working in the financial district of London, I was exposed to the arguments of those that did.

The approach taken in this book is intended to offer a new perspective on recent economic events and broader concepts, such as Thatcherism and neoliberalism, as they manifested themselves in the politics of the consumer. It applies a Foucauldian method to link recent economic problems to a much longer trend in economic thinking and policy-making. During my doctoral studies it became clear that there was little in history that had not been researched before. What was important was to ask different questions.

There are many people whom I would like to thank for their help and insights. For their help and for the use of their archives, I would like to thank the librarians at the London School of Economics and at the Conservative Party Archive at the Bodleian Library in Oxford. For allowing me access both to use its archive and to quote material from it in this book, I would like to thank the Conservative Party. A thank you must also go to the team at Routledge for giving me the opportunity to publish this book and for answering all my queries so patiently.

I would also like to thank, for all their ideas and input, members of the economic history and sociology departments at the London School of Economics. In particular, I would like to thank Fran Tonkiss and Nigel Dodd for all their thoughts, comments and help over the past few years. I would also like to thank Peter Miller, Graham Thompson, Robin Archer, Nik Rose, Claire Alexander and Paddy Rawlinson for their hugely constructive criticisms of my work-in-progress.

I would like to thank Mary Morgan for allowing me to adopt her as a mentor and for the considerable friendliness she has shown me, and for the help and guidance she has given me. It was because of Mary that I was able to spend a hugely enjoyable year at Duke University in North Carolina as a research fellow in the Center for the History of Political Economy. I would like to thank everyone, fellows and permanent staff alike in the Center at Duke for their advice, support and encouragement. In particular, I would like to thank Bruce Caldwell and Kevin Hoover for the many hours spent discussing my work.

I would also like to thank my friends and family for all of the support they have given me, listening patiently to my ideas as they developed bit by bit. In particular, I would like to thank my brother Richard, Tim Dickson, Omar Negyal, Bruce Bell, Adrian Brettle, Alun Jones, Dan and Elise Holland, Hanan Kkoloussey, Peter Rickett, Kyle and Maggie Smith, Edward Griffin, Charles Brock, Marvin Mohn, Alistair Veitch, Helen Kim, Rachel Lifter, Russell and Imogen Brooks, John and Joanna Nevin and Ian Andrews for the many hours of discussion, helping me make sense of it all. And of course my parents, Ian and Pauline, who have been phenomenally supportive, far beyond the call of duty. Their ongoing help and exemplary editing skills have made all the difference. Finally, my wife Nadia, whose patience and encouragement knows no limits. I do not know how I would have got through all the ups and downs without her.

Christopher Payne,
Washington, DC, May 2011

1 Introduction

Neoliberalism and governmentality

Every human being is a consumer.

Keith Joseph, 1978[1]

With the onset of a global financial crisis in 2007 and the return of depressions and mass unemployment across the industrialized and rich nations of the world, questions are being raised about the state of economics and about the way economies are governed. In economic crises of the past twenty-five years, in East Asia, Russia and Latin America, criticism has been focused on the dogmatism of international economic advisory bodies such as the International Monetary Fund, which have espoused a 'Washington Consensus' of market-based rules for economic policy.[2] However, this time round, perhaps because of the scale of the economic crisis, or perhaps because the epicentre of the crisis has been in countries such as the United States and Great Britain, a far deeper questioning is under way. Rather than focusing on specifics, on particular countries, governments, policies or international agencies, much criticism is being set at a level that attempts to encompass the totality of economic theorizing and governance. One catch-all term for such a discussion is 'neoliberalism'.

What does this term mean or designate? Perhaps all that is meant when using it is the free market or laissez-faire. In this line of thinking, as with the Great Depression of the 1930s, unfettered capitalism is shown to be intrinsically unstable. Neoliberalism turns out to be no more than a return to the doctrines of the nineteenth century, a new-found liberalism, reimplemented in Britain, for instance, from 1979 by the Conservative Party led by Margaret Thatcher. However this kind of argument seems to fly in the face of so much academic wisdom: the tools of economic policy-making are meant to be that much more sophisticated now than they were in the nineteenth century, and the source of so much instability, the gold standard, was consigned to history in Britain in 1931. It certainly appears as if the excesses of laissez-faire, particularly with regards to the banking sector, caused the crisis, but the dramatic expansion of credit so often central to economic cycles of boom and bust in the past was not led by corporations and businesses; it would be difficult to say that there has been too much business investment with too little consumer demand. On the contrary, it has been consumers in countries such as Britain and the United States who have been doing much of the borrowing and much of the spending that has supported economic growth in recent years. When Thatcher made her damning quip in 1975 that 'never in the history of mankind has so much been owed',[3] household debt was under 40 per cent of household income. As of the end of 2007, the same ratio stood at 160 per cent. And whereas consumer credit (overdrafts, credit cards and unsecured loans) represented 4.8 per cent of disposable household income in 1979, by 2007 this ratio had risen to over 26 per cent.[4]

While neoliberalism does represent the return of the free market, at the same time it should be recognized that its return coincided with a radical transformation of the British economy, far distant from the manufacturing powerhouse of the nineteenth century beheld by classical liberalism. As recently as the end of 1979, 49 per cent of employment in Britain was in production (raw materials and utilities) and manufacturing industries. By the end of 2005, employment in these sectors had fallen to 22 per cent of the workforce.[5] In other words, much of the British economy is now geared directly towards servicing the consumer as opposed to manufacturing consumer or capital goods. So even while the social theorists of late modernity, post-industrialism and consumerism[6] have failed to comment on the rise of consumer and household debt, their arguments do suggest that, at the very least, neoliberalism, as a set of political and economic ideas, has had to recognize a world very different from the one confronted by their classical liberal forebears. To this extent alone one could surmise that neoliberals have had to utilize language that recognizes that the contemporary economy is very different from that operating prior to the First World War.

The starting point for this book is the contention that there is a connection between the way the British economy has been governed since 1979, practising a neoliberal governing mentality, and the increased role of services, the consumer, and consumer and household credit in the economy. Put another way, the difference between neoliberalism and classical liberalism is not related to the question of free markets per se but to the question of how the population of consumers is expected, and incentivized, to exercise their market freedoms. While this book does not argue that neoliberal governments have 'created' the modern consumer identity,[7] it does represent an investigation into the way neoliberal thinkers have conceptualized the consumer, how neoliberal governments have sought to foster and elicit a consumer mentality and, at the same time, ensure that the banking system is able to respond to the borrowing needs of consumers.

The question that this book sets out to answer is: 'how did an imagined figure of the consumer, with raised levels of indebtedness, come to be identified as central to the government of the modern economy?' The question reflects the argument that the neoliberal programme of government is linked to a specific understanding and practice in government of what consumption activities represent, very much differentiated from a meaning incorporated in both classical liberal and Keynesian techniques for governing the economy. Thus neoliberalism is not to be distinguished from classical liberalism by its belief in free markets, but instead by the kinds of human agency that are incorporated into economic knowledge and techniques used for governing the economy.

This book examines how the figure of the consumer has been referenced by a particular brand of economics, within key British neoliberal think tanks, the Institute of Economic Affairs (IEA) and the Centre for Policy Studies (CPS), as well as by the politicians and practitioners of economic and especially monetary policy. A notion of the sovereign consumer was activated in arguments that responded to certain microeconomic problems that were perceived in the British economy in the late 1950s and 1960s. Later, during the 1970s, a grouping that became known as the New Right[8] undertook a full-scale genealogical project in which every aspect of Keynesian economic policy was problematized in order to explain the economic problems with which Britain was beset at the time. The consumer as imagined in neoliberal discourse became the key reference point against which to measure and gauge the health of British society. Bringing into question the human agents and the forms of knowledge represented by Keynesian progressive liberalism, with its specific articulation of 'society', 'economic security' and 'the state' laid the basis for a new political rationality; one that always took it for granted that it was necessary to govern for the consumer.

1.1 Neoliberalism and the consumer

Rather than seeking to define neoliberalism, the concern here is with its governing practices; that is, how neoliberals in Britain have addressed the problem of how to govern a modern economy. Defining neoliberalism itself turns out to be an inherently problematic endeavour, as evidenced by the fact that philosopher and historian of economics Philip Mirowski provided, in an essay entitled *Defining Neoliberalism* (2009), ten different definitional propositions.[9] No doubt putting together such a list is entirely appropriate; after all why should there be one single definition that captures all the multifarious and complex ways that government acts in the economy and society? Indeed, apart from anything else, neoliberalism has always been an intellectual project, a way in which political theorists, philosophers and economists have sought to think about the problems of modernity, of freedom and of progress, economic or otherwise. It is unlikely that a major movement in twentieth century political and economic philosophy can be reduced to a single definition.

At the very least, one needs to take neoliberal intellectual endeavours seriously rather than assuming that they are nothing more than the representations of a resurgent elite capitalist class. There is little to be gained from starting an analysis of neoliberalism within a framework in which an outcome of neoliberalism, increased economic inequality, is taken to be both its cause and explanation. In this style of analysis, best typified by David Harvey,[10] class differentiation becomes both the beginning and end of the story; and little or no time is dedicated to discussing intellectual ideas. There is, for instance, little discussion in Harvey's work on the ideas of, among others, Friedrich Hayek or Milton Friedman.

Mirowski is undoubtedly right then to focus our attention on the very serious economic theorizing undertaken by neoliberals; and to this end has highlighted what he believes to be some of the key neoliberal propositions: that businesses competing in the marketplace for customers can do little that is wrong; that political and economic inequality is entirely acceptable; that capital, not necessarily labour, should flow freely; that politics is treated as a market which, if incorrectly structured, becomes nothing more than a beauty parade of promises in an upcoming election; that the state has to be strong even if its balance sheet is shrunk; and that the fundamental experience of freedom is to be located in the choice-making practices of autonomous self-governing individuals. Nonetheless, reading Mirowski's essay one is still left with the impression that neoliberalism sets out to practise a kind of deception on its subjects. Neoliberalism, we are told, advances the plan and operation of a 'technology of persuasion' in which there is a class of all-knowing intellectuals telling everyone else that knowledge is always partial and to be discovered during the market process. The truth of neoliberalism, we are asked to believe, rests upon a contradiction in which the few reserve the right to designate appropriate forms of social and economic organization, while the majority accept 'degraded' truths and a partial freedom.[11]

Discussions of neoliberalism often highlight irreconcilable contradictions, between say, the neoliberal requirement for strong government and its inherent distrust of the state; or between the need to construct a viable market order and the naturalist metaphors through which the market is so often thought about; or between the idea that free markets promote democracy and the reality that free market regimes have, in some cases, been instituted only after undemocratic transfers of power. Given such apparent contradictions, it is not surprising that attempts to define neoliberalism have often fallen back on the idea that there must be some kind of greater historical truth explaining it all, such as class exploitation.

To avoid such an analysis, therefore, requires being very careful about what kinds of questions are being asked. For instance, to discuss the nature of neoliberalism as a history of ideas might be to put too much emphasis on its creation by 'great minds', as if neoliberalism is a conspiracy of a few elites, unconnected with the real, material world. Likewise, if we consider neo or classical liberalism as a set of philosophical and normative reflections upon rule, or as a set of reflections on how to legislate for freedom, then liberalism will often appear to be self-contradictory. After all, there will always be disagreements both about what acts constitute coercion, and the extent to which government intervention aimed at limiting this coercion itself constitutes coercion.

On the one hand, philosophers and political economists following in the footsteps of Karl Marx see the supposed contradictions of modern day capitalism as evidence for an alternative reality underneath. The falsity of the surface is explained by the 'truth' of class warfare. On the other hand, when reading from within the liberal tradition one is often left with the impression that government is primarily concerned with solving philosophical conundrums about how to minimize aggregate levels of coercion within society. In turn, the history of political ideas often becomes an exercise in tracing how the ideas of 'great men' spread and were ultimately taken up by political figures and enacted in government.

This book proceeds from a different starting point: liberalism in whatever guise – classical, progressive or 'neo' – is considered to be a political rationality, rather more focused, for instance, on providing security, whether economic or territorial for the population, than on philosophical questions about what constitutes excess coercion. Rather than searching for the truth underlying neoliberalism, to understand neoliberalism is really to understand that (neo)-liberal governments have never lost the will to govern. One therefore needs to explore the question that government asks: how to govern? More specifically, how did neoliberalism pose and answer the question of how to govern the economy, both as it problematized progressive liberalism and Keynesianism from outside government and how, once in power, it actually practised governing the economy. This book is thus an analysis of governmentality, a term that originates with Michel Foucault, intended to immediately signify that government has a will to govern, a will that practises certain kinds of 'positive' knowledge, that seeks to operate in the world for certain purposes and has never sought to make itself inactive: liberalism, it goes without saying, has never been the same as anarchy.

The term 'governmentality' implies both 'government' and 'mentality'. Government is always taken to signify a form of rule in which governors aim in a calculated and rational way to conduct or regulate the conduct of those who are governed. Government aims to shape, with some degree of deliberation, aspects of behaviour according to a set of norms and for a variety of ends. The latter aspect of the term 'mentality' emphasizes the way in which thought involved in the practice of government is collective and taken for granted.[12] One could thus go as far as to say that this method represents a sociology of government that focuses on a collective way of thinking about the world. And as with any sociological study, empirical work is focused on practice, in this case what kinds of notions of human agency are to be found both in the discursive practice of think tanks as well as in government activity itself. As such there is no narrative about how ideas filter from the academic to think tank and then legislator. Yes, certain figures become emblematic of a particular political movement; certain writings are taken to encapsulate a mentality particularly effectively. However what makes a governing mentality is precisely that each part of the collective holds in mind a set of forms and objects (for example what is society and who represents economic man) that are taken for granted and that are utilized and referenced in theory and policy.

More generally, in this perspective, government is taken to involve the conduct of conduct; that is governors pose themselves to the problem of regulating and possibly changing the behaviour of the governed. This duty of government, this will to govern has, according to Foucault, been shared by governments since at least the mid-sixteenth century.[13] In the process of governing, however, the will to govern requires governors to utilize knowledge (*connaissance*), such as natural history, the analysis of wealth, political economy, sociology, psychology and life sciences to understand the 'true nature' of those that they are governing. But forms of knowledge change, 'positivities', to use Foucault's term, shift and alter, changing the way that human behaviour is understood. Thus while, in the broadest possible sense, the role of government remains the same, that is the regulation of conduct, what government chooses to identify as the appropriate and correct conduct for their legislative programmes changes.

This means that the study of governmentality is effectively an archaeology of political knowledge, the point of such an investigation being, as Foucault suggested in *The Archaeology of Knowledge* (1969), to show how a certain form of political behaviour is

> Shot through with a particular, describable discursive practice ... this positivity would determine the element in politics that can become an object of enunciation, the forms that this enunciation may take, the concepts that are employed in it, and the strategic choices that are made in it.[14]

An archaeology of political knowledge, in this case neoliberalism, does not therefore focus on what moment this revolutionary consciousness appears, the insight, if you like, that brings a new political *savoir* into existence. Neither does it require a biography of the 'revolutionary man', say of Hayek or of Friedman. Instead, the point is to try and explain how a discursive practice and a body of revolutionary knowledge is expressed in political thought, behaviour and strategies, that is to say in discursive or actual practice.[15] This book does not represent the search for the ultimate 'origin' of the politics of the consumer in one single mind or in a small group of thinkers.

Instead this book aims to demonstrate how an imagined figure of the consumer was utilized by a political rationality, neoliberalism, both to problematize Keynesian techniques for governing the economy and as the basis for a new governmental programme. To write about neoliberalism in this fashion, therefore, is to try and bring to the reader's attention the nature of the consumer as he or she appears in the neoliberal governing mentality, in pamphlets, speeches or political acts; precisely because those practising neoliberalism reference the consumer as a 'natural' state of being that does not need to be questioned. The consumer is constantly identified without the authors ever fully questioning the complex sense of being and subjectivity they are ascribing to this figure.

However, it is essential to point out that in talking about governing for the consumer it is being suggested that this reference point, the consumer, is a distinct and unique object in history. Indeed, that economies are seen to be composed of consumers is now so taken for granted that those in government do not even have to be aware of the exceptional historically contingent nature of this object they call 'the consumer'. Here, it is being argued that the consumer, as practised by neoliberals, is an object of rarefaction, and not at all 'natural'.[16] While the consumer is most certainly a real object for neoliberal government, there was no similar object for classical liberals or progressive liberals. The latter for instance, in the early twentieth century, understood the consumer to be a citizen with entitlements to certain living standards, encapsulated in the concept of the 'living wage'.

Thus as history moves by way of disjuncture and discontinuity from one assemblage of governmental practices to another, fundamental reference points alter and, as with the consumer, come into existence. This is precisely why political programmes always seem to be talking beyond each other and never to each other. Political opponents so often fail to effectively communicate with one another because they are referencing entirely different objects of knowledge in their discussion. Neither is the neoliberal consumer an ideological reification, there is no 'great interpretative postulate' of history being posited here; the consumer is no mystification of class relations: it is what it is, it is entirely real for those that practise it in their discourse and yet it is at the same time entirely historical. The consumer is part of neoliberal discourse; in turn discourses should be understood as 'limited practical domains which have their boundaries, their rules of formation and their conditions of existence: the historical base of discourse is not some other, more profound discourse, at once identical and different.'[17]

This is not to say that nineteenth century classical liberals ignored consumption. But in the theory of political economy what counted as productive was human labour congealed into something physical, essentially food or manufactured goods. For John Stuart Mill consumption used up resources; consumer credit was essentially profligate, wasting even more resources. Mill therefore believed that political economy had nothing whatsoever to do with consumption. Consumption never needed encouragement; what mattered from a legislative perspective was that there should be no obstacle to producing for those who wanted to produce. Government certainly had no role in incentivizing consumption. If someone wanted to consume more; what mattered was that they would be free to produce something that could be exchanged for the good they desired to consume.[18] While later economic thought has not displaced the idea that one should work harder in order to earn more, in order to consume more, it has been supplemented by a new idea, totally anathema to classical political economy: the idea that consumption can be productive, can add to human capital, and be an investment in the self.

That said, the question arises, was not John Maynard Keynes responsible for the integration of consumption into macroeconomic policy, that is to say, for economic policies that aim to increase consumer demand? In this regard, it is critical to note that Keynes' theory was itself not a theory of underconsumption but one of underinvestment. Consumption was part of aggregate expenditure but it was capital investment, often financed by newly created credit-money, which was seen to provide economic growth. Keynes was no classical liberal but, as will be discussed in Chapter 2, neither did he practise the figure of the consumer that has become central to government in a post-Keynesian world. Keynes' thought was part of an assemblage of governmental techniques that, opposed to classical liberalism, required state intervention in production. But just as with classical liberalism, governing the economy meant governing for production.

Here one can find continuity between classical liberalism and the kind of progressive liberalism practised by Keynes, a continuity found in the emphasis placed on production. Yet, for progressive liberals, governing for production implied far more direct government intervention in the economy than would ever have been countenanced by classical liberals. Even so, classical laissez-faire never meant the absence of government, but instead governing for the freedom of the producer. Market freedom meant, first and foremost, the freedom to produce. In turn, the market process, if governed properly (for instance in a gold standard monetary regime) would result in 'natural' prices: values in exchange that were commensurate with their costs of production.

The market was, to use Foucault's term, a 'regime of veridiction', a site that verified that government was doing its job properly. In turn, producing truth in exchange required government to enact a multitude of limitations and controls, coercion and obligations that could often rely on threats. In Victorian Britain these took a variety of forms, from campaigns that extolled the virtues of thrift, to moral campaigns against vice and the general degeneration of individuals and families. And while Bentham's Panopticon ensured that the behaviour of 'deviants' could be corrected, the application of similarly disciplinary techniques in schools and factories meant that the conduct of individuals could be addressed to increasing profitability and productivity. 'Control was the mainspring of freedom',[19] and classical liberalism's regulation of conduct could imply a very brutal yet intrinsically 'liberal' experience.

From the governmentality perspective classical liberalism was never about freedom per se but about using free action within the market to constitute a standard of truth, the natural price. According to Foucault, liberal governmental practice

> is a consumer of freedom as it can only function insofar as a number of freedoms actually exist: freedom of the market, freedom to buy and sell. [Thus] ... it consumes freedom, which means that it must produce ... [freedom] ... [and] ... it must organize ... [freedom] ... The formula of liberalism is not 'be free' ... [an] ... immediate contradiction.... Liberalism formulates simply the following: I am going to produce what you need to be free. I am going to see to it that you are free to be free.[20]

Classical liberalism governed by taking for granted the figure of the entrepreneur, a man of abstinence and prudence, foregoing consumption for the sake of his investments. What needed to be produced for entrepreneurial freedom was the possibility of maximum productivity. As Karl Polanyi's *The Great Transformation* (1944)[21] explained, English society in the nineteenth century was reordered and restructured so that markets in land, labour and money could function unhindered; entrepreneurs would be able to produce and markets would create truthful values. Of these three markets, Polanyi's genealogy of catastrophe (depression in the 1930s followed by the Second World War) placed special emphasis on the classical liberal monetary system, that is to say a gold-backed currency for consumption purposes combined with a complex system of credit-money and bills of exchange for entrepreneurs. For Polanyi, the need to maintain the gold standard turned out to be a huge destabilizing force in the first half of the twentieth century. And while Joseph Schumpeter's narrative in *Capitalism, Socialism and Democracy* (1943) is very different, he defined capitalism as a special case of commercial society in which banks create deposits for the purposes of entrepreneurial enterprise and production.[22] In the era of classical liberalism, enterprise and economic advancement was always seen as a function of production, and government was there to create the appropriate conditions for entrepreneurs. As such the monetary and banking system was geared towards meeting the credit needs of entrepreneurs so that they could produce.

This is important for, as this book argues, in the second half of the twentieth century neoliberals came to view consumption as an enterprising and entrepreneurial practice in its own right. As a result, it was thought essential that credit also be liberally available to fund consumption practices that were deemed as productive of human capital. This in turn required a different monetary regime from those that operated in the classical and progressive liberal eras. In this new monetary system, the borrowing needs of consumers could invariably be met, in turn fostering and eliciting the 'natural' enterprising spirit in everyone, whether producing or consuming.

1.2 Governmentality as method

> The grid of governmentality, which we may assume is valid for the analysis of ways of conducting the conduct of mad people, patients, delinquents, and children, may equally be valid when we are dealing with phenomenon of a completely different scale, such as an economic policy, for example, or the management of a whole social body.
>
> (Michel Foucault, 1979)[23]

Governmentality studies begin by recognizing that history is a struggle over what has been called truth, what objects are claimed as 'natural' and 'proper' and therefore need to be governed for. Different political rationalities practise different truths, constituted by different taken-for-granted objects. Some of these truths are related to how individual human agents are imagined, such as the 'entrepreneur' and the 'consumer'; others signify larger entities such as 'society', 'economy' and the 'state'. But none of these objects should be thought of as existing permanently through time, as always meaning the same thing: everything is historical. The state, for instance, is not something stable or permanent; what is of far more importance is the 'governmentalization of the state'. It is the tactics or art of government that make possible the continual definition and redefinition of what is within the competence of the state and what is not.[24] Politics, in turn, is nothing more than 'the interplay of these different arts of government with their different reference points and the debate to which these different arts of government give rise.'[25]

Government, of course, invariably fails to recognize the historical contingency of its own projects. It assumes that the set of rules that it uses to identify what is true and what is false are permanently valid. And, as a result, the constituent objects that it makes up in theories and policies are seldom questioned as they are used to explain the world as it appears. Government practises what it constitutes as real and it takes itself to be a subject 'capable of knowing, analysing and ultimately altering reality.'[26] Neoliberal government, for example, constituted the enterprising consumer, and put this knowledge to use in identifying and diagnosing the 'British disease' with the intention of finding a cure and creating a 'healthy society' of enterprising consumers. It set out to alter reality.

On the one hand, intellectuals and governments practising a particular political mentality take for granted that certain forms of thinking and behaving are natural and proper. On the other hand, they also recognize that they have a role in trying to 'elicit, promote, facilitate ... [and] ... foster'[27] various forms of conduct. In doing this, government, by utilizing its knowledge and know-how, believes itself to be acting on those that it governs. It is nothing but optimistic about its own powers, even when, as in the case of liberal regimes, it generally does not seek to directly coerce those who are governed. Essentially overconfidence can be its undoing, as it misidentifies conduct in the population at large. This is precisely why Foucault viewed government as not inherently bad or wicked, but as dangerous all the same.[28]

To understand what forms of conduct neoliberals took to be both natural and proper and part of their governmental programme requires understanding what was taken to be problematic about the way progressive liberalism imagined society and the role of government in it. Neoliberalism was assembled, after all, in contradistinction to progressive liberalism. This earlier political mentality, also referred to 'new' (as opposed to 'neo') liberalism or Keynesianism (in its later economic policy guise), can be characterized, at least in Britain, as a governmental rationality that practised a particular articulation of freedom and society; a political *savoir* in which governing was geared towards an irreducible social sphere in which and through which individual humans would find fulfilment and progress.

Progressive liberalism was a mentality assembled in Britain in the late nineteenth century by, among others, John Hobson and John Hobhouse and various Fabian Society members, and which was practised in the welfare reforms of the 1906 Liberal Government.[29] Most importantly this mentality identified society as an organic reality that had to be governed in a way that enabled society to function smoothly, constituted by a happy and productive population, permanently released from the effects of alienation, so often associated with the experience of modernity. Social pathologies resulting from inequality and injustice, like unemployment and crime, had to be tackled on the basis of restoring society to its natural, full and functioning state. In all of this government had a special role; it was a place where politicians, always assumed to be acting for benign, unselfish reasons, informed by the relevant experts, took for granted their role as facilitators of a functioning society.[30]

The assemblage of neoliberal governmental practices emerged in a discourse that problematized all aspects of progressive liberalism. Governmentality literature has pointed to the way that neoliberalism reconceptualized all aspects of social behaviour, not just economic action, as calculative actions undertaken through the universal human faculty of choice. The economic logic of the consumer has, for instance, been extended to the provision of health and education: patients and parents are now required to choose between competing providers of these services. No longer is work thought of as an entitlement: for neoliberals, economic security is less a function of government expenditure programmes and more a function of how successful government is in fostering more enterprising and entrepreneurial thinking. While there are no more 'jobs for life', the insecurity that has resulted is often reframed as an opportunity to develop new skills and enhance one's experiences and creativity. Insecurity and flexibility are given positive ethical values.[31] To this extent, state-provided social security is seen to inhibit the ability of individuals to utilize risk as a way to create value.[32] Finally, entitlement programmes are invariably seen to be the cause of lower self-esteem, so often viewed as a cause of failure. Individuals are often required to practise positive thinking, and in so doing take responsibility for themselves.[33]

At the same time, neoliberalism problematizes experts and bureaucrats, who are assumed to be acting out of self-interest. Public choice theory constantly places a question mark over whether officials and experts can be relied upon to be benign; the assumption is that it is always safer to assume that they are not.[34] As such, new forms of public management are activated: greater accountability and performance pay are built around targets based on models that simulate market conditions.[35] Governments, in accordance with public choice theory, have attempted (with more or less success) to bind their activity to specific fiscal rules (e.g. balanced budgets over the economic cycle) and monetary rules (e.g. stable and low consumer price inflation). However, where these kinds of constitutional arrangements are not practicable, whole slurries of accounting and audit technologies have been used to regulate and check government activity. These have included the rolling out of net present value accounting to nationalized industries in the 1970s, with the aim of fostering a certain kind of managerial attitude,[36] and an obsession with the use of audit to check and verify decisions, ensuring through the construction of audit trails that decisions can always be evaluated and made visible.[37]

At each point, practices related to the social, as identified by progressive and Keynesian liberalism are problematized and replaced by new reference points that appear to the neoliberal mind to better capture and articulate with that which is out there, or should be out there if only government could regulate conduct accordingly. In all, governmentality studies have highlighted how neoliberalism has problematized the following: the state as coterminous with society, benign non-self-interested government and expertise, economic security as a governmental concern, the unemployed, community and citizenship. So much that had been taken for granted by progressive liberals is questioned and reformatted by neoliberals.

This book clearly connects with much in the governmentality literature with regards to focusing on the consumer as a motif and the importance of choice. Nonetheless its focus is on the detail of what neoliberals have written and done in relation to the problematic of how to govern the modern economy. The evidence presented comes from think tank pamphlets, political speeches, and publications by the Bank of England. In each case, the point is to show how all these different sources referenced the same kinds of taken-for-granted objects, such as the consumer and household.

These arguments take their lead from Foucault's work on neoliberalism (found in a series of lectures given in 1978 and 1979 and published for the first time in English as *The Birth of Biopolitics* in 2008). It was in these lectures that Foucault discussed the economic and social ideas of specific neoliberal theorists, from the Ordoliberal[38] movement in Germany pre- and post-1945, to Gary Becker's theories of human capital emanating from the Chicago School of law and economics. And it was here that Foucault argued that neoliberalism should not be understood as a resurgence of classical liberalism but as something much more important, representing a new art of government. Moreover, he showed how in different times and different places neoliberal theorists had practised a similar and yet non-classical notion of *homo economicus*. For Ordoliberals, for instance, the ultimate political goal of policy was to enable access to private property; thus the basic unit of society would, for them, have the form of the enterprise: 'what is private property if not enterprise? What is a house if not an enterprise?' In turn, for Foucault, Ordoliberal 'social interventionism ... entails an institutional reform around the revaluation of the 'enterprise' unit as the basic economic agent.'[39] Similarly, in the Chicago variant of neoliberalism,

> *Homo economicus* is the entrepreneur of himself. For Becker, the man of consumption, insofar as he consumes is a producer. What does he produce? Well, quite simply, his own satisfaction. Classical analysis which divides man between consumer and producer no longer holds up under neoliberalism because consumption is an activity of production.[40]

Foucault never argued that the reference points of neoliberal governmentality were brought into being and created by the authors he discussed in his lectures; rather he showed how these different authors all practised the same kinds of reference points in their work. Likewise, this book presents a detailed explication of how this human agent has been written about and conceived in the British context, in formative think tanks and in government, and of course by those intellectuals, such as Hayek and Friedman, who while not British, were of particular relevance to the history of this political rationality in Britain. The consumer-as-entrepreneur did not appear fully formed in British liberal think tanks in the late 1950s and 1960s; only over time did the imagined figure of the consumer come to resemble Foucault's characterization of the entrepreneur-of-the-self. And as the following chapters show there have been different conceptions of the consumer activated and identified by the New Right. Nonetheless they all share a family resemblance and, at the very least, all these ways of thinking about the consumer problematize Keynesian and progressive liberal conceptions of the consumer and consumption habits in society at large. Above all else the account of the British economy, economics and economic policy provided here demonstrates the fundamental role that an imagined figure of the consumer has played in recent British economic history.

Finally, it is important to stress that the narrative and analysis presented in this book has relevance beyond Britain. 'Thatcherism' is a term that is understood internationally to designate a series of economic policies that many other countries have replicated. Moreover, much of what has happened in Britain has also occurred in the United States. Indeed, the ferocity of the recent financial and economic crisis in the US has almost obscured the fact that many countries, including Britain, have faced the same problem of excess indebtedness. Rather than being infected by a crisis caused and emanating from the US, many countries facing similar economic problems currently have all practised the same political rationality. While the predominant focus of this book is the British context of neoliberalism, consideration is given in Chapter 7 to the discourse of the homeowner consumer as it has been practised in economic policy in the United States.

1.3 The cast of characters

Much of the narrative focuses on the publications of two British think tanks, the Institute of Economic Affairs (IEA) and the Centre for Policy Studies (CPS), the former established in 1955 and independent of any political party, the latter established in 1974 by Keith Joseph and Margaret Thatcher, both prominent parliamentarians for the Conservative Party. (Thatcher became leader of the Conservatives the following year in 1975, then Prime Minister in 1979, her first general election as leader of the Party.) There are a number of reasons why the publications of these think tanks represent the best repositories through which to explore the rationality of British neoliberalism. For a start the IEA was for many years the only think tank in Britain that explicitly set itself the task of espousing what it took to be liberal or free market ideals; always suggesting the application of the market as a way to resolve Britain's micro- and macroeconomic problems. Rather than being known as neoliberal, the term 'New Right', which is taken here to be entirely synonymous, was often used instead to denote these authors. The CPS, in turn, was explicitly formed to 'articulate in political terms what the IEA had been thinking'.[41] From 1974 to 1979 it was essentially the site in which the political programme of what later became known as Thatcherism was formulated. It ran a series of policy-making committees, in addition to being a speech-writing unit for Joseph and Thatcher.

Yet one can also make the claim for the impeccable historical credentials of the IEA as 'the' neoliberal think tank in Britain. There is a well-documented history of connections (see in particular Richard Cockett's *Thinking the Unthinkable*, 1995) between German Ordoliberalism, the Chicago school, the economics department of the London School of Economics headed by Lionel Robbins, the IEA and ultimately Thatcherism. Indeed intellectuals from Germany, France, Britain and the United States explicitly designated as 'neoliberals' met together in 1938 at the *Colloque Walter Lippmann* in Paris to discuss ways to revitalize classical liberal ideas and turn back the progressive liberal tide. In turn, this gathering provided the blueprint for the structure and organization of the Mont Pèlerin Society, of which Hayek was the founder and early lynchpin. Its first meeting took place in 1947 and was attended by Ordoliberals such as Walter Eucken, Wilhelm Röpke, Alexander Rüstow, as well as economists from Britain (including Lionel Robbins, John Jewkes and Arnold Plant) and from the United States (including Milton Friedman, George Stigler and Frank Knight). Another member, British businessman Anthony Fisher, founded the IEA in 1955, and by 1958 had appointed its two central figures (both members of Mont Pèlerin) Arthur Seldon and Ralph Harris, the former as general editor, the latter as general director. Arthur Seldon had studied under Hayek at the London School of Economics in the 1930s, and it was Hayek who recommended Seldon to Fisher when he was establishing the IEA.[42] Finally, Mont Pèlerin members such as Hayek, Friedman, James Buchanan and John Jewkes authored IEA pamphlets, and as if to come full circle, speaking in 2001, Friedman generously credited the IEA with changing the intellectual climate of opinion around the world and being the major stimulus for others to follow.[43]

Nonetheless, as discussed, this book is not primarily focused on historical connections, written correspondence, and the forging of political alliances. It is concerned with a particular political rationality that emerged in the context of and in response to the performance of the British economy after 1945 and especially in the 1970s. Undoubtedly, as discussed in Chapters 3 and 4, there was a genuine sense of crisis in the 1970s, a feeling that Britain's economic misfortunes and the experience of stagflation was overflowing the bounds of the economy, tearing at the very essence of British society. However this was not the same situation as post-war Germany, where Ordoliberals sought to create, what Foucault called, the world's first 'radically economic state' in order to re-establish the legitimacy of the state. Ordoliberal-style policy (largely inspired by Ordoliberal author, finance minister and later German Chancellor Ludwig Erhard) did not ask what freedoms should be bequeathed to the market by government, but instead how the economy could have a state-creating function. 'The institution of economic freedom ... will be able to function as a siphon ... as a point of legitimacy for the formation of political sovereignty.'[44]

Hayek's *The Road to Serfdom* (1944) certainly foretold of disaster for Britain should it follow its current 'socialist' course, and of course it was a highly influential book. All the same the publications of the IEA in the late 1950s and 1960s were not laced with the language of catastrophe. The context of these publications was very different in nature to post-war Ordoliberalism. Harris and Seldon were not concerning themselves with the establishment of state legitimacy. Their aims were in fact reasonably modest; their publications often guided by whom they could find to author their papers and inevitably sources of funding would play a role in determining the kinds of subjects they would tackle. Their main concern was always with providing a policy stance for a specific industry that took account of increased freedom of consumer choice made possible, they believed, by rising incomes.

In other words, who was problematized and how it was problematized was entirely specific to British history and the British context, and discussions, at least at the IEA, were limited in the early days to matters related to microeconomic policy. What this archive therefore offers is a site through which to explore the thinking of a distinct group of intellectuals as they sought to problematize certain practices of economic policy in post-war Britain. Publications, from 1960 on, most often took the form of Hobart Papers (named after the location of the IEA's original office in London) that were pamphlets written for a general audience and invariably less than 100 pages in length. Eighty-four Hobart Papers were published by the IEA before the 1979 general election, and along with other occasional papers provide an exemplary site through which to explore the dimensions of neoliberal thinking.

The 1970s was not without its fair share of paranoia; there was a genuine feeling that the sovereignty of Parliament was being threatened by some trade unionists. It was a period in which the IEA connected their detailed microeconomic focus to bigger macroeconomic issues. Many of the pamphlets in this period start to make explicit references to monetarist versus Keynesian debates; thus the importance of Milton Friedman in the British context comes to the fore. This is reflected in IEA publications, particularly between 1974 and 1977, by an increased focus on the macro debates about the British economy. The consumer was always a key reference point for their arguments but it is in this period that IEA publications begin to take very seriously the idea that conduct in society urgently needed to be redirected and changed; that a healthy society required more people to conduct themselves with consumer as opposed to worker habits of thought.

The CPS archive suggests that entirely the same thought processes that were taking place in the IEA were occurring in this enclave of the Conservative Party. The published material from 1974 to 1979 is in fact fairly limited; the efforts of the CPS were focused on writing speeches for Joseph and Thatcher that were subsequently published. But also of great and lasting policy importance, the CPS set up and ran a series of different policy working groups, dealing with a range of issues such as consumer protection and Britain's enterprise culture (or perceived lack thereof). Perhaps of greatest importance was the *Stepping Stones* project that laid out an entire strategy for what was to become Thatcherite economic policy. As Chapter 4 discusses, this strategy, articulated clearly in the *Stepping Stones* report (Hoskyns and Strauss 1977), laid the groundwork for policy that took for granted an inextricable link between inflation and trade unionism.

There are undoubted parallels to be found between the thinking of the New Right in Britain in the 1970s and Foucault's description in his lectures of Ordoliberal concerns. Of particular relevance was Eucken's position that, as

Foucault put it, competition is 'an essence' that history had proved needed to be fostered and maintained by permanent government intervention and monitoring.[45] Yet the vantage point of the IEA and CPS was not a Nazi regime and post-war devastation. A shift in politics had to be enacted in a democracy, by appealing to an electorate. The market was to be no siphon for state legitimacy. Instead the New Right believed that it was their job to change conduct so as to foster in the population at large an enterprising spirit among many who were deemed trapped in antedated and outmoded ways of thinking. Economic policy itself was designed to effect change; that is to regulate conduct so as to elicit different behaviour from many producers and workers in the population. The application of certain distinct monetary policies in Britain in the early 1980s and the rolling out of privatization were two policies that turned Britain into an economic testing ground; this was, as so many authors on the Left and Right have attested, the British economic experiment.

The history of neoliberal governmental practice in Britain provides an opportunity to write about the formation of a political rationality, about the ways in which progressive liberalism was problematized. Additionally, this book offers a history right up to the present in which it is possible to show how this rationality has been put into practice, often with the aim of fostering consumer habits of thought. The practice of neoliberalism is addressed in Chapters 5, 6 and 7 in the context of problems that it has encountered. In particular it is shown how government and monetary authorities misidentified consumer conduct and specifically consumer borrowing. Government became convinced that there were no grounds upon which they could intervene in order to slow the accumulation of consumer and household debt.

In order to construct this critical history of the present, that is a history that uses the issue of consumer credit and indebtedness to problematize and historicize neoliberalism, Chapters 5 and 6 switch attention away from the IEA and CPS towards key policy speeches made in the 1980s and 1990s. In addition, the memoirs of Thatcher, Nigel Lawson, Geoffrey Howe and other key figures of the Thatcher era, such as Alan Walters, John Hoskyns and Gordon Pepper are also important historical sources. Walters' book for instance was written in 1986 not only as a review of economic policy after 1979 but also to reinforce the case for the policies that were still being enacted. And the memoirs of Lawson, Howe and Thatcher were all written in the early 1990s before the advent of Tony Blair's New Labour. Lawson's 1992 memoir in particular provides a rich assessment of the 1980s as well as pointing the way forward to how the consumer, credit and debt were problematized or not, as the case turned out, in the 1990s and beyond. That said, the IEA and CPS also continued to offer important statements and criticisms of policy from within the neoliberal fold. These sources remain important in disputing the claims made by some that policy, especially from the mid 1980s on, veered significantly away from neoliberal practice.

This book also makes significant use of Bank of England material, essentially economic commentaries, research papers and speeches by important officials and researchers. Indeed the Bank of England is an important primary source in its own right for a number of reasons. Reform of the banking sector, making it more competitive was, apart from anything else, a central part of how to govern for the consumer, and attempts to change the way banks operate in Britain go back to 1971. Indeed, the monetary consequences of early attempts at reform played an enormous role in the formulation of Thatcherism in the mid 1970s. The Bank of England provided all policy-makers with key information and interpretation in those years. Moreover the Bank was also charged with implementing government policy and, as an open and transparent organization, it provides a clear window into the minds of policy-makers.

There was much soul-searching at the Bank in response to the economic downturn of the early 1990s, made entirely public by their publications. Officials at the Bank saw themselves as part of government, entirely responsible for monitoring monetary developments and the efficacy of monetary policy. After 1997, the Bank was given operational control of monetary policy in Britain. Given the limited use of fiscal policy as a macroeconomic tool (the government was supposed to balance its books over the economic cycle), the Bank of England was, within the guidelines set for inflation, very much governing the British economy. The central bank has been a key site in which neoliberalism has been practised and the consumer, with unrationed access to credit, has been referenced as a key foundational economic agent.

1.4 Chapter outline

There are six substantive chapters, which divide into two parts. The next three chapters deal with neoliberalism in opposition to the government of the day, problematizing the activities of British governments in the 1950s, 1960s and 1970s. The following three chapters deal with neoliberalism in government: Chapters 5 and 6 with British economic history from 1979 to the present and Chapter 7 with US economic history from the early 1990s to the present. These chapters present a consistent narrative in which the consumer is referenced as a specific human agent and object of policy. Governing the economy most definitely meant governing for the consumer, both eliciting and fostering certain habits of thought and looking for signs in economic data that consumers were acting appropriately.

The book runs as a historical narrative. Chapter 2, *Constructing the Consumer*, discusses how neoliberals problematized the articulation of economic security, society and human agency in government policy in the 1950s and 1960s. Part of the focus is on the work of Hayek and Friedman and part of it on the publications and work of the IEA in this period. It examines how these authors referenced a similar economic agent, the consumer, and how, in the context of 1950s and 1960s Britain, they saw the consumer as the obvious agent to which government should look to solve certain economic problems. In discussing the way Keynes and Keynesianism was problematized in the IEA, a contrast is drawn between the way that consumers were imagined by IEA authors and how Keynes in his *General Theory*, written in 1936, implicitly referenced them.

Chapter 3, *Diagnosing the British Economy* discusses how, between 1960 and 1977, IEA authors mounted a critique of the way in which the British economy was being governed, particularly with regard to indicative planning in the 1960s and micro-intervention strategies in the early 1970s. The experience of stagflation in the mid 1970s led these authors to construct their own critical history of the British economy in which they explained the appearance of habits of thought (especially in trade unions) that were at odds with their view of what constituted a successful and advancing society. The key years were 1974 to 1976, years in which one can see the emergence of a neoliberal will to govern in ways that are certainly distinguishable from classical liberalism or laissez-faire. Specifically, this is the period in which neoliberalism had to reconcile the notion that consumers were to them the natural and proper agents of the economy with their growing perception that a significant proportion of the population were failing to identify themselves as such and behave appropriately. To this extent the New Right recognized that the consumer is a historical object while at the same time arguing that this being was the authentic and appropriate human agent of the age. The result was that neoliberalism came to believe that it was entirely appropriate for government to foster consumer and enterprising attitudes and conduct in British economy and society.

But of course it is one thing to problematize government in theory; it is another to decide what to do about it and to articulate a set of policies that put right what it has been deemed is wrong. Thus in Chapter 4, *How to Govern the Economy*, attention switches from the IEA to the CPS and the parallel and complementary project that was conducted there, this time concerned with the practical policies that it was believed would cure the 'British disease'. It is here that neoliberals first conceived that monetarism was 'not enough' to solve Britain's problems but at the same time was a tool that could be fashioned in a particular way to address issues that went far beyond the purely economic. Encapsulated in the speeches of Keith Joseph, Margaret Thatcher and in the *Stepping Stones* project, the CPS focused their attention on how a particular articulation of state and society had produced economic agents misaligned to the needs of the time. The New Right did not deny the existence of society; instead they sought to foster a society of consumers, acting ethically because they would be free to choose. In this, the neoliberal conception of the social was very distinct from that imagined by progressive liberals.

In many respects the CPS in the 1970s was already seeking to change attitudes and behaviour in certain parts of the population. The UK election of 1979 was to be interpreted as a sign that the population had embraced all that they were saying. Nonetheless as Chapter 5, *Governing for the Consumer*, argues, Thatcher's government considered there was still much to do with regards to governing the economy. At the heart of Thatcher's first term lay a paradox, the liberalization of the banking system (ending what amounted to de facto rationing of consumer credit) and the concurrent targeting of aggregate money supply, so as to limit monetary expansion and inflation. It is argued that the explanation for this lies in the attempt both to incentivize 'rational' behaviour and to do, somewhat paradoxically for free-market liberals, the work of creative destruction in the economy. By 1985 the government believed that low inflation signified that attitudes and behaviour had changed and that Britain had adopted an enterprise culture. Thus the boom of the late 1980s should not be viewed as an abandonment of neoliberalism but instead as an act based on the belief, falsified by the ensuing bust, that consumers had become rational agents using debt to grow their balance sheets and plan expenditure across their lifetime.

In Chapter 6, *Misidentification and Crisis*, the narrative is brought up to the present day. It should be recognized that the New Labour project extended far beyond the bounds of the economy. A fairly brief look at Tony Blair's speeches from the mid to late 1990s shows that New Labour was extending the calculus of choice to many areas of the social services. As far as governing the economy is concerned, New Labour continued to practise a neoliberal conception of economic agency; that is of the consumer-as-entrepreneur. And while the Bank of England's use of monetary policy utilized New Keynesian notions of stability, there was no significant problematizing of rising levels of consumer indebtedness. Indeed, in the closing part of this chapter, it is suggested that the financial crisis and economic downturn after 2007 represents, just as with the 1980s, the confrontation of the neoliberal governing rationality, which viewed people's behaviour in a certain way, with a world in which individuals were not necessarily conforming to those envisaged norms. It is a more complex crisis than at the end of the 1980s but it highlights more than anything else the potential for the projects of government to be dangerous and for strong political visions to ride roughshod over the way others might perceive their own freedoms.

However, Britain has not been alone in experiencing an economic downturn precipitated by a financial crisis. The United States, in particular, has suffered a similar fate. In Chapter 7, *The American Sub-prime Homeowner Consumer*, the political rationality of Bill Clinton's and George W. Bush's presidencies is addressed. In particular, the discourse of the politics of home ownership is examined and the question is raised as to why the US central bank, the Federal Reserve, did not act to keep increasing indebtedness under control. The argument is made that the governmentality of neoliberalism was as pervasive in the US as it has been in Britain. Even so, the complexity of the American financial system and the role played by government-sponsored enterprises has enabled neoliberals to make strong counter-arguments about the financial crisis in which progressive liberalism is cited as its main cause. In considering these arguments, questions are raised about the possibility of ever constructing a pure, utopian neoliberal economy.

Overall this book aims to show how an imagined figure of the consumer became a key reference point for government, how this figure problematized a Keynesian governing rationality and yet did not imply that economic policy should somehow revert to a classical liberal regime. What distinguishes neoliberal economic policy is precisely that it imagines a society composed of one class of entrepreneurs, whether producing or consuming. And what essentially gives proof to that is an entirely novel way of perceiving debt. Rather than the shame of the nineteenth century, a moral scourge on the abstinence and work ethic of entrepreneurs, debt when used to finance the purchase of assets became a sign in the late twentieth century that consumers were building their personal balance sheets and making themselves more productive for society in the process. Government had not problematized the inexorable rise of household debt (as a percentage of household income) in any significant way precisely because it never problematized the parallel increase in the asset side of household balance sheets. That average household assets in Britain increased from 75 per cent of household income to over 150 per cent in thirty years of economic history was taken as a sign of increasing rationality in the population at large.

2 Constructing the consumer

From its very earliest publications in the late 1950s, authors at the Institute of Economic Affairs (IEA) sought to problematize methods for governing the economy that did not, as far as they were concerned, maximize the potential for the free expression of consumers in the marketplace. Its goal was to achieve for liberalism what it was believed the Fabian society had achieved for the welfare state; only now, these Fabian goals were to be the target of criticism. The IEA was thus founded in a world in which the practices of government were shaped by social concerns. Certain techniques for governing the economy, such as Keynesian demand management, planning and income controls, formed part of an assemblage of governmental practices that required the state to ensure economic security and with it a functioning social order.

Yet there was no crisis; 1959 was in fact the year in which the British population were told by the Prime Minister Harold Macmillan, perhaps overenthusiastically, that they had never had it so good. One might thus say that the liberal critics of the supposed Keynesian orthodoxy were simply arguing that things could be even better, that the general level of consumer satisfaction was below that which it would be if certain industries were allowed to run along market principles. At the very least, these British (neo-)liberals, along with other Mont Pèlerin liberals such as Hayek and Friedman, were determined to argue against policies that sought to extend the role of government intervention in the economy.

This chapter focuses on how these arguments were constructed, and how they referenced a particular kind of human economic agent, the consumer. Whether in the context of political philosophy, economic theorizing of consumption and the demand for holding money, or in more localized political arguments regarding controls over advertising, consumer credit and the provision of consumer goods and services, the figure of the consumer was activated to counteract and bring into question the conventional economic thinking of the time. A key part of these arguments was the recurring liberal criticism of government, that there are often negative unintended consequences of government intervention, however benign the intention. Nevertheless, the focus here is not on these well-rehearsed arguments but instead on the way the consumer was constituted in discourse so as to immediately problematize the kinds of human agents that were taken for granted by more progressive and 'social' ways of thinking. Indeed, while welfare-based political rationalities certainly activated a particular organic notion of society monitored by the state, this same governing mentality also imagined a certain kind of consumer, one who was weak in the face of corporate power and prone to habitual, as opposed to aspirational, spending patterns.

This is a key point, for to understand how the neoliberal mentality tackles governing the economy in ways that are distinctive, say from classical liberalism, it is necessary to understand how it referenced human behaviour in contradistinction to the social democratic orthodoxy of the time. This counter-revolution in economic theory and policy, to use Friedman's term, was never about restoring the initial situation (classical liberalism) but was about articulating something new.[1] The argument here is that neoliberalism, both in theory and policy, referenced a human agent that was different from that practised by progressive liberals; and one that was not referenced at all by orthodox nineteenth century political economists, the thinkers that this grouping were claiming lineage from. To look to the consumer as a transformative agent of (economic) progress required a distinctive and different view of society and the types of human beings that constituted it, discontinuous with both a classical and progressive liberal mentality of rule. In this regard neoliberal economic thinking was decidedly post-Keynesian.

This chapter asks the question: how did neoliberals conceive of the figure of the consumer and how did this figure appear in their political thinking in the 1950s and 1960s? To answer this question the early work of the IEA, as well as some of the writings of Hayek and Friedman, are examined. All these authors referenced in their publications taken-for-granted assumptions regarding human behaviour and the associated norms that they took to be symptomatic of human existence, albeit with different methodologies and audiences in mind. At the same time, it is important to understand the way this neoliberal figure of the consumer problematized the conception of individual economic conduct in the political rationality practised, although certainly not created, by Keynes. As such this chapter also examines what Keynes took for granted when writing about the economy, and how his 'revolution' can be seen as an economic theory that incorporated the idea, already in existence, that government could and should play a distinctive role in providing economic security. Post-1945 economic policy was made in the wake of the Keynesian Revolution, and it is only in this context that one begins to comprehend the formation and constitution of British neoliberalism; the way that a new kind of social realm was imagined, one composed of entrepreneurs and enterprising consumers. Understanding Keynes therefore provides the necessary background to the work of the IEA and important neoliberal figures, like Hayek and Friedman.

2.1 Economics and progressive liberalism before the Great Depression

Just as neoliberals have practised in their discourse a similar conception of the consumer, so Keynes practised a conception of workers and savers that was not his invention, but which was generally accepted by progressive liberals. Indeed, Keynes' theorizing existed in a world where the British government had long since incorporated progressive liberal perspectives, and since at least 1906, had governed in accordance with 'new liberal' principles. Keynes' own ideas formed only one version of an attempt to bring this perspective into economic theory. Prior to Keynes, John Hobson, who was a key theoretician of progressive new liberalism, tried (in 1889) to elucidate an economic theory of underconsumption.[2] Additionally, and centred in the United States, institutional economists had criticized the classical framework with perspectives that were essentially social and progressive in nature.[3] Finally, economists such as Ragnar Frisch and Michael Kalecki were also working in the 1930s on economic theories that could sanction a role for government to directly alleviate the extreme levels of unemployment caused by the Great Depression.[4] It would thus be entirely misleading to think of Keynes other than as one figure of a collective enterprise seeking to incorporate a progressive political rationality into economic theory.

That is not to say that the neoclassical economics had offered no more practical advice for governing the economy than 'leave well alone'. The leading economist of late Victorian Britain, Alfred Marshall, developed an early form of welfare economics which made use of his own style of demand and supply analysis. With the idea of the consumer surplus, Marshall was able to argue that there was a difference between what was actually spent on a good and what one would be willing to spend on it, and this represented a stock of utility for each individual buyer. So long as one made the assumption that the consumer's surplus varied in proportion to size of income (one pound was 'worth' less to the rich man than to a poor man) then demand and supply analysis could be used to assess taxation and subsidies on the basis of whether the aggregate amount of satisfaction or utility in society would rise or fall.[5]

Nonetheless this kind of analysis did not seek to address the social question that arose towards the end of the nineteenth century; that is, how government should address the problem of dire urban poverty in the midst of plenty. It is not that individual orthodox political economists dismissed the issue; the point was in the way in which they addressed it. Thus Marshall explicitly recognized in his *Principles of Economics* (first published in 1890 but frequently republished thereafter) that it was entirely legitimate to want to do something about inequality. Moreover he was happy to accept that in late Victorian Britain it could no longer be claimed that large inequalities of income were essential for the accumulation of savings for future increases in production. However in recognizing that these issues existed, Marshall was also explicit in stating that in his view many of these problems lay outside the remit of economic science.[6] These issues were moral in nature and had to be addressed that way by government. Marshall had no problem passing judgement on the ostentatious and 'socially wasteful' consumption patterns of the rich, the plight of the urban poor and the moral standing of the competitive ethic.[7] But this social perspective remained outside neoclassical economic theory; the 1906 Liberal programme of welfare-based progressive liberalism did not look to economic theory for justification.

In other words there was no will to govern the unemployed or macroeconomic policy designed to specifically address the problem of unemployment. Indeed the very notion of unemployment only appeared in the statistical lexicon of government in the depression of the 1880s.[8] For Marshall, unemployment remained a cyclical issue, its severity in any downswing a reflection of the extent of the upswing and the degree to which it had been fuelled by credit and unhealthy entrepreneurial speculation. On the way up, Marshall thought it sensible to limit credit expansion; but once in a downturn, the best solution was for wages to fall in line with general price declines.[9] Marshall did not accept the notion that there could be a general glut of production and a concomitant problem of underconsumption. His position therefore reiterated that of Stanley Jevons, the first recognizably 'marginalist' economist in Britain: while economics might provide statistics of consumer demand to help ensure that any one industry did not expand too much, the idea of the general glut was 'absurd and self-contradictory'.[10]

On this point both of these 'great' Victorian economists, Marshall and Jevons, were in fundamental agreement with their classical predecessor J. S. Mill, that political economy had 'nothing to do with the consumption of wealth ... [instead] ... it was triumphantly established by political economists that consumption never needs encouragement. All of which is produced is already consumed ... what is consumed for mere enjoyment, is gone.'[11] Both men would have agreed that production would only be undertaken in order to consume more; as Adam Smith had argued, if someone wanted to consume more meat then he or she had to appeal to the self-interest of the butcher by producing something the butcher wanted, say bread, that could then be exchanged for meat.[12] There could be no such thing as underconsumption because production was always undertaken with a view to later consumption. This was the orthodox view, accepted even by the Fabians. Any dissenters, including Hobson, who espoused an underconsumption theory in 1889 in *The Physiology of Industry*, were marginalized in the economic community. Orthodox economics, whether classical or neoclassical, remained estranged from a progressive or new liberal mentality. Instead economics retained the Victorian emphasis on production, and the need to create conditions in which entrepreneurs would be free to produce.[13]

Keynes' *General Theory* (1936) thus represented one economist's attempt to practise progressive liberalism in economic theory and therefore to overthrow this orthodoxy. This is a critical point to note, for however one argues that Keynes' ideas were corrupted, corrupted others or were simply wrong (all three positions being taken at various times by IEA authors), one of the key IEA arguments of the 1960s and 1970s about Keynes was that he had only ever been posing a politically expedient economic theory. This was in fact a major theme in IEA literature; the idea that the 'best' economists should never adjust their theories to make them politically palatable; that theory should be stated in the purest or most 'honest' form so that politicians could at least get a clear theoretical view of the issue at hand.[14] Thus the theme of the first Hobart Paperback published by the IEA in 1971, authored by William Hutt (entitled *Politically*

Impossible): Keynes was a man who invented theory to fit with what was politically possible. For Hutt, Keynes' 'tactics were to destroy the whole authority of classical economics.'[15]

The focus of Hutt's ire was centred on Keynes' dismissal of the classical and neoclassical position that unemployment could be solved by a general fall in wages. Keynes' position was that a fall in wages would lead to less demand for the products of other industries thus doing little to increase demand in the economy in aggregate. Additionally a fall in wages might well lead to more income being earned by wealthy *rentiers* who would be unlikely to spend this additional money. Finally, Keynes also made the point that it would be almost impossible in a free society to engineer a fall in the general wage level and that the inevitable industrial disputes that would follow would likely dampen entrepreneurial appetites for investment.[16] It was this third aspect of Keynes' argument that the IEA authors attacked, offering it as proof of an admission by Keynes that he was censuring himself politically; making up theory to fit political realities. This was the 'politically easier economic solution'.[17]

From this analysis came the argument that *The General Theory* was anything but general. Writing about his experiences of Keynes in 1966 (first published by the IEA in 1972 in the third Hobart Paperback, *A Tiger by the Tail*) Hayek recollected, 'though he called it a "general" theory, it was to me too obviously another tract for the times, conditioned by what he thought were the momentary needs of policy'.[18] And Hayek again offered proof for this argument in a 1975 IEA paper by pointing to Keynes' earlier views expressed in 1919 (*Economic Consequences of the Peace*) in which he had endorsed the idea that British workers were uncompetitive and wages would indeed need to fall. As with before, Hayek put the later view down to Keynes recognizing the political impossibility of achieving a general wage cut in the 1930s,[19] rather than any genuine theoretical illumination.

The position put forward here is that howsoever Keynes' theory was disliked it was an economic theory all the same; and elements of the theory, particularly as they were based on psychological insights into human non-entrepreneurial economic agency (see section 2.2), were critical to the neoliberal rethinking of economic theory and policy. Thus the 'rigidity of money-wages' problem was in many ways a side issue, and notwithstanding the above complaints, Hayek, Friedman and IEA authors practised a governmental rationality that problematized Keynesian conceptions of human economic agency, not by rejecting out of hand Keynes' ideas because they were supposedly made to be politically palatable. The point being made here, before moving on to discuss *The General Theory* in more detail, is that the discourses of Keynesianism and of neoliberalism were equally attuned to their respective conceptions of economic freedom and security, referencing distinctive conceptions of the consumer and worker, yet always addressing the problematic of how one should govern. This had little to do with political expediency. In this sense, it is perhaps more helpful to think of *The General Theory* as a 'social' theory of employment, interest and money.

2.2 Keynes, the macro problem and the social world

The 'originality' of Keynes' theory is not in focus.[20] Indeed, what was certainly not original in Keynes' work was a political mentality that sought to govern for social ends, such as equality and state-sponsored economic security. Keynes practised this mentality within his theory but this mentality of rule had dominated much British governmental thinking since at least 1906. All the same, the specifics of Keynes' *General Theory* (1936) are examined in this section in order to demonstrate that he took for granted a very particular kind of human economic agent when writing his theory; an imagined figure that was not necessarily made fully explicit but which provides the fundamental reference point for the theory. It is what made it possible for Keynes to solve, what he believed, was the key theoretical problem of the time. As he said,

> The transition from economic anarchy to a regime which deliberately aims at controlling and directing economic forces in the interests of social justice and social stability, will present enormous difficulties both technical and political. I suggest, nevertheless, that the true destiny of New Liberalism is to seek their solution.[21]

The General Theory placed a new emphasis, previously lacking in economic theory, on everyone in the economy; everyone had a role to play. Unlike the classical position it was not just to the entrepreneur that the nation looked for progress; the actions of all could affect the outcome of all. And while there was much that neoliberals took issue with in Keynes' theory of consumption, later neoliberals also recognized macroeconomics for what it was, a study of a realm that referred to all human subjects in the economy. Consumption practices in and of themselves had consequences for the future wealth of the nation, and aggregate output was a function of everyone's economic choices. This, at any rate, is what marked out *The General Theory* as different, as 'macro' in focus and differentiated it from neoclassical/marginalist theories of economic growth, development and capital.

This doubtless requires some explanation of the state of economics in the early twentieth century, the context in which Keynes was developing his ideas. Writing in 1921 in *Risk, Uncertainty and Profit* Chicago-based economist Frank Knight argued that the major problem with orthodox economics was to be found in the artificial division in theory between consumption and production, and the resulting weak account this gave of the consumer.

> The problem of consumption is considered independently, taking the form of expending value in exchange, which is worked out on its own account in accordance with the principle of rational choice or distribution of resources among competitive uses. This value in exchange on the expenditure side, becomes like the concept of exertion to Crusoe; it is an instrumental idea, with no ontological content, but extremely useful in solving the problem of

choice. The separation of the two halves of the economic problem ... [production and consumption] ... is much heightened in real life by the storing-up of value in exchange against unknown contingencies, with no thought of any particular use to be made of it. The separation is still further heightened by the tendency for the production of wealth to lose all connection with the notion of consuming utilities and take on the form of a competitive contest in which value in exchange becomes a mere measure of success, a counter in the game.[22]

The problem according to Knight was this; the marginal and neoclassical revolutions in economics practised a new theory of value: the reason something had a value in the marketplace was no longer ascribed, as it had been by Smith, Ricardo, Mill and Marx, to the labour that had been expended in production; instead each individual person made a subjective or psychological assessment of how much any particular object was worth to them. Given that the consumer had a scarce amount of purchasing power to deploy, each individual subjective assessment of value came together to form, in aggregate, the price in the marketplace. And according to Leon Walras' general equilibrium theory (1874) the market auctioneering process for goods and services, composed of producers, distributors and consumers, cleared as prices were agreed by all simultaneously. Each moment in time, each clearing of the market, ended with consumption and the using up of resources that had previously been produced at the direction of entrepreneurs.

General equilibrium, as Knight argued, involved some pretty 'heroic assumptions', which included perfect foresight and knowledge, but it also, as he said, implied a consumer with 'no ontology'.[23] What did Knight mean by this phrase? On the one hand, it was an exaggeration, within the neoclassical scheme a change in preferences by the consumer would change everything; the auctioneering process would have to start again. To the extent that consumers had the power to move equilibrium from one intersection of prices and outputs to another, it is difficult to say the consumer in neoclassical economics had 'no' ontology. On the other hand, however, the underlying human character of the consumer had become decidedly 'thin'. For Knight this figure had no intelligence, his reactions were mechanical, and he treated other human beings as if they were 'slot machines', that is pleasure machines that experience no pleasure, and no vices, virtues, desires or children, no propensities, talents or preferences.[24] One could say therefore that there was little sense of 'being' in this theory precisely because there was no notion that the figure of the consumer existed between the discrete moments of time when markets cleared and the Walrasian auctioneering process started again. Indeed, by suggesting that, in the real world, consumers store up value-in-exchange against unknown contingencies, that is to say they save money for no particular reason, Knight was alluding to a sense of being, an existential awareness of the future that consumers faced, that hitherto had played no role in economic theory with regards to the activity of consumption.

Conversely, both classical and Austrian-school accounts of the economy recognized that the entrepreneur-as-producer operated with a distinct sense of the future and of his existence through time. By the mid nineteenth century the entrepreneur was viewed as an individual who had come to realize that the only way to increase his consumption in the future was to abstain from present consumption, save, invest and ultimately produce more that could then be exchanged for more goods to consume in the future.[25] For Austrian-school economists like Eugen von Böhm-Bawerk and Joseph Schumpeter, writing in the late nineteenth and early twentieth centuries, the entrepreneur-producer was made into a figure endowed with very special capabilities and psychological propensities, someone who had overcome the human tendency to undervalue the future. This person was not 'Mr. Public', as Böhm-Bawerk labelled the consumer, but an individual of will and action, earning profits because of an ability to consider the future desires of others. Where consumers undervalued the future, entrepreneurs gained a profit by exchanging current goods for future goods and waiting until consumers realized the full value of those goods, as the future became the present. For Schumpeter, the will and action of the entrepreneur was practically Nietzschean in proportion, 'Zarathustras' reaching for the heights of their creative powers. The consumer on the other hand was weak and could easily have their desires created for them by the entrepreneur.[26]

In these accounts, the entrepreneur was afforded a sense of being, operating through time to make a profit. This figure had a purpose, a will and the ability to act on that will, and it was thanks to the entrepreneur that economies grew richer. It was only by not using up resources in the present, by building capital goods that would produce more in the future, that everyone could enjoy increased consumption and an increased standard of living. In this latter regard Knight was sceptical; suggesting instead that some entrepreneurs had become so rich that competition between them had turned into a personal battle rather than a competition to consume more. In turn it could not be definitively claimed that entrepreneurs always acted in society's best interest.[27] Nonetheless whatever position one took on that issue, Knight certainly believed that economics remained bipolar; on the one hand there was a neoclassical theory which gave consumers little sense of being and character, and on the other, an Austrian theory which both doubted the consumer's ability to contemplate the future and celebrated the entrepreneur as a human being able to do precisely that. In the wake of the Keynesian revolution, neoliberalism (even if in the hands of Friedman it shared much of the mathematical formalism of neoclassical economics) provided a much 'thicker' rendition of the consumer. The figure of the consumer, in neoliberal thinking generally, came to resemble the Austrian account of the entrepreneur. Consumption was imagined as an entrepreneurial practice.

The problematic status of the consumer in orthodox theory was exactly what Keynes addressed in *The General Theory* in 1936. His consumption function and demand for money function gave his vision of the consumer, that is the non-entrepreneurial human agent of the economy, a status in the economy that mattered. Uncertainty and a concern with the future was not just an existential condition faced by entrepreneurs but faced by everyone in society. In this sense, one might say therefore that the idea of macroeconomics[28] carried a double meaning. Clearly it referred to a new body of economic theory that sought to explain how the behaviour of one individual impacted on another, why for instance an individual's decision to save might, by lowering the income of others, result in a withdrawal of entrepreneurial investment elsewhere in the economy. However, it is also possible to think of macroeconomics as a body of knowledge that provided all human agents in the economy, not just entrepreneurs, with a sense of being, portraying key psychological propensities shared by all. It is in this second definitional sense that it could be claimed that neoliberalism was macroeconomic and necessarily post-Keynesian.

Keynes' analysis of consumer behaviour was far removed from the precepts of consumer price theory; it is an analysis in which time, existence and uncertainty play a critical role. The question he asked is why individuals consume and why they save. The answer he gave involved a consideration of both subjective and objective factors; it provided a psychological explanation of consumption behaviour in response both to personal characteristics and to outside factors (such as wage levels in the economy). On the personal side Keynes suggested, like Knight before him, that people save against an unknown future, for nothing in particular. In addition to this he also suggested that people might save for known future expenditures like education or old age, for inheritance purposes, or because of the independence it might give them in the future. Keynes also acknowledged that some people clearly enjoyed receiving interest and seeing their capital appreciate (alternatively they might simply be miserly). Nonetheless, Keynes' opinion was that overall while there were many different personality types there was ultimately a more or less permanent social structure that held sway over average consumption habits. In general there was likely to be a shared attitude to saving in society such that personal idiosyncrasies would balance out on average, having little affect on consumption and saving rates.[29]

So what did, according to Keynes, affect the general level of saving in society or the average rate of savings of consumers? The answer, as with above, was habit, but modified to some degree by the level of incomes in society as a whole. Note 'to some degree', because this was essentially Keynes' point: real incomes over time will rise, but spending, although it will also rise, will not rise in a one-to-one proportion with incomes, 'for a man's habitual standard of life usually has the first claim on his income, and he is apt to save the difference which discovers itself between his actual income and the expense of his habitual standard'. This was the 'fundamental psychological law upon which one could depend with great confidence both from a priori … knowledge of human nature and from the detailed facts of experience'.[30]

One could say therefore that human beings save because they exist through time and there are many motivations that determine saving: 'precaution, foresight, calculation, improvement, independence, enterprise, pride and avarice.'[31] However for Keynes, these factors invariably cancelled each other out; what matters is that through time people develop certain habitual consumption patterns;

they tend to spend a similar proportion of their income and thus as they get richer the absolute level of savings rises. The result is that to maintain the same circulation of money in the economy, which maintains the same level of employment, investment in capital goods needs increasingly to make up for the shortfall in spending which arises as incomes increase. And it is precisely because savings are nothing more than the residual, the leftovers of income and a fairly constant proportion of income, that new investment will be multiplied through the economy, resulting in far more additional resources being utilized than the original investment. All of which, it should be said, suggested that government expenditure should take up an increasing proportion of the slack created by rising amounts of aggregate savings, and that this spending would be non-inflationary precisely because spending and saving practices (which Keynes described as a decision either to hold money or bonds) were so habitual in nature.

However in this analysis the first step in thinking about aggregate expenditure and income, the macroeconomy, was not the fact that one person's spending is another person's income, although of course this is an essential ingredient in Keynes' theory. What makes this statement possible in the first place is that the theory referenced the behaviour, or to be more exact the consumption and saving practices, of ordinary people not just entrepreneurs. Previously, as discussed, both neoclassical and Austrian-school economics had given little attention to the consumer. Now Keynes was acknowledging that ordinary individuals also faced uncertainty and that time made a difference. For Keynes, it seemed obvious that habits formed and stuck; this aspect of human nature he was happy to take for granted. Once character was formed and spending habits crystallized, individual expenditure could be understood as a function of income received; non-habitual consumption practices were generally reduced to a minimum. Thus rather than calling this figure 'a consumer', one might rather suggest a different label, the 'worker-saver', to describe how Keynes envisaged the psychological propensities of these human agents. People work, habits invariably determine spending, what is left over is saved.

The consumer that Keynes referenced in *The General Theory* was, as shall be discussed in section 2.3, not the same figure of the consumer referenced by IEA authors, or by Friedman and Hayek in the 1950s and 1960s. Keynes' consumer or non-entrepreneurial human agent was essentially imagined as his co-Bloomsbury set writers and artists imagined him, in need of creative leadership and guidance; like E. M. Forster's Leonard Bast in *Howards End* (1910), the working classes were yearning to rise above their biological lives, yet all too often consumption was motivated by habits of emulation.[32] For Keynes in *The General Theory* the consumer was certainly far more than just the marginalist 'thin' subject that Knight had described. But at the same time the consumer as worker-saver was clearly a reflection of how Keynes and his cohorts perceived the nature of the British working-class male of the early twentieth century. At any rate what matters for the purposes of this book is that Keynes did indeed have in mind a specific typification of human agency that constituted a central reference point in his attempt to turn economics into social science and social policy.

To 'societize' economics, to make it a theory of the aggregate or macroeconomy, Keynes had described all the human agents in the economy as they moved through time. From the Austrian marginalists he took the entrepreneur, and in depicting everyone else as a 'worker-saver' Keynes was referencing what he took for granted as being the stereotypical idea of the psychology of the British working-class man. This figure no longer lived entirely 'hand-to-mouth', but instead earned enough to be able to save. Nonetheless as he appeared in theory, he was not deemed sophisticated enough to be able to plan with any great presence of mind how to save for investment or future contingencies. At the very least there was far too much uncertainty to plan with any great intent. In the theory therefore, it would be fair to say that savings were the 'leftovers' from income put away for unknown reasons. Perhaps Keynes' notion of the worker-saver was a fair reflection of the kinds of persons that had come into being in the early twentieth century. But by describing this kind of agency in theory, by 'making up' this category of person, this new social theory, in guiding economic policy, would also guide the way that people actually experienced their economic lives.[33] That is to say, if Keynesian-style economic policy required government to plan British industry and set up large corporations, then this would inevitably lead to individuals experiencing the economy in certain ways; and certainly less as the consumers that neoliberals imagined them to be.

2.3 Problematizing worker-savers, 'making up' the consumer

Recollecting their own upbringing and formation of their own political compass in an interview published by the IEA in 2001, the IEA directors Ralph Harris and Arthur Seldon commented that they found the idea that the working class were incapable of running their own affairs and making their own decisions 'offensive'. They were 'appalled by the insensitivity of governments to the efforts of the working classes to help themselves.'[34] They took issue with the way they believed workers and consumers had been made up in theory by the dominant progressive thinking inherent in economic policy-making. Freedom, when defined as the social provision of economic security, was viewed by these authors as patronizing paternalism. Thus the aim of the second half of this chapter is to demonstrate how a political rationality inherent in the early IEA publications in the late 1950s and 1960s developed around a specific problematizing of progressive and Keynesian conceptions of the worker-saver.

IEA publications in the late 1950s and 1960s practised a much stronger figure of the consumer. At the same time, Hayek and Friedman were important figures in problematizing Keynesian thinking by referencing a different conception of consumption and figure of the consumer. Nonetheless IEA authors and in particular Harris and Seldon also referenced the consumer, what they labelled the sovereign consumer, to make arguments addressed to the problem of how to govern. While it is not being argued that Friedman's 'wealth-owning unit', Hayek's 'agent of progress' or the IEA's 'sovereign consumer' were necessarily identical figures, there is clearly a very strong family resemblance in the way these and other authors were thinking and conceiving of the consumer at the time.

This section considers some of the earliest IEA publications, as well as some of the key works of Hayek and Friedman, to demonstrate how the worker-saver was reconstituted and reidentified as the consumer, and how from the start this figure was central to the question of how to govern the economy. The focus will be on three themes running through the IEA publications of the era, as well as in the work of Hayek and Friedman. First, a specific appeal was made to the idea that consumers are the foundational unit of economic progress and civilization; the same sort of calculative mental processes that are used by entrepreneurs also determine consumer spending. Second, a shift was made away from the neoclassical model of perfect competition. IEA authors consistently argued that monopoly was neither permanent, nor the size of any one individual business problematic, so long as consumers were allowed and encouraged to be sovereign agents in the economy. Finally, monetary stability was deemed as significant for the consumer as for the entrepreneur, and because it was a necessary prerequisite of undistorted consumer behaviour it was also essential for progress. This inevitably meant that Keynes' demand for money function was problematized as an inadequate description of the balance sheet of the modern consumer and, critically, this laid the groundwork for transforming the relationship in economic policy between the consumer and credit.

2.3.1 The consumer and progress

The IEA was set up in the context of Hayek's essay *The Intellectuals and Socialism* (1949); an essay which was essentially a call to arms to 'offer a new liberal programme which appeal[ed] to the imagination' as much as Fabian and collectivist ideas had previously succeeded in persuading intellectuals.[35] Hayek argued that a new political vision was required that would not just warn of the dangers of collectivism but offer an alternative. It would have to offer up images of an advancing society in which, as Harris and Seldon did indeed argue in 1958, everyone had a part to play as agents of a second industrial revolution, enacting a philosophy where all humans could assert their will[36] whether they were entrepreneurs (as with Böhm-Bawerk, Schumpeter and Keynes) or not. To this end, these authors would be doing precisely what Keynes had done, not just in terms of publicizing and popularizing theory; but critically, like him, making an argument that incorporated all the human agents of the economy.

The vision of the non-entrepreneurial class referenced by Hayek and the IEA authors was very different from Keynes' worker-saver, but theirs was a clear vision all the same, something very much lacking in their classical liberal forebears. Neoliberal theory, just like economic theorizing in the name of social ends, would reference a much more complex figure of the consumer than previously provided by classical and neoclassical economists alike. That said, there was clearly a difference in style between the IEA's pamphleteering and Hayek's more academic work. Nonetheless all of these authors were asking questions about progress and economic growth, and about the role of the consumer. Before discussing the IEA vision of the sovereign consumer, as envisaged by its directors Harris and Seldon, it is worth briefly considering Hayek's conception of progress as laid out in his 1945 essay, *The Use of Knowledge in Society*.

Hayek's essay was in many ways a rejoinder to the 'socialist calculation debate' that had raged in the 1930s. It addressed arguments concerning the possibility of constructing an economic system using Walrasian general equilibrium without market prices. However, it also marked a point in Hayek's career in which he shifted his work on capital, production and cycles into social and political theorizing, beyond the Böhm-Bawerkian focus on production and capital (the problems with which Hayek had been battling in *Prices and Production* (1932) and his *Pure Theory of Capital* (1941)) and into the realm of the social; that is to say into a context in which his arguments would address all the human economic agents that made up the economy.

On the face of it *The Use of Knowledge in Society*, which is Hayek's clearest statement of his arguments at the time, was a critique of the neoclassical assumption that the economic problem was to calculate prices and outputs. Hayek argued that the data which was needed to make these calculations was not 'given' and could never be so, because it existed solely in the minds of all the separate economic agents acting in their own specific circumstances of time and place. The notion of planning had thus been entirely misunderstood: planning rightly belonged not to a collective endeavour (such as government) but with every individual in society who constantly made decisions about how to allocate their scarce resources to a range of competing desires. Thus every individual economic act was an act of planning and no one body, whether collective or individual, could possibly know what was going on in the minds of every individual in an economy. For Hayek, only the price system, which had arisen without conscious planning, could coordinate the actions of different people without them having to know everyone else's plans. Using prices, civilization was thus able 'to extend the span of our utilisation of resources beyond the span of control of any one mind; and therefore ... dispense with the need ... [for] ... conscious control'.[37] Quoting philosopher Alfred Whitehead, Hayek was able to conclude that civilization could only advance because it was able to increase the number of important operations that could be performed without being thought about.[38]

A faulty pricing system would not only lead to irrational outcomes for an economy and society but, according to Hayek, a fully functioning price system enabled people to take actions that led to progress and the furthering of civilization. Thus working through Hayek's logic backwards: civilization was defined as the satisfaction of an increasing stock of desires, which essentially meant enabling more people to realize their own personal plans. By definition, to realize an aim by taking an economic action demonstrated rationalism, an understanding of cause and effect; and because of the dispersal of information, the price system maximized the chance of this happening. As a result, Hayek could claim that the price system was rational and led to progress and the enhancement of civilization.

Everyone was a planner and everyone would share the benefits of the price system. But what might be the appropriate term through which to capture this generalized agent of progress? It would certainly include business entrepreneurs, but there were far more individuals in society than the traditional entrepreneur-capitalists. And there was nothing explicitly written here to suggest that Hayek's vision would immediately appeal to a worker-saver, spending his income as he always had, saving what was left over. However for Harris and Seldon, Hayek's agent of progress was very clearly identifying the sovereign consumer as well as the entrepreneur. Thus in a modification of language, by directly labelling this agent the consumer, Harris and Seldon could appeal to everyone because everyone was a consumer. The consumer was thus to be imagined as the foundational unit of progress; that is the simplest unit of planning and investment, albeit in a simpler form, engaged in essentially the same thought processes as the entrepreneur.

To designate this figure the IEA authors used the term 'consumer sovereignty'. It was a term explicitly employed in Harris and Seldon's tracts *Hire Purchase in a Free Society* (1958) and *Advertising in a Free Society* (1959) to act as the foundational basis on which a free society operates. In theory it meant two things: firstly that no one could know an individual's wants more than they do themselves. This at any rate was no more than the assumption inherent in the marginalist theory of value. But additionally the point was made that no method of centralized decision-making could match the dynamic diversity of personal preferences and circumstances. Thus the consumer became the explicit human label for Hayek's decentralized sites of time and circumstance. For Harris and Seldon, the free society 'governed by man as a consumer not by man as a producer' minimizes 'resistances to change' that inevitably lead to 'impoverishment and restrictions on liberty.'[39] Progress and civilization[40] were the results of a mentality shared by consumers and entrepreneurs alike: being adaptable, having free play to act on one's desires, planning in each individual situation of time and circumstance. The agent of progress was the consumer and, as the next section demonstrates, this figure became the key motif in IEA arguments on a number of specific policy issues, including advertising and consumer credit.

2.3.2 Consumer sovereignty and the impossibility of monopoly

The sovereign consumer was the key reference for the IEA in the context of policy debates. Indeed in their earliest publications Harris and Seldon sought to debunk the notion, consistent with both classical and progressive liberalism, in which the consumer was held to be weak in the face of entrepreneurs and companies that could effectively create monopolies at will. Schumpeter (1943) for instance had argued that monopolistic practices were by definition inherent in all capitalistic behaviour; an entrepreneur would use all the means available to protect his business including patents, pricing policies and location. Schumpeter however suggested that no monopolies are permanent because of the entrepreneurial spirit of innovation and change (what he called creative destruction[41]). In a similar vein many on the Left (J. K. Galbraith is a prime example, see below) were making the argument that advertising is a form of monopolistic activity because it seeks to create desires in consumers that they previously did not have. And of course, although certainly no socialist, Schumpeter had argued that creating desires in others was a mark of the highest calibre entrepreneur, the man of will and action. Conversely for the socially minded progressive liberals it signified the very impossibility of constructing a regime of perfect competition.

Harris and Seldon disagreed with both positions. In particular they discussed the development of the monopolistic interpretation of advertising in economics in the first half of the twentieth century in the work of Chamberlain and Kaldor, the latter deriding advertising as wasteful and misleading. The apotheosis of this position, for them, was to be found in the works of Galbraith, where advertising was portrayed as creating false consumer desires, making people buy things they did not need. In turn these kinds of arguments had led to increasing calls for legislative restrictions to be placed on corporate advertising.[42] It was a position found to be totally problematic within the IEA. That is to say, they might have agreed with Schumpeter that the gales of creative destruction would always undermine monopolistic positions in due course. However that was not enough for them, for if the consumer was to be the agent of progress, the sovereign of freedom, one had to deny the very possibility that the consumer would always be weak in the face of business concerns. If entrepreneurs could create the desires of consumers through advertising techniques, how could they ever be the adaptable and free agents of change?

Harris and Seldon's response was to argue that advertising did not 'create the market ... [it] ... found the market'. In other words advertising did not instil in consumers needs that they did not previously have, needs that might turn out to be false; instead advertising offered information on new products for which a desire was lying dormant, potentially waiting to be activated. 'The appeal to spend is not merely an appeal to rush out, withdraw savings, and buy this or that product. It is an appeal to raise one's standard of living, set one's sights higher all round ... whetting appetites, awakening ambition.' In the consumer society, advertising was an essential part of consumer value creation. And if the claims being made of a product turned out to be false then the consumer as sovereign would not buy that product again and would inform others of his or her experience. Advertising could not be a monopoly practice because the consumer was sovereign. In turn, socially inspired legislation that sought to protect the consumer was for them restrictive and patronizing: it assumed that consumers did not know their own mind. Advertising performed a 'beneficent function and ... service to mankind. ... Caveat emptor is not a primitive condition from which we have to be moved, but an ideal to which we should aspire.'[43]

This argument implied that entrepreneurs and businesses should always have the freedom to advertise, set prices and output. More than anything else, competition meant being free to be able to respond to the preferences of consumers, the foundational providers of progress. Thus Harris and Seldon set the tone for much of the work of the IEA in the 1960s. The perspective was always that consumers were not in need of protection from large corporations but instead consumer sovereignty would always imply progress in any one industry because of the innate adaptability of the consumer. In the meantime as long as consumers were allowed to be sovereign, with markets constructed to maintain their sovereignty, there could be no market failure brought about by the monopoly practices of businesses.

Under the auspices of the IEA, Harris and Seldon either wrote or commissioned (and edited by Seldon) a series of monographs (in most cases they were published in the Hobart Papers series), which applied these principles to different areas of economic action. *Hire Purchase in a Free Society* (1958) argued against restricting any form of arrangement, in this case consumer credit, that would not allow the assertion of the will of man as consumer[44] (see section 2.3.3). *To Let?* (1960) argued that rent control, born of a desire to do social good, had led to a deterioration of housing stock in Britain. No consumer with savings in his or her right mind, it was argued, would want to invest in a rent-controlled house; for this author a comparison of the London skyline with Erhard's modern Germany was a permanent reminder of the failure of planning in Britain.[45] *Health Through Choice* (1961), argued that it was wrong to mistrust consumer choice in the field of health. The author argued for wholesale denationalization as, in his view, the provision of health care would always be sub par if one assumed that consumers were not able to make their own medical choices and instead assumed, wrongly, that health care was a natural monopoly best served by collective provision.[46] *A Market for Labour* (1961) began by reminding the reader that a labour market was the only means for enabling the community of consumers to express preferences between alternative ways of using their labour. The point was not to direct labour but to improve the operation of the labour market through providing better information and training to those seeking jobs.[47] *Farming for Consumers* (1963) argued that agricultural boards were set up on the basis that consumers were not capable of making accurate assessments of relative prices, quantities and qualities of food products. Policies enacted on social grounds had restricted the development of agriculture in Britain and kept prices high; instead consumers should be given their freedom and given the necessary information to make their choices.[48] Finally, *Telephones – Public or Private?* (1966) made the case for the denationalization of the British telephone and postal service monopoly on the basis that consumer sovereignty was the only way to ensure adequate investment in a telephone service. Treating a consumer service as if it were a social obligation was problematic, so the author argued, because it was impossible to define and allocate appropriate costs on that basis.[49]

It is also worth noting that the IEA were not just a publishing house for the Hobart Papers. Harris and Seldon commissioned a series of surveys in which they sought to demonstrate that given appropriately asked questions, the public was far less keen on the social provision of welfare services than generally thought by intellectuals. Social provision would always ride roughshod over consumer sovereignty and, as they suggested, even the Fabian Society in recent publications had begun to argue that, without strong reasons to the contrary, people should be allowed to make their own choices.[50] Finally, it is important to remember that the IEA's remit to explain and convince others of their case always extended beyond intellectuals and politicians into schools and universities. This they set out to achieve with the publication of research monographs explicitly intended for use in the classroom. One such monograph, written by Christina Fulop, entitled *Consumers in the Market* (1967), neatly summarized the position adopted in all the above publications, clarifying for students that it was the consumer not the producer that guaranteed progress. 'The problem for consumers' (rather than producers') sovereignty is that, to safeguard his interest as producer, man would be tempted to stultify change by suppressing invention and innovation, which would eventually lead to stagnation.' Fulop went on to explain how consumer protection agencies could be problematic, why advertising, contra Galbraith, served a positive purpose and why it was a necessity that the retail price mechanism, which allowed producers to dictate the price their products were sold at by retail businesses had, with some small exceptions, been abolished.[51]

In concluding this section it is important to draw attention to Harris and Seldon's point about Fabian Society research on the welfare state. Even while IEA authors were writing about consumer sovereignty, the Left was not without those who were calling into question the received wisdom of the welfarist governing mentality. There were those who would of course argue for more planning and economic control, and who considered the politics of appealing to the newly 'embourgeoised' working class as revisionist and wrong.[52] Nonetheless there were different voices within the Fabian and Labour movement who were giving recognition to this new figure, the active consumer. For instance, Fabian Tract 155 (1953) thoroughly endorsed the idea that nationalized industries should cooperate with consumer councils to ensure that they were meeting consumer needs as best as possible.[53] Fabian Tract 188 (1957) addressed the issue of home ownership, suggesting that while housing did represent a stock of community wealth, it was not wrong for the government to offer help for those who wanted to own their own homes. Consumers were entitled to express this desire. Indeed, the author argued that Britain needed more equity capital and that it would be better if some of the savings going into paying off mortgages went instead into share ownership.[54] Finally and perhaps most importantly, the prominent Labour politician Tony Crosland began a critique of the Labour movement in 1960 arguing that Labour policies no longer satisfied the aspirations of the new and richer working class. Social attitudes had changed and so must policy.[55] By 1971 Crosland was echoing much that had been said at the IEA; criticizing those, like Galbraith, who assumed that consumers had been brainwashed into buying things they did not need. The Left, he believed, continued to fail to connect with the prevailing positive social attitude to consumer pleasures.[56] Indeed in the same year the influential journalist Samuel Brittan suggested in the IEA's second Hobart Paperback that in future the Labour Party might even consider becoming the party of the consumer.[57]

That is not to say that this recognition of the consumer among some on the Left implied the same kind of dismantling of the welfare state that the IEA had in mind, but the point is that IEA authors were not alone in recognizing changing attitudes and patterns of behaviour in society at large. It is thus worth remembering that the IEA were addressing themselves to changes in the real world, in which consumers were now more affluent. Indeed as has been documented by the historian Matthew Hilton (2003) significant shifts were taking place in the language of consumer movements in Britain. Prior to the Second World War, the discourse of consumer politics had been geared towards concepts like 'the living wage' that stressed the rights of all individuals to a basic standard of living, that is a basic level of consumption. In the post-war era of the 1950s and 1960s, consumer movements were changing in nature. 'Affluent consumerism' of the Consumer Association's *Which* magazine was about the promotion of wise and discriminating shopping. Responsibility for purchases most certainly lay with the consumer, but the movement was guided by ideas that had parallels with the IEA message: more information would empower consumers to be more discerning about what they purchased, ultimately forcing British manufacturers to better meet their demands.[58]

All the Hobart Papers discussed above were prefaced with the same message (written by Seldon). Their 'general theme' was to address how rising incomes had given increasing scope for consumer choice and that policies needed to be designed to take account of this. In conceptualizing this emerging figure of the consumer, the IEA were laying the groundwork for future government policies that would seek to act against those who were not deemed to be utilizing a consumer mentality. Government would aim to guide the possibilities of personhood and subjectivity. All the same the figure of the consumer as understood by the IEA authors in the late 1950s and 1960s in some respects reflected and recognized that a new form of subjectivity was increasingly coming into existence in society. Commentators on both the Left and Right of the political spectrum recognized that the assumptions of the working class mentality that had guided policy-makers were becoming problematic, that there was increasingly a class, not of worker-savers, but of active consumers.

2.3.3 The consumer-entrepreneur and money

So a critique of the way that consumers had been thought about, as passive and weak, was coming from all quarters, and was directed at a range of different renditions all connected with a progressive liberal governing mentality. Keynes' conception of consumer, the worker-saver, offered just one way in the assemblage of progressive liberal governmental practices for thinking about the non-entrepreneurial class. For many, however, it was not the attitudes to saving and habitual spending patterns that, as with Keynes, took centre stage, but that in their guise as consumers these individuals were often deemed unable to make appropriate decisions regarding products in the marketplace, say in health or education. Alternatively consumers might find themselves, due to a lack of information, being unable to resist very insistent marketing techniques. But certainly in the context of neoliberal economic theory, Keynes' rendition of the progressive liberal political rationality took centre stage in the theoretical counter-revolution. And none of his ideas were more critical than those regarding money and the consumption of financial services, such as the provision of credit. The relationship between money, credit and the consumer was present from the very beginning of the British neoliberal movement.

The monetary system and the concomitant availability of credit, as this book aims to demonstrate, came to play an increasingly central role in the practices associated with governing for the consumer. And money, banking and credit played a significant role in IEA publications, as the discussion at the end of this section and the next chapter demonstrates. However it is important to focus first on Milton Friedman's ideas, particularly in relation to his work in the 1950s, not only because it became critical in government policy-making in the 1970s and 1980s but also because it provides an extremely clear image of the active consumer and of consumption as a form of enterprise. For Friedman, refashioning Keynes' social world was first and foremost a question of problematizing and thus rethinking the worker-saver's psychological relationship to money.

Two pieces of Friedman's work stand out in the way they bring into question the ontology of the worker-saver: *The Quantity Theory of Money: A Restatement* (1956) and *A Theory of the Consumption Function* (1957). And just as with Keynes, it is not being suggested that this work somehow originated a new subjectivity in theory; Friedman's theories referenced a similar human agent that was being referenced by a set of authors that included Hayek, Harris and Seldon. Nonetheless they can be read as key statements of a specifically neoliberal mind set.

Friedman's restatement of the quantity theory was an explicit demand-for-money equation, indeed for him being a quantity theorist meant 'in the first instance' working on a theory of the demand for money.[59] One might indeed say that this was precisely what Friedman meant in his famous lecture, *The Counter-revolution in Monetary Theory*, delivered in London in 1970 and published by the IEA, when he said that Keynes was a quantity theorist;[60] for Keynes had also constructed a demand-for-money equation, one in which people made a choice between holding their savings as money or bonds. Thus Friedman was not denouncing Keynes' work on the demand for money, he was seeking to extend it. The 'Keynesian Revolution' had incorporated the whole social world, entrepreneurs and non-entrepreneurs, into a theory of the aggregate economy. Where Hayek's recognition of this had been somewhat philosophical in tone, Friedman's contribution was that much more involved with economic theory, suggesting that Keynes had oversimplified his discussion of the worker-saver's balance sheet.

It should be said that Keynes had already foreshadowed much of Friedman's argument, in recognizing that changes in the value of money, windfall gains and an expectation of higher future income might all affect current consumption. Yet where Keynes concluded that these factors were of little importance both in aggregate and because the future was ultimately too uncertain to act upon in the present,[61] Friedman moved these factors centre stage in his description of the behaviour of all wealth-owning units. Human beings, whether individuals, entrepreneurs or working together in business concerns to maximize profit, were portfolio managers, allocating resources to different assets, whether money (as a store of wealth), tradable securities, physical and intangible assets. This immediately meant that because wealth was measured as a unit of account (i.e. money, which is also an asset), changes in money's purchasing power would affect reallocations of wealth between assets. This in turn could lead to a misallocation of resources.

However the main point to draw out of this is that according to Friedman, wealth-owning units in their guise as individual humans were constantly repositioning their wealth between different assets that existed through time and which provided a flow (a series of income receipts), that were regularly received over the period of ownership or during the asset's useful economic life. One might say that Friedman was suggesting that the wealth-owning unit behaved in a fashion that recognized its own movement through time. This is not to deny that, as with any neoclassical theory, the wealth-owning unit was imbued with perfect knowledge and foresight, it was just that as an asset allocator, the wealth-owning unit was having to make a decision now about how to allocate resources to assets that would not cease to exist simply because the market had cleared. Consumers, like businesses, existed through time and the arrangement and constant repositioning of their assets would have a huge impact on their wealth over the course of their lives.

All of this is taken for granted in Friedman's *Restatement* of the quantity theory of money, where an expression was developed to include both the demand to hold money as well as the demand to hold all other assets. It demonstrates precisely what assets and the nature of these assets that Friedman had in mind. A wealth-owning unit could, just as had been suggested by Keynes' demand-for-money function, make a choice to hold wealth in the form of cash or bonds. Holding money yielded a utility merely from the convenience and security of having it on hand, and the yield on a bond was dependent on its interest payment (coupon) plus or minus the effect of changing interest rates on the value of the bond over its time to maturity. Both money and bonds provided nominal returns. Wealth could also be allocated to equities, where the yield took the form of claims on the profits of companies, received as dividends and capital returns. They were similar to bonds except that income would be received in perpetuity and would be linked to the future general price levels because company earnings immediately incorporated the effects of inflation.[62]

Up to this point, Friedman had said nothing controversial; Keynes had also included money and tradable securities in his demand-for-money function. Additionally though Friedman now extended the demand-for-money function to show that the same wealth that was allocated to holding money and tradable securities could also be allocated to the purchase of physical and non-physical goods. Measuring the yield or utility of these assets was of course problematic, but the very act of placing them on a continuum of assets including money presupposed that any purchase could provide an income flow that was reducible and comparable to the income received from any other asset. That said Friedman did suggest simple ways to include these flows on his demand-for-money function. Physical non-human goods were thought of as equivalent to equities, except that the annual stream of income they yielded would be in kind rather than in money (in his model it was nonetheless assumed that the flow could be measured in monetary terms). Finally, there were the investments in human capital, which Friedman added to the equation by assuming that the income derived from these investments would be a fixed proportion of the income received from investments in non-human capital. However, as he noted, the payment to another human being did not really represent an investment because the income was actually received by the payer rather than the service provider. In general terms Friedman remarked,

> Shifts between human capital and other forms must take place through direct investment and disinvestment in the human agent ... the tastes and preferences of wealth-owning units for the service streams ... [yields] ... arising from different forms of wealth must in general simply be taken for granted as determining the form of the demand function.[63]

The wealth-owning unit could be a business or an individual, but if it was the latter, consumption no longer signified the end of the economic process in any one discrete time period. The allocation of scarce resources did not finish at the moment of market clearance, with the 'ontologically-light' consumer that Knight had pointed to. On the contrary the consumer was making asset allocation decisions that created asset holdings that would continue to exist through time. And it did not matter whether these assets were bonds, property, clothes or education; all were assets of different sorts. As such the consumer did not necessarily use up resources; consumption was now a term that signified the beginning of a whole new arrangement of investments in which each individual aimed to 'produce' themselves in their chosen way.

With regards to consumption practices, Friedman was explicit. Consumption should no longer be thought of as a habitual practice; Keynes was wrong to suggest that the marginal propensity to consume was consistent and always had a value of less than one. Instead Friedman's alternative hypothesis was that 'men do not adapt their cash expenditure on consumption to their cash receipts'. Put another way, spending, he believed, is not so much a function of income but a function of one's expectation as to what permanent standard of living is commensurate with the subjective assessment of the worth of one's own human capital. Changes in cash receipts (income) would only change spending patterns if these changes were thought to represent permanent changes in one's earning power. If a change in income were deemed temporary then the individual would aim to maintain spending by borrowing at an appropriate rate of interest.

To this extent next week's pay cheque might be totally irrelevant to next week's spending. And, as Friedman admitted, implicit in this was a definition of consumption not in terms of purchases but in terms of the value of services, that is to say the income received over time from what was bought. Thus 'much that one sees as consumption gets reclassified as savings' which of course means investment.[64] So consumption, in this sense, no longer necessarily used up resources as in the classical position. Likewise borrowing to consume was not necessarily, as Böhm-Bawerk had argued, profligate and wasteful, always increasing the depletion of a nation's subsistence fund.[65] Instead at the very least consumer credit was a way to manage cash flows over one's lifetime.

Friedman considered himself a scientist; his critique of Keynes involved an empirical investigation into spending practices. He believed that his results suggested that saving was not just the leftovers from income once habitual spending had taken place. Perhaps on a practical level he might not have declared that all consumption spending is an investment; perhaps he would have seen this as a *reductio ad absurdum* of his theory. Nonetheless where should one draw the line? In the formalism of his *Restatement* there is no guideline and no suggestion that the equation is not intended to capture all the decisions of the wealth-owning unit. Either it is or it is not; can one have it both ways? The following quote would seem to suggest that there is no exclusion intended.

> Dollars of money are not distinguished according as they are said to be held for one purpose. Rather, each dollar is, as it were, regarded as rendering a variety of services ... and the holder of money as altering his money holdings until the value to him of the addition to the total flow of services produced by adding a dollar to his money stock is equal to the reduction in the flow of services produced by subcontracting a dollar from each of the other forms in which he holds assets.[66]

The important point is that in this model spending involved the construction of a portfolio of assets that produced a yield over time. This was as applicable to the consumer as to businesses; they were all wealth-owning units. Perhaps, the neoclassical methodology that Friedman employed forces too extreme a position. At any rate there is nothing in the theory that enables anyone to claim that each item of expenditure does not involve the purchase of an asset, however short its useful economic life. Thus what matters in this description is not the positivistic method that Friedman employed, it is that consumption signifies the beginning of a process of self-investment in which flows are received through time. Keynes had made it clear that consumption was important to economic growth, that everyone's excess savings could disincentivize entrepreneurial investment. Friedman also believed that everyone was relevant to economic growth, because in his model everyone was referenced as an entrepreneur, adding to the nation's stock of yielding assets.

The consumer theory and the demand-for-money theory can therefore be read as two sides of the same coin; put together they problematized the notion of the worker-saver, practising instead an idea of human agency where individual decisions, consumption and saving became decisions regarding how best to allocate wealth and invest in oneself. Consumers were in fact often making investment decisions regarding the future streams of incomes they wanted to receive: they were entrepreneurs-of-the-self, consumers-as-entrepreneurs rather than the worker-savers described by Keynes.

Friedman was not alone in making these kinds of arguments. IEA authors referenced a similar conception of the consumer in which the distinctions between consumption and production broke down. Enoch Powell's IEA pamphlet *Saving in a Free Society* (1960) for instance demonstrated no qualms about applying a similar perspective to ordinary consumer activities. The nation's stock of capital was constituted by both the fixed assets of manufacturing companies and by consumer purchases of cars, furniture, 'for the housewife's larder' and education. Consumption of all forms was an investment akin to business investment: the only difference being that the former was an investment in the self, in one's own balance sheet. To this extent the act of purchase and the use of a consumer good did not necessarily use up resources. In terms of public policy, for Powell, there could thus be no justification for thinking that there should be more or less 'saving'; because this would assume that the government had the ability to evaluate all consumption spending in relation to the future yield it gave to each individual consumer.[67]

Harris and Seldon's 1958 monograph on consumer credit, while not worded in such definitive terms, was written in defence of the consumer and the consumer's right to borrow. Specifically on the issue of hire purchase they argued that the current debate had become mired in the restrictionist and prejudicial attitudes towards the working classes adopted they believed by those championing the social cause. Hire purchase in fact they argued often went hand in hand with saving, that is with investing in durable goods. To purchase a good did not categorically imply that a resource was being used up, quite the opposite it might imply an investment in the household. Moreover, who could say what was right for anyone to invest in? Harris and Seldon were vehement that it was not just for the purchase of tangible, consumer durable goods that credit should be made readily available; consumers should be able to buy intangible services on credit too.

Hire purchase helped expand ownership, which in itself expressed fundamental instincts and as such there was 'virtually no limit to potential demand for consumer durable goods obtainable through hire purchase.' Consumer credit provided finance for consumer investment; to restrict it was entirely wrong.[68] Even at this early stage in the life of the IEA a link had been forged between how to govern for the consumer and the acceptance of rising household debt. At the very least, these authors believed that controlling consumer borrowing was no way to control inflation.

> One day … the notion that hire purchase control could be used as a substitute for control of the supply of money will be seen as the futile dream it

> always was. On that day, hire purchase and related forms of consumer credit will be able to look ahead to new horizons. There is enormous scope for extending the use of consumer credit for durables of all kinds, including labour-saving or pleasure-giving devices not yet invented ... services as well ... [for instance] ... air transport, holidays, loans to finance home repairs.... The commercial banks must extend the scope of their services in order to make sure that the second Industrial Revolution will not be held back by financial difficulties.[69]

2.4 Concluding remarks

Knowing how to govern requires an explicit vision of the human agents for whom one is governing. In turn different governing mentalities practise different conceptions of human economic agency, whatever the form of discourse: economic theory, political philosophy or policy pamphlet. Perhaps what led to claims by the IEA authors that Keynes was more a politician than an economist was that he was such a successful one-man show, that Keynes himself translated his theories of money and consumption into an actionable political programme. Alternatively perhaps it was that what Keynes offered fell on ears that were already entirely attuned to a progressive liberal mentality of rule. 'Keynesian' thinking was already conventional wisdom; rather like the label 'Thatcherism' that appeared over twenty years after the foundation of the IEA, it came to stand for a political rationality already well constituted. This latter interpretation has been the one put forward in this chapter.

The progressive liberal perspective and reference points inherent in Keynes' thinking were not in themselves revolutionary; but by providing a role for non-entrepreneurs in economic theory, giving these consumers meaning and existence through time in a way that both classical political economy and neoclassical economics had not, Keynes was already pointing to a new possibility for liberalism: one that would include all agents of the economy in one class. This post-classical liberalism, or neoliberalism, would still be a social theory of the economy, including everyone, but one in which it was possible to assume that the economic decisions of individual consumers as asset allocators would be aligned to the economic interests of society. There would be one class of people in the social order constituted by enterprising consumers and entrepreneurs, very distinct from the class-based social order described by classical liberals composed of capitalists, landowners and workers. And as each private site of enterprise would seek to maximize self-fulfilment it was believed that there was little ground to argue that the government should act as an agent to maintain economic security.

This new figure of the active consumer was referenced in the theoretical work of Hayek and Friedman, and this figure existed both in the minds of IEA authors in the late 1950s and 1960s as well as in the minds of some on the Left and in the new post-war consumer movements. No doubt it reflected the changing nature of society at the time and the way people were living their lives. But the concern here is with a mentality of rule and the kinds of governmental programmes that follow from different perspectives on human agency, from reference points that become ingrained and locked in the minds of those who govern the economy. To say that society was composed of active consumers, rather than weak consumers at the mercy of corporations or workers saving what was left over of their incomes, meant that a neoliberal governing mentality would be referencing the whole social order, constituted at its foundation by enterprising consumers, seeking wherever possible to govern for those self-same consumers.

Problematizing Keynesianism and the progressive liberal governing mentality essentially meant identifying a human agent, the consumer, that, neoliberals believed, had been misidentified previously as a worker-saver at the mercy of large corporations. And from this perspective the assumption could be made that a whole range of enterprising units, consumers, household consuming units and business concerns constituted the social and economic order. But as the next chapter discusses, during the late 1960s and 1970s, IEA authors began increasingly to confront a world that did not appear to them as it had existed in their publications. British economic performance was deteriorating in relative and absolute terms and the New Right sought to explain and understand all facets of that performance. As the following chapter discusses, in addition to problematizing Keynes and/or Keynesian policies, these authors turned their attention to an examination of the economy as they understood it to be, and the kinds of human economic agents that existed in it. This in turn laid the groundwork for a set of policies that would seek to change attitudes and behaviour: intervention, that is, for the sake of consumer sovereignty and therefore the market.

3 Diagnosing the British economy

Much of the early work of the Institute of Economic Affairs (IEA) formed a coherent programme in which the agreed answer to certain economic problems was to be found in consumer sovereignty. As the last chapter demonstrated this was practically the opposite of saying that government needed to concern itself with consumer protection and with minimizing the power of large corporations, either through specific legislation or nationalization. The early publications of the IEA assumed that consumers were already equipped with the necessary faculties to make appropriate and discerning choices and, with their inherent adaptability, facilitate change and progress. Yet, for IEA authors, the experience of the 1960s and 1970s demonstrated that there was something wrong with the British economy; a malaise had infected it that needed to be identified and diagnosed.[1] Britain's economic growth and productivity rates were consistently below the level of other developed countries and for the IEA this meant that the consumer was not facilitating change and progress. Instead they believed that government involvement in the economy, while being well intentioned, was decidedly problematic.

Of course, the IEA were certainly not the only intellectual grouping to be concerned about the economy; politicians and think tanks representing all political viewpoints sought to understand the nature of Britain's relative decline. Even so, this chapter specifically addresses the question of how, between 1960 and the late 1970s, the IEA problematized existing techniques for governing the British economy. There were two aspects to the IEA's diagnosis, one a continuous critique of all governments' economic policies in the 1960s and 1970s, the other specifically related to the notion of crisis in the 1970s. The first aspect essentially stated the ongoing neoliberal position that government intervention in the economy was stifling consumer sovereignty, whether through Keynesian demand management, brief flirtations with indicative planning in the 1960s, or through more micro-style intervention strategies in the 1970s. Many different discursive strategies were used by the IEA: some tried to argue that Keynesian policies were a corruption of Keynes' ideas, focusing primarily on methodological issues; some argued against the whole notion that growth was always a function of fixed capital formation. Others argued, particularly in relation to Britain's financial system and the policies of Edward Heath's Conservative government of 1970 to 1974, that the meaning of competition had been completely misunderstood.

The second aspect of the IEA's critique of Keynesianism took shape in response to the historical circumstances of the early 1970s. During this period, IEA authors launched what might very well be described as their own critical history of the present. That is to say, quoting Foucauldian philosopher Colin Gordon, that criticism was practised by all these writers as genealogy: as 'a historical investigation into events that have led us to constitute ourselves and recognize ourselves as subjects of what we do, think and say'.[2] For Gordon, genealogy had last been practised in the 1930s and 1940s by figures on the Right, such as Hayek and Rüstow, and on the Left by Theodor Adorno, Walter Benjamin and Karl Polanyi. All these authors had written in various and very different ways about the collapse of classical liberalism into depression, fascism and war.

This is not to claim that Britain in the 1970s was facing catastrophe on the same scale as Germany in the 1930s. But with the advent of economic crisis and high levels of inflation in Britain in the 1970s, many IEA authors came to adopt a narrative that explained the crisis historically, as a failure of so many to adapt their attitudes and conduct to the present times. Far too few people in Britain were, so the argument went, identifying and constituting themselves first and foremost as consumers. In this narrative, habits of thought had become misaligned to social reality and methods of government had, they believed, produced conduct not commensurate with progress. However to adopt this history required neoliberals to recognize that the economy was not made up of sovereign consumers, as had been previously assumed. In resolving this tension IEA authors invoked a critical history with a remarkably social and evolutionary tone.

3.1 Problematizing Keynesianism

It was not until the late 1970s and early 1980s that the impact of public choice economics began to be felt in the publications of the IEA, with their questioning of the very possibility of benign government. The American economist James Buchanan, for instance, co-authored two IEA papers in 1978 and 1981 that argued that analysis should assume that political practice involved time-inconsistent promises and policies designed in the first instance to win elections.[3] However in the publications of the 1960s and 1970s IEA authors did not bring this viewpoint to the fore. Generally speaking, their publications did not attempt to deny that politicians had good intentions; instead they believed that governments were doing incalculable damage to the economy precisely because they had assumed that there was no limit to the power of good intentions.[4]

The IEA shared a desire to see the British economy growing and for standards of living to improve; what they questioned was how to govern with these outcomes in mind. Broadly speaking in the 1960s their concern, as discussed in Chapter 2, was with particular industries and the role that the consumer should be playing in the allocation of economic resources. As section 3.1.1 shows, when addressing macroeconomic policy, IEA authors poured scorn on the idea, whether practised in Keynesian demand management or French-style indicative planning, that investment in capital goods was the only means through which to ensure continued economic growth. In the 1970s, as well as focusing on broader issues relating to how to govern the economy, IEA authors also problematized micro-interventions geared towards making industry more competitive. These arguments are discussed in section 3.1.2.

3.1.1 Growthmanship

The IEA position on Keynesian demand management and government-led planning was very negative. Their position on Keynes himself was more ambivalent. In some circumstances, as discussed in the previous chapter, Keynes was derided as being an economist only of the politically possible. However an alternative IEA discursive strategy focused on the way in which, so it was argued, Keynes' ideas had become corroded by his followers. Thus according to Colin Clark (1961), by 1939, Keynes had come to understand lessons that Keynesians did not, that the type of work given to the unemployed was just as important as the act of doing it. Any work was not necessarily better than no work.[5] In a similar vein Terence Hutchison argued that Keynes' papers written after *The General Theory* showed that he had always recognized a natural level of unemployment below which the government should not be forcing the economy to operate. Hutchison's revelation was that Keynes had considered that in the late 1930s this could be as high as 12 per cent of the workforce, rather than the 3 per cent level that Keynesians at Cambridge University, like Richard Kahn and Nicholas Kaldor, were suggesting in the 1950s and 1960s. By propounding their own views Hutchison argued that the Keynesians were counterfeiting Keynes' intellectual heritage.[6]

IEA authors also had methodological problems with the Keynesians that they did not necessarily have with Keynes himself. Hayek and fellow Austrian school economist Ludwig Lachmann argued that Keynes' ideas had been corrupted by the scientism of econometrics. For them, translating the notion that unemployment was due to insufficient demand for labour into a statistical policy model took for granted the explanation without leaving room for alternative hypotheses based on understanding how people made decisions. They questioned the possibility of constructing testable aggregates based on information that was held in particular circumstances of time and place. Lachmann in particular made the point that Keynes had a very developed sense of the subjective nature of the entrepreneur totally at odds with an economic policy in which differences in preferences and expectations were irrelevant to the need to produce more. There was some truth to this: Keynes' understanding of the entrepreneur was in keeping with Böhm-Bawerk and the Austrian tradition. Nonetheless, for these authors, Keynes had offered the germ of an idea whose danger lay in giving politicians something to do: a temptation too difficult to resist, to be seen to be doing something, whatever it was.[7]

All these arguments were part of an almost instinctive questioning of the notion that the production of capital goods was the only proper source of increasing national wealth. One means to do this was to argue that Keynes was not really a Keynesian and, as Hutchison argued, that it was Erhard's Germany that really represented enlightened Keynesian economic policy.[8] For Clark, in his Hobart Paper *Growthmanship* (1961), the point about Keynes' 'specific' theory was precisely this, that however relevant it might have been for the depths of the 1930s depression, it had mistakenly given rise to the impression that investment in physical capital goods (rather than the production of consumer goods) was the way to grow an economy. This was, as he put it, 'the germ of the idea that has done so much harm in economic thinking'. Keynesian macroeconomists, Clark maintained, such as Alvin Hansen and Evsey Domar (based at Harvard and Massachusetts Institute of Technology (MIT) respectively) had translated this idea into econometric formulations, which had been condensed into the capital-output ratio, in which it was taken for granted that the only way to raise economic growth was through capital investment. (This of course for Hayek would have been an error of 'scientistic' thinking.) Thus if an economy had a capital-output ratio of three then three additional units to the national stock of capital would lead to output being raised by one unit per annum. If a 6 per cent increase in capital investment led to a 2 per cent increase in output and the population was growing at 3 per cent then, according the theory, the country would be stuck in a vicious cycle of poverty.[9]

On its own, the capital–output ratio was a convenient working concept but it had, according to Clark, been 'insidiously elevated' to the status of 'a general economic law'. In turn, he argued, a number of mistakes had been made. Human factors in economic growth had been ignored such as education and entrepreneurship; and the model also ignored, Clark argued, the impact that production of more consumer goods would have because their presence on the high street would act as an important incentive for people to increase their effort and output. Rather like Harris and Seldon, Clark was arguing that the activity of consumption itself was transformative and key to developing a mentality suited to change and progress. In Britain, Clark complained that channelling government money through subsidies to industries such as coal, electricity and railways had led to a waste of hundreds of millions of pounds: conspicuous investment was ultimately as wasteful as conspicuous consumption.[10]

During the 1950s and 1960s the government had in fact done much to move Britain towards more open market pricing; most wartime controls were gone by the mid 1950s and in 1964 producer controls over retail pricing were abolished. But no doubt there existed a broad consensus for the continued use of Keynesian demand management, and that the emphasis of policy would be on maintaining industrial output growth. Indeed during both Conservative and Labour administrations in the 1960s a range of policies were used to limit consumer spending in order to lower inflationary pressure (and protect the pound) while doing relatively little damage to output (and therefore employment). The burden of these policies, which included income controls, import duties, hire-purchase controls and higher rates of income tax, invariably fell on consumers.[11] In addition, IEA authors were particularly alarmed by successive governments' flirtation with the idea, first under the Conservative's National Economic Development Council

(1961–64) and subsequently under Labour's Department for Economic Affairs (1964–66), that there should be more attempts in Britain at coordinated national long-term planning. Higher growth rates in France were viewed, at least in government circles, as proof that indicative planning could make all the difference to Britain's industrial performance.

Attempts in the 1960s to coordinate a national effort to increase growth (with a focus on exports so as to counteract Britain's recurring balance of payments problems) were short-lived and failed to deliver the levels of growth that had been indicated in the plan. Indeed the Labour Party's plan was soon abandoned in favour of what appeared like a permanent battle to stop the pound devaluing; a battle, it should be added, that was lost in 1967. Even so, while in operation, critics on the Left and Right saw these attempts at planning as half-hearted.[12] Writing for the IEA, George Polanyi made an argument highly reminiscent of Hayek in *The Road to Serfdom.* Planning for Polanyi was devoid of intellectual and moral foundation because governments could never know the minds of the community made up as it was by millions of individual consumers and businesses. Moreover the government were not forcing the different parties to adhere to the plan, but instead were relying on people's willingness to work towards the guidelines. Thus for Polanyi the whole thing was half-enforced and half-believed, the result being that virtually no difference was made to economic performance. Instead to make planning a reality (even if in Polanyi's mind it would no doubt fail anyway) would require ever-increasing Soviet-style restrictions on freedom: the inevitable incomes policies that came at the end of periods of economic growth were for him just the sign of things to come.[13] British indicative planning was neither indicative nor real planning at all. Instead it was based, as Hobart Paper 35 (1966) written by the anonymous Spartacus had claimed, on 'wish-dream projections' with no idea of how to make these projections a reality.[14]

Methodological errors, a misunderstanding of Keynes (Polanyi cited Keynesian economist Roy Harrod as a particularly malign force in the development of economic policy[15]), and a desire, however benevolent, by politicians to be seen to be doing something: all these reasons were given by IEA authors when problematizing the role that government was taking in the economy in the 1960s with regard to trying to encourage and facilitate increased production. All these IEA pamphlets were attempts to demonstrate the futility of seeking growth through any means other than competition and consumer sovereignty. The IEA argued that all these interventions succeeded in doing was stopping prices working effectively as signals that would enable businesses to meet consumer demands and enable consumers to be able to design and enact their own personal plans. The solution to Britain's low relative levels of growth was thus necessarily related to consumer sovereignty. There was absolutely nothing wrong with the goal of economic growth; this was a perfectly desirable goal that entirely corresponded with the growing affluence of consumers. But for the IEA what this required was a social policy that sought to free consumers to be able to make more choices, forcing producers to compete for their custom. This, and only this, would ensure progress.

While the IEA were referencing the consumer, economic policies in the 1960s were referencing the worker-saver, with habitual spending practices: these contrasting theories of economic growth only made sense in the context of their respective political rationality. The capital-output ratio, for instance, did not capture the behaviour of individuals if one assumed that every individual was concerned with the development of his or her personal plans and human capital. But this does not mean that it was 'false science'; it was science that practised a different precept of human conduct. Thus if one's perspective was that consumption in and of itself used up resources (classical liberalism) or that consumption patterns were habitual (Keynesian progressive liberalism) then the logical conclusion from this viewpoint would be that growth was bound to be a function of production, that is investment in capital goods (plant and machinery) which would subsequently produce more consumer goods for future consumption.

This of course was not the viewpoint of the IEA authors: consumption could be interpreted as an investment or, at the very least, as an activity that affected the consumer. Thus the greater the availability of different consumer goods, the more the incentive for the consumer to better him or herself, thereby casting off the old habitual practices of the worker-saver. Keynes' theory shared the earlier perspective, not that of the IEA. He was no fan of econometrics, that is certainly true, and it is doubtful that he would have fully condoned attempts to plan the economy. Nonetheless governing the economy for the sake of producing more physical output represented a view of society and its constituent human agents that was entirely commensurate with Keynes' thinking. *The General Theory* was practising a particular mentality of rule that was equally being practised in the theories and policy implications of Harrod, Domar, Kahn and Kaldor; economic security for all of society could only be guaranteed by increasing production, whether paid for directly or facilitated by government investment. Talk of planning in the early 1960s aroused little controversy either between the political parties or between informed observers.[16]

Throughout this period economic policy practised a progressive liberal mentality. One question that Polanyi had posed in his Hobart Paper was why the Conservative government under Prime Minister Harold Macmillan (1957–63) had been so eager to adopt the mantra of indicative planning. His answer was that it fitted with Macmillan's personal outlook, which had been stated in a book authored in 1938 in which he had argued for more social regulation of production.[17] It was almost as if Polanyi was saying that Macmillan had a personal vendetta to resolve, finally getting his way. In a sense Macmillan's 'personal perspective' was anything but; it was the expression of the same governing mentality dominant at the time and inherent in Keynes' theories. And it was equally part of future Labour Prime Minister Harold Wilson's impassioned plea in Fabian Tract 309 (1957) that the government needed to do more to increase production and output; if Britain faced recurrent inflationary problems and balance of payments crises because of excess demand surely the answer was not industrial stagnation but ensuring that the right things were being produced, that capital stock was increased in areas that generated wealth and export earnings. Production was the key to social and economic stability.[18]

This was of course the same perspective that dominated the Government's *Employment Policy White Paper*, published in 1944 two years before Keynes' death, which offered a direct link between *The General Theory* and the economic policies of the 1960s. The primary aim of policy after the War was to be the maintenance of high and stable levels of employment. The problem was precisely that any one fall in demand, say for example steel, would lead to unemployment and a fall in spending for other goods. A decline in demand in one part of the economy would multiply through the economy and because workers' spending was a function of their cash income (worker-savers did not borrow to maintain spending habits based on a permanent assessment of income over their life; see discussion of Leijonhufvud later), the end result would be a bigger fall in output and employment than the original cut in steel production implied. Thus the crucial moment for government intervention was at the first onset of the depression. Moreover low interest rates were in and of themselves seen to be a weak expedient when it came to encouraging entrepreneurial investment. Instead, the report stated, the government would help encourage private enterprise to plan capital expenditure to be in conformity with the national stabilization policy. Planning would invariably require public and private bodies to submit programmes outlining the next five years' capital expenditure.[19]

This paper showed the link between indicative planning and demand management. Thus in finishing this section it should be reiterated that Keynes was just one voice in a collective of thinking that did not see consumers as active agents of progress but as worker-savers with habitual spending and saving patterns that could weigh down on society's aggregate employment potential. Keynes' ideas had not been misapplied and transformed into 'growthmanship' and indicative planning as the IEA authors had argued. Keynes was a Keynesian and had not been misunderstood by his followers; his thought shared the same progressive liberal mentality practised by government in this era.

3.1.2 Competition

The IEA's alternative to planning and production was competition and the consumer. 'Spartacus's' *Growth Through Competition* (1966) was a clearly stated manifesto for consumer sovereignty that argued for policies that would enable people to get on with the business of creating wealth. First, the pound needed to be floated in the foreign exchange markets; a fixed exchange rate just caused bottlenecks, as industry was not able to respond quickly enough to changes in consumer demand. A psychological attachment to a certain exchange rate was deemed entirely irrational. Second, private social security, much more than the public system, would be able to meet the needs of the consumers of unemployment insurance. They would be able to secure themselves insurance payouts in case they lost their job, and because this would be in the private sector and not paid for by the state, the payout would be a much higher proportion of their salary. In turn this would remove the fear of unemployment and help to create an environment where people could be mobile and move from one occupation to another as consumer tastes and relative prices changed. Finally, IEA authors argued against policies that created, they believed, excess demand in the economy. They blamed these policies for creating too high levels of employment, which in turn minimized flexibility, created yet more bottlenecks and led to the imposition of income policies; all forcing restraints on consumer sovereignty.[20]

But to those practising a progressive liberal governing mentality, competition meant something different and even those who believed that British producers should be more competitive were using the term entirely differently to the way the IEA used it. For a start, growth was viewed by Keynesians (of the Right and Left) as a function of capital investment that enabled more to be produced for future consumption. This in turn meant that it was a function of technological capability, productivity and efficiency, essentially engineering qualities. Over the economic cycle, the government would need to be active in ensuring that appropriate investment was taking place so that enough people were being employed. The 1960s was a period in which demand management and, for a brief time, indicative planning were viewed as legitimate ways in which to ensure that growth was maintained and economic security ensured. However by the end of the 1960s it was recognized that these policies had not been successful, and with Edward Heath's election as Conservative Prime Minister in 1970 a change of tactics was instigated.[21] The period from 1970 to 1974 certainly introduced significant change: new trade union legislation, entry to the European Common Market and reform of the banking sector (see section 3.2.1). Nonetheless as Heath battled with the Labour Party in his pursuit of a more competitive industrial base, for the IEA, his policies remained problematic. The Heath government represented a period in which a contested meaning of competition was brought into sharp relief.

Within eighteen months of Heath's election, the IEA were publishing indictments of his government's policies. The second Hobart Paperback, written by the influential journalist Samuel Brittan, *Government and the Market Economy* (1971) pointed out that for the all the talk of increasing competition in the economy the overall tenor of policy remained interventionist and corporatist. There was too little movement towards competition in the way that the IEA meant. Brittan was particularly scornful of intervention aimed at specific industries, where the state was supporting and protecting producers such as car manufacturers because it was deemed to be in the national interest. He was equally scathing where the government was supporting new projects, such as Concorde, which was believed to be beneficial for Britain because of its advanced technological nature.[22] This, as far as the IEA were concerned, was not competition.

Yet Heath 'believed' in making British producers more competitive especially when compared to foreign competition. How can one explain the disparity? The answer is that Heath believed in 'being competitive', in having an attitude that was 'dynamic, thrusting and go-getting'[23] and in a sense this notion of competition was entirely coincident with a mentality of governing that

Conservatives such as Macmillan had represented before in the Party, in which one made a distinction between the mentality of the entrepreneur and everyone else. Attempts to govern the economy from the top, looking down, had been unsuccessful, and this meant that economic policy in the 1970s would have to focus on the micro-level. It was not enough to encourage companies to work towards agreed targets. Although Heath did publish a 5 per cent target for economic growth, the point was that the government believed that it had to get its hands dirty if it wanted Britain's economic performance to improve and industry to be more 'competitive'.

Subsidies, preferred supplier status, support for large capital projects, encouraging large-scale mergers in order to increase efficiency were all part of a programme to make Britain more competitive.[24] In some cases the government gave business steady cash flows to enable them to plan for the long term and be more efficient. In other cases, it was thought the only way to compete internationally was to be larger and benefit from economies of scale that again would increase efficiency.[25] These, one could say, were microeconomic policies targeted at Britain's productivity and efficiency problem. Demand management had clearly not provided Britain with economic security. Instead government, so Heath believed, needed to get down to the nitty-gritty and make Britain's economy more secure by making individual industries and companies that much better. Growth would come from planning for companies to be more competitive.

The same term: 'competition', but encapsulating a completely different meaning from that used by the IEA authors. In the progressive liberal lexicon it was still about one's status as a producer vis-à-vis other producers: being the most technologically advanced and the most efficient, which in practice often implied being the largest company in any one sector. To get that right was to ensure success; the rest, sales and profits, would follow. For the IEA, competition meant something entirely different, it was made by constructing an order in which consumers were sovereign. There was no such thing as 'being competitive' as if this was a permanent ontological condition for a company to establish by itself. Competition was a process, neoliberals believed, activated and existing only in the presence of the consumer: producers could not be competitive unless they were competing with each other for the attention of consumers.

For the IEA it was not just that consumers were resistant to monopoly, as discussed in the last chapter, it was that consumers were the cause of competition. Their presence created competition; being competitive was not a state resulting from the imperative for innovation, which Schumpeter believed was personally inspired and others believed could be inspired by the state. Thus in definitional terms they believed that the microeconomic policies of the 1970s were misplaced. Brian Hindley for instance argued in *Industrial Merger and Public Policy* (1970) that policy should not be geared towards an ideal in which governments encouraged certain mergers that they had deemed would create efficiency gains and block mergers that they deemed would not.[26] Ivy Papps in *Government and Enterprise* (1975) argued that there were in fact no natural monopolies; it was an illusion invariably created by government in the belief that consumers needed protecting.

In reality government subsidies only incentivized producers to declare the wrong costs and protecting nationalized industries in this way only produced higher prices. She maintained, 'present subsidies insult the poor by refusing to accept the validity of the choices they would otherwise make if left to themselves.'[27]

Finally, John Jewkes in *Delusions of Dominance* (1977) pointed to a general schizophrenia in the mind of government since 1945. On the one hand he argued there had been a pervasive feeling that the industrial and commercial landscape was increasingly being concentrated in the hands of fewer companies. Thus given a belief in corporate omnipotence and weak consumers, the latter needed protecting either by nationalization or by refusing to allow companies to merge. On the other hand there was an obsession with size, a belief that efficiency was needed to compete. For Jewkes, this was all misplaced. There was no evidence that the largest companies were dominating more of the nation's output. In any case, for him, that missed the point: concentration ratios said nothing about the prevailing intensity of competition. 'Consumer's choice generates competition ... by price and quality.' Consumer protection that assumed a model of a weak consumer only 'weakens competition and can actually result in consumer exploitation, particularly with government controls on prices and profits.'[28]

The active and enterprising consumer on the other hand was immune to monopoly and knew his or her own mind. The presence of this figure activated the essence of competition; without consumer sovereignty to say a company was competitive was, for the IEA, meaningless. Thus government policy in the 1970s that aimed to make some British companies better managed and more competitive might be different to demand management and planning, but was still, for the IEA, very much part of the problem.

> Under the existing mountain of legislation, by which governments have so completely armed themselves to chide, jolt, threaten or lure private industry into what are supposed to be better ways of conducting its affairs, the marvel is that the patient has not collapsed beyond recovery.[29]

For these authors, all would be right with the British economy, so long as consumers were free to make choices between different and competing producers, and so long as the British population were no longer constrained by government controls. Or so the argument went. However, as section 3.2 discusses, this argument relied on the population acting as sovereign consumers, to be willing and able to be adaptable and not habitual in their spending practices, putting their interests as consumers over their interests as producers. Increasingly IEA authors began to recognize that the assumptions they had made about the British population were not necessarily entirely accurate.

3.2 Towards a genealogy of crisis

In the introduction to this chapter, it was suggested that there were two aspects to how the IEA problematized the British economy in the 1960s and 1970s. The first, as discussed above, was about how the IEA criticized Keynesian methodology and theory and attempted to draw out distinctions between Keynes and the Keynesian economists and policy-makers. By covering the arguments presented in the 1960s and 1970s it has been shown that these discursive strategies were in a sense surface features of a clash between political reference points; that is between alternative visions of human agency and subjectivity existing and being practised in political discourse. The second aspect of the IEA's problematization of the British economy involved a discursive style that was genealogical in nature, in which a range of IEA authors sought to understand, through a historical narrative, why they did not recognize in society the agents in the economy for whom they wished to govern. Problematizing government and economic policy was not enough; they now sought to problematize the human constituents of British society.

This does not mean that the IEA's position on the 'natural and proper' status of consumer sovereignty was completely displaced by this genealogical project. Indeed the former argument was continually made throughout the 1970s. To view the genealogical project as a complete change of course would be to suggest that the IEA recognized that their depiction of consumers was inaccurate, that the 'worker-saver' was somehow a better way to characterize the human agents of the economy. As will be discussed below, IEA authors were certain, for instance in their analysis of money and banking, that enterprising consumers did exist and that these habits of thought were entirely dominant in society at large. However this genealogical work did bring to light and try to explain the presence in society of habits of thought that were different. Does this then demonstrate a contradiction in IEA thinking; would it be possible to reconcile the belief that active consumers were the natural agents of the economy with the recognition that many members of the population were not acting as enterprising consumers?

Perhaps the answer to the above question is yes. However if the answer is yes with regards to the IEA, then no doubt one could find similar parallel contradictions in all the different approaches that have been taken to the question of how to govern. In other words this problematic is inherent within all forms of governmentality. Regimes of government do not create subjectivities, but they do try to elicit, encourage and foster them.[30] Therefore rather than talk of contradiction, it is better to suggest that there are tensions in any programme where it is recognized that something is not quite right, that people are not necessarily behaving according to the norms that are taken to be generally extant in society. The point is how to overcome this tension. In this case the IEA utilized social and evolutionary arguments that recognized both the problem, yet at the same time suggested that it was transitory and had been exacerbated by the distorting effect of governmental practices that, they believed, should now be made obsolete.

This section of the chapter is divided into the following parts. Section 3.2.1 considers how IEA authors criticized monetary policy in the 1960s and how they came to argue that a liberalized banking system would be much better suited to the sovereign consumer. By the end of this decade one can begin to see glimpses of the genealogy to follow, in the sense that Keynesian policies were increasingly seen as an obstacle to certain ways of thinking. This provides the background to section 3.2.2. In 1971, the British banking sector was indeed liberalized in a spirit akin to the IEA viewpoint. The new system of control was known as *Competition and Credit Control*. However, by 1974 the experience of ballooning bank lending and inflation led to the reimposition of direct controls over lending. This experience was critical for British neoliberalism in the formation of its diagnosis of the 'British disease'. Indeed this metaphor only appears in IEA literature after this period. Thus in section 3.2.3, the nature of this diagnosis is discussed, focused as it was on the use of organic metaphors to explain social change. A neoliberal mentality of rule would have to govern for this change not as an active agent in and of itself, but as midwife to a difficult birth. In this one can distinguish a very particular neoliberal mentality of economic government.

3.2.1 Banking against the consumer

In the wake of another stop-go cycle in the second half of the 1950s where inflation and a balance of payments crisis was checked by the imposition, among other things, of direct controls on lending and hire purchase, the Macmillan government set up a commission to inquire into whether monetary policy could play a more active role in economic policy. The Radcliffe Committee reported its findings in 1959, which in turn led to the publication in 1960 by the IEA of *Not Unanimous*, a short book containing a series of essays by authors all sharing the same viewpoint. Their position could broadly be put as follows. The committee's findings were said to be helpful in that it suggested that it was right to consider monetary policy in the context of a whole range of liquid assets, not just cash and bank deposits. However they believed the committee had ultimately adopted a 'fatal attitude' to monetary policy, exhibiting a 'fundamental distrust in the efficacy of short-term interest rate changes'. Monetary policy would remain, mistakenly they believed, subordinated to fiscal policy.[31]

It seemed to the authors that the Committee was endorsing the behaviour of the Bank of England, which they argued both acted to keep interest rates low to encourage business investment, but also acted with regard to the needs of government in respect of financing their fiscal deficit without recourse to bank borrowing (that is without recourse to monetary creation, or as it is euphemistically known 'printing money'[32]). There had been, so it was argued, a reluctance to raise interest rates before the sterling crisis of 1957 because the Bank of England had been concerned about the difficulties of finding private (non-bank) buyers for government debt in a falling bond market. In this regard R. F. Henderson argued that both the Bank of England and Radcliffe were totally wrong to think that high rates were damaging to the creditworthiness of the government and the confidence of investors in sterling. In fact he believed the opposite was much closer to the truth.[33]

For Victor Morgan, the Radcliffe Committee was right both to be concerned with the build-up of general liquidity in the economy outside of just pure cash holdings, and in its recognition of the link between changes in the rate of interest and capital values. But at the same time, the report had, according to Morgan, ignored the shift in expectations that had occurred in Britain since 1939; more and more people were acting to protect themselves by hedging against inflation, that is by spending their cash now on the basis that it was going to be worth less in the near future; and this in itself increased inflation.[34] As Wilfred King put it, also in *Not Unanimous*, the fatalistic attitude of Radcliffe had failed to see an increased scope for the use of monetary policy because behaviour itself had changed.[35]

For IEA authors, the Bank of England's distrust of the efficacy of short-term interest rates was based on the latter's outdated view of how individuals behaved. What these authors were pointing to was precisely the notion that individuals in the economy were no longer worker-savers but consumers with balance sheets and as such an active monetary policy could work because interest rates would affect the value of assets, which in turn would lead to the required change in behaviour. An interest rate policy could be that much more effective. And certainly if this argument was implicit in 1960, by the end of the 1960s IEA publications were arguing much more explicitly for monetary policies that incorporated the notion of the consumer as an entrepreneur-of-the-self.

Alan Walters (later to be Margaret Thatcher's chief economic advisor) argued in *Money in Boom and Slump* (1969) that the Keynesian model was essentially a too complex reading of the impact of changes in the money supply. For the Keynesians an increase in the quantity of money would lead to a decline in the rate of interest, which would induce entrepreneurial demand for labour, leading to an increase in aggregate demand and prices. However in Walters' view, following the quantity theory of money (whether Friedman's or Irving Fisher's more simplistic version), even though the relationship between money supply and aggregate income did change over time, there was enough evidence to suggest that there was a fairly direct relationship between money supply and aggregate income. In other words a change in the rate of interest, rather than passing through the economy from Bank of England to entrepreneur and finally to worker-savers' incomes, passed directly from the Bank of England to all human agents in the economy, as consumers and businesses alike reassessed the value of their assets in relation to the unit of account, money. There might be a lag before policy-makers could assume that everyone had adjusted their respective balance sheets, but in a world composed of entrepreneurs and enterprising consumers the effect was direct.[36]

In *Keynes and the Classics* (1969), Axel Leijonhufvud argued that the Keynesian model was problematic because it was macroeconomics without microfoundations. The Keynesian model assumed that increased investment spending would lead to increased incomes, thus higher demand and additional investment spending. The 'multiplier' described how the total increase in aggregate output was a multiple of the initial additional investment. In response, Leijonhufvud argued that if one had a notion of human capital as an individual assessment of worth and income over one's entire life then the multiplier effect was in fact a reflection of personal illiquidity problems. That is to say, a failure to be able to access credit at cheap prices meant that human agents could not adjust their spending to their expectations of earnings over their life but instead were being forced to spend only a percentage of their current cash income. They were 'forced to let current income be the operative constraint on their consumption'.[37] Thus, so the argument went, policy on credit was essentially forcing individuals to act like worker-savers, which in turn enabled government autonomous expenditure to have some effect on actual consumer spending and thus be multiplied through the economy, as if Keynesian theory had in fact accurately assessed behaviour all along.

In Leijonhufvud's argument one could thus see the traces of the genealogy to come, that government policy itself was creating behaviour that made its policies look as if they were effective and based on accurate theory. Worker-savers might actually 'exist', but in this argument, only because they were being constrained from acting differently. The recommendations both for monetary policy and for the banking system as a whole were clear. With regard to the former, it was certainly too early to suggest that these authors were advocating a full monetarist programme. Nonetheless the IEA maintained the view, established since *Not Unanimous*, that there was a need for a far more active monetary policy to control inflation, because monetary policy would act directly on all the agents of the economy. As regards the banking sector, it needed to be freed from its cartel structure so that it could respond to the liquidity needs of consumers. This way banking in Britain would become more competitive. Indeed Walters concluded his paper by saying that financial institutions should be free to innovate and develop new instruments to meet consumer needs; fine-tuning macroeconomic polices, such as hire purchase restrictions, discriminated against low-income groups and caused havoc, inefficiencies, unemployment and uncertainties in the consumer durables industries.[38]

Neil Gibson's Hobart Paper entitled *Financial Intermediaries and Monetary Policy*, first published in 1967, then republished (with update) in 1970, was much more specific in addressing the structure of the British banking industry. The 1967 edition began with a recognition that banking was changing. Financial intermediaries were increasingly able to provide liabilities or claims against themselves, whether deposits or shares in an investment or unit trusts. Additionally, there were markets in which these same institutions could acquire claims on borrowers (assets).[39] Put another way, if it so chose, a financial institution could create a deposit at the same time as it created a loan; it did not need to attract savings (pre-existing money) in advance of agreeing a loan. Once the deposit liability (i.e. money as a bank balance) was created, if the borrower used the loan to pay for a good or service and the receiver of that money ended up depositing it in another bank, then the original bank, in order to balance its books, would have to borrow back the deposit. Instead of this new liability showing up as a deposit in the books of the original bank, it would show up as an inter-bank loan. And of course the person or business that received the money in consideration for a good or service would not need to consider whether the money originated in the form of a bank loan, as an inter-bank loan, as a deposit of Bank of England notes and coins, or for that matter, as an exchange of gold for on-demand convertible currency.[40]

Gibson's point was this. Four banks dominated commercial banking in Britain with a payments clearing system operating between them. On the one hand they were subject to a fixed cash ratio requiring them to hold 8 per cent of their assets in cash as well as temporary direct controls over lending should the Bank of England wish to control the rate of loan growth. On the other hand, these four banks effectively operated a cartel on the pricing of loans (i.e. interest rates charged to customers); competition focused not on price but on the range of services, locality of branches, payroll services, credit and cheque guarantee cards and personal financial advice. Mortgage lending was generally the preserve of building societies that were entirely funded by the pre-existing savings of depositors (which had led to the infamous mortgage queues), and other forms of consumer credit were provided for by non-bank financial intermediaries (NFBIs). As a result, Gibson argued, there had been a significant lack of innovation and productivity gain in the banking industry. And although consumer demand for borrowing had been met by a shadow banking system that in size had grown from 75 per cent of the clearing banks' deposits in 1920 to 240 per cent in 1969, direct controls over one part of the financial system were not being completely offset by NBFIs; consumer demand for borrowing was not being met in full and this was detrimental to the development and efficiency of, among others, the motor industry.[41]

Post the Radcliffe Committee the financial system was still being run, according to Gibson, on the basis of keeping interest rates low and bond prices high so as to ease the sale of government debt. In turn there was a general lack of competition in the banking sector. There was, he believed, too much scepticism in the Bank of England about the direct relation between money, income and economic activity, and a failure to realize that the demand for a whole group of liabilities was sensitive to interest rates. Indeed the very fact that the community as a whole was accumulating financial assets at a rate faster than its growth in income was offered as proof that behaviour had changed. Monetary policy that targeted total money supply was possible because, as enterprising consumers with assets, ordinary people could be expected to adjust their balance sheets to changes in the Bank Rate. Competition in the banking sector would thus be activated by innovators and entrepreneurs in the banking industry, either by innovating products to meet consumers' borrowing needs or by 'finding' desires in consumers to consume financial products that had hitherto remained dormant. To this end Gibson recommended abolishing the fixed cash ratio, abandoning direct controls, subjecting all financial institutions to one regulatory regime and subjecting them all to the sovereign consumer.[42]

3.2.2 Monetary mayhem

It is not necessarily being claimed that these IEA pamphlets were instrumental in changing policy in the early 1970s. They may have been one among many voicing alternative ways to govern the economy. Either way the implementation by the Bank of England of a new monetary regime, *Competition and Credit*

Control, in 1971 provided precisely the kind of measures that the IEA were arguing for, aimed at increasing competition in the banking sector. It was not perfect; Brian Griffiths suggested there was potentially a muddle over controlling inflation. The Bank of England was unclear as to whether it intended to use the reserve requirement or open market operations to control money supply. Moreover Griffiths believed using the former would be problematic given a very open definition of what constituted reserve assets.[43] Nonetheless, the new regime abandoned all forms of direct control over bank lending, leaving banks free to respond to demands for borrowing. As the Governor of the Bank of England at the time put it in a speech in May 1971,

> We are permitting the price mechanism to function efficiently in the allocation of credit, and to free the banks from rigidities and restraints which have for far too long inhibited them from efficiently fulfilling their intermediary role in the financial system. ... At the same time, it is hoped that these changes will favour innovation and competition, and in their way make some contribution to faster and sounder economic growth. These changes are consistent with the broad policy aims of the present government of the United Kingdom.[44]

From the IEA perspective the banks were now free to be activated by the consumers of their services to compete with each other for the business of borrowers, whether pent-up or newly found demand. The consumer might of course literally be a consumer or it could be a business; the distinction was irrelevant.

It is worth remembering that for Heath and his finance minister, Chancellor of the Exchequer Anthony Barber, setting the banks free meant first and foremost enabling industrial corporations and businesses to have greater access to funding. This was part of the 'dash for growth' strategy that it was hoped would change the nature of business practice in Britain by making it more 'competitive', that is larger and more efficient. As Brian Sewill (Barber's special advisor) wrote in 1975, all these policies were about creating a 'dynamic, thrusting, go-getting economy ... with a pride in achievement, and new challenges for management', such as entry to the Common Market.[45] (Of course this was more managerial in nature than necessarily about consumer sovereignty.) Growth would come from active micro-interventions, increased output by the nationalized industries and of course increased private investment too.

And certainly between mid-1971 and mid-1973 economic growth accelerated; the economy was booming and inflating in all aspects: private sector investment, nationalized industry investment, government spending (including cuts in the rates of income tax), consumer spending, the stock market, and the property market. Accompanying this boom was a sharp increase in the money supply, as measured by M3 (a broad measure which included notes and coins and sterling deposits in the banking sector). Table 3.1 provides an overview of the financial years from April 1971 to the end of March 1977. The point in demonstrating these numbers is to show how the IEA's interpretation of what was happening in

Table 3.1 Public sector borrowing, GDP, inflation and sources of monetary expansion 1971/72 to 1976/77 (all numbers in £ millions, unless otherwise stated)

Fiscal year ending 31 March	*Public sector borrowing requirement (PSBR)*[a]	*Unfunded PSBR*[b]	*Government money printing*[c]	*Private bank money creation*[d]	*Increase in broad money*[e] *(%)*	*GDP growth (%)*	*Inflation*[f] *(%)*	*House price increase*[g] *(%)*
1971/72	1,024	–679	1,199	2,703	15.5	3.0	7.6	11.9
1972/73	2,515	1,400	86	4,654	24.1	10.0	8.2	33.8
1973/74	4,450	1,739	424	5,328	22.6	–2.9	13.5	36.2
1974/75	7,959	3,780	552	1,916	8.5	1.9	21.2	8.3
1975/76	10,604	5,264	3,710	–1,607	7.0	1.3	21.2	5.9
1976/77	8,501	1,323	51	2,512	7.6	2.4	16.7	8.9

Source: UK Office of National Statistics, Bank of England.

Notes

a Public sector borrowing requirement: the excess of government spending over revenue.

b Unfunded PSBR: the borrowing that is not paid for by the sale of government bonds to the non-bank private sector.

c Before the abandonment of foreign currency capital controls, the Bank of England held the nation's reserves of foreign currency. If there was a net outflow of foreign currency and the Bank had sufficient funds, then sterling received as consideration for foreign currency could be used to pay for domestic government spending.

d With all sources of sterling used up (issuance of bonds, foreign currency sales), the remainder of the deficit was financed by the banking sector. This is known as printing money and adds directly to money supply.

e Private bank credit creation is essentially new lending, not financed from pre-existing savings.

f Increase in money supply (M3) caused by addition of public and private sectors monetary creation.

g House prices increases are for calendar years, not fiscal years.

the economy changed. Up until 1974 the explanation for Britain's economic woes continued to reference the active consumer, as if the population was constituted entirely by these 'agents of progress'. After that, the IEA narrative shifted towards a more genealogical tone and recognition that society was not entirely composed of sovereign consumers ready to activate competition. This period in Britain's economic history led to the identification and diagnosis of the 'British disease'.

In late 1972 three economists closely related to the IEA, Harry Johnson, Alan Walters, and Victor Morgan wrote an open letter to Edward Heath, *Memorial to the Prime Minister*, in which they argued that the economic boom that was reaching its peak at the time was unsustainable and based on a desire to keep unemployment at a level far below the natural rate. Their argument was that the prices and incomes policy that Heath had imposed in November 1972 meant that when wage claims were settled by management in nationalized industries above originally agreed levels, the difference was being paid for by government borrowing. People did not realize, they claimed, that a ballooning budget deficit necessarily involved adding to the amount of money in circulation. In other words, it was not wages themselves that were causing inflation, but money printing to meet those wage claims.[46]

However this was not the full story. As Figure 3.1 shows, although the budget deficit was expanding rapidly in the two fiscal years of the boom only a small proportion of the deficit was actually financed by printing money (that is by government borrowing from the private banking sector rather than from the non-bank private sector). In fact bank lending to the private sector in the three years 1971/72, 1972/73 and 1973/74 was four times the amount of unfunded public borrowing (and a much higher multiple of the actual amount of new money that was created to fund the deficit). So the money supply expanded rapidly in these years, but it was not the case that this was as a result of the government printing money. The authors of the *Memorial* in 1972 were no doubt aware of this. As such they proceeded to suggest that the new money that was being created (in the private sector) was the result of individuals and companies borrowing heavily from commercial banks (invariably either to build property or buy property) on the basis that this was a hedge against inflation. Or to be more exact a hedge against inflation that would come after a suitable lag of twelve to eighteen months. Thus as inflation accelerated to over 20 per cent in 1974/75 and 1975/76, the argument was that house prices had already factored in both this past and future monetary debasement by rising over 70 per cent in the two previous years. As these authors said 'in a word, this new money was going to meet the demand for hedges against inflation – in houses, property companies and land.'[47] Consumers and businesses were acting in a rational and similar fashion.

Competition and Credit Control had only represented one half of the IEA policy programme, the other being the need to control money supply. This had been acknowledged in the papers of Gibson, Griffiths and Walters in the late 1960s, and the *Memorial* made it clear as well. And although the Bank of England were not charged with targeting money supply, the Governor, Gordon

Richardson, stated in December 1973 his opinion that the Bank had been late to raise interest rates, but they had at least acted in July by raising them from 7.5 per cent to 11.5 per cent.[48] Commentary, it should be said, from the Bank in the same quarterly report, while admitting mistakes, also made it clear that the addition to money stock had come from the private sector.[49]

Nonetheless by early 1975 it appeared as if Harris, now referring to himself as a 'self-confessed monetarist', was allowing the nuance of what had happened to be forgotten. Trade unions, he argued, could not cause inflation through wage bargaining alone; the government had to have been a colluding agent because only by creating more money to finance the pay rises could inflation occur. Inflation after all, in this view, could only ever be a monetary phenomenon. The inflation of 1970–74 was, according to Harris, to be explained by money supply growth, a result of the government creating money to pay for its deficit. Money supply, he said, 'admittedly' had been boosted by the replacement of credit controls by competition in banking, but this key factor was now of less interest to Harris in his March 1975 account. Inflation was the result of the printing press at the Bank of England; it was not the result of wage claims per se.[50] Thus to fight inflation the government would have to refuse union demands for pay rises.

Even so, there was an ambiguity here. While monetary policy was ultimately to blame, union demands for pay increases, although one step removed from the printing press, were part of the problem. Unions had long been singled out for attack by IEA authors and by neoliberals generally like Hayek and Friedman; but what if the problem was not just with union leaders but with their vast membership as well? Moreover, if large parts of society were sympathetic to the union cause, could they be counted on to act as sovereign consumers, activating a mentality of adaptability, change and progress? Over the next two years a decidedly different narrative began to emerge among IEA authors matched, as is shown in the next chapter, by work that was being done at the Centre for Policy Studies (CPS). This was the genealogy of Britain in crisis and the diagnosis that society was infected with a disease. Put another way, there was a new sense that while for all this time the IEA had been assuming that Britain was a nation where sovereign consumers were ready to ensure companies were competitive, there was a new-found belief that to govern for the consumer would mean eliciting and encouraging particular ways of thinking, while at the same time discouraging habits of thought that represented a past era. Only enterprising consumers and entrepreneurs, so they believed, utilized habits of thought properly aligned to the material conditions of a wealthy capitalist economy and society. Conversely neoliberals came to argue that policies that accepted different non-consumer and non-enterprising habits of thought reinforced ways of thinking that were now bringing Britain to the edge of crisis, to a breakdown of society.

3.2.3 The genealogy of crisis

Before discussing this discursive shift in more detail it is worth saying something of the nature of its cause or at least something about the characterization of

British society at the time. Of course Britain was not alone in struggling with the aftermath of the collapse of the Bretton Woods fixed exchange rate regime in 1971, competitive currency devaluations and the effects of oil price rises around the world in 1973; average inflation rates in the ten Organisation for Economic Co-operation and Development (OECD) nations rose from 4 per cent in 1968 to 13.5 per cent in 1974. But it was also clear that Britain was suffering more than other nations that seemed to have brought inflation under control. Victor Morgan reported that West German inflation between 1967 and 1974 was 48 per cent versus Britain's 74 per cent, representing, he argued, domestic inflation that had been superimposed upon imported inflation.[51] IEA authors were forced to confront the issue: was it fair to say that everyone in Britain was a rational sovereign consumer?

Indeed it was generally accepted that Heath's government had failed to be re-elected in 1974 and had been replaced by a Labour government, led by Harold Wilson, on the understanding that only Labour was capable of negotiating a peace between unions, management (of both private and nationalized industries) and government itself. This was the 'Social Compact', a peace treaty and voluntary incomes policy, which it was hoped would bring inflation under control. Of course the IEA position, this time represented by Gordon Pepper (a bond market analyst, monetarist and a key advisor to Thatcher up until her election in 1979) and Geoffrey Wood was that inflation should never be concealed, that this only further distorted the ability of prices to signal information. The answer was not to conceal inflation but to control it in the open by targeting and controlling the money supply. Nonetheless, as Pepper and Wood argued, once money was scarce, this policy would lead to a 'battle for funds' between government and private sector. If the government insisted in winning, that is fully funding its deficit by raising interest rates, this would crowd out the private sector, limiting their access to new funds with which to invest. The remedy, for these authors, was a shallow, prolonged recession to bring money supply and inflation under control.[52]

Nonetheless, Pepper did not address the social problem, 'the battle' itself; there was nothing to suggest that the government could keep control over competing claims for scarce money. This became for the New Right the problem at the heart of the 'British disease', the main diagnosis that both the IEA and the CPS propounded. Unless Britain was pervaded by a 'classless' consumer subjectivity, all attempts to control inflation via imposing monetary scarcity were likely to lead to serious social disorder. Hobart Paper 67, *The British Disease* (1976) was entirely dedicated to this topic. Nonetheless, before discussing this paper it is important to note that this diagnosis of the problems with which Britain was beset was certainly not just the product of the New Right. Indeed during 1975 the IEA published two papers, one by the influential and leftwing *Times* journalist Peter Jay (son-in-law to James Callaghan, Labour Prime Minister from 1976–79) and one by Brian Sewill (in a paperback with commentary also by Harris), who had been the special economic advisor to Barber from 1970–74. Both authors pointed to concerns that were explicitly taken up by the IEA in 1975.

Sewill began by stating that there was 'literally no truth to the allegation that the Bank of England printing press worked overtime'. Instead the acceleration of broad money supply was due in the main to the new liberal policies encapsulated in *Competition and Credit Control.* Indeed the secondary banking crisis that broke in December 1973 could, he believed, largely be seen to have resulted from the overstimulation that easy money brought. The real issue for Sewill was the power of the unions to push up pay and prices. Thus, he said, 'the only way monetary policy alone could stop inflation is by creating so much unemployment that the unions were brought to their knees'. None of the political parties in Britain were, he thought, capable of standing up to the unions, and as a result inflation could get out of hand. The Social Compact was nothing more than a temporary truce,[53]

> There are signs that the structure of civilized society is beginning to crumble. Money depreciates, hoarding is endemic, shortages multiply, public services deteriorate, respect for law and order declines as more and more groups come to feel that a display of strength is the way to get what they want.[54]

Perhaps Sewill was being overly paranoid; all the same there was clearly a feeling shared by many, not just the neoliberals, that Britain was veering towards crisis. For Peter Jay the crisis was so 'deeply rooted' that Britain was 'near to where tensions within the system could overthrow it'. There was, he believed, a 'contradiction' between a political system in which political entrepreneurs could make promises to the electorate, such as full employment, which were so grand that people were 'almost forced' to vote for them, and an economic system in which the economic entrepreneur always had 'to ask himself what people want most'. The logic of the ballot box had created a structure in which the freedom of unions was endangering the freedom of all: according to Jay 'democracy has itself by the tail and is eating itself up fast'. What was needed was the removal of the general influence of collective bargaining. In specific terms Jay was suggesting a transformation of economic mechanisms and a new approach that emphasized consumer and employee sovereignty. On the one hand this meant the competitive marketplace deciding the allocation of resources; on the other hand it meant bringing workers directly into the management decision-making process and thus democratizing industry. This was, Jay believed, about changing minds and attitudes,[55]

> They … [the workers] … need somehow to be 'dis-alienated' enough to become infected with the entrepreneurial realities which confront their present employers, so that they will accept a non-inflationary market-determined environment as setting the level of rewards that can be afforded.[56]

Clearly this 'true socialism', as Jay described it, was not what the IEA had in mind. However looking back at the transition of discursive style at the IEA between 1975 and 1976 one can see this open dialogue across the political spectrum as a link between the way consumer sovereignty had been taken for granted by the IEA since its foundation in the late 1950s and a modified, sociological perspective in the late 1970s; an acceptance that the problem was not just government and loose control over spending, but something inherent in the ways of thinking that had become dominant in British society. It was more than just government printing money, as the 1972 *Memorial* suggested.

This new perspective was evident in George Allen's Hobart Paper, *The British Disease* (1976) and in Harris' contribution to the Hobart Paper *Can Workers Manage?* (1977), the latter a response from the IEA to the sorts of policies regarding worker participation in management that Jay had expounded on and which had been recommended by the Bullock Report, a government commission to examine these specific issues. Arthur Seldon's preface to *The British Disease* spelt out precisely what was at stake in this new critical history. Britain's relative decline was about 'a failure of attitudes and institutions to adapt themselves to a technological–industrial society ... the government ... [had] ... failed to make the economy competitive so that people and institutions would have been impelled to adapt themselves to change.'[57]

Being adaptable to change was at the very core of the IEA definition of a progressive mentality, a consumer mentality that was essential for competition, and which defined competition. So on the one hand, attitudes had failed to adjust to what was natural and proper for an advanced rich industrial country. On the other hand, Seldon was berating government for policies that had failed to make people think like sovereign consumers so that they could be and act as sovereign consumers. Consumer sovereignty was the appropriate mentality for the age, but, all the same, throughout large parts of British society, the IEA was coming to the opinion that the government needed to create a consumer mentality such that there would be competition. In a sense then, this enunciated the problematic tension inherent in any governing mentality that comes to recognize a disparity between the norms of behaviour it had hitherto taken for granted and a reality that is different.

In the body of the paper itself, Allen set out to tackle what hitherto he believed economists had 'tended to ignore', that is the intangible problems, the attitudes and practices of workers and managers: the very stuff of the British disease. He proceeded to problematize the British economy in five ways. First, all people, he said, wanted to be better off but the contemporary British were not willing to submit to the necessary exertions and changes in their ways to get there. Second, energies needed to be concentrated on enterprising ways of thinking that produced economic growth; there were, according to Allen, far too many inconsistent ways of thinking prevalent in society. The next problem was by way of a question: if it was true that Britain's social and economic institutions and attitudes were out of tune with the requirements of modern industrialism, how had this come about? Next, partly in response to this question, Allen suggested that Britain was characterized by bad investment decision-making due to defects in the selection and training of civil servants and business executives, i.e. in the public and private sectors. Finally there was clearly a highly anachronistic system of industrial relations that also fostered unprogressive attitudes.[58]

In diagnosing the British disease, Allen was casting the net far beyond government itself; this was a problem about business training, investment decisions, public opinion, and worker attitudes. Britain had failed to create the 'virtuous circle' that Japan had created in the 1960s, which 'depended upon directing a large share of their investment into forms of capital that yielded their returns quickly in marketable goods and services'.[59] Two aspects of this comment are worth highlighting. First, the comment about the quickness of return: Allen was reiterating the point made in the 1960s, that too much investment had gone into capital goods at the expense of consumer goods. In the IEA view only a high street full of goods for consumers to buy would incentivize people to raise their standards of living. Second, the comment about the marketable goods: this referred directly to the importance of the market as a siphon through which to ensure that producers were competitive, that they responded to consumers activating the market as a process rather than as a state of being.

The word 'marketable' was a new word to the IEA lexicon, which was popularized in 1976 by an influential monograph, written by economists Robert Bacon and Walter Eltis. The title of the book, *Britain's Economic Problem: Too few producers*, on the face of it suggested the need to build more factories; it sounded distinctly Keynesian. In fact the authors made the argument that those who worked in the public sector as civil servants, social workers, teachers and medical workers, whose output was thus unmarketed were in fact not 'producers'. The real problem was that these workers straddled two zones of practice; on the one hand they still consumed in the marketed zone, but on the other hand they did not produce anything in the marketed zone. Thus they were being paid for out of the profits of producers, which in turn lowered the amount of funds available for investment. This was destroying the British economy.[60]

Bacon and Eltis were not arguing about productivity and efficiency (Heath's version of being competitive), but about consumers and entrepreneurs sharing wealth in the marketed side of the economy versus non-producers in the other side of the economy adding no wealth yet still wanting to be consumers at the same time. To say that there were too few producers meant saying that there were too few people who were conducting the entirety of their lives in the marketable sector of the economy, producing and consuming there. Neoliberalism pointed to a division in society not between consumption and production but between consumer sovereignty and no consumer sovereignty. Where there was a market process in operation, the consumer and producer shared the same habit of thought, one entrepreneur, the other enterprising consumer. In other words the consumer was the foundational unit or way of thinking, a necessary condition for entrepreneurial habits of thought. There was no Schumpeterian distinction between the passive consumer and the active entrepreneur in the neoliberal mentality of rule.

The problem, returning to Allen's diagnosis, was that British economic policies had obstructed adaptation to change, not deliberately, but because the institutional structure of British society itself, created originally in an era of market liberalism, had become filled with 'routineers' suspicious and dismissive of entrepreneurialism and incapable, so Allen believed, of comprehending the importance of the market process, that is of marketability. Using distinctly evolutionary metaphors, Allen suggested that there was a late adaptation to change in British business management, in attitudes to business and in the attitudes of the workforce, which like management, had become stuck in anachronistic ways of thinking. Industrial unionism, he said, was failing in the face of a determined craft union mentality, which constructed a permanent opposition to management.[61]

> Britain is a victim of its past, institutions and attitudes have persisted long after they have served their purpose ... institutions and attitudes that are not well-fitted to the task remain entrenched ... the process of recovery is likely to be long and perhaps painful ... [and] ... is conditional upon a shift in values and the transformation of institutions.[62]

In consequence, the government had to take steps to 'encourage the desired changes and to foster the attitudes consonant with a progressive society'. Success had to be rewarded and subsidies ended such that the market process could work. Rewards could no longer relate to status, an attitude from the past. Training and educational standards had to be raised from primary school, to civil services, to managerial training and this training had to be geared towards intellect, character, science and technology., and of course the proper rules of business decision-making.[63]

Finally, there were the attitudes of the workers in their unions addressed by Harris and others in 1977 in *Can Workers Manage?* The idea for these authors, that workers should be represented on the board, was a serious misjudgement precisely because the worker 'tunnel vision of output' had done so much harm to consumers and national well-being. Instead only owners and shareholders could be expected to properly monitor business activity. Erhard's Germany again provided the model for Britain to follow: in Germany closed shops were illegal, union membership was voluntary, and there were no special legal immunities from being sued for loss of business if a strike was later deemed illegal. And because they could be trusted, representatives of workers in Germany were allowed to sit on advisory (although not main) company boards, to help them understand the rationale behind some of the decisions that management were taking.[64]

Harris' essay in this volume took up Allen's language, and in it one can see a clear development from the 'self-confessed monetarist' of two years previously. For Harris the lesson of history was now clear, 'the chief source of economic progress is compounded of energy plus enterprise in adapting the arts of production and distribution to supply the changing goods and services demanded at home and abroad'. This was the rational mind of progress, which could be found in both the consumer and the entrepreneur. However, these attributes were not necessarily there in nature; as he says 'to bring these qualities into effective operation they must be animated and harnessed'. In the nineteenth century, so Harris argued, British statesmen had pioneered a framework of laws, which had made a market economy possible by giving entrepreneurs maximum freedom. Yet Harris now believed that 'a competitive market does not emerge from laissez-faire'.[65] Rather than just harnessing entrepreneurs through the granting of appropriate property rights, consumers too needed to be harnessed and animated by government so that producers could not entrench themselves in monopoly positions.

The mistake that had been made, according to Harris, was to give special privileges to workers on the basis that one needed to redress the balance between master and servant. This had both increased and maintained attitudes that were opposed to the interests of a consumer society; that is 'in choice, cheapness, change and other fruits of progress'. There was, Harris believed, a 'schizophrenic conflict' taking place in the minds of workers that would need to be resolved in order for Britain to progress again. The subjectivity of the producer, exhibited as 'stability, comfort, continuity and security', was not necessarily about knowingly keeping others unemployed, likewise the unemployed who supported unions were not voluntarily unemployed: they all just held beliefs that were the result of a historical process that had led to a society stricken with disease. Harris believed that the Bullock report on workers in management was even worse than Jay's earlier proposals because the Bullock report had not even mentioned the consumer.[66]

What mattered in this was that the market was not a place of equality but a process in which the consumer could maintain an active competitive tension. One had to be adaptable. Consumer sovereignty would ensure that producers were adaptable; but more than that, the consumer mentality was meant to be the bedrock from which enterprising habits of thought developed. Some consumers would become entrepreneurs, locating the desires of others; most consumers would no doubt remain as just consumers. Either way it was this consumer mentality of energy and adaptation that remained the foundational, rational and progressive mental disposition. Government had to learn how to govern the economy always and only in the name of this mentality, harnessing energies that were suitable to a modern and wealthy capitalist society.

3.3 Neoliberalism and social evolution

This chapter has outlined the development of neoliberal thinking from the mid 1960s to the late 1970s in Britain through the publications of the IEA. In this discourse there is both a continuous narrative and a significant shift. The IEA authors always maintained that competition was the appropriate policy response to Britain's economic woes and as such they consistently problematized Keynesian policies. In doing this, these authors were happy to accept that successive British governments were full of good intentions; in a sense, this they believed was half the problem. They argued that a focus in policy on production was based on methodologically unsound economic theory that had misunderstood

Keynes and that 'growthmanship' by 'conspicuous investment' gave no significant thought to the consumer's position in the economy. At the very least there was more the high street could be doing to awaken dormant consumers and incentivize them to want to improve their living standards.

This was a political *savoir* in practice, built upon a particular understanding of what was the 'natural and proper' mentality of the human agents of the economy. Conversely, Keynesians, whether theorists (and very much including Keynes) or policy-makers, were not false scientists as charged but were practising a progressive liberal governing mentality. Specifically this meant that the human agents they took for granted were 'worker-savers', consumers with habitual saving patterns only ever using up resources that were produced and created for them by entrepreneurs and businesses. When the latter became derelict in their duty, the government needed to step in as early as possible to ensure the fall-out from unemployment did not multiply unduly through the economy.

Moreover this progressive governing mentality often took it for granted that businesses could dominate consumers, bending their wills where need be. There was no image of the sovereign consumer. For the IEA the notion that government should help businesses to be bigger and more efficient, so long as consumers were given due protection (say through nationalization and/or regulation) missed the point about competition. For neoliberals competition was a process initiated only in the presence of the discerning consumer. There was no such thing as a permanent natural monopoly when consumers were allowed to be sovereign.

The IEA authors never dropped this argument, but in the context of the early 1970s they were confronted by a problem, a seemingly intractable situation in which they recognized that many of the human agents in Britain were not acting in accordance with behaviour that they had taken for granted. Entrepreneurs were making consistently bad decisions and consumers were responding more to their instincts as workers than as consumers. This new language was developed in response to the historical circumstances of the early 1970s. In particular it was responding to the inflationary boom that followed the new competitive reorganization of the banking sector, which had created a financial system that could do exactly what the IEA believed it should be free to do, that is to meet the demands and needs of borrowers, whether consumers or businesses.

In confronting this problem the IEA were confronting a problem with which governmental programmes are beset, that is recognizing that norms of behaviour that have been taken for granted are in fact problematic. The response within the New Right was to construct a genealogy, a critical historical trail that explained for them the formation of problematic subjectivities with a view, hope or expectation that the future would be different. Specifically, the IEA's genealogy was constructed in social evolutionary terms, as a story in which habits of thought that belonged to previous eras had remained extant long past their due date; nurtured and protected as they were by government. In constructing this narrative they were able to maintain a notion of the consumer as a natural agent of competition and progress, as well as providing an explanation for why not all behaviour could be recognized as such. This tension was only resolved by suggesting that the government needed to act in such a way as to create an environment suitable to the conditions of a modern society. How the government should act and practise this political rationality was a matter for the CPS, a think tank existing within the Conservative Party. The next chapter demonstrates that a parallel genealogical narrative was being constructed there which shared the same rationality yet by necessity took a much more direct approach to the question of how to govern the economy.

As for the evolutionary tone of language in IEA thought, questions remain about where it came from and what kind of thinking it represented. The following is a quote from Veblen's *The Theory of the Leisure Class* (1899):

> The evolution of social structure has been a process of natural selection of institutions. The progress which has been made and is being made in human institutions and in human character may be set down, broadly, to a natural selection of the fittest habits of thought and to a process of enforced adaptation of individuals to an environment which has progressively changed with the growth of the community and with the changing institutions under which men have lived.... The institutions are, in substance, prevalent habits of thought with respect to particular relations and particular functions of the individual and of the community ... they may, on the psychological side, be broadly characterized as a prevalent spiritual attitude or a prevalent theory of life.... The habits of thought ... are ... received from an earlier time; they have been elaborated in and received from the past ... and are therefore never in full accord with the requirements of the present ... this process of selective adaptation can never catch up with the progressively changing situation in which the community finds itself at any given time.... A step in ... development requires ... a new adaptation; it becomes the point of departure for a new step in the adjustment, and so on.... The institutions of today ... do not entirely fit the situation of today.... Mental attitudes and aptitudes ... are therefore themselves a conservative factor. This is the factor of social inertia, psychological inertia, and conservatism.... The evolution of society is substantially a process of mental adaptation on the part of individuals under the stress of circumstances, which will no longer tolerate habits of thought formed under and conforming to a different set of circumstances in the past. ... Social advance, especially as seen from the point of view of economic theory, consists in a continued progressive approach to an approximately exact 'adjustment of inner relations to outer relations'; but this adjustment is never definitively established.... The degree of approximation may be greater or less, depending on the facility with which an adjustment is made. A readjustment of men's habits of thought to conform with the exigencies of an altered situation is in any case made only tardily and reluctantly, and only under the coercion exercized by a situation which has made the accredited views untenable.... Freedom and facility of readjustment, that is to say capacity for growth in social structure, therefore depends in great measure on

> the degree of freedom with which the situation at any given time acts on the individual members of the community. If any portion or class of society is sheltered from the action of the environment ... that class will adapt ... more tardily; it will ... tend to retard the process of social transformation.[67]

There is a great deal of similarity in language between Veblen and the tone of Hobart Paper 67: Seldon believed there had been 'a failure of attitudes and institutions to adapt themselves to a technological-industrial society'.[68] Allen referred to attitudes that were showing a 'late adaptation to change ... institutions and attitudes have persisted long after they have served their purpose'. The solution for him was a 'deep-seated adaptation to industrial society ... a shift in values and the transformation of attitudes'.[69] Of course Veblen was writing about habits of thought in a different era; he was referring to more socialistic, interconnected and engineering ways of thinking and behaving; he thought attitudes were adapting away from a pecuniary culture towards a taken-for-granted acceptance of society as organic, and that hitherto progress had been impeded by competition to make one's own wealth as conspicuous as possible. And in this new modern world Veblen argued that consumption habits had changed; consumption was less about emulation and being conspicuous and far more about instrumental behaviour. The new consumer bought things to use them, the consumer now primarily had a personal relationship with the things that he or she purchased and consumed.[70]

However the essence of Veblen's institutional argument is to be found in the IEA, not just with regards to his description of consumption in the machine age, but critically in the resolution of the tension in neoliberal thinking in Britain in the mid 1970s, the tension between assuming that the population at large had the mental attitudes of the sovereign consumer and the recognition that many were not behaving that way. For the IEA the mentality of the sovereign consumer represented the proper way of thinking; it was entirely right to think that way, but there was no need to assume that had always been the case. Moreover it was perfectly reasonable for government to act in a way that helped elicit and smooth the process from one societal form to another. Invoking Veblenesque terminology, government would have to find a way to coerce people into giving up views that society had decided had become untenable. The above quotations are intended to demonstrate that the neoliberal governing mentality was sociologically minded, even if society itself was to be privatized into discrete entrepreneurial units consisting of consumers and their households. In this mentality one had to govern for all human agents in the economy (not just entrepreneurs), doing society's evolutionary and organic work.

Seemingly, the IEA came to accept this new role for government, this role as the agent of change, in the context of the specific economic conditions in Britain in the early 1970s. These years thus represented a tension in governmental thinking that in the end proved not insurmountable. Indeed the evolutionary perspective on society was not new for the New Right; it had already made an appearance in the opening section of Hayek's *The Constitution of Liberty* (1960).

> Man did not simply impose upon the world a pattern created by his mind.... If we are to advance we must leave room for a continuous revision of our present conceptions and ideals, which will be necessitated by further experience. Some of our ... habits and skills, our emotional skills ... may be retained long after they have outlived their usefulness and even when they have become more an obstacle than a help ... Thus every change ... creates a 'problem' for society ... solved by the establishment of a new over-all adjustment.... Who will prove to possess the right combination of aptitudes ... is ... little predictable: it is the product of individuals imitating those who have been more successful and from their being guided by signs ... such as prices. What is important is not what freedom I personally would like to exercise but what freedom some person may need in order to do things beneficial to society. This freedom we can assure to the unknown person only by giving it to all. All that we can know is that the ultimate decision about what is good or bad will be made not by individual human wisdom but by the decline of the groups that have adhered to the 'wrong' beliefs.... The ineffective will be discarded and the effective retained ... and the ends of the successful group will tend to become the ends of all members of the society.... Our only way of confirming this is to ascertain whether it continues to prove itself in competition with other standards observed by other individuals or groups. The argument for liberty is not an argument against organisation ... but an argument against all exclusive, privileged, monopolistic organisation.[71]

Hayek's argument was clearly not advocating government intervention per se, but by the mid 1970s this way of thinking, this mentality of rule, had identified and explained to itself the need to act. Knowing how to act is the subject of the next chapter.

4 How to govern the economy

> We all talk today about social morality, social justice, social responsibility. We'll only get those things when you have a high proportion of individuals of worth and responsibility.
>
> Margaret Thatcher, interview in the *Observer*, April 1979[1]

In the previous chapter the focus was solely on the Institute of Economic Affairs (IEA); how individual authors writing under the banner of the IEA shared a definition of competition as a process and not an a priori state of being, and how they came to recognize the existence in society at large of attitudes and conduct that were not commensurate with the social market economy they wanted Britain to adopt. Certain ways of behaving seemed to these authors to represent attitudes consonant with an older version of the market society in which classes confronted each other and government's role was to arbitrate between conflicting interests in the marketplace. For neoliberals, exchange in the marketplace created value: all participants, by exchanging, could increase their capital or self-worth, whether businesses, entrepreneurs or consumers; there was a continuity of 'proper' thinking between the entrepreneur and the consumer. What this perspective required then was a fundamental change in the practice of government; it would need to govern for all forms of entrepreneurialism and against a non-marketed, non value-adding side of the economy. From 1974 to 1979, the Centre for Political Studies (CPS), a think tank operating from within the Conservative Party, took on the task of putting together such a new political programme. This is the topic of the current chapter, which is asking how the CPS thought the economy should be governed.

The CPS was an overtly 'political' think tank, given its connection with the Conservative Party, designed, according to one of its co-founders Nigel Vinson, to 'articulate in political terms what the IEA had been thinking.'[2] From its inception in 1974 up until 1979 it was the think tank of a political party in opposition, not actually in government. Its job was essentially to prepare for government; it was a think tank for the politicians who were to be at the centre of the Thatcherite political programme: Keith Joseph, Geoffrey Howe, Nigel Lawson and of course Margaret Thatcher herself. In this capacity, its primary role was to support the speech-giving programme of Thatcher and Joseph, particularly the latter, as he went around Britain making speeches to audiences both hostile and receptive. Nonetheless, these speeches had a double role, both aimed at winning support but also directly aimed at the key problematic; that is how to foster an environment in which people shared the attitudes that the New Right believed were consonant with civilization and progress. To this extent, if one takes the Foucauldian position that government is always concerning itself with the conduct of the governed, these speeches represented the actual job of government; an attempt to change behaviour, not just an attempt to win support for the cause.

This, at any rate, was the explicit strategy of the *Stepping Stones* project, written at the end of 1977 by John Hoskyns and Norman Strauss at the CPS. For them, winning the election in 1979 had to mean that attitudes had already changed; the election itself was to be a sign that the majority of the country was ready for something different. Nonetheless, the point of this chapter is to demonstrate that certain themes that had been constantly in play in IEA writings since the late 1950s were also present at the CPS. Of course one way to establish this would be to trace the personal interconnections between the staff of the IEA and CPS, showing how specific ideas circulated. But the aim here is different: it is to demonstrate that the CPS practised a neoliberal governing mentality and that this was evidenced in the words that were written and spoken by members of the CPS in the 1970s. Certain themes are thus apparent: the consumer and entrepreneur were the rational agents in the economy, much trade union activity was not commensurate with the realities of modern society, and although the existence of the social world was not denied, it was argued that it could never be embodied in the state.

The chapter itself is divided into three sections. Section 4.1 deals with the first two years of the CPS's existence up until 1976, a period in which its publications were dominated by the speeches of Keith Joseph. The language in these two years portrays a fairly classical liberal view of the economy, although in 1976 Joseph was becoming increasingly explicit about how active the government would have to be; as he put it, 'monetarism was not enough'. Section 4.2 deals primarily with the *Stepping Stones* project, itself a document that tackled head-on the CPS's views on trade unions. In the last part of this chapter, section 4.3, Thatcher's speeches and opinions are dealt with directly. This section draws out an underlying theme of Thatcherism, that society very much existed in the minds of the New Right but that it needed to be privatized and remoralized in order to function properly.

4.1 From Preston to Stockton: 'monetarism is not enough'

Having been a long-serving Conservative Party Member of Parliament, Keith Joseph underwent a self-proclaimed 'conversion to conservatism' in 1974 at the height of Britain's experience of stagflation.[3] What might Joseph have meant by this? The answer can be found in the speech that announced the birth of the CPS in June 1974, *This is not the time to be mealy-mouthed*, and in his more well-known speech, *Inflation is caused by governments*, delivered at Preston Town Hall in September 1974. Essentially Joseph was announcing himself to be a classical liberal. His attention in these speeches was focused almost exclusively on entrepreneurs and the role that government had taken in undermining them.

The analysis in June 1974 was straightforward enough; Britain was consuming its capital stock faster than it was being replaced or, in other words, not enough profit was being generated by free enterprise. The private sector, Joseph argued, created resources that were needed for general prosperity and these were being undermined by high taxes, by the unrealistic wage demands of unions, inflation and the inability of companies to operate in an environment of high uncertainty created by continuing government intervention. Profits, he said, should be welcomed and defended rather than criticized. Thus there was nothing particularly 'neo' about this classical liberal statement. Indeed the speech ended by recalling Schumpeter's view in *Capitalism, Socialism and Democracy* (1943) that free enterprise would die only because it would lack defenders.[4] Profit, in this view, reflected two things: either that consumers wanted to buy the goods that entrepreneurs had produced for them, or that a business had successfully found a new way of producing a good that saved production costs and enabled freed-up capital (represented by cash profits) to be used for alternative and new investments.

Joseph's new-found classical liberalism was again on display in Preston in September 1974. As if to underline the point, the speech argued that economic policy had gone wrong after the 1930s; 'we fight the battles of the 70s with the weapons of the 30s'. Thus the solution lay in a rediscovery of ideas that had predominated from before the Great Depression. British governments, he believed, by creating persistent inflation, had in recent years made it even more difficult for private firms to do their job. The goal of full employment through Keynesian demand management had now, so Joseph thought, been falsified by inflation that was 'threatening to destroy society'. As for a new policy, he argued, 'we should not give up our efforts to rescue people wherever possible and help them become productive members of the community. But creating excess demand for labour by printing money is certainly no way of doing it.' All that this money printing had done was to create 'outrage and widespread resentment' at 'soaring rises in property values', which was a 'by-product of inflation', among those whose incomes were held down by incomes policies.[5]

To some extent, then, Joseph was repeating the argument that had been made in the *Memorial to the Prime Minister* in 1972 by Johnson, Walters and Morgan, albeit in more simplistic terms. As discussed in the previous chapter, in the years 1972 to 1974 inclusive, the Bank of England had in fact engaged in very little 'money printing'; they were able to successfully finance the fiscal deficit from the sale of bonds to the non-bank private sector. The rapid expansion of money supply had come from private banks lending to the private sector following the introduction of the new liberalized monetary regime in 1971, *Competition and Credit Control*. One might therefore restate Joseph's argument by suggesting he was saying that the rise in property prices was a hedge against future inflation that was bound to come because everyone knew (or at least those buying property knew) that the government would have to finance the ballooning fiscal deficit by printing money. Clearly, Joseph had a lot of faith in the inherent economic rationality of the British people. However, whatever the cause of inflation, he believed that the government was creating too much employment where there was no natural demand for labour. The economy should be allowed to find its natural level, after which the government could help people in different ways to be more productive, say through retraining programmes or advice on how to start a business. These comments still very much suggested the exclusively classical focus on production as the source of growth and progress.

Joseph's speeches through 1975 and early 1976, many of which were published by the CPS, all suggest a similar focus. He argued in 1975, again in Preston, that the only cure for unemployment was restored profitability and that the many 'scroungers … keeping useless jobs' were wasting government money. At the Oxford University Union Joseph suggested that the 'real thrust of nationalisation was devoted to the interests of the producers'. The Government, he said, needed to 'hold the ring', rather than participate as a 'pseudo-entrepreneur'. Education, he said, was failing to teach young people 'to be sufficiently well-informed and self-disciplined … to be motivated and enabled to earn their living by making the best use of their talents in existing opportunities for productive work'. And in March 1976, in Harrow (in north-west London), Joseph declared that 'government over-spending has depressed the level of employment below what it would otherwise have been'. Excess taxation and borrowing were 'important components in the sluggishness of the private sector'. Britain needed less 'tax-based jobs' and more 'self-sustaining jobs' in the private sector.[6]

To reiterate, it is fair to argue that there is nothing in these speeches that suggests more than a classical liberal approach, and this probably very much reflects the influence that Alfred Sherman had as the director of the Centre for Policy Studies (CPS) and chief speechwriter. Too much interference from the government was holding business back, creating a poor business environment. Government was not doing all it could to make sure that teachers were preparing people for work, providing them with the right attitudes of self-discipline and motivation to join society as a productive member of the workforce. There was little talk here about the meaning of competition and the habits of thought persisting in society at large.

Joseph's lecture in Stockton in April 1976, *Monetarism is Not Enough*, can be seen as the culmination of his classical liberal arguments. Thatcher and Joseph were later to openly distance themselves from the term 'laissez-faire' in a way that was very reminiscent of the German Ordoliberal movement and Erhard's social market economy. However in this lecture, Joseph was still content to be seen to be advancing a laissez-faire programme. Indeed Britain's 'fall from grace' could be accounted for by precisely the failure to return to a classical liberal regime after 1918. The inter-war governments, so Joseph argued, had not in fact operated a policy of laissez-faire but instead had intervened to return the British pound to its pre-war parity almost as an act of nationalistic defiance, 'looking the dollar in the face'. This had nothing to do with orthodox economic theory, but instead marked, he argued, the beginning of a move towards the belief in the 'virtual omnicompetence of state intervention.'[7]

The 'sinews of the economy' were now being eaten away, the economy 'haemorrhaging' even while the government 'stimulate[d] the blood supply'. More than anything else there was a 'declining birth rate of new enterprises' because the government had 'driven out some of the wealth creators … [and] … shrivelled the impulse to expand … [It had] … throttled enterprise'. Most importantly though, Joseph was now explicitly invoking the idea of a zero-sum economy in which the public sector detracted from the private sector's ability to create wealth. 'For every job preserved in British Leyland, Chrysler and other foci of highly-paid outdoor relief, several jobs are destroyed up and down the country.' This comment of course begged the question as to why the private sector alone was capable of creating value. The answer was, as Joseph put it, that the 'public sector is relatively insensitive to economic conditions; it does not spontaneously adapt; it exerts a huge force of … inertia'.[8]

So Joseph was invoking the Hayekian notion of spontaneous adaptation; without the ability to adapt, to find new products and new markets there could be little or no wealth creation. And it was clear to him that the public sector was not adaptable; thus it formed a part of society whose activity, having not passed through the siphon of the market, acted as a drain on the rest of the economy. Joseph believed the public sector to be unproductive, in exactly the same way as was argued by Bacon and Eltis in *Britain's Economic Problem: Too few producers* (1976). Additionally though, and of course making the same argument that Pepper and Wood had made in *Too Much Money* (1976), if money supply growth was limited then there would be a battle for funds which would hit disproportionately on the private sector, that is the private sector would lose this battle and find itself 'strangled' and 'constricted'[9] in a way that the public sector was not.

Monetarism Is Not Enough was thus a direct response to the Labour government's introduction of money supply targeting in 1976; which itself was presented by the then Prime Minister, James Callaghan, as an explicit acknowledgement of the failure of Keynesianism. Indeed in the fiscal year ending March 1976 the government were being forced to 'print money' to finance their deficit, and even though private lending had slowed rapidly (this was due to the recession rather than the ending of *Competition and Credit Control* and the reimposition in 1974 of direct Bank of England controls, known as the 'supplementary deposit scheme' or 'corset'), money supply was still growing. Addressing the Labour Party conference in September 1976, Callaghan famously announced:

> We used to think that you could just spend your way out of recession to increase employment by cutting taxes and boosting government spending. I tell you in all candour that the option no longer exists and that insofar as it ever did it worked by injecting inflation into the economy.[10]

Joseph's speech at Stockton took place before the money supply targeting began, but after the policy was announced. As he said, 'the government's intention to contract the money supply is welcome and potentially beneficial to all. But it is not enough.' The state sector, he argued, would remain protected, and thus would win the battle for funds, crowding out the private sector. The private sector would be 'punished for the state sector's profligacy'. Thus it was essential to reduce the state sector at the same time as encouraging enterprise with substantial tax cuts.[11] Britain's problem was to be understood through the lens of unproductive producers versus productive producers, as demonstrated aptly by the Conservative Party's paper on economic policy, published in 1976, *The Right Approach*:

> The fundamental problem has been the erosion of the cornerstone of the whole edifice of industrial enterprise – profits and profitability. These provide both the incentive and the financial resources out of which expansion comes. If fewer people are embarking on new ventures to make profits, the reason is that fewer such possibilities exist.[12]

4.2 Stepping stones to the 'healthy society'

No history or discussion of Thatcherism or neoliberalism in Britain is complete without a discussion of the *Stepping Stones* report, written between August and November 1977 at the CPS by John Hoskyns and Norman Strauss,[13] both of whom had been brought into the CPS by its director, Alfred Sherman, at the end of 1975, on the basis that the Conservative Party was lacking any form of strategy for actually turning the economy around. And it was on this basis that Joseph asked Hoskyns and Strauss to prepare a report in 1977, a single strategy, as Thatcher later called it, to reverse economic decline. Key to this new strategy was the idea that government involved changing public attitudes, especially with regard to unions, thus turning the union issue from 'the Labour Party's secret weapon into its major liability'.[14]

In discussing this document, the point is not to prove how critical it was in the formulation of Thatcherism, but to use it to demonstrate the nature of thinking in the CPS in 1977 and how specific solutions for government were being developed. These 'solutions' addressed issues raised in Joseph's 1974 to 1976 speeches yet, at the same time, set out a plan for tackling attitudes and conduct in the population at large that, it was argued, needed changing. The argument presented here is that *Stepping Stones* represents a specifically neoliberal agenda, laying the groundwork for policies that sought to foster and elicit appropriate habits of thought from significant parts of the population who were, according to the authors, far too attached to their unions and worker instincts. That said *Stepping Stones* in no way represents the finished product of the New Right mentality of rule; speeches by Joseph, Lawson and Thatcher (discussed below) represent more complete statements of Thatcherite political rationality. All the same it provides a key primary resource through which to explore the genealogical work that was being done at the time, both at the CPS and, as discussed in the previous chapter, at the IEA. That is to say it offers a narrative in which the authors problematized certain habits of thinking, exploring those habits and explaining how to they came to be. Moreover the document is explicit in arguing that to reverse inexorable decline these attitudes needed to change, and that government had a role in doing this.

Stepping Stones is a document about government and how to govern the economy. In it, Hoskyns and Strauss envisaged a strategy that, if successfully enacted, would enable a future Conservative government to govern a society that had already become what it needed to be. The population would have accepted the need for legislation to limit the power of the unions before it was passed into law. The new government would only be formalizing the transformation through judicial modifications. The point was to win the next general election, but winning it for the right reasons was more important to these authors than winning it for the wrong reasons. As the report stated, there was 'no point in the Tories winning the next election unless the people are ready, at last, to move calmly and sensibly back to the sanity of other Western democracies'.[15]

Explicit economic policies were thin on the ground in the report; *Stepping Stones* did no more than provide a list from *The Right Approach*, published the year before. These policies included stabilizing the currency through balanced budgets, monetary discipline and public sector wage restraint; shifting personal taxes from income to expenditure and allowing capital gains to be treated as income; deregulating the private sector through scrapping price, profit and dividend controls; and finally using North Sea oil revenues to cut the public sector borrowing requirement so that interest rates could be kept low and investment encouraged.[16] But these authors believed that to do all of this required first and foremost a 'sea-change' in Britain's political economy; a fundamental change in attitudes.

Stepping Stones' focus was on attitudes that were, the authors argued, anathema to a healthy and growing set of private enterprises. And this clearly included the idea, already present in Joseph's speeches and most succinctly stated by Bacon and Eltis, that the public sector was a user-up of the wealth and value created by private industry. Britain was infused with wrong attitudes. The right attitudes, commensurate with a 'Healthy Society' involved a 'desire for something better – for unity, effort, quality of work, fairness, trust, and straight dealing'. On the face of it then the right attitudes related to attitudes towards work. However, focusing on that misses the point, because the purpose of *Stepping Stones* was to expose wrong attitudes, linked as they were to the perceived conduct of workers and unions alike. The very possibility of enacting the kind of legislative programme outlined in *The Right Approach* would already have meant, in the minds of Hoskyns and Strauss, ensuring that unions were not in a position to block change and that rank-and-file union members had already stopped supporting shop stewards and their more radical and explicitly socialist ideals.[17] The point of *Stepping Stones* was to present a strategy that insisted that the work of government had to be done immediately, even though it was going to be done outside the actual executive functions of government itself. In short, it was an attempt to change people's conduct, operating in a zone of ambiguity between a belief in the need to change attitudes and a belief that attitudes were changing or were poised to shift, just given the right nudge.

> The rising tide of public opinion is already transforming the trades unions from Labour's secret weapon into its biggest electoral liability … what we have to show is that the real conflict, which is already happening, is the direct result of the union status quo.[18]

In fact these authors were not alone in claiming that attitudes were changing. During the 1979 election, Callaghan is reported to have commented that he knew Labour were going to lose, that he could sense that there was a sea-change in politics, that the British public were going to vote for something different from government.[19] *Stepping Stones* is not being credited with this change; nor is it being necessarily claimed that British attitudes had 'in reality' changed; only that the report reflected a belief that attitudes were changing and that the New Right believed that they reflected this new consensus and knew how to 'finish the job off', so to speak. Of course the 1979 election did mark a huge shift in voting from Labour to Conservative, but the important point, as far as the question of how to govern is concerned, is that reports such as *Stepping Stones* demonstrate that the New Right were convinced that what they were saying and what they stood for represented attitudes that were commensurate with a healthy society; an electoral rejection of the Labour Party would mark a public rejection against old habits of thought. 'A landslide is needed, but it must represent an explicit rejection of socialism and the Labour–trade union axis; and the demand for something morally and economically better.'[20]

So *Stepping Stones* laid out a strategy for dislodging the average voter and rank-and-file union member from supporting the so-called Labour–trade union axis. This was to be no easy task, for, according to Hoskyns and Strauss,

> The individual worker and his union are closely linked. It would never occur to most workers that it could be otherwise, even though he may be inactive and attend no meetings. Exile from the union would be like banishment to Siberia. Between him and the terrors of being on his own in a society which, as yet, offers fairly unequal opportunities, stands his union – that is, his tribe, his clan, his own small society. Inside it he is warm, and to a large extent, safe. Outside, he is nothing. If he is to desert Labour – and thus by close connection, qualify his loyalty to his union – it must be for something better and equally reassuring to him. We have to create a situation where he can openly resolve the 'dissonance' between these feelings and his own opinion poll response to union power and socialist policies, by voting Tory.[21]

This is not to say that *Stepping Stones* blamed Britain's 'gradual decline … [to a] … low-wage second-world economy' solely on the unions. Much union behaviour, they argued, was a response to poor management and poor government; yet the unquestioning support for unionism in its current form was viewed as a permanent obstacle to recovery. In this account, recovery without an imposed period of austerity, in which consumers in Britain would be forced to adjust their expenditure so as to balance Britain's external account, was based on three preconditions: large-scale de-manning, an end to collective bargaining (and the linking of wages to productivity) and a natural shift from industry to services. This was all (only just) possible. Certainly it would have to involve the right kind of fiscal and monetary policies, as documented in *The Right Approach* (1976), but above all else de-manning and ending collective bargaining was positioned as the first necessary obstacle to overcome. In turn given their legal powers and huge membership, the unions were deemed an obstacle to any change. By electing a Labour government in 1974, the country had turned, according to Hoskyns and Strauss, towards a party that they believed could at least cope with unions, forming a satisfactory relationship with them, managing decline rather than precipitating crisis. Conversely, crisis was exactly what had been precipitated by Heath's Industrial Relations Act of 1971, which had led to large-scale strike action and a coal miners' strike that forced the country onto a three-day week at the start of 1974.[22]

The report classified those that 'needed to see economic reality' and adjust attitudes and behaviour accordingly on the following basis. The rank-and-file union members were really just ordinary people who could be convinced by the right political marketing that their interests lay elsewhere than with 'their tribe'. These people were no different from large numbers of Labour voters in 1974. Within the union hierarchy, however, there were potential allies, the economically confused and the political opponents. The latter, according to Hoskyns and Strauss, were the only true socialists, essentially Marxists who by marshalling and controlling members on the factory floor were increasingly turning unions into a political force that would celebrate the demise of the private sector, suffering under high rates of interest required to finance a fiscal deficit that itself enabled the public sector to continue to function. These were the people that the report argued had to be isolated and discredited.[23]

However, it is important to point out that none of these groups necessarily constituted the kind of cartel behaviour invoked by classical liberals such as Adam Smith, or by Hayek in *The Constitution of Liberty* (1960). That is to say, *Stepping Stones*, just as with George Allen's IEA paper on the British disease and Ralph Harris' essay in *Can Workers Manage?*, did not start from the supposition that the legal privileges afforded British unions had created self-acknowledged job protection cartels. Of course they would have argued that unions could be coercive organizations that erected barriers of entry to a particular form of employment so as to protect remuneration and benefits. And they would have whole-heartedly endorsed Hayek's view that 'a plant or industry cannot be conducted in the interest of some permanent distinct body of workers if it is able at the same time to serve the interests of the consumer'.[24] But the motives behind union behaviour at all levels were problematized in a different fashion. The agents of Britain's 'sick society' ('class war, dishonesty, tax fiddling, intimidation and shoddy work'[25]) were invariably not 'knowing' monopolists in the supply of labour but simply people with the wrong habits of thought, habits that belonged to a different time and to a different society.

Changing the law in itself was clearly something that the New Right believed needed to be done. This would include banning the closed shop and secondary picketing, as well as ending the legal immunity, granted to unions in 1906, from being sued for damages caused to a company's profits by union action that was not directly related to the dispute in question. However in the mid 1970s, in the context of stagflation, industrial disputes and a sense of crisis, these authors began to argue that new rules would only work if attitudes had first changed; or at the very least if those that refused to change attitudes could be marginalized so as to minimize the inflationary impact of their wage claims. And to change attitudes required first accepting that the opposition was not constituted by knowing, destructive monopolists; that unionists did not wake up every day and plan how best to protect their jobs. *Stepping Stones* was about accepting that for many unionists, their trade union was society, that supporting the union meant supporting a certain social structure and collective way of thinking. There was, one might say, a certain realization that if the worker-saver had been the image of ordinary human agent incorporated into the mind of the progressive liberal or Keynesian mentality of rule, then the union was often the way in which individuals had articulated themselves with this practice of rule; unionism and a progressive liberal governing mentality were two sides of the same coin. One could problematize these ways of thinking without necessarily claiming that they were deliberately malevolent.

So how was the *Stepping Stones* strategy supposed to work? How was a sea change in public opinion supposed to come about such that the Labour–trade union axis would be linked in people's minds to the sick society? The answer was through a communications strategy that took account of the 'not … strictly rational process … of how we think'. Like any product, a political product had to be marketed, advertised and differentiated, so Hoskyns and Strauss believed, 'at the level of ideology' by 'what sort of society is being proposed'. Marketing would, however, have to appeal to the three different groups of people that made up society: the thinkers, the feelers and the doers. The authors were confident that the intellectual argument could be won with the 'thinkers' and they thought that the 'doers' could be convinced by the results of change and reform; it was the vast majority, the 'feelers' who would need convincing to switch sides through some kind of emotional appeal. The appeal would have to be made as an 'emotional bridge' to help the feelers resolve the dissonance that they felt between wanting to be part of the union ('the tribe') and a feeling that the same union might in some way be restricting their freedom of action and self-expression. Images of the healthy and sick society and appropriate slogans would effect a shift in values and disturb existing mental states, preparing the ground for election victory and the acceptance of the legislative programme to come.[26]

The key message was that 'mental sets' had to change. Each person, Hoskyns and Strauss believed, had 'a more or less stable set of opinions, values, interests and purposes', which meant that responses to all kinds of events would be predictable unless the mental set changed.[27] The argument, which had also been heard at the IEA, was that the government had a role in realigning the population's attitudes and conduct to the requirements of modern British economy and society. Hoskyns and Strauss were not saying that union members were involved in a deliberate job protection operation. They were literally saying that their perspective on the world, which in itself referenced a certain kind of image of society and required a corresponding economic role for government, needed to change.

In discussing *Stepping Stones* it is of course tempting to ask the question, did it work, or was it successful? On the one hand, one can point to the frustration that Hoskyns felt and talked about in his memoirs *Just in Time* (2000); his diary entries suggest a continued annoyance that the Conservatives had not understood the central point: that battles needed to be picked with unions in order to make them appear to the public as synonymous with the British disease; the point was that attitudes had to change before legislation could be passed. And in government itself, at least in the first few years, legislation was much 'softer' on unionism than he had hoped, drafted as it was by one of the so-called 'wets', Jim Prior; government also, much to Hoskyns' annoyance, chose to settle pay disputes rather than battling the unions.[28] But certainly for Geoffrey Howe (Chancellor of the Exchequer from 1979 to 1983) the report continued to offer guidance throughout the years in government[29] and with the miners' strike of 1984–5 one can see its influence: the battle was prepared for and executed; opportunities for compromise were deliberately passed up.

Nonetheless, none of this addresses whether the strategy was successful in changing attitudes; whether attitudes were correctly characterized by the New Right before 1979 and whether, even if they did change, their political programme had anything to do with it. Of course finding reliable answers to these questions would be very difficult. However, this is not really the relevant point. Instead what all this is intended to demonstrate is that the New Right understood their role to be one in which government had to change conduct for the betterment of society. This was the job that they had given themselves; but how would they recognize the success of their policies? Having fewer working days lost to strike action was clearly one way in which government could convince itself that it had been successful and that things had changed. A more important way of recognizing success, however, would be to see the decline of the supposed inflationary effects of unionism. Inflation was seen as a monetary phenomenon; yet this was not contradicted by the belief that it was caused by weak government and management giving in to the wage demands of unionized workers.

That the demise of inflation would be the key signifier to the New Right that they had succeeded in their task of changing habits of thought was made clear in one of Joseph's speeches published by the CPS just before the 1979 election, *Solving the union problem is the key to Britain's recovery* (1979). This idea will be returned to in the conclusion to this chapter, for it is an essential point in understanding the following two chapters; but for now it is enough to say that, for Joseph, inflation in itself left 'people frightened and angry'; it 'upset … rational economic behaviour', causing 'everyone to try to seek the largest possible share of next year's bank notes'. In other words, everyone, Joseph believed, was 'forced into destructive action', but none more so than unions who appeared, to him at least, to be 'uniquely fortunate': collective action seemed to give them a strength that others did not possess. Crude monetarism was an insufficient response because with powerful unions refusing to moderate their wage claims, real damage due to high interest rates was being inflicted on the private sector.[30]

To abate inflation, the public sector, Joseph believed, would have to shrink. But in order to remove the fear that inflation would soon return, the present power of the trade unions needed to be curtailed. This was no more than 'a few stepping stones on the way to national recovery'. Ultimately the government under Thatcher would set in place a legislative framework that encouraged 'mature behaviour'. But, and in this he was of course reiterating Hoskyns' and Strauss' main point, 'it is rarely – except *in extremis* – prudent to pass laws unless the majority of people understand the need for them'. Laws could only be passed in the context of having already effected a change in habits of thought, only after and not before; and the demise of inflation would be the sign that everyone was ready for the new legislation. 'Debate' was therefore 'an essential prelude to practical action'. And as part of this debate, there was a need to focus on attitudes. One had to know the mental set out there before one could elicit and foster a new one. Thus they came to accept that union members believed what they believed, not that these beliefs were cynically deployed covers for colluding monopoly suppliers of labour. 'We should never forget that many union members are prisoners of a set of wrong assumptions and of a system which has gone wrong. It is the system we criticize, not the people involved in it.'[31]

4.3 How to govern the economy and reconstitute society

There are many reasons why by the late 1970s the New Right were publically distancing themselves from being linked with the term 'laissez-faire'. One reason might simply have been that they were worried that the term gave an immediately bad impression in the minds of voters. The argument being put forward here is that these denials were more than mere electioneering. During her first Conservative Party conference address as leader in 1975, Thatcher stated that she had never believed that the economy should run itself; governments were under an obligation to create a framework in which each individual could make the best of his of her talents.[32] In 1977, she argued in another speech that laissez-faire was a 200-year-old doctrine used by industry and commerce to fight monopoly and interference. In the current day and age, there were different battles, and there was no denying that the government had a role in economic life; 'there is much that the state should do, and do much better than it is doing.'[33] For a start, as discussed, changing attitudes and conduct in society would be a central task of her government.

However, any discussion of a whole assemblage of New Right ideas and practices would have to include not just economic issues, but also positions on law and order, defence, international relations, national identity, community, housing, health, education, and the control of government itself, whether local or national. The government was to be very active on all these issues after 1979, and before returning to the discussion of the formation of the policy programme in the 1970s, it is worth briefly touching on some of the different aspects of the New Right economic and social programme as enacted in the early 1980s. And of course these policy areas were interconnected. For instance, a properly functioning housing market was vital to the labour market because without a large stock of private houses for rent it was thought that it would always be difficult for workers to move and find new jobs. Legislation in 1980 and 1988 aimed at establishing tenancy agreements that, by giving landlords more control of leased premises, would stimulate the growth of the private rented sector.

Much was done to break up local government housing estates that were seen as fostering attitudes that were not progressive. For Thatcher, living in local government housing caused 'the worst source of immobility ... [tenants] ... not only have every incentive to stay where they are: they mutually reinforce each other's passivity and undermine each other's initiative'.[34] Thus in the 1980s the government instigated a massive programme of local government or 'council house' sales. This was linked to another target of New Right distaste, local government itself. Local governments were seen as an area of non-productive output that needed to be shrunk,[35] where a cosy relationship between council and tenants fostered habits of thought that were opposed to entrepreneurialism and wealth creation. Rather than allowing local governments to sell housing stock if they chose (a right that dated back to Harold Macmillan's Conservative government of 1957), the new 'right to buy' led by 1990 to one-and-a-half million families buying their homes from local councils. These houses were invariably sold at a significant discount to the current market value in order to incentivize as many as possible to become homeowners. Moreover, funds received in consideration for the sale of council houses were not to be used by local government for the construction of new social housing estates. Finally, the perceived incestuous relationship between local government and its tenants was further undermined by the 1988 Housing Act which allowed whole estates to vote for a transfer of ownership from local government to non-government associations. Such was the determination to shrink local government balance sheets, the voting system was set up such that those that did not vote were assumed to have voted for transfer out of local government control.[36]

The government also concerned itself with directly encouraging and incentivizing entrepreneurial (as producers not consumers) activity. This was of course a key and ongoing part of the New Right vision; fostering a better 'supply side' of the economy in which people were more productive, responsive and adaptable to consumer demand. And the Thatcher government believed that they could act directly to foster a more entrepreneurial spirit. Lower taxes for instance might have been part and parcel of shrinking the public sector, but fiscal policy was also to play a role in new behavioural incentive structures. The changing nature of taxation policy, for instance, was signalled almost immediately by Geoffrey Howe's first budget in 1979 when he instituted a huge shift from direct taxes on income to indirect taxes on expenditure (value added tax or VAT). The top rate of tax on earned income was lowered from 83 per cent to 60 per cent, and VAT on basic goods was increased from 8 per cent to 15 per cent. As he said, this was a hugely important and lasting change to the tax structure that was meant to enable high achievement to be rewarded and incentivized with commensurately high salaries. Moreover, VAT as opposed to income tax was thought to be less distorting to the consumer decision-making process.[37]

Nigel Lawson's first budget as Chancellor of the Exchequer in 1984 was equally important, extending the remit of VAT from 50 per cent of consumer goods to almost all goods. He also abolished tax surcharges on investment income, part of the policy of ending the distinction between income earned in work and income earned on savings. In the same year Lawson also changed the tax system so that corporate capital purchases were no longer immediately tax deductible. Following on directly from the neoliberal critique of investment theories of growth, he explained that this change reflected the long held and incorrect prevailing belief that investment in physical plant and machinery was good per se and should be subsidized. Having abolished these tax allowances, he was able to bring down significantly the rate of corporation tax charged on profits.[38] Taken as a whole, changes to the tax system were aimed at incentivizing enterprise whether at the corporate or individual level and removing a highly variable tax structure that, the New Right believed, distorted the allocation of capital in society.[39]

For Lawson, speaking at a lecture given in 1984 entitled *The British Experiment*, this all represented an appropriate switch in policy. On the one hand, macroeconomic policy was all about creating conditions conducive to growth and employment; fiscal policy could only be part of that if it was operating in harmony with declining monetary growth. Microeconomic policy, on the other hand, was now all about removing controls and allowing markets to work better.

> The abolition of pay controls, price controls, dividend controls, foreign exchange controls, bank lending controls, hire purchase controls, industrial building controls – all these have been beneficial in themselves, but will bring even greater benefit to the nation as part of the process of rediscovering the enterprise culture.... In the field of microeconomic policy ... what we are seeking to do is to change a psychology, to change a business culture.[40]

At a push one might say that with regards to economic policy the substantive goal was the re-creation of a society in which laissez-faire was possible. However, even this is problematic in that, as the last chapter discussed, competition was viewed as a process that the government had to maintain, that resulted in an active tension between consumer and producer. To drop one's attention from the economy for even a short time might mean that producers were no longer serving consumers. Laissez-faire for neoliberals was only possible if there was competition, but competition, as the above quote from Lawson suggests, was an artefact of having the right psychology. Competition would have to be constantly monitored; as such the conditions of possibility for laissez-faire could never necessarily imply a laissez-faire governmental regime. Habits of thought in society at large and in business culture had to change. And there would have to be a permanent vigilance by government to ensure these attitudes persisted: that businesses were not adopting monopolistic practices and that the population at large was using its consumer instincts to subject businesses to competition.

This is a discussion that will be returned to in the following chapter and is directly related to the role of monetary policy and the ongoing monitoring of monetary developments in the economy. However, the remainder of this section will pick up on another theme running through this chapter: the emergence within the CPS of first classical liberal, and then later neoliberal ideas. The early speeches of Keith Joseph spoke heavily of his discovery of classical liberalism. By 1976, in the midst of crisis Joseph was making a sharp distinction between a right-minded and wealth-creating zone of productive practice and a non-wealth creating public zone in which resources were used up. Unless this latter zone was deliberately shrunk by restricting access to funding (money from the government), then limiting total money supply growth in the economy would fall disproportionately on the private sector wealth creators.

This is where *Stepping Stones* was so important; everyone had to accept the need for pay restraint so that collective bargaining would not add to inflationary pressure. In time these new arrangements for collective bargaining would be enshrined in union legislation. Six Acts of Parliament were passed between 1980 and 1993 that successively removed union privileges and legal immunities. But the very fact that they were not passed all at once was part of the plan. Hoskyns, Strauss and Joseph had all made it clear that the public had to already have changed attitudes and be exhibiting new habits of thought in order for the new legislation to be accepted and be effective. Knowing when to govern for these new habits of thought was going to require some significant signals in order that government could be certain in their belief that attitudes had changed.

All the same, one question remains unanswered: what were the new attitudes to be? So far, one might say, that discussions and speeches had taken a certain negative character. The New Right was pretty sure what was wrong, that uncritical support for unionism created regressive thinking. Moreover they believed that the maintenance and build-up of these attitudes was a result of economic policies that had overinflated demand for employment, always holding in mind what had happened during the 1920s and 1930s. In the neoliberal mind the sick society and the British disease did not have to be described in great detail because the symptoms were manifest for all to experience in Britain in the 1970s. Thus in the material so far considered in this chapter, there is a certain lack of detail in regard to what the healthy society would look like, and what, in human terms, it would consist of. It would certainly consist of good business managers and entrepreneurs. Indeed Joseph in part held business responsible for not standing up to unions and for not 'convincing them of the facts of economic life. ... Management had been shell-shocked by the shift in power, without responsibility, to the shop floor.'[41] The government, as discussed above, would do what they could to incentivize private business. They would also do much more, as the next chapter will demonstrate, to try and eradicate bad management.

However Joseph also recognized in a speech in 1978, *Conditions for fuller employment*, that entrepreneurship was a great skill and talent that not everyone had.[42] He wanted everyone to respect entrepreneurs as leaders rather than considering them, as he believed others did (especially the 'well-intentioned social workers and misguided left-wing teachers'[43]), as morally dubious seekers of profit. But a healthy society was not simply constituted by two classes of people: workers (who respected all that entrepreneurs did) and entrepreneurs. This was the Schumpeterian perspective. There had to be something else to this vision of society, not just that it would appeal to everyone and win votes, but that everyone was included and played a vital role. Certain key habits of thought had to be part and parcel of everyone's economic behaviour. 'For full employment to happen involves adaptability and co-operation by people.' The worker (as unionist or as 'worker-saver') was, in the hands of Joseph, a label that applied to attitudes that damaged the interests of the whole of society. The worker needed to cease to exist as a central category of self-identification in people's minds, and instead needed be reconstituted in different forms; 'the worker as consumer wants low prices; the worker as investor, as beneficiary of occupational pension funds, wants high dividends; the worker as job-seeker wants high profits, yielding extra jobs'.[44]

'Work is a creation of value by service to the consumer.' This, according to Joseph was its social function, creating value by satisfying wants. 'Full employment and rising standards are by-products of adaptability. Repress the adaptability and you diminish the degree to which demand calls forth supply, and supply generates demand.' To think in a way that stressed adaptability was therefore the way to exercise habits of thought that were commensurate with progress, economic growth and the least possible unemployment. Desire, in this view, was not appropriately satiated by inappropriately created jobs but instead by appropriate consumer behaviour, whether on the high street or whether in ownership of more long-term assets, such as houses or shares.

> Every human being is a consumer. The consumers vary in number, tastes and effective demand. There are more consumers than producers. The population as consumers will keep occupied the population as producers provided, of course, that the financial system is so managed as to allow this to happen. The reverse is *not* true; producers will not satisfy consumers by producing the same pattern of goods and services.[45]

For the New Right there were still far too many people who thought of themselves as workers rather than as servers of the consumer,[46] that is as employees of the consumer. There was far too much governing that was done in terms of a model of the worker-saver and there was much that government could do to incentivize and facilitate entrepreneurs to create new products and foster new demands. But at the same time neoliberal governing had to proceed on the basis that society was also composed of individuals who were at the very least thinking of themselves as consumers, not as workers, with the connected instincts of ownership and adaptability.

The neoliberal mentality of rule divided society in a fashion that was entirely distinct from the classical liberal division between classes: landowner, capitalist, worker. No longer should government aim at producing a population of people who would learn to properly exercise their respective class responsibilities; nor should government arbitrate so that these classes could meet in equality in the marketplace. As far as economic agency was concerned, on the one side of society there was the private sector and consumers working together for progress, both exhibiting adaptability, willingly responding to change; on the other side there were workers and the public sector. Either one was doing all that one could for oneself, maximizing one's own potential through work or through investing in oneself, or one was using up the wealth and resources being created by agents doing the former.

This was, therefore, a social argument, an argument about what constituted a moral society. And no one expressed this idea more so than Thatcher in her speeches between 1975 and 1977. In *The new renaissance* (1977) she argued that for forty years the progressive up-to-the-moment belief in Britain had been in the virtues of collectivism. But now there was a new form of progressiveness that began with 'the individual, with his uniqueness, his responsibility and his capacity to choose'. The moral side of the economy was thus composed of people who made choices for themselves, whether consumers or entrepreneurs. 'Choice is the essence of ethics; good and evil have meaning only insofar as man is free to choose.'[47]

> People must be free to choose what they consume in goods and services. When they choose through the market, their choice is sovereign; they alone exercise their responsibility as consumers and producers.... Choice in a free society implies responsibility. There is no hard-and-fast line between the economy and other forms of personal responsibility to self, family, firm, community, nation, and God. A moral being is one who exercises his own judgement in choice, on matters great and small, bearing in mind their moral dimension – right and wrong.... A man must choose between spending and saving; between paying for his children's education and accepting whatever the state provides.[48]

Thatcher's vision of the healthy society was one that was founded on the idea of personal responsibility; that every citizen could 'develop his full potential both for his own benefit and for the community as a whole'.[49] Indeed every person had 'an obligation to make the best of his talents', and in turn government had an 'obligation to create the framework' within which each person could do that.[50] Only once people had taken responsibility for themselves, ensured that they had used the resources available to them to maximize their self-worth, only then would a healthy society come into existence. Being responsible for oneself and one's family first would lead to a feeling of being a responsible member of the community and wanting to ensure the well-being of that community. Ultimately 'the voluntary spirit of the community … [would] … be mobilized'.[51] To consume the services of the state was not taking responsibility for oneself; only consumption that was marketed represented a signal of wishes and preferences,[52] and only this kind of consumption was commensurate with the moral society.

Neoliberalism did not deny society, quite the contrary; but it was an individualized form of society neither embodied in separate classes nor the state but in one class of entrepreneurs, either in business or 'of-the-self'. That is not to say that the Conservative Party did not recognize income differentials although, as Thatcher argued, to act so as to iron out differentials would ignore how they arose, and to do this would be 'to ignore the fact that society is a living organism resting on processes and changing relationships'.[53] Simply put, class division ought to be nothing more than income differentials. Or to be more exact, the persistence of allegiance to the working class was deemed wrong; everyone should be allied to the progressive society of consumers and entrepreneurs. As the policy document *The Right Approach* (1976) put it:

> It is not the existence of classes that threaten the unity of the nation, but the existence of class feeling. So long as success and ability are rewarded, there will be classes. But class is rapidly ceasing to be the main determinant of political behaviour.[54]

More than anything else the New Right took offence at the idea that the state was the embodiment of society. And this lies at the heart of a certain irony; that Thatcher was a great believer in a certain form of society, even though she is famous for her comment 'there is no such thing as society'. Understanding the neoliberal mentality of rule is to recognize that its vision of the social market economy was based on a set of economic ideas which were post-Keynesian, which referenced a vision of the economy in which all humans were active agents of economic prosperity, not just one class (of entrepreneurs). Thatcher's infamous statement was made twice in an interview in 1987. On the first occasion it was in the context of saying that people who cast their problems on society were ignoring the fact that they were casting their problems on other individuals because it was individuals and families that made up society. In the second instance, she followed the comment by stating that she believed there to be a living tapestry of men and women and the beauty of that tapestry depended on how much each person took responsibility for themselves and was prepared to help others through their own efforts.[55]

Her memoirs are more revealing in that she defended the statement by making the key differentiation between society and the state; the whole problem she believed was due to the evolution in people's minds of the confusion between society and the state, as helper of first resort. 'Society was not an abstraction ... I expected great things from society ... because I believed that as economic wealth grew, individuals and voluntary groups should assume more responsibility for their neighbours' misfortunes.'[56] Thatcherism was meant to be a project to improve society, to make it function better, and to govern for those who shared the appropriate habits of thought. But in this political rationality society was not embodied in the state; instead society was to be privatized and reformulated so that it was constituted by responsible consumers and entrepreneurs.

4.4 Conclusion: inflation first

At this stage it is worth recapping some of the major themes running through this book. To start, it is necessary to reiterate Foucault's position that liberal government 'is a consumer of freedom ... which means that it must produce it ... [Government says] ... I am going to see to it that you are free to be free.'[57] The question remains however, free to do what? In both classical liberal and progressive liberal or Keynesian regimes, the freedom that was invariably prescribed and produced was the freedom to produce more. For classical liberalism it was a freedom in which nothing should be allowed to get in the way of the entrepreneurs' right to funds (whether obtained from personal savings or the bank) so as to accumulate capital equipment that would increase output in the future. Discipline might be required for some of the non-entrepreneurial classes to ensure that they were fit for work; thus one could always discern a distinction between the deserving and undeserving poor. For progressive liberalism this right to produce changed nature and shape, now everyone in society had a right to work. And as nations got wealthier and average savings rates rose it was more likely that governments would have to take a role in providing work. After all was it not better to make people useful, getting them to build houses and roads rather than just hand out cash or dig holes in the ground, fill them with cash, and ask the unemployed to dig the cash out again?

For neoliberals, however, increasing general levels of wealth meant that there was a new freedom to be actively addressed by government: the freedom to consume. It was not that people had not been free to consume before, but that this freedom was one that did not need to be spoken of. Adam Smith's *Wealth of Nations* began with a recognition that the whole point of political economy was to understand how the nation was able to provide more for itself to consume, that the poorest in a rich nation still consumed more than the richest in a poor nation. But there was nothing to say about consumption itself, other than excluding eating, which was ultimately limited to the human stomach; Smith knew of no limit for 'the desire of the conveniences and ornaments of building, dress, equipage, and household furniture'.[58] Nothing more needed to be said on the matter, and Ricardo, Mill and Marx essentially followed suit. One cannot find in the practices of liberal government any sense of the need to produce sovereign and enterprising consumers. The idea of the consumer as an agent of progress, imbued with a mentality of adaptability and the sense of self as a site of human capital had been anathema.

The IEA from its inception posed the right to consume, to use hire purchase, and to be addressed by advertising as something that needed to be actively encouraged by government. For these authors being free to choose, being free to consume was an essential part of being free to maximize self-fulfilment, not just as immediate gratification but in the lifetime process of self-discovery, in which one maximized one's potential self-worth and one's intrinsic value. This was a foundational element of being. And, as Thatcher was to remark many years later, it was a duty on each individual to maximize self-fulfilment and in turn the community's worth would be maximized as well.

This conception of the consumer was a fundamental reference point in the neo-liberal mentality of rule. It was always present as an ultimate foundation to draw upon in problematizing how the economy was governed. However, it was not until the 1970s that this reference point was fully activated in the minds of the New Right in Britain as a governmental concern for the conduct of those who were governed. Intellectuals and politicians came face to face with the problem that they might have to 'produce' active consumers in the population at large. A distinction in society had been drawn between the thinking of entrepreneurs and sovereign consumers on the one hand and workers and the public sector on the other; being part of this latter pairing meant that the authenticity of one's economic activity was questionable because it not had passed through the siphon of the market. However as the 1970s progressed, and this genealogy of crisis was constituted in the IEA and CPS, government policies came to be blamed for exacerbating habits of thought that, these authors believed, should have passed into history. Moreover, and critically, these habits of thought were increasingly problematized as attitudes and conduct that acted as obstacles, blocking and detracting from the activity of the marketed side of the economy. How could one be thinking appropriately as a self-responsible consumer when one was part of a union, part of 'a tribe' supposedly opposed to the concerns of business? How could one be an entrepreneur, endowed with special talents, if one was constantly compromising with the factory floor on pay and conditions, rather than being focused on the bottom line, the creation of profit and funds for reinvestment?

In the minds of the New Right, in a world of rising affluence it was time for people to take responsibility for themselves, to become individualized consumers, free to choose all the goods and services that they might need. And by bringing this dissonance into the minds of workers, the 'rational' desires and habits of thought that were lying dormant would become active. There was much for government to do here with regards to trade union legislation. There was also, as the next chapter discusses, much that could be done within the financial system to foster and encourage consumer ways of thinking. For, as Joseph had said, 'the population as consumers will keep occupied the population as producers provided, of course, that the financial system is so managed as to allow this to happen.'[59]

However, as this chapter should have made clear, the New Right saw many different and interconnected roles for government; there was much for it to be doing with regards to the economy. Attitudes prevalent in the public sector, in nationalized industries and in unions had, they believed, also undermined businesses, often creating managers who were not 'doing their job' vis-à-vis wealth creation, let alone explaining 'economic reality' to their workforce. Incentivizing and promoting entrepreneurial activity and increased productivity was very much part of the ongoing neoliberal project and, as is discussed in Chapter 6, was taken up by the Labour Party in the late 1990s as a way to reform services that remained in the public sector. The figure of the consumer was clearly not the be-all-and-end-all of governing the economy or society. The Thatcher government betrayed a distinct awkwardness when addressing public services, but there was no reluctance to tackle the economy and to command business managers to be more creative. Thatcher, for instance, exhibited this very point when addressing the Institute of Directors in 1976, when she said,

> The politician's role is to set the circumstances in which the wealth creator can use all his talents to play his chosen role in society. We fail you if we do not provide them; you fail us if you are not then enterprising.[60]

The focus here is however on governing for the figure of the consumer. Governing the economy this way was always of course related to production; competition for instance was throughout the IEA literature explained as an active tension between consumers and producers. The next chapter shows how, in the early 1980s, policies were enacted on the economy that were intended to a have the effect of unsettling workplaces, whether in the private or public sectors, where managers and workers had, rather like Thatcher's depiction of the local government housing estate, established a cosy relationship and reinforced, at least in her belief, passive attitudes that were contrary to the general economic interest of the nation. Monetarism was both about bad management and certain types of worker habits of thought. Moreover monetarism did not mark both the beginning and end of policies for increasing productivity; that the following chapters do not focus more on the 'supply-side' legislation is a reflection of this book's concern with how governments have governed for the consumer. This focus is not meant to imply that the government did not continue to concern itself with the productivity of producers or with the productivity of government itself.

However to finish this chapter it is important to revisit the notion that the economy was seen as the starting point of the New Right governmental programme. The *Right Approach* (1976) opened by stating that the priority of any government should be the reduction in the debt burden and the mastering of inflation. This would mark the beginning of economic recovery because, so it was argued, economic failure lay at the heart of Britain's economic problems, sapping the self-confidence of the people.[61] Indeed, in a speech in 1975 Joseph stated his belief that it was the poor government of the economy that had led to the 'declining rationality ... in our society's workings' and the 'deterioration in ... defence provisions, law and order, levels of behaviour and freedom from fear'.[62]

The consistent message was, get the economy right, and then everything else can follow, from finding the money to sustain a strong military force, to paying for social services that (at least for the time being) were to remain in government ownership and control. Inflation was the key priority; after all as Joseph had said it was inflation that was threatening to destroy society. But tackling inflation meant controlling the money supply, cutting government spending, and controlling the unions' collective bargaining practices; all of which would ultimately provide the framework in which companies could start offering consumers what they wanted and thus, in the process, be returned to profitability and therefore to wealth creation.

But how would government recognize that their policies were working? Well of course, the Thatcherites could take pleasure in high corporate profits and less working days lost to strike action.[63] But all of these signs could just be temporary, manifestations of a cyclical pick-up in economic activity that could prove short lived, and not the result of rational wealth-owning units maximizing profits or self-potential. The only sure sign that things had changed, that conduct had changed, would be permanently low inflation. Only the ongoing price level would fully betray what was going on in people's minds; was the government printing money, were companies giving in to wage claims that were not matched by productivity gains, were workers demanding inflationary pay increases? Nigel Lawson put the matter very clearly in two lectures in 1981 and in 1984 respectively. In discussing *Thatcherism in Practice* (1981) Lawson noted that the Thatcher government had inherited a 'legacy of psychology and attitudes bred by decades of economic miseducation'. The 'overriding objective' of policy now was to be 'the conquest of inflation'.[64] In 1984, when discussing *The British Experiment*, Lawson made it crystal clear that inflation was the central barometer of success; 'to achieve stable prices ... implies fighting and changing the psychology of two generations. That cannot be achieved overnight. But let there be no doubt that that is our goal.'[65] The enterprising society of consumers and entrepreneurs was to be identified and governed by a persistent monitoring of consumer price inflation.

5 Governing for the consumer

In the previous chapter, it was argued that the programme to change British attitudes and behaviour began in the mid to late 1970s, as Margaret Thatcher and Keith Joseph toured Britain delivering speeches to the public imploring them to abandon their union instincts and imagine themselves in a healthy society composed of entrepreneurs and enterprising consumers. This chapter explores the strategies and tactics of neoliberalism practised in government in the 1980s to make these changes permanent. In the broadest sense, this chapter asks the question, how did the Thatcher government govern for the consumer? More specifically, it explains key elements of Thatcherite economic policy in the context of the society being imagined by the New Right. If neoliberals were to govern for certain ways of thinking, encouraging and fostering habits of thought that would enable consumer sovereignty to be reasserted, then the strategies and tactics to be employed had to be geared towards changing attitudes and behaviour in the economy.

Many of the economic policies enacted in the 1980s appear paradoxical; one historical account of the period, E. H. H. Green's *Thatcher* (2006), goes as far as to say that, unlike other areas of the government's agenda, Thatcher's political economy was 'often contradictory'.[1] In this chapter it is being suggested that these paradoxes can be explained in the context of the New Right's political rationality and *raison d'être* in government. The interpretation presented here is different from accounts that have focused on Thatcher's pragmatism, such Hugo Young's *One of Us* (1989) and William Keegan's *Lawson's Gamble* (1989).[2] Equally, this chapter argues against economists of the New Right, such as Gordon Pepper and Tim Congdon,[3] who viewed the consumer boom of the late 1980s as an explicit abandonment of monetarism. Milton Friedman's own assessment of monetarism in practice, presented to the House of Commons Select Committee in 1980, was that government was not following the kind of monetarism that he had outlined over the previous ten years.[4] All the same, the argument that follows downplays the notion that policy was muddled and confused. The substantive goal was not the practice of monetarism but the readjustment of attitudes and behaviour. Monetarism was just a tactic of government used at a particular time for a particular governmental purpose.

There was a fundamental continuity in policy, where at first glance government actions appeared paradoxical and problematic. For instance, why fully liberalize the banking sector yet at the same time restrict money supply growth? Why, when the stated intention is to reverse Britain's economic malaise, 'squeeze' the private sector as much as the public sector? And why, having worked so hard to bring money supply growth within target range, abandon targets and do little to control a consumer spending and housing market boom? These paradoxes can be explained when one considers that Thatcherism meant governing for the consumer, and that making the consumer sovereign was a key goal of government.

In keeping with these themes, this chapter is divided in the following way. Section 5.1 focuses on the monetary squeeze enacted in Thatcher's first term of government between 1979 and 1983. This period can broadly be divided into two halves, the first in which the private sector felt the brunt of monetarism, the second, commencing with the spring 1981 Budget, when attention was turned towards limiting the flow of funds to the public sector. Section 5.2 focuses on how financial sector reform formed part of enabling and establishing the enterprise culture. In turn, liberalization and its results precipitated the abandonment of money supply targets in 1985. The chapter argues against the view that this change in policy was a betrayal of neoliberalism. Finally, in the conclusion to the chapter, the boom and bust of the late 1980s/early 1990s is presented as the first crisis of neoliberalism, a crisis of governmentality brought about by a confrontation between the behaviour of the consumer-as-entrepreneur, that had been imagined by the New Right, and the realities of excessive consumer and household borrowing.

5.1 'The quiet revolution'[5]

According to the politicians of the New Right, British industry, whether in the private or public sectors, acted against the interests of the consumer in two distinct ways. First there was the view, regularly espoused by IEA authors, that industry and management failed to produce goods and services that British consumers wanted. Whether this was because industry had been subsidized by government or badly educated in business practices, the end result was that British consumers seemed to prefer to buy goods that were made elsewhere. For IEA authors, consumers were giving a consistent message about the poor quality of British industrial output, and this in part was held responsible for Britain's low economic growth rate and its regular balance of payments crises. Then, second, there was the view that had increasingly come to the fore in the 1970s, and had been put across on several occasions by Keith Joseph,[6] that bad British management, by failing to stand up to unions and not educating its workforce about business realities, was in part to blame for the continuation of habits of thought among the population at large that were not commensurate with progress and adaptation. How, so the view went, could one have consumer sovereignty while producer and unionist attitudes predominated?

In what follows it is argued that Thatcherism enacted a severe monetary squeeze on the economy between 1979 and 1982 in order to directly counter these problems. Thus although the depth of the recession between 1979 and 1981 was accentuated by global economic problems and the problematic application of monetarism, the core group of New Right economic policy-makers, including Thatcher, Howe and Lawson, believed that a severe recession was a necessary part of changing the attitudes of workers and managers alike. The monetary squeeze (nominal interest rates peaked at 17 per cent in November 1979 and stayed above 14 per cent until March 1981) was for them 'a blitz on overmanning'[7] in British industry. Between mid-1979 and the start of 1981 total output fell 5.5 per cent, manufacturing output by 15 per cent (in 1980 alone), and the manufacturing workforce by 10 per cent. Overall during the recession unemployment doubled, rising to 10 per cent, and it stayed high for the next five years, during which time a total of two million manufacturing jobs disappeared (representing 14 per cent of total employment).[8] But job losses were seen as a sign that the policies were right and that attitudes were changing, that retrograde inflationary psychology was being eliminated. In its place government believed that a society of entrepreneurs and consumers, operating in a marketed zone of practice, could come to the fore.

Nonetheless, by saying that job losses were a sign that attitudes were changing, it is not necessarily the case that policy was deliberately aimed at producing unemployment. As discussed in the previous chapter, lowering inflation was the goal; rising unemployment signalled to government both that their prognosis was correct and that change was occurring. Essentially, high interest rates, they believed, would only affect companies where management was poor in the first place. As the Governor of the Bank of England, Gordon Richardson, put it in December 1979:

> The moral of what I have been saying is plain. How badly firms are hit will depend, in quite large part, on how well they can control their costs; it will depend on the ability of management and workers to back wage increases with comparable strides in efficiency. The situation no doubt varies widely. Many industrialists I have met remain confident, especially those successful in new product areas. But in general the future will depend importantly on co-operation by all concerned to produce much better results.[9]

And the following year, at the end of 1980, Richardson was talking in more optimistic terms; things were indeed beginning to change. Rising unemployment proved to government that the quality of management had been poor, leading to overmanning; at the same time increased unemployment now proved that things were improving.

> We can discern some benefits beginning to emerge from the policies which have been pursued.... Over decades our productivity performance has been poor ... we had been ... resistant to change.... It is encouraging to hear

> reports that attitudes may be changing. The Bank's wide contacts with industry suggest that managers are more alert to the need to manage, and that workpeople are more concerned with success of firms in which they work.... When ... [the recession] ... ends many companies will be in a better condition to grasp the opportunities that an upturn presents.[10]

The goal of policy was the eradication of an inflationary psychology based upon the belief that inflation was the result of management (in both the private and public sectors) not standing up to wage demands that were in excess of productivity gains. Bad managers, so the argument went, had all too often given in to demands for wage increases and had not sufficiently rationed their workforce. This, it was believed, was the ultimate cause of inflation. Any policy which both decreased inflation while at the same time increasing unemployment was taken as evidence that the theory was right, i.e. it proved the policy presuppositions were right in the first place. Writing in a pamphlet in May 1982, *Financial Discipline Restored*, Lawson argued that unemployment was the inescapable casualty in the war against inflation. Job losses, he said, 'are neither intended nor are they unexpected. They are a sign of neither wickedness nor incompetence. The object is quite simply to win the war ... against inflation.' Unemployment was not targeted but it was entirely to be expected that if inflation fell, then 'a change in attitudes on both sides of industry' representing 'a new realism' was emerging. Management suddenly awakening to the need to cut overmanning and return companies to higher profitability would represent the 'return to rationality'. This was the 'quiet revolution' that was perceived to be taking place in British industry.[11]

5.1.1 Good managers and bad managers

What might be taken to be problematic about the above account is that it presents the early Thatcher policies as if they went entirely according to plan. This is not the case; the application of monetarism was fraught with difficulties. But to focus on Britain's supposed failed experiment with monetarism is to miss the point. The standard account of the period is that, having induced an excessive monetary squeeze in the early 1980s due to a misreading of monetary data, monetarism was replaced in the mid 1980s by a pragmatic and essentially Keynesian policy, whereby government reverted to 'stoking up' demand in the economy; only this time promoting household consumer expenditure, in part financed by credit.[12] The 1980s, in this view, represents the beginning of an era of, what social scientist Colin Crouch has called, 'privatized Keynesianism'.[13] As discussed, this interpretation follows from ignoring that the purpose of monetary policy in the early 1980s was to change habits of thought in society at large and redirect conduct. Nonetheless, it is important to examine some of the problems that were encountered in money supply targeting, for to do so explains why other accounts of this period have so heavily focused on the 'failure' of monetarism or on the idea that the government got it wrong or did not mean to do what they did.

The Thatcher government inherited from Labour in June 1979 a money supply target for Sterling M3 (essentially notes and coins and all sterling deposits in the banking system) of 8 to 12 per cent, which Howe immediately reduced to 7 to 11 per cent for the twelve months ending March 1980. In the Budget of March 1980 monetary targets were incorporated into what became the centrepiece of Thatcher's economic policy, the *Medium Term Financial Strategy* (MTFS). This document incorporated targets both for the public sector borrowing requirement (expressed as a percentage of gross domestic product) and for monetary growth (using Sterling M3). The point of the MTFS was to demonstrate the resolve of government; to show that it was not going to waver from its belief that bringing down inflation was the primary goal, and that the way to achieve that goal was by slowing money supply growth. Including a target for public borrowing that was consistently shrinking as a percentage of GDP was meant to ensure both that the government would never have to 'print money' to cover the deficit and that funding the deficit would not put additional upward pressure on interest rates, thus crowding out the private sector. Any shrinkage in the private sector was intended to be entirely the result of bringing down inflation (via slowing monetary growth), rather than because the 'non-productive' government sector was taking up too much of the 'economic pie'.

But as Figure 5.1 demonstrates, the Government's record between 1979 and the end of 1983 in meeting its targets for money supply was poor. Foremost, it should be said that monetarism, as propounded by Friedman, entailed the use of open market operations to ensure that money supply actually fell within the target range. Essentially, if money supply grew too fast then money would be taken out of the system directly by the central bank. In the British version, however, money supply growth was targeted by the use of interest rates, on the basis that there was a consistent relationship (that had supposedly been previously established) between the rate of interest and the demand for money, and in turn that there was a consistent relationship between money supply growth and the rate of inflation. Goodhart's Law, coined by the monetary economist Charles Goodhart, summed up the problem: every time a new money supply measure was adopted on the basis that a correlation had been statistically established, the relationship between that measure and interest rates broke down. For the sake of clarity Figure 5.1 only demonstrates the failure to target Sterling M3; nonetheless other measures were also used in addition to Sterling M3. Thus M1 and M4 (both narrower and broader measures of money respectively) were also targeted between 1982 and 1984, as was M0 (the narrowest measure, essentially notes and coins) after 1984. All measures used were found to be equally problematic, supporting Goodhart's Law.

But Goodhart's Law is not an explanation for what happened, just a description. The problem was that interest rates targeted the counterpart to money in the balance sheet of the financial system (that is private bank credit) rather than money supply itself (which only open market operations could affect directly[14]). Given this, it is easy to understand the two key problems faced by the Bank of England in their attempts to target money supply. First, higher interest rates put

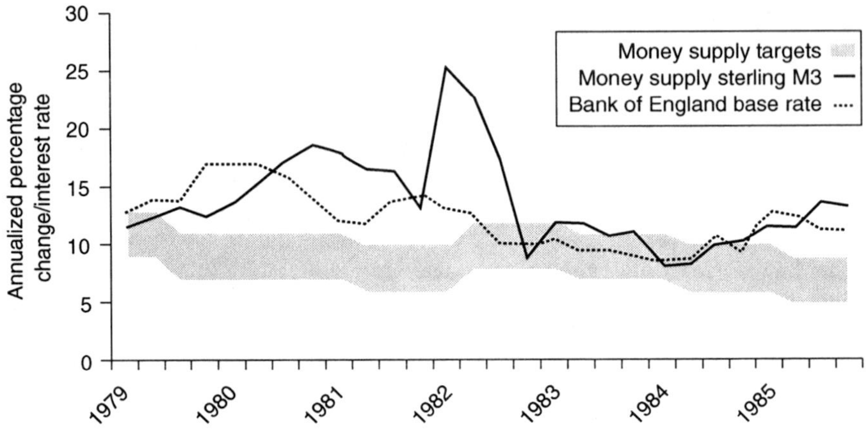

Figure 5.1 Money supply growth targets, actual money supply growth and interest rates 1979–85 (source: Bank of England, HM Treasury).

pressure on the cash flows of private companies forcing them to borrow even more from the banking system. According to the Bank of England, bank lending was fuelling 'unruly' money supply growth, but was itself a response to the cash flow pressures caused by a high interest rate policy aimed at lowering money supply growth.[15]

Second, the deregulation of the banking system, specifically the removal of exchange controls in October 1979 and the ending of the supplementary deposit scheme (or 'corset') in June 1980, meant that banks were now free to lend. Both measures were intended to remove distortions in the systems for monetary control and to ensure that there could be no direct control over lending.[16] The government could no longer ration credit; the banking system would be free to create deposit money (the other side of the double entry in their books that created the loan) on the basis of its own assessments of the risk worthiness of the borrower and need to keep reserves. These measures, as discussed in the following section, formed part of a long-term programme aimed at fostering entrepreneurialism and an enterprise culture. However, in the short term they played havoc on attempts to target money supply. Not only did the removal of the corset mean that it was easier for companies in distress to raise funds, but reintermediation of bank lending (bringing off-balance sheet lending back onto balance sheets and ending the 'bill leak') following the corset's removal added 7.75 per cent to Sterling M3 between July and September 1980 alone.[17] And while this latter increase might only have been an accounting issue, it seemed to almost immediately draw into question the powers of the government and the Bank of England to bring money supply into target range.

By liberalizing the financial system at exactly the same time as trying to target money supply growth through interest rates, monetary policy was essentially chasing its own tail. Interest rates needed to be raised so as to meet targets that were being missed partly because interest rates were being raised. Does this mean that the government was enacting a monetary squeeze far harsher than they had intended? Comments at the time and after from New Right politicians and advisors at the Bank of England all seem to suggest not. However, this does mean that policy was running smoothly, and that there were no disagreements; but it is important to be clear on the nature of these disagreements. Indeed both John Hoskyns (the co-author of *Stepping Stones*, who had moved to the No. 10 Policy Unit after the 1979 election) and Alan Walters (monetarist and IEA author, who became Thatcher's chief economic advisor at the start of 1981) did become increasingly convinced that by the end of 1980 monetary policy was too tight. The latter in particular was concerned that high interest rates had caused a dramatic appreciation of sterling (from 3.8 to 5 deutschmarks to the pound from November 1979 to February 1981) making the operating environment ever tougher for manufacturers.[18]

But Hoskyns' and Walters' main bone of contention was that up until the end of 1980 the brunt of the monetary squeeze was being felt by the private sector, and thus the public sector was 'getting off lightly'. The original forecast contained in the MTFS for public sector borrowing was 4.75 per cent of GDP for 1979/80, 3.75 per cent for 1980/81 and 3 per cent for 1981/82. However the depth of the recession had led to smaller tax revenues than expected and, much to Hoskyns' annoyance, the government had chosen to settle on pay awards of 16 per cent and 17.7 per cent for British Rail and British Steel workers respectively.[19] The result was that even with cuts in public spending, the deficit for 1979/80 and 1980/81 was 4.9 per cent and 5.4 per cent of GDP respectively. Moreover, and of course contrary to everything that had been planned and entirely conflicting with the goal of tight monetary conditions, the overshooting of government expenditure in 1980/1 meant that about 20 per cent of the deficit had to be funded through 'money printing'. To some extent the government was repeating the experience of the 1970s, and it was this that really crystallized the view, held by the Thatcherites, that the public sector was not being squeezed enough, that they were being given far too much access to funding.

These internal criticisms were to culminate in the Budget of March 1981, which according to Lawson was the political equivalent of the Battle of Britain.[20] Indeed all the major figures within the Thatcherite camp believe that this Budget marked a major watershed for them.[21] Essentially, the decision was taken to raise the tax burden at a very low point of the economic cycle, cut spending, and force the Treasury to adopt a system of cash planning, rather than volume budgeting with some cash ceilings. Walters describes it as 'one of the most severe fiscal squeezes in recent history,'[22] and it enabled the government to bring down the public sector borrowing requirement from £12.5 billion or 5.4 per cent of GDP in 1980–81 to under £8.6 billion or 3.2 per cent of GDP the following year.[23] To paraphrase Lawson, it no longer appeared as if the public sector was 'getting off lightly'.[24]

The Budget itself initiated a torrent of criticism, famously summed up by a letter published in *The Times*, three days after the Budget speech, and signed by

'364 economists', in which it was stated that there was no basis for believing that deflating the economy would permanently bring inflation under control, and that the present policies would simply deepen the recession and further erode Britain's industrial base.[25] But of course the Budget was not itself about deflating demand, it was about ensuring that the public sector, the unmarketed sector of the economy, was forced to rationalize at least as much as the private sector had done. Indeed Howe's Budget speech made it clear that there was to be no fiscal aid for the private sector, that is no return to subsidies that might help struggling companies through the recession.

Nonetheless the important point is that this tactical switch (interest rates were lowered by 2 per cent in the Budget) reflected a belief that attitudes in the private sector were changing, that there was a new air of realism among workers and managers alike. Only because of this could a tactical switch be countenanced. Indeed Patrick Minford's response to the '364 Economists', also published in *The Times*, reiterated the position of the New Right. While manufacturing output had fallen 15 per cent and employment in the sector was down 10 per cent in 1980 alone, there was, for Minford, 'no evidence that those with sound long-term prospects were going to the wall'. Instead he was pleased to see that there had been rationalization, a reduction of overmanning and a sharp reduction in wage settlements. The point for him had always been that there needed to be 'political courage and determination' to reverse the inflationary process, that is 'to break the inflationary psychology'.[26]

Those that shared this governing mentality, the belief that government could and should affect a change in habits of thought were all of the opinion that attitudes were changing. The tactical switch in 1981 was just that; it did not in any sense imply that there were misgivings about what had happened before. Indeed, the Bank of England reported in March 1981 that their observations suggested that, 'in many cases the attitude to wage claims, to improved efficiency and to more rational manning levels has moved towards greater realism'[27]; and in the same month the Bank of England Governor, Gordon Richardson, resolutely denied that the Bank was intervening to help save companies from bankruptcy. 'Unviable companies' were not being kept alive; the Bank could not be criticized for allowing monetary control to be 'eroded'. Indeed there was for Richardson, in the build-up to the March 1981 Budget, much to take heart from: 'redundancies, though painful, have been resolutely declared and in many areas new manning levels give promise of much improved efficiency. Wage settlements are taking place at a lower level.'[28]

Likewise, within the Conservative Party Research Department, ministers and policy-makers were making it very clear in individual submissions to the Budget writing team that there were clear signs their policies were producing the desired results. One submission, by analyst Chris Mockler, written in February 1981, read:

> Things have changed quite dramatically since last year. Largely as a result of the rise in the sterling exchange rate and the speed of severity with which

> the recession has developed, the rate of price increases has fallen faster than we could have hoped a year ago. On this, the central objective, progress is ahead of target. Wage increases too are now very clearly moderating.... The shakeout of labour may mean that industry is able to compete with higher productivity.[29]

Another submission by researcher Barry Baldwin suggested that any attempts to help industry by lowering the exchange rate would be a 'retrograde step, and would remove the edge which exists at present to make British industry become more competitive'.[30] That said, Baldwin recommended that,

> Steps should be taken to ensure that managers of our independent enterprises, which survive 1981, are left in no doubt as to the role which they can play in our recovery and that recognition of that role be at the heart of government policy.[31]

For the Thatcherites, things had gone well, but just because there was a new acceptance that the public sector needed to be disciplined and that most of the changes had taken place in the private sector, this did not mean that the government should let up on the private sector; the job was not fully done. Peter Lilley's policy paper, written in April 1981 made it clear that there was:

> More scope for anticipation of the medium-term targets by unions, lenders etc.... The potential benefit from moulding expectations and thereby reducing unnecessary unemployment ... depends on how rapidly wage bargainers learn to abandon habits acquired in a period when monetary policy invariably accommodated the going rate of pay increases.[32]

5.1.2 Creating destruction and the new economy

There was a muddle over the application of monetarism; Lawson was entirely right in his memoirs when he says that it is a myth that there was ever a golden era of monetarism in Britain.[33] But it is also clear that throughout the process the government was generally happy with what it was doing; it recognized rising unemployment and higher productivity among the remaining workforce as a sign that attitudes and behaviour were changing and progressing. As Lawson put it in a speech in January 1981, *Thatcherism in Practice*:

> The British people, and British industry, now know that they have a Government that means what it says.... It is this that has led to a new climate of realism, the breath of fresh air that is blowing through British industry today. The water may be choppy, but we are on course, and intend to remain so.[34]

What was of supreme importance to the government was that inflation, which was over 10 per cent at the time of the June 1979 election and which had risen to over 20 per cent in 1980 was, by the beginning of 1983, down to around 5 per cent. And as Figure 5.1 shows, Sterling M3 was also finally growing just within target range, albeit with the Bank of England having to use a form of open market operations, known as 'overfunding' the fiscal deficit, so as to offset private sector monetary creation (see section 5.2). Of course the '364 economists' were arguing that inflation was falling because demand was depressed by high interest rates. But the Thatcherites believed something different: there had been a 'quiet revolution' in the country, and a change in psychological attitudes, evidenced by a lower inflation rate. There was a belief that policy had successfully addressed conduct that was deemed to be destroying British society.

Even if the MTFS targets were missed, what really mattered was that in raising interest rates so as to hit those targets, everyone had to be made aware that this was a strong government insistent that it achieve its goals and that no one, whether in the public or private sector, should escape from being confronted by the government's requirement for attitudes and conduct to change. Indeed, no one in the New Right fold had ever shied away from stating the collective belief in the need for strong government. At the inception of the CPS in 1974, Keith Joseph had called for a government with strong nerves.[35] And speaking to the *Observer* newspaper in April 1979, Thatcher made the same point: 'limitation of government doesn't make for a weak government – don't make that mistake. If you've got the role of government set out, then it means very strong government *in that role*. Very strong indeed.'[36] The size of the government's balance sheet was irrelevant to its need to act and the need to exhibit to all that it had the will to act in its new role.

That Thatcherism combined a strong state with a free market is a consistent theme of historical and political analysis.[37] Certainly there was never any doubt in the minds of the New Right that if they were going to change attitudes this was going to take much resolve on their part. But rather than suggest that this somehow points to an underlying authoritarian tendency in neoliberalism, the point being made here is about the interpretation of economic policy between 1979 and 1983. However muddled the application of monetarism, the general outcome appears to have been the one that was broadly intended. Lawson, writing in 1982, in a pamphlet entitled *Financial Discipline Restored*, made it clear that:

> We have to go back to basics. We have to restore and maintain financial discipline.... We have to restore and strengthen market forces throughout the economy.... My own judgement is that we have got it roughly right.... If you leave on one side those who believe that there should be no discipline at all, roughly a third of our critics complain that our policy is too tight, a third complain that it is too lax, and the other third complain on both counts at the same time.[38]

Restoring financial discipline had always meant the same thing to the New Right, requiring managers and workers to be more 'rational', to give up habits of thought that they believed were unsuited to the modern economy. It was, for neoliberals, time for a revolution in the way the that resources were allocated in the British economy; why, Geoffrey Wood wrote in the IEA's journal *Economic Affairs* in July 1981 in response to the '364 economists', should the government respond to the pleas of industry? 'Will the industrial base of the economy be eroded? What if it is? Do economies have to be industrialized to be prosperous?'[39] Lawson's response to this question was a resounding 'no'. His view, propounded in a speech given to the International Monetary Fund in September 1984, was that governments 'should not be seduced by the wonders of high-tech'. 'Many of the jobs of the future', he said, would be in 'labour intensive service industries – not so much low-tech as no-tech.'[40] Along with his 1984 Budget changes, which ended all fiscal distinctions between business investments in machinery and in the service industry, Thatcherism was demonstrating its absolute commitment to the long held IEA position that growth did not have to come about through investment in fixed assets; that the high street was at least, if not more, as important for economic growth as the factory floor; that appealing to consumers through the direct sale of goods and services was critical to the future of Britain. Job losses in manufacturing would be compensated for by job gains in the consumer services sector.

The British economy was changing; in the minds of the New Right, it had to be helped to change, as too many of the human agents of the economy were 'stuck' in industries that could not be returned to profitability, or that encouraged conduct in workers and managers alike that were not adaptable or progressive. For these neoliberals it was now left to them to be the agents of change, to embody the will and action required to break the British out of their mental sets: the psychology of the worker, the compromising manager, all encapsulated in a psychology of inflation. In this view the entrepreneurial spirit had been so undone that government had to step in where the market could no longer act; where consumer and entrepreneurial attitudes should be, but where instead the New Right could only see attitudes which were attuned to a progressive liberal governing mentality.

The government would have to do the job of the market; there were not enough entrepreneurs or consumers to usher in the creative destruction that was the normal process of capitalism. On this Alan Walters was clear; writing in 1986, he said 'we are engaged, like the process of capitalism itself, in what Schumpeter called creative destruction.'[41] This is the crux of the arguments of this section of the chapter, and a statement of the openness found in the neoliberal mentality to the need to create the conditions of the market, to monitor those conditions and to maintain them. It was, they believed, left to the government to activate competition and this activation was, for them, about ensuring that consumer and entrepreneurial habits of thought were evident and dominant in society at large. This meant that attitudes that were not appropriate had to be acted against, whether bad managers, factory workers, unionized workers, or public sector workers. The Thatcherites had accused the Heath government of trying to do the impossible, of trying to pick winners. Neoliberals believed that governments could never pick winners; instead winners emerged only through competition for consumers in the marketplace using prices as signalling devices. The New Right had no intention of picking winners, just making economic conditions difficult enough such that only the winners would emerge.

5.2 Freedom for the consumer

Governing for the consumer invariably meant acting against those agencies that inhibited the consumer's adaptability. Those agents might have been bad managers unable to understand that the consumer was sovereign. In most cases, the New Right saw the human obstacle to consumer thinking, so Ralph Harris had put it, as the individual suffering from a schizophrenic conflict between producer and consumer instincts. The battles against unions and the application of monetarism were tactics employed to 'cure' people of this condition. And as discussed at the end of Chapter 4, there were other fiscal measures that were also taken to encourage entrepreneurialism. However, governing for the consumer also meant providing positive freedoms for the consumer as if he or she were an entrepreneur, but with their own balance sheet or self as the product.

For neoliberals, the consumer needed to be free to actively 'do' things that were previously not so easy; and these new opportunities would serve a purpose. On the one hand, consumers were being made sovereign; by being able to be as adaptable as possible in as many markets as possible, the conditions were set for as much progress as possible. No longer should politicians be attuned to 2.5 per cent annual GDP growth; 4.5 per cent was 'a realistic vision', so Herbert Giersch (Mont Pèlerin Society President at the time) argued in the annual Wincott lecture in 1986, published by the IEA. All one needed to do was free 'activities and resources on the supply-side'. And so long as expansion was led by the supply side it would never be inflationary.[42] On the other hand, these freedoms would foster, incentivize, encourage and maintain the 'right' consumer attitudes. More of the economy geared towards the high street would incentivize people to work harder and be more successful so as to be able to benefit from new innovations and fashions. More importantly though, consumers as entrepreneurs-of-the-self, whether individually embodied or coalesced in the 'household', now had to be free to construct their own balance sheets, their portfolio of assets from which they could derive income and satisfaction over time.

Privatization of housing and of government-owned industries could do much to provide appropriate assets for the balance sheet. Banking reform was essential also, both so that consumers could fund their asset purchases and at the same time become consumers of financial services, provided with a range of other more liquid investments, such as deposit accounts. This was the very stuff of governing for the consumer. However, before moving on to this discussion it is important to highlight that there were significant problems that arose in relation to these policies, specifically with regard to the emergence of the asset-heavy yet debt financed consumer. The discussion in section 5.3 will bring into play questions over the nature of neoliberal government and the difficulties of governing for what is essentially an imagined notion of being human. It is the utopian nature of governmental programmes and their confrontation with something different that acts as a catalyst for crises of governmentality. Section 5.2.1 on the enterprise culture, on building the balance sheet, sets out in detail the imagined and utopian notion of the consumer that was subsequently problematized by the economic boom and bust of the late 1980s and early 1990s.

5.2.1 Building the balance sheet

One can interpret the notion that Thatcherism wanted to create a 'property-owning democracy' or a 'people's capitalism' in a variety of ways. One obvious interpretation is that the politician selling a government-owned house to the occupier at a discounted rate is buying support at the next election. A more sophisticated version of this might be to say that the vote has not been 'bought', but that the buyer might vote for the party that they believe has given them the opportunity to own their home. Alternatively, they might not vote for the other party for fear that the house will somehow be taken back into public ownership. And even if all these explanations are accepted as valid, this does not necessarily deny that the politician is selling off publicly owned houses because he or she feels it is the right thing to do. The politician might feel they have deserved electoral support on the basis that their policies were popular and responded to some perceived innate human instinct to own the property in which one lives. All of these explanations no doubt have some basis in truth. However, the argument here is that neoliberals were trying to produce an enterprising and entrepreneurial population of consumers, producing a certain kind of free action that in turn would lead to a certain kind of progress. All of this implied that consumers were being enterprising, investing and arranging their individual portfolios of physical and non-physical assets and liabilities in such a way as to maximize self-fulfilment.

The government believed that they could change conduct, that the population could become sophisticated consumer-investors. To understand what this consumer know-how might entail it is useful, as an example, to think through how the government bond market yield curve describes to investors the expectations implied for future interest rates and inflation. The yield curve plots interest rates against durations for different bonds. However, to be of use as a signalling device there needs to be a 'deep market', that is to say a broad range of readings that can be taken. One wants to be able to plot a curve that shows the interest rates for as many bonds with as many durations as possible, from one day to thirty years, to give the interpreter of the yield curve the maximum information. If there are more assets to invest in and more choices to make, there is much more that can be known about current investors' expectations of future interest rates and inflation, and it is easier to match one's own schedule of liability durations against a corresponding set of assets. A bond market with only a limited amount of traded bonds offers few of the advantages of a deep market.

So this is how one might think of an imagined figure of the consumer in its most 'developed' form, not just sovereign and moral but as a producer of human wealth capitalized in the individual. This human agent is essentially the embodiment of an internalized yield curve, whose very functioning improves the deeper the market: more information available, more financial discipline, and an enhanced ability to match the duration of assets and liabilities. The potential to portfolio-manage oneself might always be present but it can only be activated by first creating the assets that form the yield curve. Thus the discipline of the market and the ability of the individual to arrange his or her assets entrepreneurially needs to be monitored by government so that asset markets remain liquid. Likewise sudden drops in the value of assets could distort the ongoing asset allocation process. There is much for government to do, for instance enabling the private sector to have a ready supply of assets and credit, so as to ensure the effective operation of the internalized market, for if the market dries up and becomes non-functioning there is nothing to say that habits will not revert to previous forms. For neoliberals, the entrepreneur-of-the-self is rational and natural but his or her ongoing existence depends on the ongoing availability and liquidity of available assets, all with different durations and income flows.

This is the emphasis adopted here for interpreting aspects of economic policy in the 1980s such as financial liberalization, privatization, selling publicly owned housing and reform of the rental market. Assets of different durations were now freely available to invest in. Selling off government assets at a discount is of course an incentive to get individuals to participate but the point is, what in? Specifically, people were being asked to participate in investing in themselves as sites of enterprise, to build their own portfolio of assets. In government, the collapsed distinction between entrepreneur and entrepreneur-of-the-self (the fact that both types of agents existed as operators in a marketed zone) was practised within the notion of the 'enterprise culture'. The term itself, used in policy-making groups and by politicians alike, referred to the one class of consumers and entrepreneurs.

The Conservative government was also much concerned with small businesses, start-ups, and wealth creation through new business ventures; this was very much how they imagined Britain's economic renaissance. But the attitudes that accorded with business were, they believed, to be found in the homeowner consumer, and this opinion is evident by looking at the minutes of a series of meetings hosted by the CPS and the Conservative Research Department in 1981 and 1982 to discuss the enterprise culture. For a start, the chairman of the first meeting in February 1981, the economist Terry Price, defined the enterprise culture in terms far exceeding the activity of business: it was an attitude that pervaded the whole of society, and was of direct political concern: 'the social and political context which determines a nation's ability to exploit its physical and human resources.'[43] And the topics under discussion varied seamlessly and without reflection between the household consumer unit and business. Three meetings took place at the end of 1982 to cover different approaches to promoting enterprise. The first discussed possible fiscal incentives such as spreading enterprise allowances, reforming social security; even encouraging academics to go into business. The following meeting moved on to home ownership, arguing that only 56 per cent of the nation were homeowners, whereas as much as 80 per cent of the nation probably wanted to be. As such, more land should be made available, and that hopefully with banks competing more in the mortgage market, mortgages would also become more easily available. The following two meetings were back to business: more could be done in the accounting profession to help, self-employment could be encouraged, and employees could be increasingly incentivized with profit-related pay and share options.[44]

Discussions of physical property or home ownership could reference both consumer and entrepreneur; these assets signified that both agencies shared attitudes commensurate with adaptability and progress. The 1976 policy document, *The Right Approach*, announced that, 'private ownership of property is essential if we are to encourage personal responsibility and the freedom that goes with it. ... Property diffuses power, increases choice and is an important source of independence.... Enterprise comes first from independence.'[45] Nonetheless houses were illiquid long-term assets and any portfolio of assets should also include liquid holdings, such as money and equity, as well as a range of investments in non-physical and physical assets.

A wave of privatizations and the introduction of portable contribution-based pension schemes rapidly increased the extent to which shares formed part of the personal balance sheet. Both measures of course had other purposes. In particular selling off large nationalized industries was one way for the government to raise finance and ease the fiscal burden. The temptation to interpret it this way is helped by the fact that only aerospace, shipbuilding and the National Freight Corporation were specifically mentioned in the 1979 election manifesto as targeted for privatization. Nonetheless it should also be noted that receipts from privatization represented only 0.4 per cent of government expenditure in the first four years of the Thatcher government, and it was during these years that the government was in significant deficit. Receipts from privatization increased later (representing 0.8 per cent, 1.4 per cent, 1.7 per cent and 2.6 per cent of annual government expenditure in the following four years respectively), but in none of these years could it be said that the government was looking for emergency financing.[46]

How did Thatcherites explain privatization? In presenting privatization as *The Way Ahead* in July 1981, Howe argued that it was only since being in government that the Conservatives had begun to be convinced that competition was best served through the financial discipline of the private sector.[47] Privatization was a way of ensuring that certain industries did not escape the monetary squeeze, if there should be a need for one. But privatization increasingly also came to be seen as a way of filling out household balance sheets: the investor and consumer were natural comrades, sharing certain habits of thought, forcing businesses to compete either for sales or for capital, managing their own stock of investments. Thus speaking at the time of the British Telecom privatization in November 1984, Lawson remarked:

> Investment in shares has begun to take its place, with ownership of a home and either a bank or building society deposit, as a way for ordinary people to participate in enterprise and wealth creation. We are seeing the birth of people's capitalism.[48]

This perspective was very much shared among other intellectuals of Thatcherism. For John Redwood, in the CPS pamphlet *Equity for Everyman* (1986), a lack of ownership produced Marxist thinking and, just like property ownership, share ownership needed to be encouraged. For Redwood, one way of doing this was to increase the use of portable pension funds with contribution-based as opposed to benefit-based pension plans; this way overnight, up to eleven million people could be turned into owners of stakes in British business and commerce.[49] This also raised the question of universal share ownership; the idea that shares in nationalized industries should be given to everyone rather than sold in huge share offerings. This was something worth considering as it would 'introduce the habit of owning shares and spread the responsibility of ownership'.[50] In the end, Redwood concluded that the scheme was impractical. Nonetheless, in *Every Adult a Share Owner* (1986), another CPS pamphlet, Shirley and William Letwin argued that the case for universal share ownership was becoming urgent, in that it was the ideal form of property owning, the very foundation of a property owning democracy which could act to demolish once and for all the myth of wages versus profits. Ownership of shares was for them a way to counteract the divisive and destructive attitudes 'encouraged by the enemies of capitalism'. 'Owning anything gives one a rational interest in understanding it.'[51]

Making more assets available for ownership, and incentivizing the purchase of those assets by selling them at a discount to generally accepted fair value had a double purpose. On the one hand it was believed that by increasing ownership, government was creating an increased stock of enterprising and appropriate attitudes in the economy. This was the cultural change in Britain that Thatcherism wanted to foster and encourage. For instance, speaking at the Party Conference in October 1987, Lawson talked about the property owning democracy as the essential means for entrenching the political, economic and cultural changes that Thatcherism had sought to bring about. This was, as he later remarked, the objective that increasingly came to preoccupy him at that time.[52] On the other hand, however, these attitudes were always thought of as somehow natural and proper. Making more assets available to own would match the inclinations of a population rejecting their own identification with a more progressive liberal creed of government. To provide the possibility for an expanded balance sheet was seen as providing the conditions necessary for people to be entrepreneurs-of-the-self.

The enterprise culture that incorporated consumers and homeowners did not however just stop at dwellings, equities and pension plans. The yield curve also included high liquidity items, such as deposit accounts as well as longer term more durable assets or even assets held in perpetuity such as human capital accumulated through education of one sort or another. Investing, as Lawson had said, in a deposit account was just another form of property investment, just like shares or a home.[53] And removing controls over lending and hire purchase (i.e. consumer credit) was every bit as much part of creating the enterprise culture as removing pay controls, price controls, dividend controls, foreign exchange controls, and industrial building controls.[54] Consuming financial services, using credit to augment consumption in the present, helped consumers to maximize their self-worth over the course of their lives. The increased availability of credit that came with financial reform was about enabling consumers to construct balance sheets of assets. Credit was a tool that could be used to enable consumers to better maximize their income streams in the future. As the Bank of England Governor from 1983–93, Robin Leigh-Pemberton, put it in a speech given in January 1988:

> There is nothing fundamentally reprehensible about personal credit: in fact the reverse.... It must be an advantage for the individual to have more choice between different types of borrowing facility, and greater flexibility over the timing of his expenditure and in the arrangement of his portfolio of assets and liabilities.[55]

Rising debt was seen as being integral to the management of one's personal portfolio and, as a corollary of this, neoliberal government could not identify falling savings rates and rising consumer debt as problematic. This is discussed in more detail below, but for now it is important to highlight the point that as the average personal savings rate fell in the late 1980s (see Figure 5.3), Lawson was approving, identifying it (as did Alun Budd's commentary in the IEA pamphlet in which Lawson's speech was published) as a matter of financial planning, a decision being made by private individuals and businesses about their own financial affairs.[56] There was no iron law, Lawson believed, to suggest that the private sector's finances must be in balance. What really mattered was that investment was rising rapidly and, as part of this, that individuals' wealth would rise rapidly too.

At the start of the 1980s, average personal net financial wealth was only 25 per cent higher than annual disposable income; at the end of 1987, it was over double.[57] This was all taken as a sign of a successful transformation to the enterprise culture. The building of the consumer balance sheet had provided, so it was believed, precisely the right and secure footing in which consumers-as-entrepreneurs could recoordinate and reconstitute their portfolio of assets and take on expenditure, financed in some cases by debt, that could maximize their ongoing self-worth.

> It is thus not surprising that individuals now feel they can safely spend more – in many cases by adding to their borrowing rather than by spending their capital. This, too, is in essence a reflection of increased confidence. So as a result net saving is low and consumer spending is running at a high deficit.[58]

5.2.2 Neoliberal versus neoliberal

From the very beginning the implementation of Thatcherism proved problematic. The government wanted to put a monetary squeeze on bad companies and the public sector, with the aim that management and workers (often unionized) would change their attitudes and give up conduct that it was believed was backward and symptomatic of the British disease. Policy was heavy-handed in its approach, not just because it was believed that government should be strong and demonstrate that it meant to do what it said, but because at the same time there was a parallel endeavour to foster enterprising attitudes in society at large. That is, enterprise was not just about productivity and entrepreneurs competing with each other; enterprise was a culture shared by entrepreneurs and consumers in the marketed zone of economic practice. And central to this endeavour was a series of monetary reforms that, while making monetarism more difficult to implement, deliberately set banks free to be able to respond to the needs of supposedly legitimate borrowers, both consumers and entrepreneurs seeking to build or change the composition of their balance sheets. Embedded in the financial reforms was the unstated presupposition that the borrowing needs of consumers were every bit as essential and entrepreneurial in nature as the borrowing needs of business. Maximizing self-fulfilment was the same as maximizing profit: both wealth-owning units were under the same duty.

Banking reform took place swiftly in Thatcher's first term in government (1979–83), amounting to a series of almost irreversible legislative acts that gave monetary force to a new consumer service-led economy. Foreign exchange controls and direct controls over lending ('the corset') had gone by mid-1980. Following that, between 1982 and 1985 there was a continuing relaxation of banking controls, all of which gave consumers more access to borrowing. Hire purchase controls were abolished in 1982 and clearing banks re-entered the mortgage market after the abolition of the corset in 1980. But now the major high street banks were offering specialized mortgage plans that were vigorously marketed. As such, all demand for mortgage finance could now be met; there was no more government-imposed rationing.[59]

The transformation in the banking market was both dramatic and swift. The entry of clearing banks into the mortgage market led to a swift increase in lending; total mortgage lending grew from £3.75 billion in 1978 to £6 billion in 1982.[60] By the middle of the following year this was having a direct impact on property values, which in June 1983 were rising at a 10 per cent annual rate.[61] Banks were taking a significant market share away from the building societies, who were still operating a cartel pricing system for their products, and still reliant on savings to fund their loans. Whereas the banks had previously had a 5 per cent market share, by the end of 1982 they were providing 40 per cent of all new loans. Furthermore, they were also beginning to compete for personal savings by offering interest bearing current accounts. In response the Bank of England hoped to see a break-up of the building society pricing cartel, and more competition for consumers. Speaking in May 1983, the Governor applauded some of the building societies for offering more services, like cheque guarantee cards, or high interest accounts. However, he believed the 1983 Finance Act would help the building societies compete more effectively for consumers as they were to be granted more access to wholesale markets, enabling them to borrow from other banks rather than rely on private savers for funding.[62] In the Bank's September bulletin, a research article on British banking suggested that the 1983 Finance Act and technological innovation in money transmission mechanisms (for instance cash machines and electronic transfers) would mean yet more competitive innovation and a blurring of the roles of banks and building societies. This was very much to be welcomed.[63]

Even in the early stages of economic expansion, it was very clear that this upturn was being led not by investment from industry but by the consumer. In September 1983, the Bank of England reported that GDP had increased in the second quarter of the year at an annual rate of 2.9 per cent, yet consumer spending in the previous twelve months had increased by 4.25 per cent. 'To a large extent, the recovery has been credit-financed. Consumers have been able to reduce their rate of saving without, apparently, reducing their accumulation of financial assets.'[64] Indeed, by March 1983, it had already been noted that there had been a steep decline in savings rates (see Figure 5.3), which had peaked at 16 per cent of income in 1980, and had since fallen to 9 per cent by the end of 1982. The Bank's own commentary on this suggested that perhaps 2 per cent of this could be explained by the fall in real disposable income over the intervening period; 2 per cent because inflation was lower (as it was taken as read that higher inflation increased savings rates as people attempted to offset the value of assets that were being eroded by inflation). It was speculated that the remaining fall was due to the availability of loans, and the ending of hire purchase restrictions.[65]

Such buoyant consumer demand for borrowing was causing immense problems for monetary targeting. As Figure 5.1 showed, money supply growth was far in excess of the target range in 1982. Lending, particularly in the private housing market, was making the targets very difficult to achieve. Actual sterling M3 growth for fiscal years 1982/3 and 1983/4 was 14.6 per cent and 13.5 per cent respectively, but would have been much higher (19.7 per cent and 15.7 per cent) without the Bank of England significantly overfunding the government deficit. This meant that they were issuing bonds to the non-bank private sector far in excess of that required to fund the budget deficit. It was as the monetarist Tim Congdon argued (in a retrospective CPS pamphlet written in 1989) one of the four mechanisms of a functioning monetarist regime: the other three being a broad money target (that included both government and deposit monetary creation), no targeting of the exchange rate, and keeping the fiscal deficit in control.[66] And as Figure 5.1 demonstrated, putting aside the experience of 1982, a combination of these monetarist techniques enabled money supply to stay within target range in the calendar years of 1983 and 1984.

As far as monetarists such as Congdon and Pepper were concerned, the decisive change in policy came in November 1985 when Lawson announced at the annual Mansion House speech that he would no longer be targeting specific measures of money supply. In its place there would be a discretionary approach to monetary policy in which money supply, market interest rates, inflation forecasts, labour market conditions and the exchange rate would all be used as guides for setting interest rates.[67] The speech was published by the CPS in a volume in 1985 entitled *Whither Monetarism?* which also included three essays by monetarists, two of which were very critical of Lawson. The Conservative backbench MP, Jock Bruce-Gardyne, in an essay entitled 'Monetarism was dead' labelled Lawson 'Chancellor Reagan', and likened his actions to Heath and Barber. For him, this was nothing to do with policy sophistication, but just a sign of a boom to come that would end in inflation, just as all previous monetary booms had ended.[68] Congdon saw these actions as the 'start of a somersault'; the past lessons of booms had been forgotten, monetary growth would accelerate from here and by getting rid of the targets he believed Lawson was admitting his own mismanagement.[69] Finally, Patrick Minford, while being more generous to Lawson on his supply-side improvements and acknowledging that Sterling M3 was clearly a defunct indicator also warned that there had to be a renewed commitment to a different money supply target, such as M0 (notes and coins could at least be controlled), otherwise inflation was a real future risk.[70]

From these perspectives, the remainder of the 1980s played out exactly as these authors had expected, as shown in Figures 5.2 and 5.3: a boom in the

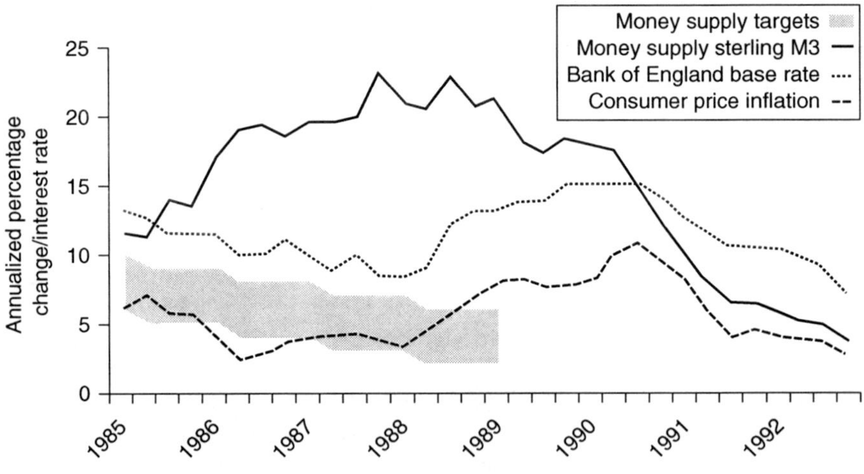

Figure 5.2 Money supply, inflation and interest rates 1985–92 (source: Bank of England, UK Office of National Statistics, HM Treasury).

Note
Although money supply targets were officially abandoned in late 1985, Figure 5.2 includes the final targets set in March 1985. In 1987, Sterling M3 was replaced by M4 as the key target because the distinction between banks and building societies was no longer relevant. Measurements of Sterling M3 were discontinued at the end of 1988. During the period of overlap the average of the two measures has been shown.

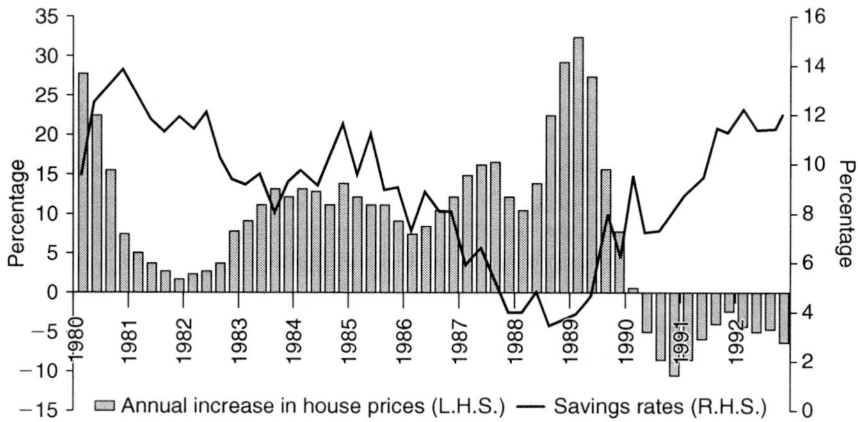

Figure 5.3 House prices and household saving rates 1980–92 (source: Nationwide, UK Office of National Statistics).

housing market, rising debt and ultimately higher inflation on the high street. Both Congdon (1989) and Pepper (1990) argued that there had essentially been a betrayal of neoliberal values. For Congdon this was just a reversion to a Keynesian model in which the direction of causation between the economy and money was thought of the wrong way round: that is the government were acting as if they believed the economy determined the level of money. In fact the right view for Congdon was that the limit to what can be spent is set by productivity; therefore a rise in aggregate expenditure above this level, caused by monetary expansion, would always be inflationary. The Treasury/government view was, he believed, a Keynesian view with a monetary aspect bolted on. It was one thing to recognize that the relationship between broad money and the rate of inflation had changed; it was another thing entirely to say, as Lawson seemed to be saying, that there was no stable and exploitable relationship at all.[71] For Pepper, as inflation rose to 10 per cent at the turn of the 1990s, it was clear that monetary policy was entirely to blame, because the cause of monetary expansion was entirely to be found in private sector bank lending. The boom of the 1980s was, for him, remarkably similar to the early 1970s except for inflation, which instead of showing up in producer prices, had shown up first in asset prices. Thus he concluded there had been bad monetary management that had been politically motivated. As he said, 'the government interpreted … [house price increases] … as a measure of people's increased confidence in the government, and this of course the politicians enjoyed. The argument that … house price rises was a form of inflation was dismissed'.[72]

The Thatcher government was being accused of vote buying by those who had been key figures in policy formulation in the 1970s; it was essentially being accused of betraying the neoliberal cause. But is this right; had neoliberalism been abandoned along with money supply targets? The answer proposed here is that it was precisely because neoliberalism was a mentality of rule concerned with changing conduct that one should view this moment as a parting of the ways between neoliberal government and a stricter, more utopian version still being offered up by the think tanks of the New Right (see Chapter 7). That is to say, the government were looking for evidence that homeowner consumers were building up portfolios of assets, that a new set of attitudes had been embraced and that conduct had been aligned to an adaptable and progressive society. On the one hand, inflation was the result of additional money being created to meet the needs of bad managers, government and workers unwilling to match their wage demands with increases in productivity. On the other hand, monetary creation for entrepreneurs and enterprising consumers, borrowed for the purposes of balance sheet expansion and better portfolio management, was not and could not be inflationary.

Broadly speaking, from 1986 to 1988, through the eyes of this political rationality, the data would have been interpreted as conforming precisely to expectations, as clearly identifying signs of the enterprise culture. As Figure 5.2 shows, in these two years there was no extra inflationary pressure on the high street, which meant, at least from this perspective, that all the money that was being created was being used to expand personal balance sheets. Thus while new money balances had been created, say for the purchase of houses, once used this money was ending up on deposit and not being spent on the high street; nor for that matter was cash being held on the balance sheets of corporations being used to finance higher wage settlements. Monetary targets could no longer work because, as Lawson said, 'the boundaries of the banking system have become blurred.... The problem is gauging what is excessive ... [There] ... might be a genuine desire in the private sector to build up liquidity.'[73]

Monetary targets had been used to monitor the conduct of human agents in the economy, and to ensure that those who continued to choose to identify their agency with the unmarketed zones of practice faced restrictive funding. However contradictory it might appear to liberalize banks while at the same time control money supply, the latter was a necessary part of encouraging and enabling a different kind of behaviour that matched the components of the healthy and enterprising society. And if governors assumed that they had done their job and succeeded in changing attitudes and behaviour then there was nothing to fear from the expansion of money supply. Monetarism was a disciplining regime that was unsuited to an era when the expansion of personal credit went hand in hand with the expansion of personal balance sheets.[74] Enterprise and a healthy economy meant low inflation on the high street. Rising asset prices, to Thatcherites, represented something entirely different: a sign that more people were becoming buyers of assets, expressing their choice from a broader portfolio of assets for a more self-fulfilling and adaptable experience of life.

The neoliberals believed that whereas past incomes policies had transmitted no information to government, now 'the inflation rate would be judge and jury'.[75] All the while inflation remained low then the build-up of liquidity, that is deposits, in the banking sector could be taken as a sign of the enterprise culture; that entrepreneurial thinking was prevalent in both the personal and corporate sectors of the economy. Indeed this was precisely the conclusion that the Bank of England came to; in a society which they now believed was constituted by enterprising conduct, the rules devised by the monetarists were simply no longer appropriate. In a speech in December 1985, Leigh-Pemberton (the Governor of the Bank of England) asked the question, 'does Sterling M3 represent a behavioural change without necessarily adverse implications for the future course of inflation?'[76] His answer was that it did. Inflation was currently falling and expectations about the future pace of business activity did not portend undue pressure.[77] And this was the message to be repeated over the next couple of years. Speaking at Loughborough University the following year, Leigh-Pemberton had no problem stating that he would be recommending to Lawson the complete abandonment of targets. The build-up of debt through monetary expansion was entirely rational. The ratio of household debt to income had peaked at 45 per cent in the early 1970s, falling back to 40 per cent at the end of the 1970s. By 1986, it had indeed risen to 70 per cent but with the availability of credit, homeowner consumers might well choose to hold less of their assets in the form of equity built up in their homes. Gearing was seen as perfectly rational, and the adjustment to higher gearing ratios in an environment of easier credit did not appear to have come to an end.[78]

The following August (1987), Leigh-Pemberton spoke broadly about Thatcherism in the 1980s:

> Since 1981, after a severe recession – which was instrumental in breaking the inflationary psychology of the 1970s ... output has grown at an annual rate of almost 3 per cent ... but by 1985 it had become clear that much of the faster growth in broad money relative to the growth of nominal income was due to changes in financial behaviour and the increasingly competitive and innovative financial system, with less disturbing implications for future inflation and nominal income growth. In these circumstances it would have been inappropriate to continue to pursue – whether through funding policy or interest rates – the original path for broad money which had been set on the basis of different assumptions about the relationship between money and income.... My own view in that instance is that the combined financial pressure from interest rates and the exchange rate was necessary to break the inflationary psychology and I doubt whether we would have reached our present relatively favourable position without it.[79]

Thus for the Bank of England, like the government, there was nothing to worry about; the economic statistics and facts around them were precisely what they wanted to see, they were to be identified as the demonstration of enterprise in society at large. Monetarism for them had just been a tactic to rescue the British economy and society from the clutches of irrational forces. That period was now over, and the huge build-up of monetary balances via credit creation was in the hands of the 'right' people.

That said, the policy practitioners were not oblivious to economic signs that were interpreted differently by others. They had, for instance, closely monitored savings rates and the accumulation of household debt; commentary was required on the rapid rise in household debt to income levels. The pattern of these responses was set in September 1986 by the Bank of England. Yes, the proportion of income spent on servicing debt had risen from roughly 4 per cent to 9 per cent in the past decade, and this was linked to overall gearing: liabilities as a percentage of annual income had risen from the low 30s per cent in the late 1960s, to 40 per cent in the mid 1970s, and to almost 70 per cent by the end of 1985. But the value of assets in personal portfolios had more than compensated for this.[80] As the *Quarterly Bulletin* from December 1986 reported, between 1980 and the end of 1985, the stock of assets had increased 16.5 per cent per annum, liabilities (i.e. debt) 17.5 per cent, yet the absolute rise in assets was far greater because at the start of the period, the value of assets was three times that of liabilities.[81] Therefore there was nothing alarming about the increases in consumer debt.

In February 1987, even as outstanding consumer debt was increasing at a rate of 20 per cent a year, helping to finance private consumption growth of 5 per cent, the same story was reported. The growth of liabilities, and the fact that average mortgage advances to incomes had exceeded a ratio of two to one for the first time since the Heath–Barber boom, was just a reflection of increased ownership. Debt to income might have risen to 70 per cent, but thanks in part to the stock market, and house price inflation which had risen to 17 per cent per annum the previous summer, assets were now on average 160 per cent of annual disposable income. It was certainly the case that the owners of assets were not necessarily the same people as those accumulating debt, but, as the Bank reported, there was very little detailed information on this.[82] All in all, there was much on which to be congratulated, habits of thought had changed, inflation had gone from the high street even while the stock of money and assets had grown rapidly. What more evidence could there be that throughout Britain entrepreneurialism could be identified everywhere, that government could affect a change in conduct, and that Britain was now free from the 'dead weight' of attitudes of the past.

5.3 The first crisis of neoliberal governmentality

There is no doubt that monetarism formed a major part of the neoliberal technique for governing the economy but in 1985, as private sector lending started to expand rapidly, rather than raising interest rates to excessively high levels or imposing direct restrictions on bank sector lending, the decision was taken to abandon money supply targets. The charges of political expediency and of betrayal of neoliberalism do not seem far-fetched by any means. However it has been argued here that Thatcherism, like other rationalistic governmental programmes, was a project that required government to produce a certain type of conduct in the population at large. Monetarism was a tool for limiting the flow of money to the 'bad' managers and workers in both the public and private sectors. It was heavy-handed and its application flawed from the start. Nonetheless for the Thatcherites it did what it was meant to do. Increased productivity, a reduction in 'overmanning' (unemployment), lower wage claims, and lower inflation were all taken as signs that the project had succeeded and that attitudes had changed.

No doubt mobilizing the consumer was not something that was solely taken on by government; marketing, advertising, and education for instance all incorporate techniques that worked to foster a particular way of perceiving oneself in relation to economic forms and practices.[83] However, government was heavily involved in this project as well, practising a particular imagined figure of the consumer as it had been conceived in academia, think tanks, opposition and government itself. Moreover this figure was defined with the tools of modern economics, tools that gave a psychological rendition of a human being existing through time, building a balance sheet, remaining adaptable and progressive. The entrepreneur-of-the-self, the consumer-as-entrepreneur, belonged to the same category of individuals as the entrepreneur and together they belonged to the healthy society, which daily practised an enterprise culture.

Enterprise, however, requires finance. Capitalism, Schumpeter argued, was dependent on certain habits of thought, but it also required a system in which money could be created if need be to aid the entrepreneurial process. Capitalism is, so he said, a special case of commercial society defined by the additional phenomenon of credit creation, 'of financing enterprise by bank credit', i.e. by money (notes or deposits) manufactured for that purpose.[84] During the era of the gold standard in the nineteenth century, this credit creation took the form of reasonably short term circulating bills of exchange. It was fundamentally unstable and required the Bank of England to regularly step in and act as lender of last resort to the discount houses, small weakly capitalized finance houses that arranged and accepted bills from businesses needing finance. In the twentieth century, corporations increasingly raised finance either by direct listings of commercial debt and equity securities or from clearing banks which increasingly offered overdraft and other lending facilities, creating deposit money in the process which was only partially backed by government currency. Enterprise required this banking function.

Neoliberalism referenced consumers as entrepreneurs; as such they too would need access to finance, access not rationed by the availability of savings, but finance that could be granted by the creation of deposits against loans, priced on an assessment of risk. Credit could be used to expand one's balance sheet or to rearrange it in relation to the different durations of alternative assets. This was enterprise; signified by an expanding broad money supply that was not inflationary on the high street. To cut off finance just at the moment when one was recognizing the fruits of government would be to betray entrepreneurial habits of thought. It was not a betrayal of the British experiment in monetarism because the goal was never the experiment itself but conduct in society at large, in the imagined one-class-only society of 'right-minded' thinking.

All neoliberals viewed inflation as an evil that could threaten society and the economic prospects of a nation. At the very least, for them, it effected an unjust redistribution between debtors and creditors. Economists such as Congdon and Pepper chose to recognize house price rises as inflation, as caused by the increase in money supply. The government on the other hand chose to identify rising debt, lower savings and rising house prices as the natural correlate of increased ownership. Households had taken up the opportunity to use gearing to restructure personal balance sheets, and this in part reflected increased confidence in the state of the British economy and in their personal outlook for future income and standard of living. And it was not as if the government stood alone, somehow opposed to neoliberal academics: the new classical economist Patrick Minford suggested that any attempt to control deposit money creation made use of 'concepts appropriate to a financial environment that had now passed away into history'.[85]

As he said, in the enterprise economy, deposits are just one form of asset to invest in:

> The demand for any one of these interest-bearing assets is not given or easy to determine. There is literally an infinite number of asset-liability combinations in which the private sector can hold its savings.... The banks become just like unit trusts, distinguishable only by the bundle of deposits that they invest in (loans rather than shares). Just like the unit trusts in our earlier example, should banks expand credit and deposits, nothing other than the balance sheet structure will have been affected. Credit and wide money measure will be driven by the supply-side technology of the financial system and be of no significance for consumers' savings and firms' investment plans. High street banks are being compelled by competition to make themselves more efficient; it is hardly surprising that they seek to expand their operations sharply.[86]

Credit was there for consumers and businesses, to help balance sheet restructuring: nothing more, nothing less. Thus the excesses of the boom in 1988 and 1989 and the recession that followed were problematic for government, not because house prices rose by 34 per cent in 1988 alone, or because broad money supply was growing by over 20 per cent per year, or because low savings rates were seen as a threat to economic growth. Instead what really concerned policymakers was that excessive borrowing was now precipitating inflation on the high street (6.8 per cent in December 1988).[87] As Governor Leigh-Pemberton said, interest rates had to rise rapidly for fear that Britain would suffer from a relapse in which there would be a resurgence of double-digit pay claims, untethered to productivity gains.[88]

By April 1990, interest rates had been increased to 15 per cent, necessary, according to the Governor, to keep inflationary pressure under control. Added to this, and rather like the early 1980s, high interest rates had led to a high exchange rate that was seen as helping keep inflation under control, enabling employers to resist wage pressures. Nonetheless, policy-makers were not oblivious to boom and bust: to quote Leigh-Pemberton from a speech given in early 1990, 'it is clear that something has gone quite badly wrong.'[89] But what exactly? This had been no investment-led boom, with producers bidding up the prices of factors of production; the root cause was a consumer boom, fuelled by debt that had grown so much faster than disposable income. Increased optimism about long-term growth prospects had led to lower savings and rapid credit growth, a large proportion of which had involved mortgage equity withdrawal, that is borrowing against the added value to one's home. Consumer optimism had turned to overconfidence and excess personal gearing. But at least for Leigh-Pemberton, real gains persisted: better management and a workforce now operating more realistically.[90]

One might almost say that in the mind of Leigh-Pemberton, government had been let down by the population who had not delivered on their side of the bargain; they had not abided by a moral code that was expected of them. The policy was still deemed right even if those in society were not behaving appropriately.

> I have few regrets about this policy in so far as it has spurred innovation and competition, increased consumer choice, and ended what amounted to de facto rationing of personal credit. But it has had some quite startling effects … net savings of the personal sector in this country – that is gross savings less borrowings – have fallen from 13 per cent to 5 per cent as a proportion of disposable income.… This is, I would suggest, both a symptom and a cause of wider cultural change in our society. Thrift has gone out of fashion. Indeed, the all too prevalent outlook on life has become 'I want it, and I want it *now*'.[91]

The boom and bust of the late 1980s and early 1990s in Britain can be understood as a crisis of neoliberal governmentality, a moment in which the taken for granted is confronted by a reality which is different. That is to say that policies which practised a particular imagined figure of the consumer, where debt could be used for 'rational' purposes, had led to outcomes that were surprising and taken to be problematic by the government. The question then becomes, what next, what to do with this new knowledge, how should one interpret the crisis? In the 1970s invoking an evolutionary narrative for society provided a theoretical solution to the problem that banking liberalization had thrown up. Politically this was matched by the idea that government could encourage habits of thought that were natural correlates of a progressive and modern society. However, at the end of the 1980s, neoliberalism was confronted by the negative side-effects of its own policies. But as the next chapter will discuss, there was to be no disillusionment or questioning of the premise of governing for the consumer. Indeed Lawson had already foreshadowed the problem in 1980 when he said, 'those liberated from the dungeons of state control are often at first blinded and bewildered by the bright sunlight of freedom'.[92]

And in 1992, in his memoirs, he again acknowledged the problem, and the crisis that neoliberalism had encountered. Credit liberalization remained a key tenet of freedom but 'it admittedly brought problems as well as benefits. Freedom always does, until people learn how to use it properly.'[93] This crisis, the first crisis of neoliberal governmentality, had in this view come about because the population's habits of thought were not entirely attuned with the enterprise culture. However, this was not insurmountable. It was perhaps, so Lawson believed, a necessary crisis on the road to freedom and away from serfdom; a crisis that would act as a reference point for the population at large, supposedly providing invaluable lessons for the enterprising mind.

6 Misidentification and crisis

This chapter completes the historical narrative of how the figure of the consumer has been practised by government in Britain since 1979. It brings this history up to the present, showing how the British government has continued to preside over a regime that was laid down in the early 1980s and allowed to operate, effectively unfettered, ever since. There has been neither an attempt to cap the sovereignty of the consumer nor an attempt to recognize debt as anything other than the correlate of appropriately modern attitudes. Household debt as a percentage of household disposable income has risen steadily from 100 per cent in the mid 1990s to 160 per cent in 2007.

This is not to say that the Labour Party, led by Tony Blair and returned to government as New Labour in May 1997 after eighteen years of Conservative rule, represented nothing more than the same. As will be discussed, New Labour took on the role of governing the public sector and regulating the conduct of those who provided social services with a gusto lacking among Conservatives. Public services were the traditional heartland of the Left, and New Labour clearly felt qualified to address the perceived shortfall in standards, productivity and funding. That their reforms often practised the neoliberal notion of the consumer and responsible citizen does not necessarily mean that these policies would have been enacted to the same extent by the Conservatives had they stayed in government after the 1997 general election.

However in terms of governing the economy, New Labour did not unwind or step back from the fundamental reference points of neoliberalism: that is they continued to promote and identify in entrepreneurs and consumers a mentality of progressiveness and adaptability. An exploration of the key policy texts of Tony Blair, Gordon Brown and Ed Balls (the latter two central architects of economic policy formulation and practice in the New Labour project), as well as the speeches and research of the Bank of England in the 1990s and 2000s, demonstrates this point quite clearly. The genealogy of the financial crisis and economic downturn can be traced, at least in part, to the continuation of a regime that failed to recognize in actual policy prescriptions that increasing debt and perpetually rising asset prices (including and of key importance, housing) was problematic.

The current chapter is divided in the following way. In section 6.1, there is a brief discussion of the New Labour project and the way in which it attempted, to use Blair's words, to reassert the social in the practice of government.[1] In doing this some limited comparisons will be made between the vision encapsulated in 'Third Way' politics and the political programme, as it was being assembled by the Conservative Party, for a revitalization of Thatcherism in the mid to late 1990s. These two programmes are shown to have shared a great deal in outlook and intent. Section 6.2 deals specifically with how New Labour addressed the question of governing the economy in major speeches both prior to forming a government and once in government. Did New Labour's leaders seek, and if so how, to problematize economic policy and specifically monetary policy in the 1980s? Both inside New Labour and within the Bank of England one can discern a deliberate and self-acknowledged shift to the language of New Keynesianism. Thus section 6.3 explores what this shift in language meant in policy terms. It is shown that in practice this change of tone implied little difference between the monetary policy of the 1980s and 2000s.

The ongoing accumulation of debt and associated rising asset prices that ultimately led to crisis after 2007, in being so reminiscent of the early 1990s, evidences that since 1979 government has continued to operate with the consumer-as-entrepreneur as a key reference in the practice of economic policy. In turn, in the conclusion to the chapter it is argued that the ongoing economic crisis, a crisis of the neoliberal political rationality, provides an apt example of the dangers of liberal government and of visionary government in particular.

6.1 Reasserting the social?

A political vision is essentially the enunciation of a governing mentality. Thatcher's first speech as the Conservative Party leader in 1975 was appropriately entitled *Let me give you my vision*, and Blair's 1994 speech, *Socialism*, published by the Fabian Society was equally clear in expressing the need to 'present a clear vision of the country's future'.[2] Perhaps then the economist Patrick Minford was right to suggest that Thatcher and her companion in the Centre for Policy Studies (CPS), Keith Joseph, were political entrepreneurs of great ability;[3] perhaps Blair was one of equal standing? However, one has to be careful in thinking of political vision in entrepreneurial terms because, as this book has consistently aimed to show, political visions do not necessarily express something profoundly 'new'. Instead they often reiterate a political rationality, that is to say, they practise already existing ways of seeing the world and presuppositions about what is natural and proper conduct. Yes, tensions arise when there is no complete overlap between vision and reality; then government attempts, to some extent, to make reality that which it thinks it ought to be. Nonetheless, in a democratic society where governments need to be elected there is invariably some overlap between vision and reality. As Blair said in a speech in 1995 (*Let us face the future*), 'the genius' of the 1945 Labour government, which among other things implemented the 1944 White Paper on employment policy and set up the National Health Service, 'was to capture the national mood and at the same time lead the national mood'.[4]

The 'national mood' of 1945 can be thought of as one in which the social as an objective realm was seen as a space in which human agency could find security, fulfilment and thus freedom; the counterpart to this version of society in economic theory was the imagined figure of the worker-saver. Conversely, for Keith Joseph, there was a different national mood in the mid 1970s; the New Right were seeking to 'articulate' a new set of 'values and aspirations'.[5] In turn, Blair perceived that there was a new popular mood in the mid 1990s that he could articulate in Third Way politics: 'notions of the Left', he believed, were back in the national mood including social justice, cohesion, equality of opportunity and community. His new vision thus reasserted the existence of the social, the notion that people are socially interdependent human beings and therefore owe a duty to one another and to a broader society. That said, he also paid homage to a neoliberal interpretation of twentieth century British history, that as the majority of people had become more prosperous a reaction had occurred against the manner in which power was exercised, and that this attack had come in the name of the individual.[6] This latter statement encapsulated precisely what Arthur Seldon was intimating in his prefaces to the early Institute of Economic Affairs (IEA) Hobart Papers.

In *Let us face the future* (1995), Blair explicitly connected his political project with the New Liberalism of Hobhouse, T. H. Marshall, Beveridge and Keynes, none of whom were Labour Party members or supporters, but all of whom had progressed liberalism, as Blair argued, into something that recognized that 'theoretical liberty was of little use unless people ... [had] ... the ability to exercise it.' The state could act to achieve this 'positive freedom even if it infringed traditional laissez-faire liberal orthodoxy'.[7] New Labour, or the Third Way, was thus intended to be like New Liberalism; that is to take seriously government's role in producing and providing for the governed what they 'needed' in order to function in a prosperous and globalized world. In one sense, this would mean equipping citizens with the right kind of skills and education; but it also meant that it was 'vital' for government 'to equip citizens with the ... aspirations they need to succeed in the modern economy.[8]

Liberal government, for Foucault, involved needing to produce a population that was free to be free.[9] The key question and what distinguishes classical and neo varieties of liberalism is the latter's concern with producing a certain kind of consumer mentality in society at large. To be an entrepreneur-of-the-self, purchases have to be made with a view to investing in physical and non-physical assets that exist through time, providing a yield to the owner. Consumption is not the final moment of fulfilment but the arrangement of being oriented to the future. And there is no better way of expressing this than in terms of aspirations; a word that signifies habits of thought that are immediately future oriented and at the same time of course incorporating a sense that one wants to better oneself, to be as good as one can. Government, to use Blair's words, has to involve giving 'each citizen the chance to develop their potential to the full'.[10] It is, for Blair, the duty of government to equip citizens in this way; it is the duty of citizens to be aspirational.

In fact there is little difference between the reference points invoked here in these statements and those invoked in the early 'visionary' speeches of Thatcher. For her it was the duty of every citizen to 'develop his full potential both for his own benefit and for the community as well'. Each citizen had an 'obligation to make the best of his talents'. In turn government had an 'obligation to create the framework' within which each person could do just that.[11] Similarly the state, for Blair, was the 'enabling force' in a world in which success was about individual 'knowledge and creativity', and where value and competitive advantage resulted from the development by individuals of 'human and intellectual capital'.[12] So on the one hand, New Labour explicitly acknowledged the role of consumer interests ('producer interests have over the century become increasingly varied and diffuse ... and in any event they need to be balanced by the needs of consumers'[13]). On the other hand, these speeches practised a specific kind of imagined human agent very much in keeping with the New Right; and just as with Thatcherism, government was required to act so as to elicit and foster certain conduct.

That said it would be churlish not to recognize that the imagined figure of the consumer in Third Way politics was addressed to issues outside the purely economic domain. The consumer of social services was a cousin of the consumer-entrepreneur, whose sovereignty was to be applied to the social sphere, in areas such as education and health. Thus individuals would need to be empowered in order to maximize the opportunities that would become available in a society and economy dynamically created by already-empowered sovereign citizens. Communities and schools for instance could then be denationalized, 'free to run their own affairs' and the National Health Service could be 'rebuilt as the people's service' with citizens enabled and empowered to share in decision-making that affected them.[14] Thatcherism had always practised a firm belief in the distinction between the marketed and non-marketed zones of practice, never really knowing what to do with the latter, assuming that there was never going to be a full-scale privatization of health and education. Here New Labour was much more comfortable with re-engineering social services, granting them more money yet at the same time acting to improve them as supply-side services. The government, by activating the consumers of these services and by directly setting performance targets believed that it could ensure their increased productivity without full-scale recourse to the private sector.

New Labour was willing and able to roll out neoliberal solutions beyond the specifically economic with much ease. Target setting, supply-side reforms in the public sector, audit, empowerment, community, 'responsibilization', all features of a neoliberal governing mentality that showed that New Labour did not have to stick rigidly to the economic division between marketed and non-marketed.[15] Even so, these policies still referenced the same neoliberal kinds of human agent and attempted to foster attitudes that were deemed as appropriate to the hospital as to the high street.

Indeed, many of the public sector reforms of the Blair era were imagined and proposed by Conservatives in the 1980s and 1990s. *The Unfinished Task*, so Ronald Butt argued in a pamphlet published by the CPS in 1986, was precisely about extending choice to the public sphere, giving parents, for instance, the choice over their children's school because 'people get fulfilment through endeavours to exercise control over their own lives and families.'[16] For Peter Lilley, in *Thatcherism – the Next Generation* (1989), again published by the CPS, the point was that the market was only ever 'shorthand for the combined efforts of individual choices.... Why should not patients, parents and pupils have a measure of choice between schools, hospitals and other medical services?'[17] Neither of these authors was actually suggesting a wholesale dismantling of the welfare state; just a reorganization around active citizen-consumers, rather than passive recipients of social services.

New Labour's social programme was not as original as Blair promoted it to be. Its policies were neither alien nor anathema to Thatcherites. But it would seem that it was easier for representatives on the Left to act with regard to public services, whereas those on the Right found it difficult to act in an area that they remained permanently untrusting of. Instead many of the intellectuals on the Right in the 1990s retreated into questioning the morality of the welfare state without exactly knowing what to do about it. For Michael Portillo (*The Blue Horizon*, 1993) the welfare state encouraged 'entitlement' and government needed instead to act preventatively to 're-establish and nurture the relationships that can help people before they find themselves in real difficulty'. The state, for Portillo, just 'crowded out ... [moral] ... responsibility'.[18]

For Malcolm Rifkind (*Conservative Britain in the 21st Century*, 1996) there was a definite sense in which government needed to be 'reinculcating a sense of personal responsibility and returning to the individual control over their own destiny and that of their families'. Conservatism was thus a moral crusade that could be extended to health and education. For Rifkind the biggest risk was that the project would be undermined by the supposedly undemocratic statist practices of the European Union.[19] That the welfare state was a moral issue was most clearly stated by the American neoconservative Michael Novak in the CPS paper *The Crisis of the Welfare State* (1993),

> The subjective sense of personal responsibility has atrophied.... Yes – we need a necessary sense of security and stability, but insurance mechanisms should not be anchored in grand state apparatuses.... The project of self-government depends on the capacity of citizens to govern their own passions, urges, habits and expectations. The project of self-government is moral.[20]

In many ways, Thatcher and Blair shared a very similar vision of society as a moral institution comprising strong families and civic institutions. For Thatcher this was the strong and rich tapestry that she envisioned arising from the voluntary spirit of the community; she had, as discussed in Chapter 4, great hopes for society.[21] Blair essentially had the same moral vision of community, except that Third Way politics identified a need for government to act in order to create the necessary framework of attitudes for this vision to be activated. Thatcher envisaged that the tapestry would emerge voluntarily; that the 'healthy society' would emerge on its own once the economy was free of an inflationary psychology. And in 1993 Portillo was still arguing that government could not alone make society; that morals essentially arose from a variety of institutions including churches, business, media and government.[22] Blair's vision was that government could foster a strong society[23] in precisely the same way as it fostered a strong economy, extending consumer sovereignty into citizen-sovereignty, not through state apparatuses, but by encouraging the right kinds of attitudes.

In a sense it was rather strange that the New Right were willing in government to try to foster, through a heavy hand, what they believed were the right attitudes for a progressive economy and yet were more reluctant to apply these same ideas to trying to build their vision of a moral society, equally based on an imagined congruence of individual responsibility and compassion. Where Conservatives stumbled or were slow on the uptake, New Labour had no qualms about rolling out the image of the active consumer across the social domain. In fact, Novak, writing for the IEA in 1998, argued that Blair had indeed recognized the moral crisis of the state and had therefore made the project of self-government his own. Novak proceeded to congratulate Blair on a set of policies that he found entirely coincident with the values of the New Right: reducing passivity, nourishing families as sites of independence, nourishing personal habits of creativity, initiative and enterprise, and helping families establish a capital fund that could be transferred across generations.[24]

Over time, and after a period of reticence, the Conservative Party has come to embrace a brand of 'libertarian paternalism' in which they are happy for government to take a role in activating an image of society correlated to the image of the economy that they believe had already come into existence.[25] Thus Thatcherism transformed The Labour Party.[26] In turn, New Labour's 'Third Way' has led to Conservative Prime Minister David Cameron's vision of the 'Big Society'. This vision, enunciated before and after his election in 2010, is another iteration of the neoliberal concern for activating citizen-consumers; applying government pressure to the governed in order to elicit 'voluntary' society-building associations.

6.2 Revamping monetary policy

If New Labour were comfortable with making the morality of society a political project in Britain in the 1990s and 2000s, believing that it needed to foster the attitudes of active consumers of social services, then it should come as little surprise that New Labour did not see the need to problematize the neoliberal figure of the consumer within economic policy itself. The Governor of the Bank of England, Mervyn King, suggested in a speech in May 2005 that there were two key speeches from within government that, he believed, encapsulated current approaches to economic policy. The first was Lawson's 1984 Mais Lecture, *The British Experiment*, the second Blair's 1995 Mais Lecture in which was discussed New Labour's proposed framework for curing economic ills.[27] In making this statement, was King suggesting that these two speeches provided the two key parts to current policy, or was he simply saying that the two speeches were the best two summaries available of a single approach to policy?

A reading of Blair's speech would suggest the latter interpretation; there was little that was 'new' in it. It endorsed the idea that monetary policy should target low and stable inflation, and that this should not be by way of intermediate money supply targets. And certainly almost immediately in government in 1997, the New Labour Chancellor, Gordon Brown, announced that the Bank of England was being given operational independence to set interest rates so as to meet the target of 2.5 per cent annual retail price inflation. However, this was not a new regime; inflation targeting began at the start of 1993 with the publication of the first inflation report that introduced an ongoing target range for retail price inflation (excluding mortgage interest payments) of 1 to 4 per cent per year. In tying his flag to this regime, Blair was stating his belief that the policies of the 1980s (not 1990s) had failed to appreciate the extent to which macroeconomic policy measures could 'swamp improvements' in both the supply side and government attempts to reform the supply side in microeconomic policies.[28] This comment was in many ways specifically referenced to Lawson's 1984 speech in which the latter began by arguing that policy in the post-war era had put micro and macro policy the wrong way round. For Lawson macroeconomic policy would no longer be about producing growth and employment but about producing the conditions conducive to growth and employment.[29]

In many ways, Blair's speech was designed to calm nerves in the City of London, to confirm to the financial world that there would be fiscal prudence; that the government would not renationalize, but in fact would seek to make the public sector more productive. Priority would still be given to the control of inflation because even 'temporary failures over inflation have permanent adverse effects on the real economy'.[30] One might say that the speech emphasized a commitment to stability that might previously have been lacking. The reality of monetary policy since 1979 was certainly not stable: recession, boom and then another recession in which interest rates had risen as high as 15 per cent in September 1992 in a failed attempt to keep the British Pound tied to a basket of European currencies. Now, everything possible would be done to maintain stability; the real failure of monetarism, so the architects of New Labour believed, was that it had failed to provide precisely that.

Both within the New Labour camp and within the Bank of England there was no dissension from the idea that inflation was still the enemy that needed to be battled, and that there was indeed a moral aspect in fighting it: 'inflation is a country where nobody speaks the truth. That is why there is a moral element to controlling inflation.'[31] For Ed Balls, writing in 1992, it was Britain's 'inflationary psychology' that had 'encouraged consumers to borrow excessively in the mid 1980s'.[32] It had nothing to do with a financial system competing to advance credit, nor with the vision of consumers and households as active balance sheet builders. There was no question, therefore, of letting up in the neoliberal battle against the old inflationary psychology. So, the question naturally follows, how did New Labour problematize economic policy in the 1980s? Certainly as the discussion in section 6.1 suggests, they made supply-side improvements a key New Labour policy, applied as much to the public as private sector. In the public sector it meant acting directly on productivity, making those that were deemed unproductive productive not, as the Thatcherites had done, by limiting the supply of funding but by setting a series of specific performance targets. In the language of Gordon Brown there was to be 'necessary modernization, wholesale modernization and nothing but modernization'.[33]

Conversely, in the private sector this meant continuing to foster conduct in order that markets could function; that is to say, that consumers could always and everywhere assert their sovereignty and not have decisions distorted by inflation. Yes, there were certainly difficulties measuring inflation, which suggested that consumer prices recorded a higher level of inflation than was actually experienced on the high street, but fundamentally, according to the Bank of England, 2.5 per cent retail price inflation was essentially no inflation. Governor Leigh-Pemberton cited the Chairman of the United States Federal Reserve, Alan Greenspan, in expressing the view that price stability did not refer to zero per cent inflation but to an economic environment in which general changes in the price level 'do not materially enter business and household decisions.'[34] And to reiterate, Brown believed that the first priority in 'equipping Britain for the 21st century' was establishing 'monetary stability that allows businesses and families to make their plans for the long term.'[35]

Inflation was still, as the Bank of England's first inflation report stated, very much a 'monetary phenomenon.'[36] Nonetheless something had clearly gone wrong in the late 1980s and early 1990s, which needed to be addressed by policy-makers. Balls, in two papers in 1992 and 1997 respectively, set out the New Labour position. Combining the medium-term financial strategy with the easing of credit controls had made policy-making highly unpredictable, permitting another upsurge in inflation. Indeed deregulation, technological advances and widening consumer choice all ultimately made, he believed, intermediate money supply targets unworkable. The Thatcher government had tied their credibility to these targets, only to have their credibility undermined. In the process Lawson had taken his 'eye off the ball to such an extent that the information that double-digit growth of M4 did transmit from the mid 1980s on was not given the attention it was due'. Balls wanted credibility to be re-established in a way that signalled it was not just going to be another false dawn. This time credibility would stick and stability would follow as the 'very essence' of policy.[37] Moreover a pre-commitment to stability implied that no government could 'cheat in a pre-election dash for growth'.[38]

The notion that Lawson took his eyes of the ball is critical because in Balls' view his inattention allowed an inflationary psychology to creep back into people's minds. One has to be very clear, therefore, about what was being put into question. Rising asset markets, the rapid rise in home ownership (that net financial wealth was twice annual disposable income in 1987 versus only being one-quarter more in 1980) was not being positioned as problematic in and of itself.

Only when inflation had started rising on the high street had it become apparent that rapidly rising house prices were a problem; they had been revealed to be the result of an inflationary psychology only by the rise of consumer prices. Without the return of inflation in the late 1980s to signify the problem, there was nothing to suggest that house price rises were at all problematic. Increasing the size of one's balance sheet with the use of debt was the result of a perfectly rational psychology. That many households had chosen to reorganize their portfolios at exactly the same time, thus putting upward pressure on prices because there was more demand, was not a symptom of anything malign. It was only the appearance of inflation that led authorities, retrospectively, to see that there had been a problem, where previously none had been perceived.

The criticisms brought to bear on the operation of monetary policy in the 1980s by the New Labour establishment never suggested an underlying critique of consumer sovereignty or the possibility of disabling in any way the ability of enterprising consumers and households to use debt to bring into being a balance sheet that would exist through time providing a range of different income flows. New Labour economic policy was about the technicalities of establishing stability; that is to say, that stability would only come from a credible policy that ensured that people understood that an inflationary psychology would not be tolerated by the monetary authorities. The measure of inflation was high street prices, retail prices excluding mortgage costs, the measure established in 1993 and retained by New Labour in 1997 that did not include house prices or asset prices generally.[39] Changes in asset prices were not viewed as problematic so long as consumer prices on the high street signified that there was no inflationary psychology in the population at large.

The Bank of England and New Labour were absolutely united in their position on this and, in a sense, both implicitly accepted Lawson's view from 1992, that the boom in the late 1980s had spiralled out of control (that is inflation had returned to the high street) because people needed time to learn how to use their new-found freedom in the credit markets. As King, Deputy Governor of the Bank, put it in August 1994, the problem with financial liberalization was that it was essentially a supply-side reform that had potential effects on the demand side as well; which if not properly managed, that is with a view to ongoing monitoring of retail price inflation, might give rise to associated inflationary pressure. The Bank would not make the same mistake again, allowing excess inflationary demand to impinge on a supply side of constant consumer prices. However the lack of credit rationing was not seen as a problem and would not be reintroduced. After all, 'credit denied to potentially good borrowers is capable of doing more harm to an economy than credit advanced to bad ones'.[40] The message from the Governor Eddie George that 'we must never let things get out of hand again'[41] was not targeted at debt or house prices per se, but at consumer price inflation. New Labour and the Bank of England agreed that using intermediate targets, such as money supply, was so problematic that one could end up distracted. Instead monetary policy would remain solely focused on the inflation rate as the beginning and end of the targeting process.

Of course the rule, that inflation should not deviate by over 1 per cent either side from the target of 2.5 per cent, also gave a place for reasoned discretion: it did not necessarily tie the hands of policy setters, because to set interest rates meant using discretion to assess the information available.[42] If the target was 2.5 per cent over the medium to long term, then one had to use one's judgement now as to what economic statistics were indicating about the future. Whereas a fixed rule might say for every 2 per cent that M4 rises more than 10 per cent per year, interest rates will rise by 1 per cent, there was now no fixed rule about how much interest rates should move by, only that the Monetary Policy Committee (MPC) should assess the likelihood of inflation moving outside the target range and adjust interest rates accordingly.[43]

So clearly this was no strictly monetarist regime; stability of output and inflation were of equal importance to the target. For King (speaking in November 1997) the new regime had two variables, inflation and stability. The latter was captured in the belief that there was a permanent trade-off between the volatility of inflation and the volatility of output. One should use 'constrained discretion', a term used by both King and Balls, to respond to exogenous shocks that might cause a temporary rise in inflation. That is to say, if oil prices were to rise it is not necessarily correct to respond in 'the first round' with interest rate rises, but instead to 'accommodate' the price level effect in the short term, knowing that once the effect of higher prices has worked through the system, and assuming that these prices are not leading through into higher wage demands (above productivity gains), the inflationary effect will disappear. The idea is that to raise rates in response to the initial rise in prices might unnecessarily cause volatility in inflation and be detrimental to the long-term path of sustainable economic growth (delivered by a flexible and adaptable supply side).[44]

Complementing the idea of constrained discretion is the idea of symmetry, the notion that it is as important that inflation be kept from falling below 1.5 per cent as it is to ensure that it does not rise above 3.5 per cent. On the one hand, and as discussed above, this policy was acceptable given that 2.5 per cent inflation was essentially no inflation, as Greenspan had said; it did not impact the decision-making process of businesses or households. On the other hand, symmetry ensured more stability and meant that interest rates were never set prohibitively high to achieve a goal of zero per cent inflation, which was thought unnecessary in the first place.[45] Thus symmetry and constrained discretion together, one might say, suggested a 'New Keynesian' remoulding of the anti-inflationary policies of the 1980s. This was not the hard and fast regime of money supply targets; there was a new leeway, an acceptance that some inflation, as long as it was stable and (very) low, was fine, possibly even desirable; and that a certain amount of discretion was required because volatility in inflation was almost as disturbing as volatility in output to the attempts by government and monetary authorities to guide the economy on a path of 'non-inflationary consistent expansion', or as King called it, a 'nice' trajectory.[46]

To what extent, therefore, can one talk about a disjuncture in policy between the New Right and New Labour with regards to theorizing the role of monetary policy and banking and its connection to the homeowner consumer? Certainly, by removing the strictures of money supply targets, or exchange rate targets, a 'softer' regime could be practised in which short-term cost cycles could be accommodated. Rules now referred to the ends not the means, thus introducing expertise and discretion in the interpretation of data, rather than requiring a fixed response to data presented as fact. Nonetheless, there was, and has been, no questioning of the figure of the enterprising consumer. Consumers were still to have their borrowing demands met unrationed as if they were businesses in their own right. There was to be no modification to the liberalized banking system. Inflation on the high street was still the indicator and sign of an inflationary psychology. All the while consumer prices were stable; movements in other assets, however much affected by new 'innovations' in the funding market were ultimately seen as benign. This is not to say that questions were not asked; for as section 6.3 discusses, the Bank of England in the decade from 1997 to 2007 became increasingly obsessed with the increase in house prices and consumer debt. It was only that they knew no way to provide a judgement on the matter all the while consumer prices remained within target.

6.3 Practising New Keynesianism

In terms of policy formulation one can see therefore the emergence of a regime formed by those at the Bank of England who had been part of policy-making under Lawson and Thatcher, and those at New Labour seeking to impose their stamp on the process. Monetary policy was to be more 'sophisticated' but broadly the same; that is to say, macroeconomic policy continued to be focused on interest rates and the fight against an inflationary psychology, microeconomic policy on the supply side. Financial liberalization (the end of credit rationing) and the belief that inflation was always and everywhere a monetary phenomenon would continue to live side by side without reflection upon their potential paradoxical statuses. The consumer was still central to governing the economy. This mentality was as much embedded in inflation targeting as it had previously been in money supply targeting.

It was equally embedded in the regulatory reform introduced by New Labour in June 1998 which transferred the responsibility for banking supervision and surveillance from the Bank of England to the newly formed Financial Services Authority (FSA). Perhaps the best way to understand this new arrangement is in reflecting that there was seen to be no contradiction between free monetary creation and a monetary view of inflation. The extent to which private banks chose to grow their balance sheet, the nature of the funding they used and the models of risk management that were practised were of little relevance to the Bank of England in so much as the latter was concerned predominantly with consumer prices. Low inflation on the high street was all the evidence the Bank needed to be convinced that there was no excess monetary creation or systemic risk issues. The events of 2008 (involving the near collapse of the British banking system) show that the FSA had failed in its task of monitoring the behaviour of the banking sector and in protecting consumers. But it also demonstrates that monetary policy and banking supervision were disconnected; policy had practised the belief that the supply side, i.e. the availability of funding in the banking sector, would have no effect on the demand side. That is to say, demand for credit was perceived as being entirely related to individual decisions of portfolio management undertaken by consumers and entrepreneurs.

On the face of it, the FSA's concern was primarily with consumer protection,[47] and this appears problematic. If it was accepted that consumers were now behaving as entrepreneurs, they would not need protecting; so long, that is, as there was sufficiently intense competition for their business. Indeed this was precisely the criticisms of regulation made by IEA and CPS authors, both as the new regulatory regime was being set up and afterwards. For George Benston (*Regulating Financial Markets*, Hobart Paper 135, 1998), much of the reasoning for any form of regulation was that it paid government revenues, whether from the requirement for banks to hold non-interest bearing deposits at the Bank of England or by forcing banks to make discounted loans to favoured sectors. Additionally, protecting consumers where there was unfair treatment or to ensure that there was sufficient information so that a reasoned decision could be made by the consumer was one thing, but this could too often raise the issue of moral hazard, whereby deposit insurance, for instance, removed the incentive for depositors to monitor the activities of deposit providers (see discussion in section 7.4).[48] For these authors there was the matter of cost, on which a key statement had been made in 1988 by Charles Goodhart in another IEA publication (*Financial Regulation – or Over-regulation*). The direct cost of having regulatory bodies, Goodhart estimated, was over £100 million per year. This he suggested was much higher than the cost of identified scandals. This alone suggested regulation was not worth the cost, and this did not even include other unseen costs such as how the burden of regulation might stifle business activity in general.[49]

Whether these criticisms from the IEA were justified is not the point. What they show is that as far as these authors were concerned any kind of paternalistic protection for the consumer required too much regulation. Competition was all that was required to protect the consumer: as long as the consumer was sovereign then best practice would be enforced because consumers could walk away from poor suppliers. Benston's point was simple enough: 'why should financial services be regulated more so than other services?' Only very limited regulation on capital requirements was needed.[50] The focus, as Oliver Lodge argued for the CPS in 2002, 'should always be on encouraging innovation and competition so that banking can respond with increasing speed and effectiveness to customer needs and technological change'. Instead legislative measures were, Lodge believed, obstructing competition. All government needed to do was leave well alone; for Lodge, the information revolution and the internet had addressed the concern with information asymmetry. It could no longer necessarily be said that consumers knew less than the businesses that supplied their services and products. As such, the market should be allowed to operate unfettered, for 'the consumer has become generally better educated and more discerning.'[51] Simply put, for these authors, there was already too much in the way of regulation; any interference raised the spectre of disempowering the sovereign consumer. To try and make suppliers of financial products follow best practice was to miss the point: only the consumer could do that.

For some then the FSA represented too much consumer protection. In fact regulation never problematized the consumer and the consumer's right and need to be able to access finance so as to build a portfolio of investments in human and non-human capital. On the contrary, the question of the excess debt, systemic risk in the financial sector, inflated and unsustainable asset prices was subordinated to the information found in a basket of consumer prices that the Bank of England was required to monitor. Consumer protection, which for some already assumed too little competence on the part of individual borrowers, practised the notion that in society there existed a firm division, as King had said in 1994,[52] between good and bad borrowers. Regulation would ensure that financial products were not misrepresented to borrowers and that enough information would be available to good borrowers to make their portfolio decisions. Bad borrowers, perhaps lacking moral fortitude, perhaps infused with an inflationary psychology, were not to be allowed to derail the system for the good borrowers; there was to be no credit rationing. Given that consumer price inflation remained benign, government could conclude that the majority of the population were good borrowers, identifying themselves to the monetary authority as entrepreneurs-of-the-self, embracing the enterprise culture. To default on a loan was to reveal that a good borrower was in fact all along a bad borrower. That circumstances outside the control of a 'good' borrower might lead to default was not something that FSA consumer protection took account of. As long as the consumer was provided with information, as long as the advisor had passed a regulatory exam, an enterprising culture could never cause systemic problems to the financial sector.

The role of the FSA as a regulatory body was clear; to protect consumers from deliberate misrepresentation. Banking supervision needed only to be a systems audit because it was assumed that consumers were doing the real supervision of banking practices. Banks in turn were supposed to be making risk assessments of individual borrowers. The audit of the aggregate of enterprising consumers was carried out by the Bank of England in the form of an ongoing monitoring of inflationary psychology: no high street inflation, no cause for concern, such has been the continuing governing mentality of British neoliberalism. Except of course the Bank of England always retained a nagging doubt, a certain degree of reflexive self-questioning. This never took the form of an out and out rejection of the theory, but occasionally doubt crept in, variously in the form of questioning what had gone wrong at the end of the 1980s, persistent worries over the rise of house prices and consumer debt in the 2000s, or in monetary action throughout the period in response to the ever-present concern that debt deflation might set in.

One might say that whereas low inflation proved to policy-makers that everything was operating without the dangerous and damaging effects of an inflationary psychology, there was also a realization in practice that the enterprise economy, evidenced by the expansion of personal balance sheets and wealth, was so heavily reliant on bank financing that monetary authorities were forced to ensure that the value of that newly found wealth was not allowed to collapse unduly in times of crisis. Put another way monetary policy was asymmetrical: take little or no action on debt and asset prices as they rise, always act against the slightest suspicion of deflation. This did not go unnoticed by Goodhart who, in discussing the extent to which it was always highly problematic to include asset prices in the process of interest rate setting, pointed to the fact, in a lecture in 2003 published by the IEA, that although some account was taken of asset markets it was 'probably more often in response to asset price declines than to increases, for rather obvious reasons'.[53] Presumably Goodhart was referring to the fact that if asset prices fall, and the purchase of these assets is financed by debt, there is always a risk of debt deflation, which in turn can threaten the banking system. And any potential failing of the banking system always raised the spectre of a repeat of the 1930s Great Depression, generally accepted, following Milton Friedman and Anna Schwartz' account, to have been accentuated by a collapse of the banking system in the United States, as each bank called in lending in a hope of shoring up its own capital and reserves.[54]

For some, this asymmetry in monetary policy is no doubt evidence that the goal of economic policy has been to protect the wealth of vested interests and the *rentier* class. Here, the focus has been on an alternative explanation. The asymmetry alluded to by Goodhart has not only been related to the fear and paranoia associated with deflation, it has also entailed deploying monetary policy to protect wealth in order to protect the culture of enterprise, assumed to be writ large in society. Building a portfolio of assets took place concurrently with falling savings rates; any dramatic fall in the value of assets could always risk a return to higher savings and an unwinding of the perceived successes of neoliberalism. With this in mind, monetary authorities have been more attuned to the suggestion that markets have overreacted to negative news, thus justifying emergency cuts in interest rates, than intervening when an equal number of arguments could be made that interest rates need to rise to respond to 'irrational exuberance' in rapidly booming assets markets.

This mentality was on display for the first time in the wake of the mini-crash of the stock market in October 1987 in which central banks around the world responded with coordinated rate cuts. The November 1987 Bank of England quarterly bulletin opened with the following statement:

> The level of equity … and real estate prices … had been a cause of concern for some time.… But the pattern, speed and magnitude of the collapse was out of all proportion to the quantity of new information relating to any relevant fundamentals.… The deflationary implications of the loss of wealth for a global economy already growing quite modestly, together with the damage done to the confidence and liquidity of markets, made it appropriate for the world's monetary authorities to adopt a supportive stance, and in some cases short-term interest rates have been allowed to fall by an much as 1.5 per cent.[55]

These kinds of concerns have remained permanently fixed in the minds of policy-makers ever since. They were in operation after the Asian economic crisis of 1997–98, the Russian sovereign default in 1998 and the collapse of the 'dot-com' stock market bubble in 2000. The Bank of England for instance cut interest rates in 1999 on the back of fears of a 'general credit crunch'[56] and because they believed that they needed 'to stimulate domestic demand to offset export weakness'.[57]

So on the one hand stability was the key, and this was captured most succinctly by the persistent stress on the symmetrical nature of the inflation target. But this symmetry (2.5 per cent inflation target, with 1 per cent movements either side permitted) was underscored by a fundamental asymmetry in regard to asset prices. When consumer prices were within range and stable, monetary authorities would, more often than not, cut interest rates to support large falls in asset prices; but, again with consumer price inflation in target range, they never increased rates when asset markets rose, however dramatically. Rising asset prices, particularly in the housing market, were never taken to be problematic so long as high street inflation did not rise above the target range. In this way, and as Figures 6.1, 6.2 and 6.3 show, interest rates remained rooted to targeting inflation as debt and house prices continued to rise unabated. Indeed, in some years, most notably in 2001 and 2002, the Bank endorsed consumer borrowing and spending in the belief that this was a necessary antidote to debt inflation.

As Figure 6.3 shows, by 2004 household debt to disposable income had risen to over 140 per cent, from just over 100 per cent ten years earlier, and consumer debt (composed of mortgage equity withdrawal and unsecured credit) from 2 per cent of post-tax household income in 1998 to about 10 per cent. Savings rates had also fallen below 5 per cent, dropping to the levels of the late 1980s boom. How were these data points interpreted by the Bank of England? Were they

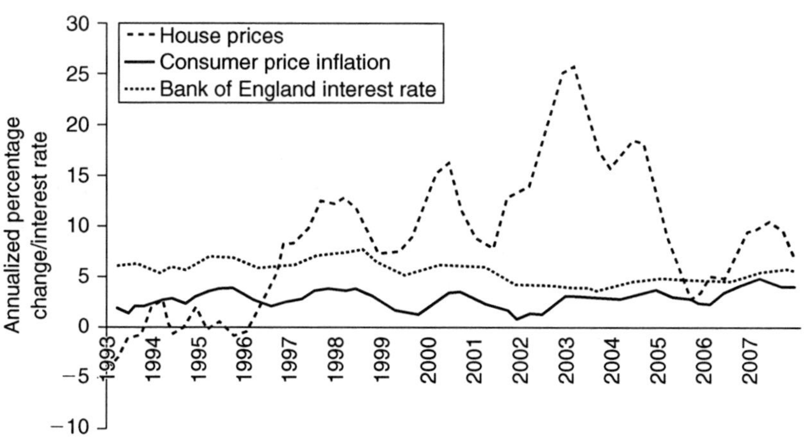

Figure 6.1 House prices, inflation and interest rates 1993–2007 (source: Nationwide, UK Office of National Statistics, Bank of England).

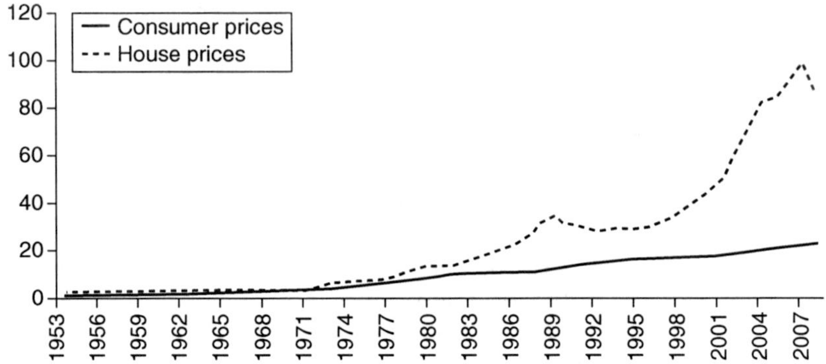

Figure 6.2 House prices and inflation 1953–2007 (source: UK Office of National Statistics, Nationwide).

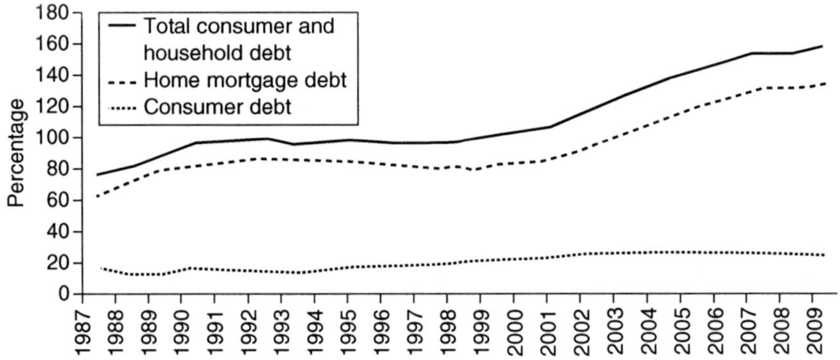

Figure 6.3 UK household debt as a percentage of household income, by composition 1993–2009 (source: UK Office of National Statistics, Bank of England).

problematized in any significant way; were they recognized as requiring policy redress? The simple answer is that, rather like in the late 1980s, the data was always explained away; the Bank of England could not say in definitive terms that there was anything wrong. That is not to say that monetary authorities were not monitoring the situation; one might even say that their research, reports and speeches showed little concern for anything else. But the conclusion was always that the outlook was most likely benign and, at any rate, it was not for the Bank to intervene all the while high street inflation remained subdued.

According to the Deputy Governor, Andrew Large, the rise in debt was a logical response to lower nominal interest rates and the wish to spread consumption over one's lifetime. It was entirely consistent with monetary stability and was in any case 'the logical accompaniment to monetary stability at a time of [global] imbalances'. The balance of probability was with the optimists; at any rate, the strength of the financial system was, according to Large, guaranteed by new techniques of risk management. There might be a long-term problem with regards to retirement savings, but this was not a problem requiring an immediate policy response. If there was a build-up in financial assets this was related to supply-side factors in the banking industry: more competition, new entrants and new credit instruments.[58] Likewise, in September 2004 the monetary policy committee (MPC) member Stephen Nickell opened a speech on household debt, house prices and consumption with the words, 'it is said we are in the middle of a long-lived consumption boom in the UK funded by a tidal wave of debt ... this statement is more or less completely wrong.' Nickell's point was that while savings rates as a proportion of income were low, they had only decreased by one or two per cent over the past few years. Rather than having a consumption boom showing up as rising consumer prices, instead the rate of financial asset accumulation had been rapid, nearly doubling between 1998 and 2003. A 'good part' of this was to be 'associated with the accumulation of housing assets by individual households'. There was no consumption boom and there was no need for concern as, for Nickell, 'the increasing rate of accumulation of debt has been closely matched by the increasing rate of accumulation of financial assets.'[59]

So while the housing boom of the early 1970s was explained by the New Right as a deliberate effort on the part of the few to hedge against the effects of inflation, the housing boom of the late 1990s/2000s was explained as a rational response of consumer-entrepreneurs to lower rates of interest and a belief that rates would remain low as long as inflation remained low. In other words, an upward revaluation of assets was to be expected from the permanent establishment of stability. This is not to say that the upsurge in debt went unnoticed, quite the contrary in actual fact, but it was seen as the congruence of a number of factors on both the demand and supply side. As MPC member Paul Tucker put it,

> The more or less structural changes in the supply of credit have been occurring during a period in which borrowers and lenders have also been adjusting to a low inflation, low nominal interest rate environment, and during which official interest rates have been cyclically low. The upshot has been lots of borrowing.[60]

Lots of borrowing: yes, but was this problematic? No. As such, the question might fairly be asked, what was the difference between what was happening in the 2000s and what happened in the 1980s? Was New Labour/New Keynesianism any different from the monetary policy practised by Lawson in the late 1980s? Well in one obvious sense the language being used to analyse data and make interest rate decisions was very different. Indeed, as both Governor and Deputy Governor remarked on separate occasions, the language utilized in the decision-making process was remarkably reminiscent of the language used in the early 1970s.[61] There was no reference to money supply growth, which was growing at a rate not seen since the late 1980s. Thus whereas the monetary authorities focused on explaining money supply in the early 1980s, as a reflection of a new kind of rationalism to be found in society at large in the 2000s, house price rises were now explained as a rational response to the success of establishing low inflationary expectations. In the 1980s the fact that money supply was growing so strongly and yet was not following through (at least until 1989) into high street inflation was taken as proof that habits of thought had changed. Under the New Keynesian regime, the population no longer had to prove their rationality, this was taken for granted; instead the focus came on explaining why asset markets were producing right and rational signals. So long as one assumed that the participants were practising the right habits of thought (i.e. non-inflationary ones) then how could the prices be anything other than a signal of information for a rational market. The job, performed so successfully by the Bank of England, was to explain to everyone why asset prices were moving upwards and why no one should be unduly concerned by it.

Macroeconomic policy had never really veered away from that which had been established by Lawson: high street inflation was still the judge and jury of an economic policy that took for granted that society was composed of entrepreneurs and enterprising consumers, building portfolios, balancing income and expenditure through time and over their lifetime, constantly making adjustments, with the use of debt, to their balance sheets. One could not arbitrarily intervene. Again this is not to say there were not risks, for as King argued in 2006, one could interpret prices as being signposts of potential problems in the future. In his opinion though, current prices reflected underlying (real or non-inflationary) preferences for saving and investment and not the underpricing of risk.[62] The Bank's base case, discussed in research in the first quarter of 2007, was that even though the stock of household debt had doubled since 2000, this debt had been used to finance assets, thus the net position of households was little changed. It was not inflationary nor was there any evidence to suggest that higher debt raised the sensitivity of consumer spending to any future economic shocks. As Bank of England research put it, 'overall it would appear that there are enough buffers on both the household and lender balance sheets for the build-up of household debt not to complicate the operation of monetary policy in the current conjuncture.'[63]

New Keynesianism certainly took its eye off the monetary ball; that is to say off the money supply. But as the 1980s had proved to those who believed that they had enacted the quiet revolution in the conduct of the British population, it was not possible to incorporate money supply into monetary policy when it could be assumed that those whose borrowing practices had initiated its growth were using this new money to make portfolio adjustments rather than push up high street prices. Indeed at a very simplistic level so long as government believed that those in the market were operating with the right attitudes, then it would be impossible ever to say that prices were wrong. Even if the monetary authority suspected there might be a bubble, then trying to 'prick it' might cause more damage than just letting it run on. If value ultimately stemmed from the individual subjective assessment of demand then unless one could prove that those making the assessment were somehow infected with irrationalism (say an inflationary psychology), who could say that anything was not the right value? Instead all government could ever do was protect consumer-entrepreneurs, that is wealth owners, from another potential irrationalism: debt deflation. This fundamental asymmetry in policy was the outcome of governing for the consumer and with the consumer in mind.

The Bank of England were not unaware of more unorthodox work in which macroeconomists were claiming to demonstrate that there was a link between the availability of credit, the accumulation of debt and the concurrent rise of asset prices; that is to say that there were causal explanations for the data that brought into question the behaviour of the household consuming unit.[64] Nonetheless their position was always that there was no causality here: people borrowed in order to rearrange their balance sheet, consumption patterns and house prices were concurrent variables, likely to be coincident and caused by a common factor, say confidence in the future as opposed to uncertainty. Indeed, in this neoliberal mentality this had to be the case because all consumption, of whatever kind, whether short term or long term, was expressed in the same functional relationship (as per Friedman's restatement of the quantity theory) based on the rate of interest and in units of account defined as money. To suggest that changes to the value of one of these variables affected another variable would be to bring into question the human agents as they were imagined in the theory. Policy simply could not practise anything other than the assumption that house prices and consumption patterns were complementary not causal variables.

Additionally, there is the question of the shift in language; did referring to 'real' expenditure variables in the economy signify a departure from neoliberalism back to Keynesianism? Certainly, discussions at the MPC tended to sound pre-Thatcherite. The notion that it was the job of economic policy-makers to stimulate and encourage expenditure certainly had a decidedly Keynesian demand management tone to it. However the focus remained inflation: stable and low high street inflation simply meant that money could be omitted from the conversation. But this was only for the time being: no one was suggesting that a concern with the money supply was essentially wrong. As Deputy Governor, John Gieve, put it in June 2007, 'if anyone is in any doubt, monetarism is not dead but only resting.'[65] And as far back as 2002, King was warning everyone that, 'it would be unfortunate if the change in the way we talk led to the erroneous belief that we could turn Milton Friedman on his head.' He fully expected at some point for money to regain its 'important place in the conversation of economists'.[66]

As the British and global financial system became increasingly under strain in 2007 and 2008 many commentators, as will be discussed in the following section, blamed easy monetary policy at the start of the decade and central banks around the world, especially the Federal Reserve of the United States, for being too slow to raise interest rates as economies recovered from the 'dot-com' boom and bust of the late 1990s and early 2000s. But in terms of high street inflation, there was no reason to raise rates: the key signifier of the population's economic psychology, high street prices, exhibited no untoward signs. All the same, it is right to say that lower interest rates were used to increase demand in the economy in the early 2000s: it was hoped that strong consumer demand would offset weak external demand and associated low manufacturing investment expenditure in Britain. But this policy was not about growth per se; but about the belief that without this extra demand, inflation would fall below the target range, jeopardizing the new economy with deflation.

Thus in finishing this section it is important to point out that one of the things that is so striking about the macroeconomic policy conducted in the New Labour years is that demand management, in being focused on inflation targeting, has made anathema the suggestion that there is anything to distinguish consumption expenditure and household investment from business investment. It was recognized that the British economy was unbalanced, i.e. coincident weak manufacturing output and strong consumer expenditure. But this was never problematized in itself. If growth needed to be maintained (so as to minimize the risk of deflation) then growth that came from consumer expenditure was 'as good as' growth that came from anywhere else. This of course would make sense to any political mentality that did not distinguish between an entrepreneur and a consumer entrepreneur-of-the-self.

While it might be said that practising a policy of equivalence of consumption and investment was both an artefact of Keynes' work on aggregate demand as well as a result of the development of national income accounting ('national income = consumption + investment + government expenditure + exports − imports'), from the 1930s on, as discussed in Chapter 3, the actual practice of Keynesian demand management always gave a special emphasis to the idea that sustainable growth resulted from investment in production equipment rather than consumption itself. This was the legacy of production so important to classical liberalism and retained in the minds of progressive or new liberalism. Thatcherism practised this distinction as a mirage: both consumer and entrepreneur belonged to the same of class of thinking. And in this chapter it has been demonstrated that the New Keynesians were practising exactly this same mentality in their monetary policy. It is thus perfectly reasonable to say that interest rates should have been raised in the early 2000s: it is entirely wrong to think that a neoliberal mentality of rule could have found any way to justify that decision.

6.4 The crisis of neoliberal governmentality

The point of this chapter has essentially been to answer the question as to whether the New Labour economic regime problematized in any significant way the neoliberal political mentality and its taken-for-granted rendition of human agency. The position taken here is that it did not. It has been shown that in many ways the New Labour government expanded the neoliberal focus on the economic into an assemblage of policies directed to other domains of the social. This redirection however should not be taken as being synonymous with progressive liberalism that understood the state as needing to play a direct role in the provision of economic and social security. Instead social and public policy sought both to empower individuals and at the same time make them responsible for themselves. Concurrently, it was believed that the voluntary and spontaneous assemblage of 'community' would provide moral guidance. Likewise, the use of certain Keynesian language does not necessarily mean that the practice of economic policy was Keynesian in the original sense of the word. Economic policy never gave a special place to manufacturing concerns (practically, if anything, the opposite). Consumer and entrepreneur were equally valid domains of aggregate expenditure. There were no unemployed worker-savers here, in need of new government investment projects. The consumer as imagined by neoliberalism was not problematized; the imagined figure of the entrepreneur-of-the-self, with raised levels of indebtedness, was consistently practised as a positive reference point for economic policy.

Nonetheless somewhere along the line government misidentified what people were doing. The deposit-run on the British bank Northern Rock and the near collapse of the British banking system in 2008, followed by its partial nationalization, suggests that the build-up of liquidity (essentially money held in deposit accounts) and the rise in asset prices reflected, at the very least, a spillover of supply-side effects on the demand side. Put another way, it seems entirely reasonable to argue that whatever roles economic agents were performing in the British economy they were not necessarily conforming to the models of action held in the minds of policy-makers. This era in Britain's economic history was not entirely performed by a class of entrepreneurs-of-the-self; policy-makers had misidentified the population to be something that it was not. Thus Lawson was wrong to think the late 1980s boom was a one-off psychological adjustment to freedom; and it would be very difficult to argue that the policy practitioners of the New Labour regime were doing anything other than practising an imagined figure of the consumer as previously practised by the Thatcherites in the 1980s.

That said, there are a myriad of factors behind the recent global financial crisis. The IEA, for instance, in its publication *Verdict on the Crash* (2009), provides a long list of various causes. According to these authors the necessary conditions for systemic collapse included flawed risk-modelling techniques associated with untested financial innovations, the remuneration structure of bankers that incentivized short-term revenue growth, international banking regulations that allowed banks to set their own risk weighting, the regulation of capital rather than reserves, the 'capture' by investment banks of credit rating agencies and regulators, and mark-to-market (and 'to model') accounting principles.

However, the underlying theme of the IEA's volume reiterates the general neoliberal response to the crisis that government is to blame and not bankers. First, in the context of the United States, it is argued that governments, by proselytizing home ownership, distorted the credit system, and forced banks to behave and lend in ways they would otherwise not have done. This response is discussed in detail in the next chapter, in relation to sub-prime lending and the politics of home ownership. Second, it is argued that central banks left interest rates far too low for too long in the early 2000s, creating excess money that led to a housing bubble on both sides of the Atlantic. For instance, in her essay in the IEA volume on the crisis, Anna Schwartz (co-author with Friedman of *A Monetary History of the United States, 1867–1960*) argued that by waiting until 2004 to raise interest rates the Federal Reserve made monetary policy far too accommodating. As she says, 'Greenspan claimed there was nothing he could do about … [the housing market bubble] … But there was no explanation as to why they could not have run a less expansive policy.'[67]

Both Greenspan and his successor Ben Bernanke, who took over the role of Chairman of the Federal Reserve in 2006, have, not surprisingly, disputed this account. Greenspan has argued that as the most popular mortgages in the United States are thirty-year term fixed interest rate mortgages, they are more sensitive to interest rates set in markets for longer dated bonds, whereas the Federal Reserve's policy rates only affect interest rates in very short-term money markets.[68] All the same, variable rate or adjustable rate mortgages became much more popular during the boom in the US,[69] and these mortgages would have been much more sensitive to the exceptionally low interest rates set by the Federal Reserve. In response to this argument, Bernanke has cited econometric studies undertaken by the Federal Reserve that purport to show that higher interest rates would only have had a small effect on payments made on adjustable rate mortgages. Ultimately, for Bernanke, regardless of monetary policy, 'both lenders and borrowers became convinced that house prices would only go up.'[70] In such a circumstance and following this line of argument, there was little that the Federal Reserve could do: as Greenspan has said, 'there are no examples, to my knowledge, of a successful incremental defusing of a bubble that left prosperity intact.'[71]

Even so, it is becoming increasingly part of conventional wisdom to attribute part of the blame for the crisis on the monetary policy of central banks such as the Federal Reserve and the Bank of England.[72] Indeed in pointing to Greenspan's unwillingness to raise interest rates, authors such as Anna Schwartz and Lawrence White (a prominent Hayekian in the United States) are alluding to the same asymmetry (acting to limit the fall in asset prices, doing nothing to limit increasing asset prices) in monetary policy that has been discussed in this chapter. Nonetheless the account presented here has focused on explaining why there has been this asymmetry and why monetary authorities around the world were unable to recognize a bubble for what it was, a giant and unstable pyramid scheme fuelled by credit. Certainly policies, such as the sale of local government housing into private ownership in the 1980s, do suggest that the British government has actively marketed the notion of home ownership. Yet, at the same time, and critically, it was house price rises and the availability of credit in Britain in the 2000s that incentivized people to opt in to ownership for fear of missing out on the gains.

The financial system was changed in Britain in the 1980s so as to allow consumer demand for borrowing to be met. Huge demand for borrowing was taken by government as a sign that populations had chosen to identify themselves as consumers, aspirational, adaptable and aligned to the mental habits of the enterprise culture. These signs were misidentified. The explanation for this is not necessarily that an ideology was 'thrust' upon the population, as Schwartz and White and many others have argued (see Chapter 7), but that government and monetary authorities practised a form of human agency that was taken, without question, to be representative of human behaviour in society at large. Government disbarred itself from acting to curtail the rise of indebtedness in the population.

However to reiterate, the fact that the financial crisis has far surpassed in severity any of the systemic issues raised by the boom and bust of the late 1980s gives proof to the fact that there was a unique intensity and complexity to this credit boom. While banking practices such as inter-bank lending and securitization enabled borrowers' demands for credit to be met, it is also clear that this credit boom was writ large across society and societies everywhere; credit was being used to open new asset positions, from Asian exporters using dollar revenues to buy United States government debt (Ben Bernanke's 'savings glut'[73]) to a search for yield that led trillions of dollars to be invested in geared bets on corporate solvency (credit derivative swaps). New credit relations were infused into almost any gap available, leaving the financial system as a whole and its human agents vulnerable to sudden reverses brought about by an absence of new credit-money to support the already existing positions and assets prices that the previously created credit-money opened up in the first place. Governments were not capable of recognizing behaviour as problematic, whatever the form of the wealth-owning unit, whether consumer, entrepreneur, business or investment bank.

All credit bubbles share common features: new ways to create credit-money that boost market prices allied to a belief that this time things are different, that valuations really do reflect reality. Likewise when the bubble bursts, sections of society are invariably singled out for supposedly being inherently greedier than everyone else. However what gives recent history a certain rarefaction is the extent to which the vast majority of the population owned assets that were incorporated into the boom. The excesses of leverage, the expansion of balance sheets was not limited to City of London coffee houses or to isolated developments in local markets, or even to those who chose to invest their savings in stock markets. The point is that so much was financed by credit for so many. However, debt having become a central experience and component of economic life does not of course mean all human agents have become entrepreneurs (of whatever sort) or that a new classless society of portfolio managers has come into existence. Indeed, what has proved so dangerous about the neoliberal governing mentality has been its inability to recognize the need to act to reverse the rise of indebtedness. Neoliberal government thought that it had been successful in changing habits of thought: the danger lay in thinking that it had been the agent of change; that the political programme had succeeded and that its vision had been realized.

This is why Foucault considered government to be dangerous.[74] So often government fails to realize its vision of how people should conduct themselves;

actual conduct invariably fails to be aligned to the human reference points taken for granted in the vision of governing mentalities. Yet along the way, political practitioners can misidentify behaviour and come to believe that their project has been successful; that, as in this case, conduct has changed, that behaviour has been aligned to that which is deemed both appropriate to the times and fundamentally 'rational'. This does not mean that government is inherently wicked or bad; that it should 'give up'. This book is not intended to add yet another voice to the list of those that Foucault believed suffered from 'state phobia'.[75] But government must be careful and critically aware of its presuppositions; it must permanently unpack the reference points upon which it has come to rely.

Such is the task of genealogy itself, the task, that Foucault believed, updated the Enlightenment, reformatting Kant's challenge 'dare to know' for the current times. Foucault's challenge, one might say, is not to find out what it is possible to know, the conditions of possibility of knowing anything so as to launch a challenge on received wisdom and authority. Instead one must launch a permanent critique of man's relation to the present, man's historical being and constitution of the self as an autonomous subject.[76] Perhaps it is too much to ask government to do this, especially given that government itself is a key player in the constitution and practice of historicized being. Yet this is in a sense what political rationalities do, at least in part, as they problematize other mentalities of rule, before they become too rigid and dogmatic. Indeed to some degree this is exactly what Hayek was doing when he argued that a political rationality (progressive liberalism) was undoing much that had come into existence spontaneously, without the rational reflection and subsequent planning of governments.

However mentalities of rule cannot help themselves but problematize from a vantage point, from their own reference points and, writers such as Hayek and Friedman, neoliberals at the IEA and CPS, and neoliberals in governments after 1979 persistently practised their vantage point, that of the human agent as an enterprising consumer. When Foucault problematized, revolutionizing the writing of history,[77] he required that there be no vantage point, no vision, no reference point, perhaps even no human agent, for to have a human agent is to define a human agent. But just like other forms of knowledge claiming to know the human subject, political rationalities do the opposite; government moves from one assemblage of practices to another in no predetermined order, bringing with it new conceptions of state, society, human agency and freedom.

Liberal regimes in particular rate 'freedom' very highly, but one has to be very careful when deploying the term. If the definition of freedom becomes fixed, say around home ownership, and expectations of conduct become linked to that definition (more people become home owners), then there is always the possibility of having to ensure that people practise their freedom in a certain way. The same is of course true for progressive liberalism: one might attain a certain kind of 'freedom' because the state acts as a guarantor of economic security (say providing employment or insuring deposits) but as Keynes realized only too clearly in his preface to the German edition of *The General Theory*, a positive freedom somewhere is a negative freedom somewhere else. For, as he says 'the theory of output as a whole, which is what … [*The General Theory*] … purports to provide is much more easily adapted to the conditions of a totalitarian state.'[78] Indeed, perhaps it is a myth of liberalism generally to suggest that there is a distinction, as Isaiah Berlin drew it, between positive and negative freedom. Classical liberalism sought to produce workers fit for duty, neoliberalism seeks to produce entrepreneurs of everyone, even consumers; no longer users-up of resources but individual human agents aspiring to enhance their human capital through their consumption purchases and the permanent reorganization of their balance sheets.

That is why liberal government is an art, the best practitioners of which are aware that there is always a balancing act, that there are non-freedoms embedded in the politics of freedom. In fact one has to question the permanent compatibility of 'freedom', as always undefined, with strong visionary politics. Electorates appear to want visionary politicians as if drawn to those that display a strong sense of intent with regards to the future. Yet the allure of a strong vision of what it is that one should become is not necessarily the same as saying that populations are able to be and want to be the willing accomplices of that vision. This is where the loss of freedom can begin.

Foucault referred in his lectures in 1979 to crises of governmentality, where an art of government becomes the victim of itself, of its own political rationality. This may be due to 'an increase in the economic cost of the exercise of freedoms', for instance the cost of the welfare state or the costs associated with wealth lost due to collapsing asset markets and the defaulting of a multitude of borrowers. Alternatively a crisis might arise 'due to the inflation of the compensatory mechanisms of freedom',[79] for instance anti-monopoly legislation and the expansion of property rights can create a litigious straightjacket for all. Finally and most importantly for Foucault, 'there are processes of clogging such that the mechanisms for producing freedom, precisely those that are called upon to manufacture this freedom, actually produce destructive effects which prevail over the freedom they are supposed to produce'.[80]

For some the image of the consumer is liberating, the availability of credit provides the means through which possibilities are opened up and human capital is happily enhanced. Perhaps for others debt becomes burdensome, even ownership is not liberating but stressful and anxiety inducing; the requirement to borrow, invest and aspire experienced more as pressure from without than as freedom from within; the inequality that society produces experienced as a coercion to act, say to buy a house, where one would otherwise not. There are two perspectives, both of which can be compelling. Problematizing the imagined figure of the consumer must take account of both.

7 The American sub-prime homeowner consumer

This book has explored the political rationality of neoliberalism as it has been practised within a British context. Clearly, however, neoliberalism has never been just a British phenomenon. As discussed in the introduction, some of the earliest academic attempts to formalize this shared way of thinking and to address questions related to government were international in nature. Before the Second World War, in 1938, the *Colloque Walter Lippmann* brought together American, British, French and German liberals to discuss how liberalism might be re-engineered and reconceptualized in the face of a wave of Keynesian and progressive liberal economic policies. Likewise, after the war, Hayek was instrumental in bringing together a similar group of intellectuals, known as the Mont Pèlerin Society, to address the same issues. Anthony Fisher, one of the British members of this group, later founded the IEA, and its two directors, Arthur Seldon and Ralph Harris, were long-time members of Mont Pèlerin. Given that many governments were utilizing progressive economic policies in the 1930s to tackle depression and high unemployment, it is not surprising that there was an equally international flavour to those that wanted to problematize this approach to governing the economy.

Neither should it be surprising to find that many governments have responded to the perceived failures of Keynesianism by rolling out similar neoliberal programmes of government. And neither is Britain unique in experiencing a crisis of neoliberal governmentality associated with a housing boom financed by a banking system freed to find new ways to create credit-money. Many other countries and city-states, in Asia and Europe, have experienced housing booms that have followed periods of financial legislative reform. And of course it goes without saying that this is particularly relevant to countries that have a shared language, and a similar culture and history, such as Britain and the United States.

In the past twenty years or so, the term that has become central in signifying these shared supra-national changes is 'globalization'. In this context, political leaders have often presented globalization to populations as an unstoppable force that the country faces and to which they must respond by activating and realizing their enterprising potential. Tony Blair, for instance, in his 1994 speech, *Socialism*, made the case that 'old' progressive liberalism was an ideology that had become redundant largely due to major changes in the world economy.

Globalization meant increased economic interconnectedness that had brought with it an 'explosion of service industries coupled with the development of a consumer culture, where people regard themselves as economic consumers as well as producers'. In this context there was much for government to do to prepare its citizens to be competitive and entrepreneurial.[1]

In this political rhetoric, globalization is rarely referenced as a function of financial flows, created and operated by financial systems that have been deliberately and actively liberalized. Indeed Gordon Brown's assessment of the crisis is that it was the first crisis of globalization. Brown does not deny that there were many problems generated by British banks, such as Northern Rock and the Royal Bank of Scotland, yet the defining feature of the crisis was that it was global in nature and caused primarily by the interconnectedness of the global financial system. As he said, many European banks, unbeknownst to governments, had bought large portfolios of US sub-prime mortgages. For Brown, the 'storm was brewing ... [in the US] ... and was certain to come rolling across the Atlantic'.[2] Because the crisis was global in nature, a global response was required. There is no doubt that some of Brown's prescriptions are Keynesian and progressive in nature, giving credence to academic arguments that suggest that New Labour always stood ready, if needed, to activate a coarse version of Keynesianism.[3] And his message also carries with it moral indignation against the behaviour of bankers worldwide.[4] Yet there remains little recognition of an active governmental role; one which sought to foster attitudes and behaviour in the population, and which required banks to provide the necessary and sufficient credit.

Moreover, the parameters in which Brown discusses this crisis of globalization make it very difficult to differentiate this crisis from the global depression of the 1930s. Indeed, Karl Polanyi's 1944 text, *The Great Transformation*, focuses on the role of international finance in the years preceding the Great Depression, and points to how the gold standard created destabilizing financial flows across nations and specifically across the Atlantic. To differentiate this crisis from previous banking and economic crises requires that it be understood as referring to a unique political disposition: neoliberalism.

This is, of course, not to deny that financial contagion is a real phenomenon; European banks that held large portfolios of US sub-prime mortgages that had gone bad were clearly exposed to the US housing market. Alternatively, if one government faces difficulties funding its budget deficit, and interest rates start to rise, it is likely that investors will focus attention on other countries whose economies appear to be structurally similar, thus spreading a crisis from country to country. All the same, rather than being concerned with the interconnectedness of the global financial system, this chapter seeks to bring out the similarity of the neoliberal political rationality as it has been practised in relation to the consumer and household beyond Britain, specifically in the United States. The implicit point being made in this chapter is that what is global about this crisis is not globalization per se, but the rationality of neoliberalism which has been played out globally in a number of domestic contexts, and with similar results.

This chapter seeks to demonstrate this parallel application of neoliberal governmentality in the US. Just as the argument has been made that Thatcherite and New Labour governments shared ways of referencing and governing for the consumer, one can also see a shared mentality operating in aspects of economic policy in the Presidencies of Democrat, Bill Clinton and Republican, George W. Bush, from 1992 to 2000 and from 2000 to 2008 respectively. This chapter will explore the language of policy as it related to questions regarding consumers, housing and credit. And in a parallel fashion to the previous two chapters, speeches from key figures at the central bank (the US Federal Reserve) can be used to address the question as to how the property boom in the 2000s was (mis) identified. As in the case of Britain, the question needs to be asked as to why nothing was done to slow the rise of indebtedness in recent years leading up to the collapse of the housing market and the ensuing financial crisis.

However, this chapter also addresses, in the US context, the question of how the crisis has been interpreted: what or who is being problematized among academics, think tanks and politicians alike? Specifically, the US housing market is differently structured to Britain; a far greater and more explicit role has been taken by government institutions and government-sponsored enterprises in the housing market, going back to Roosevelt's New Deal of the 1930s. As a result, government has become that much more directly implicated in the crisis and there has been much more open debate in which neoliberals/libertarians have blamed the crisis on, what they see as, overtly progressive liberal policies. In this chapter, some of these responses are explored. In turn this will lead on to an exploration of some of the more radical ideas of Hayek and Friedman, as they grappled with problems of what they may have considered to be an always unfinished neoliberal project. Rather than problematizing the consumer, the issue for some neoliberals is that government failed in its task of constructing a monetary system that would foster and ultimately ensure rational action in everyone.

7.1 The politics of home ownership

Throughout this book care has been taken to put the right emphasis on how Thatcherism promulgated the vision of the property-owning democracy. While there was an explicit effort made to raise home ownership in the 1980s with the mass sale of public-owned 'council housing', much of the focus of policy was on creating a financial system able to meet the needs of borrowers who, it was believed, wished to get credit for a variety of purposes, including buying a home or investing in a buy-to-let house. It was taken for granted that if credit could be made available for consumers and households then it would follow, naturally, that the population would take up the chance to borrow. For governments, this was precisely what one should expect from a population of enterprising consumers building personal balance sheets. That rising prices were incentivizing many to buy into the housing market, which ultimately turned out to be a giant pyramid scheme, did not form a part of governmental discourse.

In contrast, in the US the political project to raise the levels of home ownership, certainly from the early 1990s on, was always that much more explicit. One could go as far as saying that by the early 2000s, and the Presidency of George W. Bush, home ownership had become a, if not the, central goal of domestic economic policy. Bush's policy document, *A Home of your own: expanding opportunities for all Americans*, published in June 2002, proudly announced that, 'the Administration is committed to ensuring that home ownership opportunities are available to all Americans and to policies that will help more families open the doors of home ownership.'[5] Speaking at a conference convened at the White House in October 2002 on the topic of minority home ownership, Bush was very clear when he said, 'you see, we want everybody in America to own their own home.'[6]

In a sense, one should not be surprised by the directness of Bush's language, for in the American national rhetoric there has been a long history of conflating the promise of the new world and the 'American dream' with having a safe and secure home. Indeed, Bush regularly linked his own policies on home ownership to this concept: 'the American Dream starts with owning a home'.[7] As far back as 1918 there had been national campaigns extolling the virtues of home ownership. The 'Own Your Own Home' campaign, for instance, was launched in 1918 by a network of industry groups and the Department of Labour. The government's objective in this campaign was to defeat radical protest by encouraging urban workers to become homeowners. Then, in the 1930s, first President Hoover and then President Roosevelt addressed the homeowner issue; Hoover by establishing the Federal Home Loan Bank System (1932), and Roosevelt by establishing the Federal Housing Administration or FHA in 1934 and the Federal National Mortgage Association or Fannie Mae in 1938. The FHA was set up as a mutual mortgage insurance system; Fannie Mae was set up to buy FHA-insured mortgages, thus increasing the availability of funding in the mortgage market. Thus, policies aimed at increasing funding for mortgages were a key element in raising the level of home ownership to 61 per cent in 1960 from 40 per cent two decades earlier.[8] Correspondingly in Britain, home ownership after 1945 was roughly 40 per cent.[9] It had risen to 49 per cent in 1971/2, and in 1998/9 it stood at 69 per cent, with the vast majority of this increase occurring in the 1980s.[10]

In the late 1960s in the US, however, there was increasing concern about the reliance that Savings and Loan (S&L) institutions (the equivalent of British building societies) were placing on deposits as a source of funding. As a result, in 1968 Fannie Mae was turned into a privately owned government-sponsored enterprise (GSE), and another GSE, the Federal Home Loan Mortgage Corporation, or Freddie Mac, was created in 1970.[11] Both GSEs were allowed to buy S&L mortgages (that conformed to certain prudential standards of underwriting, including size limits and loan-to-value ratios of around 80 per cent), pool them together and sell them off to investors (a process known as securitization). Throughout the 1970s, both Fannie and Freddie developed a range of mortgage-backed securities.[12] Since 1980, the outstanding amount of these securities has risen from $200 billion to $4 trillion. Additionally, in the 1970s, a private market in mortgage-backed securities developed for 'non-conforming' mortgages. This market in private label securities was very small in comparison to Fannie and Freddie issuances until the late 1990s. However, as of August 2007, just before the onset of crisis, the private label market accounted for around $2 trillion in residential mortgage debt. In aggregate, 56 per cent of the home mortgage market is now securitized, compared with only 10 per cent in 1980 and less than 1 per cent in 1970.[13]

Even with Fannie and Freddie competing to buy, securitize and sell off conforming mortgages, by the late 1970s concern was rising about the inability of S&Ls, limited by 'Regulation Q' in the deposit rates they could offer, to compete with newly developing money market mutual funds. Like Thatcher, President Reagan supported legislation in the early 1980s to make the banking system more competitive. The Garn-St Germain Depository Institutions Act of 1982, for instance, allowed the S&Ls to compete with money market funds for deposits by offering higher deposit rates. For Reagan this Act was 'pro-consumer, granting small savers greater access to loans ... [and] ... a higher return on their savings'.[14] Moreover, Reagan made explicit the link to home ownership:

> What this legislation does is expand the powers of thrift institutions by permitting the industry to make commercial loans and increase their consumer lending.... This is turn will make the thrift industry a stronger, more effective force in financing housing for millions of Americans in the years to come.[15]

The US, like Britain, experienced a financial crisis primarily related to consumer banking in the late 1980s and early 1990s. By phasing out interest-rate ceilings in 1980 and by passing the 1982 Act the scene was set for the Savings and Loan crisis of the late 1980s. While the house market boomed in the mid 1980s, by 1994 over 1,600 banks had failed as a result of the margin between lending and deposit interest rates being squeezed and because of falling house prices in many regional property markets. All of which could be directly linked to Garn-St Germain, as it had removed statutory restrictions on property lending and relaxed loan limits to single borrowers.[16] The Act had enabled a rapid increase in lending and overbuilding; essentially a boom and bust that mirrored what was going on in Britain at the same time.

The experience of the 1980s however did not diminish the role that home ownership was to play in US politics; if anything quite the reverse. Within the first two years of his administration, Bill Clinton had announced a series of measures designed specifically to address what he considered to be a key failing of economy policy in the 1980s, the 'dramatic' decline in home ownership: as he said, 'in 1980 more than 70 per cent of our children lived in homes owned by families. In 1991, that had fallen to less than 63 per cent.' This, he went on to say, had to be turned around: 'we have to move this measure of our national prosperity forward.'[17] Clinton's administration thus enacted a series of measures all aimed at increasing home ownership. In 1993, the GSEs, Fannie and Freddie, were set new targets for facilitating credit access and home ownership among lower-income and minority households; a higher proportion of their mortgage guarantee business had to be directed to these households.[18] Targets were increased substantially in 1997, 2001 and in 2005, such that low and moderate income households were to account for 30 per cent of Fannie and Freddie's business in 1993 and 55 per cent in 2007. In turn this required the GSEs to lower their underwriting criteria and guarantee riskier loans.[19]

To complement these targets, Clinton introduced, in 1994, his National Homeownership Strategy with the specific target of raising the number of owner-occupiers by eight million to 67.5 per cent by the year 2000.[20] (In fact in one of his last radio addresses as President in December 2000, Clinton spoke proudly of how he had given 'nearly ten million more families the opportunity to own their own homes', raising home ownership to 68 per cent).[21] According to a 1995 report by the US Department of Housing and Urban Development (HUD), this policy was to be achieved by 'drawing on the resources and creativity of' among others 'lenders, builders, real estate professionals, community-based non-profit organizations, consumer groups, state and local governments and housing finance agencies'. Among the many policies were measures that would lower housing production costs, make finance more available, affordable and flexible, raise awareness of home ownership opportunities and provide home ownership education and counselling.[22]

There can be little doubt then about Clinton's desire to increase home ownership, and he did much during his Presidency in the name of that goal. Even so, for the purposes of this chapter, the key question is, why was this so important? What was the rationality for these policy actions? In Clinton's own words there were reasons that were 'economic and tangible, and reasons that are emotional and intangible, but go to the heart of what it means to harbour, to expand the American Dream'.[23]

For Clinton, the economic argument was fairly straightforward:

> Homeownership encourages savings and investment. When a family buys a home the ripple effect is enormous. It means new homeowner consumers. They need more durable goods, like washers and dryers, refrigerators and water heaters. And if more families could buy new homes and older homes, more hammers will be pounding, more saws will be buzzing. Homebuilders and home fixers will be put to work.[24]

At the same time, these investments being made by homeowner consumers would provide 'some permanence and stability' while they were dealing 'with all the changing forces ... in this global economy'. In the global economy, according to Clinton, there could be no guarantee of a job; instead through facilitating increased home ownership, the government aimed to 'guarantee to people that we're going to empower them to help themselves'. Thus a link was forged between the economic and intangible argument: 'when we boost the number of homeowners in our country, we strengthen the economy, create jobs, build up the middle class and build better citizens.'[25]

This was Clinton's political vision for the citizenship of the US. It was a vision in which all people in America could share in the same benefits and opportunities that home ownership could provide: essentially a vision in which there was only one class, the home owning class. And to this extent, Clinton was very clear that this policy should break down barriers for 'undeserved populations ... [and] ... tear down the barriers of discrimination wherever they are found'. Everyone should be able to share in the benefits that would come from the realization of the vision.[26]

> The biggest untapped market in America for many of us are the millions and millions of people that the economy of the 1980s left behind – people who live in cities, people who live in our isolated rural areas; people with productive capacities who, if they can become consumers, can explode the American economic growth rate well into the next century.[27]

To spread this vision there would have to be 'new strategies for educating those who haven't considered becoming homeowners' and government would have to do a better job of 'reaching the underserved; of eradicating discriminatory practices that prevent "minorities" from finding, financing and buying a home of their choice'.[28]

So it was a message about enabling people to fulfil their own personal (American) dreams, that it could be assumed were ever present and prevalent. At the same time there was much for government to do to educate and foster the appropriate desires for home ownership: especially guiding the conduct of those that had hitherto been excluded from these opportunities. Finally, the very act of buying a home and taking a stake in property could have transformative effects on those becoming home owners for the first time, essential to continued national economic success. The programme was aimed at 'building better citizens'[29] by empowering them and providing them with the appropriate levels of aspiration and self-esteem: both of which were seen as critical ingredients in success.

> The idea of having your own home is the ultimate expression of optimism. Homes are for families. They make a more secure environment for your children. They create pride and self-esteem. They are an extension of personality, our hopes and dreams.[30]

This was, according to Clinton, precisely what government should be doing. Rather than directly intervening in the economy, say through fiscal policy, the government should be establishing the conditions in which it could be assumed that the population were acting appropriately for the benefit of all. Speaking in 1994, Clinton linked home ownership directly to his vision of government.

> The truth is, in my opinion, as we move toward the 21st century government should be seen as an instrument that seeks to create opportunity in the private sector. It seeks to empower people, and then challenges people to

> assume both individual and community responsibility, because that's where most of the action is in America today.[31]

And this was a consistent message throughout his Presidency. Speaking in 1998, Clinton spoke in similar terms about government.

> You know, when we came ... [to Washington, DC] ... we had a philosophy of government that we thought was appropriate to the 1990s and beyond. We wanted to get beyond what I thought was a completely sterile debate in Washington about whether government could solve all the problems or government was the source of all the problems. We thought our job was to empower people, to be a catalyst, to be a partner, to give people the tools to solve their own problems and make the most of their own lives and build strong personal lives, strong families, strong neighborhoods, strong communities.[32]

In many respects, then, Clinton's vision of government was the perfect statement of the neoliberal political rationality. Government had a job to do which was to guide conduct in ways that were deemed to be both beneficial to the individual and to the economy and to the community. Government would both respond to the aspirations of those they were governing and foster aspirations in others essential to their well-being. Thus to Tony Blair, Clinton was a 'new Democrat', a modernizer like him who shared a 'third-way philosophy' that attempted to 'liberate' old progressive politics from its 'outdated ideology'. In the process this would 'reform the role of government and the state', creating a 'modern relationship between the responsibilities of the citizen and those of society'.[33]

Nonetheless, while to Clinton and Blair this was a new style of politics, much of its language, as shown in the previous chapter, was shared in Britain by Thatcherites in the New Right, who equally wanted to transform the relationship between the government and the governed. This does not mean that there is a perfect overlap between all the policies of Thatcher, Blair, and for that matter Clinton, only that there was a vision of the citizen-consumer shared by these politicians on both sides of the Atlantic which necessitated similar practices and approaches to governing for the consumer and thus governing the economy. Throughout this book these practices have been labelled neoliberal. And while in the British case, a course has been charted from 'Right' to 'Left', from Thatcherism to New Labour, this chapter takes an opposite direction: from 'Left' to 'Right'. That is to say, whether Clinton or Bush, there is an almost identical discourse in relation to the consumer, home ownership and the economy.

Indeed, as has already been noted, a central part of Bush's economic policy was dedicated to raising levels of home ownership. On the one hand, this meant ensuring the supply of affordable housing; one of Bush's goals was that by 2010 there would be seven million more affordable homes. On the other hand, Bush was determined to close what he considered to be the an 'ownership gap' in which 'too many minorities do not own a home'. And just as with Clinton before him, this policy was couched in the rhetoric of the American dream; 'owning a home is part of that dream, it just is. Right here in America if you own your own home, you're realizing the American Dream.'[34]

Bush's policy document, *A home of your own: expanding opportunities for all Americans*, published in June 2002, made 'minorities' and new immigrants the central target, by announcing that before the end of 2010, there should be 5.5 million more minority homeowners. Even though home ownership was already at historic high levels (68 per cent), statistics showed that there was a persistent gap that Bush wanted to close. Census data from 2002 showed that non-Hispanic whites had a 74.3 per cent home ownership rate, while African-Americans had a 48 per cent rate and Hispanics a 47.6 per cent rate.[35]

In response, Bush offered a number of new proposals. The *home of your own* programme would include 'downpayment assistance' to help families that could not afford the deposit on a house; tax credits would increase the supply of affordable homes; there would be increasing support for self-help home ownership programmes, such as Habitat for Humanity; and the home buying process would be simplified and refashioned to include increased education and counselling for those wanting to buy a house for the first time. This would involve establishing multilingual, consumer-oriented web sites to help 'minorities' overcome barriers to home ownership. At the same time, Bush wanted to see the lending industry responding to these new opportunities, finding new ways to meet the borrowing needs of potential buyers. The policy document laid down the challenge to lenders to develop new mortgage products so that conventional market alternatives would be available for 'minorities'. Finally, Fannie Mae and Freddie Mac were to be asked to increase their efforts as 'they lag behind private lenders in this regard'.[36] Thus during the Bush presidency Fannie and Freddie's targets for minority and low-income groups were raised three times. By 2007 these targets were almost twice the level originally set by Clinton in 1993.[37] And in 2004, Bush committed the Federal Housing Association to insuring mortgages on which there was no deposit paid at all.[38] (Whether the GSEs were 'successful' in meeting these targets is another matter, discussed in Section 7.2.)

It would be difficult to see Bush's policies as anything other than a continuation of Clinton era policies on home ownership. Indeed, the rhetoric used by Bush to explain their rationale strikes a very similar tone. Just as with Clinton, this policy reflected 'a chance for … [government] … to empower people … so they have got choices over their lives'. It would also be good for the economy: 'the idea of encouraging new home ownership and the money that will be circulated as a result of people purchasing homes will mean people are more likely to find a job in America.'[39]

More than anything else, however, this was a project not only with the economic good in mind but which was also considered 'good for the soul of the country'. Owning a home was what defined the right kind of attitude; home ownership signified it and at the same time fostered these right kinds of attitudes in those that were choosing to become owners.

> All of us here in America should believe, and I think we do, that we should be, as I mentioned, a nation of owners. Owning something is freedom, as far as I'm concerned. It's part of a free society. And ownership of a home helps bring stability to neighborhoods. You own your home in a neighborhood, you have more interest in how your neighborhood feels, looks, whether it's safe or not. It brings pride to people, it's a part of an asset-based society. It helps people build up their own individual portfolio, provides an opportunity, if need be, for a mom or a dad to leave something to their child. It's … an important part of America.[40]

Here again, as with the case of Britain, was to be found the same political rationality that perceived the human agents of the economy to be represented by their balance sheets and in the choices made in assembling individual portfolios of assets. Extending home ownership meant improving the stock of the population, fostering better attitudes and an increased association with the virtues of American life. It meant enabling and encouraging people to be a part of the American dream so that they could have a 'vital stake in the future of the country', precisely because they were now an owner. For Bush the 'great dream about America is, I can own my own home … or I can own my own business'.[41] The habits of thought associated with these two kinds of ownership were necessarily deemed, in this mentality of rule, to produce the same kind of rationality.

Of course there are many explanations that can be provided for both Clinton and Bush's politics of home ownership. There were many different vested interests associated with these policies including banks and other financial institutions, construction companies and estate agents (realtors), all of which were poised to reap significant financial benefits. Also, wanting people to take a stake in the American dream could equally be interpreted as a politician looking to increase their voter base. Indeed, this is particularly true when one considers that Bush was targeting minority home ownership, a group that historically has tended to favour Democrats in elections.

No doubt these explanations are valid; but neither do they necessarily contradict or exclude the explanation that has been provided here. For it is important to remember that Bush's vision was not his alone, it was shared by Clinton and by politicians and thinkers in Britain and America spanning over fifty years. Perhaps instead one might therefore interpret the focus on 'minorities' and immigrants in the same way that Thatcherites focused on local government-owned housing estates and unionized workers in their communities. These were the elements in society and in the economy that were deemed in most need of directing. Low home ownership was itself taken as a sign of unenterprising and, in the US, un-American habits of thought. Home ownership was a policy that could, in the minds of government, Americanize America, a country in which the proportion of 'minorities', especially Hispanics, and immigrants was increasing. For Clinton and Bush, one can venture that this was a battle for, what they perceived to be, the soul of the country.

7.2 Financial innovation, debt and home ownership

The premise of this chapter is that Britain was not alone in practising a neoliberal political rationality; the same kinds of ideas about the human agent and the consumer have been played out in America, specifically in relation to the politics of home ownership in the Clinton and Bush administrations. And like the UK, the US has also experienced a financial and economic crisis emanating from the expansion of home lending and the bursting of a property bubble (see Figure 7.1). Indeed, such was the scale of the financial boom and bust in the US, given the size the economy, that it has almost overshadowed the fact that many countries, such as the UK, have faced parallel problems. However one apportions blame for the financial crisis, the answers are not to be found in blaming contagion, but instead are located in the structure of domestic financial systems and in governmental oversight of those financial systems.

All the same it is important to be clear about the role of government in the politics of ownership. While some of the policies focused on setting higher targets for Fannie and Freddie, requiring them to buy, pool, securitize and insure increased amounts of mortgages for 'minorities' and low-income households, there is no indication that the GSEs were actually meeting these targets. Indeed, according to Ben Bernanke, targets were raised in 2004 precisely because a study conducted by the Department of Housing and Urban Development and submitted to Congress found that Fannie and Freddie were failing to meet them.[42] On the contrary, much of the 'success' in raising home ownership was attributed to financial innovation, and the ability of the unregulated 'shadow' banking system to respond appropriately to the needs of borrowers. Specifically, through a complex chain of securitization and debt, arranged and operated by mortgage originators, special purpose vehicles and investment banks, private label mortgages were being financed, at least in part, by retail savings held in money market mutual funds.[43] And in a parallel fashion to the members of the monetary policy committee at the Bank of England, Governors at the Federal

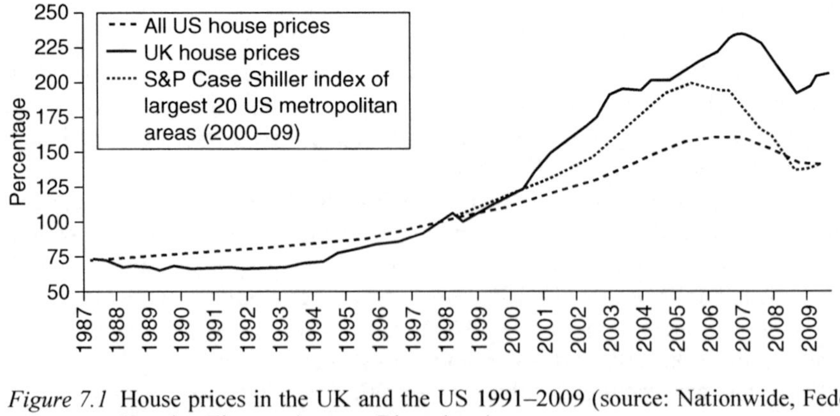

Figure 7.1 House prices in the UK and the US 1991–2009 (source: Nationwide, Federal Housing Finance Agency, Bloomberg).

Reserve rationalized the rising housing market and the associated financial mechanisms that funded it, without sufficiently problematizing rising indebtedness or growing wealth inequality.

There can be little doubt that the Federal Reserve was entirely supportive of the politics of home ownership; and that these opinions were built upon the conception of the homeowner consumer as a wealth-owning unit constructing a balance sheet of assets, using debt wherever appropriate. From 2000 through to 2006, governors were extolling the virtues of home ownership and arguing against those that worried about a housing boom and rising indebtedness. The two governors in this period responsible for 'consumer and community affairs', Edward Gramlich and Mark Olson, both openly supported the political rationality of Bush and Clinton. Gramlich, for instance, speaking in November 2001, argued that:

> Home ownership has significant social and economic implications for all of us and ranks high on our list of personal and national priorities.... Home ownership is often characterised as the 'American Dream'.... For a family, a home is generally its most significant asset and serves as its primary wealth-building vehicle.[44]

For Gramlich, by 2001, 'great progress had been made' with ownership reaching new highs every year since 1995. Success in raising home ownership rates among black and Hispanic households was particularly to be welcomed.[45] Likewise for Olson, home ownership was one form of ownership, along with investment in education (the consumption of human capital) or in a small business that constitute 'the most important components of economic and social success'. It was the most tried-and-true path to wealth accumulation and it could be 'a transforming experience for individuals and families'. Either way, for Olson, 'immigrants instinctively understand that America is an ownership society and, in fact, come here in search of the ownership opportunities that increase the well-being of family members'.[46] It was therefore to be celebrated that there was a way that these immigrants, often without complete credit histories, were able to get mortgages.

Mortgages made predominantly by the private sector shadow banking system were known as sub-prime mortgages; that is mortgages that did not conform to the standards that would enable them to be pooled and securitized by Fannie and Freddie. Some instances of sub-prime lending were simply loans that were larger than the GSEs' limits; these were called jumbo loans. In most cases, however, they did not conform to important underwriting standards that had been established for the GSEs. (Not surprisingly, delinquencies on GSE conforming loans have been much lower than in the private label sub-prime sector. In 2008, for instance, the respective average delinquency rates for non-GSE and GSE loans were 28.3 per cent and 6.2 per cent respectively[47].) The mortgages that ended up in private label mortgage-backed securities (and often then in even more risky collateralized debt obligations) were granted with far smaller down payments and often with far less documentation. While GSE conforming loan-to-value standards were relaxed, from 80 per cent in 2001 to 88 per cent in 2006, the percentage of 100 per cent mortgages (i.e. no down payment required) increased from 5 per cent of mortgages in 2001 to a third of all mortgages in 2006.[48] On the one hand, the relaxation of standards was something that Bush identified as being a necessary part of his 'a home of your own' initiative; he viewed, for instance, a 3 per cent down payment on a Federal Housing Association mortgage as a potential stumbling block to ownership and an unnecessary limit.[49] On the other hand, this was part of deregulation: Bush was not forcing a relaxation of underwriting standards on private mortgage originators and their funding sources. He wanted consumers to borrow, for home ownership to rise, and he wanted the financial system to be able to respond to those demands for borrowing. With this, of course, came the expectation that banks would be acting in their best interests and that this rational and rationalizing project would ensure its own success.

To this extent, the Federal Reserve drew a very clear distinction between sub-prime and predatory lending. To Gramlich, there was a 'vast difference between the two'. As he said, 'it is important that the distinction between the generally beneficial sub-prime market and destructive predatory lending be kept clear.' Gramlich recognized that much of the increased lending to 'minorities' was related to the sub-prime sector, but abusive lending practices, he believed, were relatively limited. Such destructive practices involved deliberate attempts to conceal the true nature of the loan, inducing a borrower to refinance a loan repeatedly, and making unaffordable loans based on the assets of the borrower rather than on the borrower's ability to repay the loan.[50] Gramlich was generally happy that the 1994 Home Ownership and Protection Act was enough to ensure that high-cost usurious loans were not being made. These he defined as a mortgage with an interest rate 10 per cent above Treasury bonds of similar term maturity and where fees exceeded 8 per cent of the value of the loan.[51]

In the view of the Federal Reserve, the key defence against predatory lending would always be consumer education rather than imposing too many restrictions on the market. As Olsen put it, 'constricting the market by pinpointing what might be considered predatory lending and returning to a situation where some borrowers have limited access to credit is not an ideal situation.'[52] This would undo the work that had been done by an assemblage of financial institutions, government agencies, secondary market institutions, community-based organizations and home ownership and credit counselling services to 'create eligible borrowers'.[53] What was really required to solve the predatory lending problem was increased consumer education. In Gramlich's view:

> We should all recognize that the best defence against predatory lending is a thorough knowledge on the part of the consumers of their credit options and resources. Educated borrowers who understand their rights under lending contracts and know how to exercise those rights can thwart predatory practices.[54]

While the Federal Reserve was not overly concerned with issues regarding predatory lending, neither were they necessarily concerned with rising indebtedness and gearing in the banking system. Speaking in 2000, Alan Greenspan made comments that were often repeated until his retirement and replacement by Ben Bernanke as Chairman of the Board of Governors in 2006; 'the final decades of the twentieth century witnessed remarkable advances in financial engineering, financial innovation, and deregulation.' This new innovation, he said, allows 'risks to be separated and reallocated to the parties most willing and able to bear them'.[55] On the other side of the coin, technologies related to assessing the individual creditworthiness of individual borrowers had, according to Greenspan 'enabled lenders to reach out to households with previously unrecognized borrowing capacities'.[56] Speaking in 2003, Bernanke made the same point: 'although some legitimate concerns have been raised about lending abuses ... overall the expansion of the sub-prime market is a positive development, opening as it does new opportunities for borrowers previously excluded from credit markets.'[57]

The politics of home ownership had increased the available stock of homeowner consumers who could be trusted to use debt as an effective means of managing their personal balance sheets. This does not mean that the Federal Reserve were unaware of concerns being raised about household and consumer indebtedness and the fall in savings rates (see Figures 7.2 and 7.3), only that, just like with the Bank of England, changes in borrowing patterns could be explained as rational and enterprising if one referenced the consumer and household balance sheet. Speaking in 2003 in a speech entitled *Balance sheets and the recovery*, Bernanke specifically addressed both the balance sheets of businesses and households as a way to measure the health of the US economy and to ask whether 'consumers ... [were] ... overburdened, financially speaking'. His answer was that they were not. On the one hand, there was, he believed, little evidence of a serious systematic overvaluation of the residential housing market. On the other hand, the large increase in mortgage debt could be explained by 'one very positive factor ... [the] ... secular increase in home ownership rates'. Much of the new mortgage debt was also due to refinancing of existing mortgages, which roughly 10 per cent of households, according to Bernanke, had done in the 18 months from the beginning of 2001, to take advantage of lower interest rates. He believed that mortgage equity withdrawal had added to consumer spending, but that a substantial portion of this new finance had been used to pay off far more expensive consumer credit.[58] In conclusion he argued that:

> Much of apparent recent increase in the household sector's debt burden reflects a combination of increased home ownership, partial liquidation of the home equity of long-tenure households, and balance-sheet restructuring by households towards a more tax-efficient and collateralized form of debt, that is, mortgage debt.[59]

In this perspective, household balance sheets were changing entirely as should be expected, given the increased availability of mortgage finance. And this was

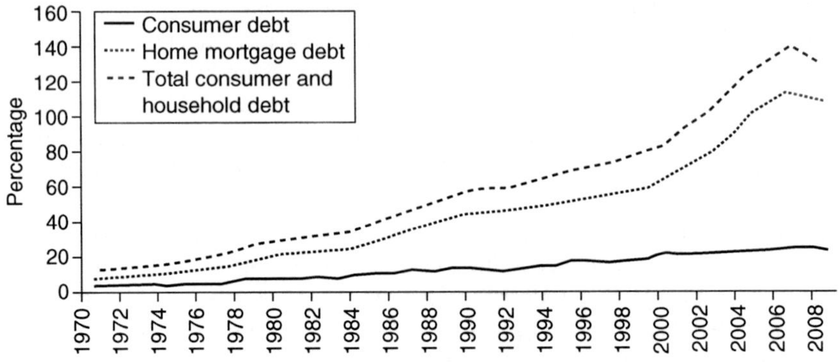

Figure 7.2 US household debt as a percentage of household disposable income, by composition 1970–2009 (source: OECD, Federal Reserve, US Census Bureau).

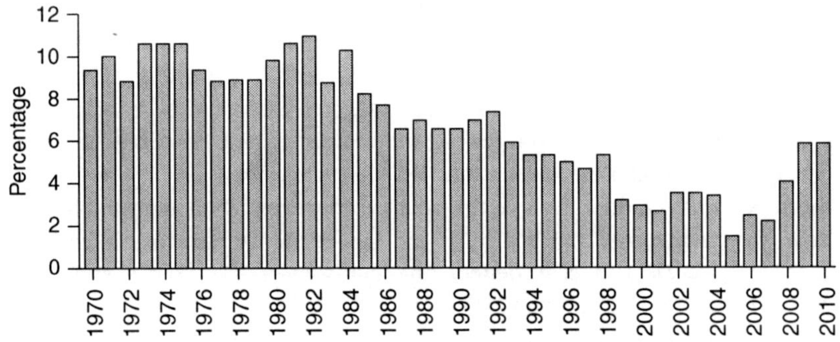

Figure 7.3 US personal savings as a percentage of income 1970–2010 (source: US Bureau of Economic Analysis).

precisely the same narrative used by Greenspan in a number of speeches between 2003 and 2005. In March 2003, for instance, Greenspan directly addressed concerns that there was an emerging housing bubble by arguing that there was little indication of such things. Moreover, he suggested that the increase in home equity extraction to directly finance the purchase of goods and services was generally a positive sign, once one considered the benefits of being able to manage the household balance sheet over one's lifetime, rather than being entirely dependent on current income.[60] In his own words:

> There can be little doubt that the availability of ready sources of home equity has reduced the costs and uncertainties associated with income volatility, retirement, unexpected medical bills and a host of other life events that can unexpectedly draw down savings. Home equity extraction may be

the household sector's realization of the benefit of a rapidly evolving financial intermediation system.[61]

Greenspan used a similar line of reasoning in September 2005 to discuss both the fall in savings rates among US households and consumers and the rise in home equity extraction. He proposed two explanations for the phenomenon. On the one hand, the fall in personal savings rates could be explained as a direct consequence of financing consumption by mortgage equity withdrawal, or 'cashing-out'. This approach could suggest overspending and would view income and spending patterns in a simplistic, Keynesian pattern, giving no account of the long-term balance sheet decisions being made. On the other hand, there was the Friedman-style approach, in which it could be assumed that 'the decline in the saving rate over the past decade could be explained by the decline in interest rates and by the increase in overall household wealth', both housing and non-housing wealth.[62] In this view spending and saving was a function of wealth (i.e. the balance sheet which existed through time) and was not the function of income received in the present.

This same line of reasoning could also be used as a way to analyse the problem of rising household debt as a percentage of household income, which had risen to 120 per cent by October 2004. Speaking at the time, Greenspan accepted that some of the concerns could not be readily dismissed. At the same time though, he argued that this was part of a long-term fifty-year trend, and that this did not imply as much stress to households as some were conjecturing. After all, as he said, there had been an increase in assets as well as liabilities, and the ratio of households' net worth to income had risen to over five times. Thus 'taking into account the higher level of assets, all in all, the household sector seems to be in reasonably good financial shape'.[63] Indeed, speaking earlier that year in February, Greenspan had noted that while measures of debt service levels of homeowners had seemed to worsen, this reflected that new homebuyers with less of a down payment had higher levels of credit card debt. For him, this was acceptable because changes in technology now enabled lenders to manage risks that much better, 'thus the movement of renters into home ownership was to be applauded'. To conclude, Greenspan noted that 'so long as financial intermediation continues to expand, both household debt and assets are likely to rise faster than income'. This was nothing to be overly concerned about; overall household balances were in good shape.[64]

In essence, the Federal Reserve referenced the same explanations for consumer behaviour as the Bank of England. They rationalized increasing indebtedness, whether from mortgages or other forms of consumer debt, by referencing the same imagined household consuming unit who, as they saw it, was making borrowing and spending decisions on the basis of the assessment of their balance sheet as it existed through time. Debt was simply a way to expand the balance sheet and reduce reliance on fixed cash flows. The similarity between Britain and the US was commented on in a speech by Governor Gramlich in 2002. Both had seen 'remarkably similar' increases in the ratio of household wealth to disposable income in recent years; which meant that governing either economy required a close attention to analysing data in the context of how balance sheets were changing and evolving:

> Besides sharing a common history, language, and legal structure, the United States and the United Kingdom have something else in common. In the past few years, both countries have experienced a significant wealth effect – so significant that understanding the wealth effect has become an important aspect of conducting monetary policy.[65]

In this political rationality, and in what was perceived as a new historical context, monetary policy was not seen to be about protecting the consumer, perhaps limiting the access to credit and mortgages. Instead monetary policy was about governing for the consumer, ensuring that the flow of credit was not constricted. So long as consumer prices on the 'high street' or on 'main street' remained relatively stable, there was nothing else for those charged with governing the economy to do.

7.3 Blaming government, not bankers

The central argument of this book is that the consumer, with raised levels of indebtedness, came to be viewed as central to the government of the economy because the consumer was identified as an enterprising economic agent. And in referencing the consumer, the government's role was determined. It had to ensure that the financial system was free to lend to those who required credit in order to expand and reorganize their portfolios of human and non-human capital. At the same time, by acting in such a fashion it could foster increased levels of enterprising thinking in the population. In Britain the targets of such thinking included unionized workers and those living in local government-owned housing. In the United States, under Clinton and Bush, the target included 'minorities' and immigrants.

However in the US, apportioning blame for the crisis has become politically charged and highly polarized. Progressive liberalism has been reactivated as a political force and policies are being advanced with the aim of re-regulating banking practices. At the same time, fiscal policy in the US and UK has been used to provide economic security. As such it is arguable that what Clift and Tomlinson have called 'coarse Keynesianism'[66] continues to exist within the parties of the Left: Labour in the UK and Democrats in the US. That the Third Way has been the ascendant tendency in these parties since the early 1990s does not mean progressive liberalism ceased to exist as a political rationality. At the same time, though, both Mervyn King and Ben Bernanke have committed themselves to ensuring that deflation does not become a reality. Going back to the early 2000s, and in the context of Japanese deflation, Bernanke made it very clear that deflation was to be avoided at all costs, given the impact that it has on borrowers. The Federal Reserve, he argued, would always be willing to use its power to induce inflation by expanding the money supply. Ultimately it could always create money and buy assets in the markets[67] (a policy that is referred to as quantitative easing, and by the Federal Reserve as large-scale asset purchases). In late 2010, Bernanke argued that these policies would aim to encourage households and consumers to increase spending, by expanding their balance sheets.

> Easier financial conditions will promote economic growth. For example, lower mortgage rates will make housing more affordable and allow more homeowners to refinance. Lower corporate bond rates will encourage investment. And higher stock prices will boost consumer wealth and help increase confidence, which can also spur spending. Increased spending will lead to higher incomes and profits that, in a virtuous circle, will further support economic expansion.[68]

As far as the Federal Reserve is concerned, and at least for the time being, the economy continues to be governed in the name of the consumer. Indeed, many politicians and commentators from Alan Greenspan to Gordon Brown have argued that global economic growth needs to be rebalanced by encouraging more consumer behaviour in fast developing export-oriented economies, particularly China. For Greenspan, the 'savings glut' that added to the easy monetary conditions in the West was caused by a developing world in which 'consumption restrained by culture and inadequate consumer finance could not keep up with the surge in income.'[69] As a result there was too much savings and too little consumer spending. For Gordon Brown it is essential that the world offers support to the Chinese as the policy-makers try to implement a structural shift towards domestic consumption from saving and exports. A key part of this is opening up financial services and reforming banks' lending practices.[70]

Many of these policy solutions involve prescriptions that seek to revitalize consumer balance sheets in developed countries and create consumers with increased access to credit in developing countries. To this extent these policies carry with them a neoliberal understanding of the consumer and consumer practices. And Bernanke's policy response to the crisis (quantitative easing) is straight from his reading of Friedman and Schwartz (1963) and their argument that the Great Depression of the 1930s was caused by a failure of monetary policy and not by primarily by overinvestment.[71]

Even so, libertarian authors in the US have heavily criticized the Federal Reserve's policy response. The Hayekian, Lawrence White, writing for the Cato Institute (a US-based sister organization of the IEA) has argued that by their very nature the Federal Reserve's large-scale asset purchases channel funds in government, rather than market, favoured directions, while also threatening inflation. The rush to avoid a financial meltdown has, in his opinion, led to a 'constitutional meltdown'.[72] In a broader sense, and in the context of a revitalized progressive voice, debate rages between those that see the crisis and subsequent recession as resulting from a lack of regulation over lending and financial practices and those that maintain that the crisis resulted from direct government interference, at least in the US in the mortgage funding markets. In the latter view at every stage the government is blamed for the crisis. Writing again for the Cato Institute, White argued that, 'the housing bubble and its aftermath arose from market distortions created by the Federal Reserve, government backing of Fannie Mae and Freddie Mac, the Department of Housing and Urban Development, and the Federal Housing Authority.'[73]

White accepts that there were elements of private miscalculation and imprudence that made matters worse; but for him, the real problem lay with policies that aimed to increase home ownership by pushing Fannie Mae and Freddie Mac into a massive expansion of their holdings of sub-prime mortgages. This expansion was funded by borrowing at rates below equivalent private sector banks, which the GSEs were able to obtain because they had an implicit government guarantee.[74]

Peter Wallison, writing for another US libertarian/neoliberal think tank, the American Enterprise Institute, has argued along similar lines that:

> The current financial crisis is not – as some have said – a crisis of capitalism. It is in fact the opposite, a shattering demonstration that ill-considered government intervention in the private economy can have devastating consequences. The crisis has its roots in the US government's efforts to increase homeownership ... from the misuse and manipulation of banking and credit by government.[75]

In Wallison's view, it was the politics of home ownership that forced lower lending standards onto the banking system; 100 per cent mortgages and self-certification mortgages, he argues, would not have happened without government interference. In contrast, many commentators and economists have pointed out that the housing bubble was a result of additional credit supplied entirely by the private sector, by a highly complex and opaque shadow banking system in which mortgage originators and investment banks worked together to seek funding, often ultimately relying on money market funds, in which retail investors believed they were placing their savings in highly secure securities and not investing in the US housing market. Levitin and Wachter, for instance, believe that the only way to account for the pricing of private label mortgages, relative to other bonds, is to explain the housing bubble as a consequence of an expansion of housing finance supply in the private shadow banking sector.[76] After all, by 2005 and 2006, Wall Street investment banks were securitizing one-third more loans than Fannie and Freddie. Sub-prime mortgages rose from 8 per cent of mortgage originations in 2003 to 20 per cent in 2005.[77]

Bernanke has also cast doubt on Wallison's explanation of the effect on the market of Fannie Mae and Freddie Mac's purchases of private label mortgage-backed securities. As they were issuing bonds to purchase these securities, then the net effect on funds going into the housing market was ultimately zero.[78] Indeed, Fannie and Freddie's actions in 2005 to 2007 were largely taken in response to shareholder concern that they were losing ground and market share to the entirely private sector-funded shadow banking market.[79] Wallison's claim that federally mandated programmes, such as the 1977 Community Reinvestment Act (in many ways a forerunner of Clinton and Bush's target setting for the GSEs) and other programmes to lower Federal Housing Association loan-to-deposit ratios, influenced what private lenders were willing to do is dubious. He himself admits that it is difficult to prove.[80] Fundamentally, the private sector, at the very core of the mortgage and housing boom after 2003, was free to act in any way it chose.

However, there are certainly affinities with what these authors are pointing to and the arguments expressed in this book. Throughout, the claim has been made that governments wanted to set consumers free and enable them to borrow; they were also keen to see banks expand their lending operations and compete for the business of consumers. And a core part of this borrowing was certainly intended to be for the purchase of homes. Governments in both Britain and the US were proud to see home ownership levels rise and house prices rise under their stewardship; policies in the US, as have been demonstrated, were particularly pronounced under Clinton and Bush. Yet, while both this account and some libertarian accounts have pointed to political issues in discussing the crisis,[81] the argument in this book has been that neoliberals sought to operationalize their politics of ownership through liberalizing the banking sector and granting consumers unfettered access to credit, rather than directing banks to advance credit in cases when it was obviously imprudent. To blame the crisis on progressive liberalism, a mentality of rule, which, as discussed in earlier chapters, references an entirely different notion of the citizen-consumer and consumption, seems problematic.

Finally, it is important to stress that there are, as was intimated in the last chapter, a variety of reasons that can be used to explain the rise of indebtedness and the housing boom and bust in the US and in Britain. The key focus in this chapter and the last is on trying to account for why increasing levels of debt were not problematized by government; and why it was not considered necessary to enact measures that would control the balance sheets of homeowner consumers. In the case of Britain, this was a reasonably straightforward story, in that from the early 1980s, the financial system was liberalized in order to create more competition and enable more borrowers' demands to be met. The banking system responded to borrowers' demands for credit because they were able to. There is little suggestion in any literature that the banks were under duress to lend more.

The American version of this story is more complicated in that a major funding mechanism in the mortgage market was government sponsored and was directed by government to behave in certain ways, for the sake of encouraging increased home ownership. Many neoliberals/libertarians believe that the role of the government in causing the crisis is paramount. Yet ultimately these arguments fail to account for the role the private shadow banking sector played in the boom and bust. Moreover, they fail to take into account the fact that the UK experienced a very similar set of historical circumstances without the involvement of government-sponsored enterprises, such as Fannie Mae and Freddie Mac. The case of Britain would therefore appear to act as a corrective to those in the US who choose not to recognize the private sector's role in the boom and subsequent financial and economic crisis.

At the same time though, it should be remembered that in both countries the government deliberately acted to change and liberalize the banking system; it then chose to interpret rising debt and home ownership as a positive indicator of the success of their policies. It should be clear in this narrative that government is being problematized; but what is being problematized is not direct intervention in the economy, but the referencing of an imagined figure of the consumer that the government sought to foster and subsequently misidentified. What has been called in question is therefore not capitalism per se; this is no 'crisis of capitalism' as such. Capitalism has already taken different forms within different political rationalities, classical, progressive and neoliberal, and will no doubt continue to be reconstituted as practices, and the human agents they reference, change. Instead, in the United States, as with Britain, the neoliberal will to govern faces a crisis in which consumer practices and the institutions designed to serve consumers have been brought into question.

7.4 Relying on others: setting the limits of possibility for neoliberalism

While some of the explanations being provided by libertarians in the US for the crisis appear to be slightly tenuous, they do raise some serious issues. On the one hand, they bring into sharp relief, just as with Nigel Lawson's abandonment of monetarism in 1985, the distinction between neoliberals in government and neoliberals out of government. In this book it has been argued that the genealogy of this crisis, whether in Britain or the US, is to be found in the neoliberal repositioning of economic thinking and in the priority given to governing for a particular imagined figure of the consumer. Neoliberalism as practised in government, activated as a will to govern, sought to guide and foster certain forms of conduct. Neoliberals identified an active programme of government that could be facilitated by the liberalization of the financial sector. Yet at the same time, some neoliberals, outside government, have increasingly come to problematize these projects.

These neoliberals have consistently focused on problematizing government action as always potentially distorting to the allocation of resources and capital in an economy. The main line of reasoning seems to be that we were never neoliberal enough and that government was always acting as a malign force. Thus, and as discussed above, lax lending standards in entirely private sector mortgage finance are seen as resulting from specific government lending programmes operated by the Federal Housing Association. The very existence of Fannie Mae and Freddie Mac (even though there are no equivalent institutions in the UK) are viewed as causes of unscrupulous and/or imprudent lending practices in some mortgage origination companies and in investment banks' securitization process.

But whatever the value of these arguments there remains a greater concern, that the very structure of both British and American banking systems, with their implicit and explicit guarantees for depositors and other creditors of banks, produces human agents that are not behaving as they should precisely because the market is not being allowed to function properly. Put another way, in this argument, conduct has become distorted by moral hazard.

To understand and address this point, it is worth posing the following thought experiment: what would Hayek and Friedman say about this crisis and how did they imagine an economy devoid of moral hazard? An answer from Hayek and Friedman to these questions will be suggested and discussed. In response, this position will be problematized by arguing that the imagined figure of the enterprising consumer will always remain problematic and such an object of political knowledge cannot be produced by government. The starting point for this discussion is the neoliberal position that the real problem is that we have never been neoliberal enough; that government never finished the task of ensuring that the population practised conduct required for consumption to always be productive. That is to say, in the neoliberal view, government never ensured that money was only ever a 'part of the self-steering mechanism by which individuals are constantly induced to adjust their activities to circumstances on which they have information only through abstract signals of prices'.[82] For Hayek and Friedman, there was only ever a society of part-entrepreneurs because consumers were never forced to take responsibility for the security of their own money holdings. While Knight and Keynes had suggested that consumers save for no particular reason or with unknown future contingencies in mind (see section 2.2), Hayek and Friedman imagined an economy in which savings were the result of active investment decisions.

The argument would go that in a free society human agents make choices over all their spending decisions and there is no guarantee from vendors (from education providers to fashion designers) that the goods and services bought actually deliver the (human) capital enhancement that the buyer had in mind. Hayek and Friedman would wonder why it should be different for the consumption of money, that is with decisions over where to deposit it, how to invest it and when to borrow it. For in this line of argument, by making money different from all the other items in the personal balance sheet, they would argue that other spending decisions are skewed. For example, excess debt and spending and inflation (both of assets and on the high street) would be seen as the result of a lax attitude towards money and a lack of due regard for its security. In other words, in the neoliberal perspective, the banking and shadow banking systems can create too much money for borrowers precisely because when those borrowers spend that money, the recipients are happy to accept it, leaving it on deposit or in a money market fund, sure in the knowledge that government will make good any losses resulting from the failure of the financial institution to which they have entrusted their savings.

This is a neoliberal argument about moral hazard, the idea that if a government bails out depositors, returning their savings to them when a bank goes bust, there will be no incentive for people to change their conduct in the future. Thus banishing the very possibility of moral hazard is essentially how neoliberals have dreamed of completing the political project, making full, not part, entrepreneurs of those that are governed. It is the dream of reason (that is, consumer's reason) implicit in the utopian monetary plans of Friedman and Hayek, as laid out in *A Program for Monetary Stability* (1965) and *The Denationalisation of Money* (1976) respectively. Both plans for the reorganization of money, though very different operationally, aimed to de-socialize money and ensure, to quote Friedman, that 'individual choices ... should have no influence on the stock of money'.[83] Both aimed to establish the conditions of 100 per cent reserve money. This was enabled in Friedman's scheme by forcing all banks to hold government bonds as reserves against all lending, buying them when necessary. In Hayek's scheme 100 per cent reserves was the outcome of removing the government's monopoly over notes and coins, making banks compete for consumers to use their currency. Hayek believed that consumers would be incentivized to insist that there are always reserves from which they can redeem their money. In different ways the point was simply to ensure that society 'would apply the same policy to deposits that we have applied to currency'.[84]

One hundred per cent reserve money would de-socialize money because it would mean that individuals could retrieve 100 per cent of deposits in notes and coins. In the current banking system this cannot happen because notes and coins represent less than 10 per cent of deposits. Thus in practice depositors only share the right to convert deposits into notes and coins; they cannot all do it at the same time. It is because private banks can create deposits and other forms of funding endogenously that can be spent as money, that far more deposits are owned than exist in notes and coins (exogenous money) and thus, effectively, owners of deposits duplicate their potential claims on notes and coins in circulation. For neoliberal purists, this is where the problem of moral hazard arises and is the problem which Hayek and Friedman were each trying to eliminate: 100 per cent reserve money would mean no duplicate ownership of notes and coins, each deposit would be represented by its own reserve. In this arrangement a bad loan in the system could not have a knock-on effect elsewhere, undermining confidence in a bank and causing it to collapse in a run, leading to losses for 'good' depositors. No longer would the government have to step in to rescue good depositors and in the process also rescue 'bad' ones. De-socializing money would force each and every member of the population, as an entrepreneur and consumer of money, to take personal responsibility for his or her own money, ensuring either that savings were warehoused securely (for an appropriate fee) or allocated to a financial intermediary offering consumers a choice of investments, none of which would have government insurance. There would be no recourse to government if a bank made bad lending decisions with consumers' deposits.

The position taken in this book is that neoliberals misidentified the behaviour of consumers. It is being suggested that Hayek and Friedman would respond to this by arguing that it was monetary arrangements and progressive liberal government paternalism that were responsible for systemic moral hazard and the ensuing crisis. Through government deposit insurance schemes, they would say that consumers were only ever partially entrepreneurial because it was never ensured by government that all decisions (including those regarding money) had to be thought of as investments made by the self, with regards to the self, and with responsibility residing with the self. The way forward for neoliberalism in this view would therefore be to intensify, to close off the possibility of moral hazard and foster a society where everyone's habits of thought no longer needed government to provide security. Everyone would know how to properly exercise their freedom.

What is problematic about Hayek and Friedman's ideas? Of course one could argue that de-socializing money would create precisely the kind of uncertainty that led to the excess savings that Keynes was so worried about, especially given the difficulty of trying to get everyone to understand the system in the first place. However here a different argument will be made, that if, as these monetary schemes suggest, being fully neoliberal means that everyone is a complete entrepreneur responsible for all their economic decisions, then even these monetary plans do not go far enough. The problem will always remain that the individuals fail to adopt the morality of a person who is knowingly fully responsible for his or her economic action. Indeed, how can most individuals be fully responsible in a modern economy, where the division of labour also requires a division of responsibility? Can individual employees truly claim that they are completely responsible for their income? Of course every employee is responsible for ensuring that they fulfil the requirements of their particular employment contract, but ultimately the security of income is dependent on decisions and events that go far beyond each individual person's function in any one organization. If one followed the logic of responsibilization to its ultimate conclusion then surely the ultimate moral hazard is that individuals take on debt, for which they have an individual responsibility to repay, and yet at the same time rely on income streams to pay off that debt, for which they have only partial responsibility and control. One can only speculate over the levels of anxiety and concomitant sense of lost freedom that would be created by a society that somehow succeeded in stripping away a generalized economic reliance on others.

So to recap, there remains the challenge that the 'real' cause of crisis was the moral hazard that came from governmental provision of security for money created in the banking system, thus releasing depositors from the need to view the holding of money as every bit a vital investment decision as any other consumption decision. And while it is not being claimed that the utopian monetary schemes of Hayek and Friedman have necessarily been taken seriously, all the same, these schemes do illuminate the entrepreneur-of-the-self, the imagined figure that represents the single class of human agents in society, as a being who is not reliant on others for economic security, especially not on the government. For neoliberals the hope remains that an economic agent can be forged that makes decisions on price signals alone which have not been skewed by the mispricing that necessarily results from relying on others without first fully pricing that reliance as a separate property right.

In response the argument has been made that the very structure of the modern economy disbars the possibility of non-reliance. Industrial integration has advanced far beyond the point at which most people can truly claim to have complete responsibility for their income. What limits uncertainty, enabling people to take on debt without the dread of the unknown future, is precisely a reliance on unknown others which has become the mainstay of modern habits of thought. There is a contradiction between the personal responsibility for debt and the collective responsibility for the income to repay that debt: it is not that by becoming a bad debtor, borrowers suddenly reveal themselves as having been immoral, it is that the necessary reliance on others means that one can never make the kind of assessments of risk suggested by those who allege crimes against moral hazard.

De-socializing money cannot undo the basic social fact that society depends on interconnectedness and reliance. It is a pipe-dream and wishful thought that once dispelled, sets limits on the possibilities of neoliberalism. That, as Veblen argued in 1894, 'advancing industrial organisation has gone far enough to obtrude itself as a vital fact upon the consciousness of an appreciable fraction of the country'[85] suggests, at least in the way it is argued here, that the dream of making everyone an entrepreneur-of-the-self, the dream that is of making everyone see that their consumption decisions belong to a single function called 'wealth', made up of human and non-human capital, has reached its limits. Instead government needs to step back from the brink and fundamentally reconsider and problematize the precepts of the consumer.

8 Conclusion

Problematizing the consumer

This book has presented the arguments and ideas of theorists, policy-makers and politicians since the late 1950s, predominantly in Britain, as they have sought to refashion the way the economy is governed. Throughout it has been shown that this discourse always referenced a particular vision of the consumer. The different permutations of the consumer that neoliberals have practised, such as the sovereign consumer, the active consumer galvanized by choice on the high street, the agent of progress, or the entrepreneur-of-the-self are not necessarily identical. But even as there are differences, each concept represents references to the consumer that have been practised by neoliberals in similar ways.

These concepts have always represented so much more than the neoclassical notion that human beings are rational, have perfect knowledge and have stable preferences. Of course, the assumptions made in neoclassical economics are, as Frank Knight said back in 1921, entirely 'heroic' precisely because they are overly ambitious and, at the very least, problematic in a world full of uncertainty about the future.[1] Clearly, no human being can be so rational as to know exactly what they want in the future, how to get it and, at the same time, be assured that they will never change their mind. Nor is every member of society entirely independent. Changes on the supply side of the economy, say in the provision of credit, can have an ongoing effect on behaviour and desire on the demand side. But, all the same, there is an ontological depth to the ways in which the consumer has been imagined in the neoliberal political rationality.

The very activity of consumption, rather than just being seen as the end-point of the economic process, the moment that ascribes a price to a resource prior to it being used up, is recast as 'value-creating' and potentially transformative for the consumer; and transformative in a way that has positive economic consequences for the wealth of the nation. As Harris, Seldon and other early Institute of Economic Affairs (IEA) authors in the late 1950s and early 1960s said, it is man as a consumer who would usher in the future, who would enable the second industrial revolution. In this view, focusing government policy on increasing the production of capital goods rather than consumer goods, would continue to inhibit consumers from judging the output of British business, and would perpetuate an environment which failed to galvanize consumers to want to be more productive so as to be able to consume and own more. Finally from increased ownership would come increased responsibility, the desire to better oneself and to be able to use more resources so as to better plan and direct one's own life. As far as IEA authors were concerned, consumers should be free to be advertised to, free to consume financial services, and free to invest in goods that would have a useful economic life extending into the future.

Consumption has been viewed as a process that can change the consumer. Certainly, it is in the marketplace that prices are attached to goods; but critically, at the same time, the active consumer, by consuming, is assumed to develop habits of thought that have been deemed to be commensurate with progress and development. Perhaps it was not until the 1980s that neoliberals fully practised the figure of the consumer as an entrepreneur-of-the-self, using debt (consuming financial services) to reorganize his or her balance sheet. But from their earliest publications, neoliberals in Britain assumed that consumption was far more than a habit; it was enterprising and, in the right circumstances, properly freed from government control, it could create an enterprising mind.

The consumer could always be used as a means through which to bring into question Keynesianism or progressive liberalism. The figure of the consumer could be used to problematize both economic theories of consumption and money, as well as industrial organization in the 1950s and 1960s: from the provision of milk, to the provision of financial services. Additionally, macroeconomic issues were at stake. Demand management, indicative planning, the assumption that government investment would be multiplied through the economy to create jobs, and the notion that government could make companies more efficient and competitive vis-à-vis foreign competitors, were all policies that were viewed as anti-consumer and therefore entirely problematic. These were policies that for the IEA authors were doomed to failure because they assumed, contrary to neoliberal thinking, that consumers were nothing more than habitual spenders, were not willing to borrow to smooth their cash flows over time and would not hedge against government inflationism. Moreover, for these authors, only the consumer could ensure competition for producers. Competition was a process that meant nothing without the consumer. However large, however seemingly dominant the business corporation, IEA authors saw the sovereign consumer as more powerful, always able to turn against a producer if they were not satisfied with the product on offer. Consumers would be in charge so long as the government did not act in such a way as to deny them a choice.

As such, one of the central premises of this book is that there is far more to be said about neoliberalism than its championing of the free market. Certain strands of positive economics may appear naïve to other social scientists who concentrate on providing 'thick' descriptions of human motivations, meaning-making and institution building (within which it is argued that markets are embedded),[2] but to criticize the 'simplicity' of economic models is to some extent missing the point. Neoliberalism and the very possibility of a governing mentality informed by economics relied upon a style of economic thinking in which the consumer was thought of in ontological terms. It was only in this post-Keynesian economic discourse that the consumer was given a sense of being, existing through time rather than just operating at disconnected points in time, using up resources as markets cleared. Thus ridiculing the neoclassical assumptions of perfect competition provides little basis for which to problematize the neoliberal figure of the consumer. This figure of the consumer, imagined as he or she may be, exhibited certain habits of thought through time that were specific, governable for and, moreover, have successfully appealed to significant proportions of the electorate, not just in Britain, but across the world and certainly in the United States.

However, the above only relates part of this book's narrative. In particular emphasis has been placed throughout on the emergence of a problem for neoliberals; a tension between identifying the consumer as a natural and proper agent in the economy and the recognition that not enough people in British society were prioritizing their consumer instincts. The failed experiment with banking liberalization and the subsequent experience of inflation in the 1970s pointed the neoliberal New Right towards identifying habits of thought in society at large, particularly prominent in trade unions, that they believed needed changing, or for those that refused to change, marginalizing. This realization provided the backdrop not only in which the Centre for Political Studies (CPS), in the late 1970s, put together a programme for governing, but also for actual government of the economy under Margaret Thatcher after 1979. This political rationality made a distinction between psychological propensities that were progressive and regressive, that is to say, between economic action that passed through the siphon of the market and action that did not, remaining forever unmarketed and unproductive.

Nonetheless, even as workers and unionists were being identified as having an inflationary and anti-consumer psychology, the New Right were no longer seeing this behaviour simply as 'knowing' job protection strategies of monopoly suppliers of labour, but as conduct created in past circumstances, perhaps appropriate to the working conditions of the nineteenth century. These workers, so the New Right believed, needed to be 'set free' from the belief that their freedom was experienced through the solidarity of the union and society as actualized through the state. On the one hand, being set free would involve allowing the population to consume financial services in order to build balance sheets that would better enable them to maximize the value of their human capital, whether contained in physical or non-physical assets. On the other hand, the government of the early 1980s would need to become the agent of creative destruction in the economy: making access to credit and funding very expensive to those in the private sector who had lost sight of their entrepreneurialism and to those in the public sector who, they believed, were misguided about their role in the economy and had failed to understand that value is created by consumers and entrepreneurs.

The New Right came to embrace the notion that there was a 'British disease' and their genealogy of crisis attempted to explain it through two distinct discursive strategies. First, specific Keynesian policies were blamed for holding back the development of a consumer mentality and for maintaining worker-saver habits of thought. Deemed particularly problematic were policies that controlled prices, incomes and levels of output as well as those that maintained tight control over the operation of the financial system, prioritizing the government's need to raise finance ahead of consumer demand for credit. Second, there was the argument that these attitudes were anachronistic, out of keeping with a new world of affluence, in which many now had more money and were able and willing to consume more durable goods and services, that previously would have been too expensive. Both these narratives, but particularly the latter, came to recognize that habits of thought, that is the ways in which human beings interpret the world about them and conduct a meaningful existence, are historically contingent. This went somewhat against the classical liberal tradition that tended to see the human agents of economic and political theory as existing naturally.

This does not mean that neoliberals necessarily thought that people had somehow become more rational (although human beings might get more adept at following trails of cause and effect in certain domains of action if following such trails becomes a more dominant part of everyday experience[3]); rather that what people take to be part and parcel of constructing a meaningful and free life is historicized and changes through time. What appears obvious in one time might appear strange in another. Thus the belief that freedom comes from economic security, that security is to found in a certain kind of human interdependency called 'society' and that society can be activated by government, might appear obvious at one time only to be questioned in another. In problematizing progressive liberalism, a political rationality was practised that not only sought to govern for consumer sovereignty but also accepted the tenet that government had a role to play in producing the human objects of a progressive economy, i.e. that the government had to elicit and foster modern consumer attitudes. So, during a critical ten-year period in Britain, roughly from 1975 to 1985, the New Right planned for and enacted policies that both referenced the consumer as the natural and proper agent of the modern economy while also explicitly identifying that government had to create, in the population, conduct that matched their imagined figure of the consumer.

The argument that has been made here has much in common with the argument of Ian Hacking in his essay *Making up People* (1986). Referring to the constitution of subjects in knowledge (the example he gives is homosexuals and heterosexuals), he states that:

> The claim … is not that there was a kind of person who came increasingly to be recognized by bureaucrats or by students of human nature but rather that a kind of person came into being at the same time as the kind itself was being invented. In some cases, that is, our classification and our classes conspire to emerge hand in hand, each egging the other on.… Who we are is not only what we did do, and will do but also what we might have done and may do. Making up people changes the space of possibilities of personhood. … By and large what I am deliberately doing depends on the possibilities of description.[4]

By always being focused on the consumer, the New Right were, from their inception, identifying in their discourse a new subjectivity that was emerging in society at large, no longer limited to the rich few. For these authors, the consumer was no longer someone who consumes merely to exist or someone who follows habits formed over a lifetime, but a new active agent, the sovereign force in the economy, acting on instincts of adaptability and change. And the New Right were not alone in noticing that society was changing. For instance, a new post-war affluence began to transform consumer movements from those that focused on the need to provide all members of society with a 'living wage', to movements that sought to provide information on products to consumers, often housewives, looking to buy durable goods.[5] Likewise, writers on the Left, such as J. K. Galbraith were writing about how the affluent society was undermining the presupposition of scarcity, so central to the development of economic thought.[6]

However, while the neoliberal conception of the consumer certainly appealed to the population, that appeal did not necessarily imply the accuracy of the figure of the consumer as he or she was imagined to be. For instance, social historian Avner Offer (2006) has argued that the rise of affluence in Britain and the United States has undermined conventions, habits and institutions of personal commitment, leading to less saving, more debt and an increased focus on satiating immediate desires.[7] While for neoliberals, the consumer is assumed to manage their balance sheet over the long term, for Offer, the opposite is the case: the consumer has become more focused on the short term. Yet, by identifying the consumer in the way they did, neoliberal policies, particularly with regards to money and credit, actually accentuated consumer conduct, such as borrowing. While government assumed that homeowner consumers were rational portfolio managers, consumers were making fallible choices with regards to spending and saving, without being fully cognizant of the future implications of such actions. Even so, this does not undermine the point being made, that neoliberals were responding to and identifying real changes in the behaviour of the population.

In assuming that the consumer 'out there' was identical to the consumer in their minds, government changed and altered the possibilities for people's activities. The transformation of the banking system enabled consumers to borrow more and increase both spending and levels of ownership. In turn, governments and monetary authorities interpreted this behaviour in a benign way, as a sign of increased freedom in society. This, as was argued at the end of Chapter 6, demonstrates how the politics of freedom can run into crisis; the very freedom to borrow that consumers were granted has become, for many, the cause of anxiety and stress, that is, anything but freedom.

Government is clearly a key institutional site whose activities can have a great impact on those that are governed. To gain electoral acceptance, it must offer something that connects and articulates it with conduct that exists in society at large. But this does not imply that the reading and interpreting of human conduct is accurate or remains accurate as government responds to the vagaries of the situations it encounters. Moreover, highlighting the failure to make the world appear as it has been represented in thought does not necessarily imply that the government should work harder to achieve its goals, to make the world conform to the way it is being thought of. The past thirty years of British (and American) economic history suggests it is problematic to think that a society can be constituted in which each and every consumer or homeowner consumer can establish a portfolio of assets with the use of credit that maximizes human capital over a lifetime, in isolation and without affecting the behaviour of others.

All the same, in making this statement, the point is not simply to reassert an older role of government, as if freedom should again be understood as arising out of the state's provision of economic security, as if the guarantee of employment is the mainstay of freedom whatever the costs elsewhere of operating such a policy. This older style of governing was relevant to the world of Keynes and the Great Depression, and its emergence was perhaps best described by Karl Polanyi in *The Great Transformation* (1944). Society for Polanyi 'came to protect itself against the perils inherent in a self-regulating market system'[8] which sought to subordinate all social organization, with its traditional bonds and interpersonal responsibilities and duties to the 'fictitious' capitals of labour, land and money. Opposing Hayek's argument in *The Road to Serfdom*, that liberalism collapsed into depression, war and fascism because it was never allowed to operate unfettered from social concerns (and concomitant government interference), Polanyi argued that it was simply impossible to think that human beings would ever allow their humanity to be permanently redefined and remoulded as no more than labour power on the factory floor.

Classical liberalism was so focused on production and the role of the entrepreneur, so involved with disciplining workers in order that capitalists could be free to produce, that the experience of labourers became untenable. The rise of progressive liberalism was, for Polanyi, the inevitable reassertion of society against pure market forces. In the language of Thorstein Veblen, writing in 1894, new habits of thought had arisen in which there was a general conviction that, rather than being at the mercy of capitalists, society, that is the state, owed every honest man a living: 'so instead of life, liberty and the pursuit of happiness, we have life, liberty and the means of happiness';[9] the 'means' being guaranteed by government.

Polanyi's historical narrative sought to confirm the inherent impossibility of establishing a pure laissez-faire regime, not because of the inherent contradictions of the capitalist process per se (as the 'scientific' studies of Marx had tried to do) but by arguing that there were many in society as a whole (no doubt including Marx) who had correctly recognized the intolerable position that the classical liberal regime had created for labour. But it would be wholly wrong to think that the liberal tradition would not respond to this, setting out to refashion capitalism in a way that would make it more sustainable. This new capitalism, neoliberalism, was post-Keynesian, in that it gave much more prominence to consumption practices; but most importantly, it recast the human agents of the economy, no longer just 'labour', but as entrepreneurs in their own right.

Under neoliberalism, there would be no dehumanizing of the worker in production-based capitalism, but instead an exaltation of the consumer in a classless consumption-based society. Clearly the market system still relied on each individual selling his or her labour; but each provider of labour was now viewed as a site of human capital. The project of the self was to maximize that human capital. Society was not subordinated to Polanyi's fictitious circulating capitals but instead composed of individuals maximizing their human capital with money, freed from its link to gold, made available for all enterprising endeavours. Government's new role would be to facilitate and enable human agents to behave this way and to foster conduct, that is attitudes and aspirations, associated with this way of thinking. This did not mean a return to nineteenth century laissez-faire. However problematic, this new capitalism had a distinct democratic intent: entrepreneurialism for the many not the few.

8.1 Capitalism and governmentality

In a sense, the narrative of this book forms part of a larger question that government and political economists alike have asked since the late eighteenth century: 'what counts as productive?' The question asks what kind of human activity produces value and can both sustain human life and fulfil human desire. And as Foucault argued in *The Order of Things* (1966), the very question presupposes that we first recognize a living human being as a point of reference for knowledge and value, instead of trying to the classify the world, and man's position in it, as part of a table of representations and signs originating with God.[10] This modern way of economic thinking stands in contrast to late pre-moderns, such as the Physiocrats of 1770s France. These thinkers believed that the only human activity that was productive was farming the land, because only the land, provided by God, afforded a natural surplus that could then be exchanged in markets, through the population, providing food for the farmer's landlord and manufacturers in the towns. The latter class were however 'sterile': what they produced could be exchanged for food but did not afford a natural surplus that provided sustenance for the population as a whole. Man on his own was not productive; only God or nature produced a surplus that could meet the demand of everyone.

Writers such as Adam Smith and David Ricardo incorporated into political economy the idea that human production was, in and of itself, the source of value, not God. Labour created the surplus, not nature, and labour's creating value could equally be embodied in manufactured goods as it could be in agricultural products; labour was the real measure of the exchangeable value of all commodities. Even so, for these authors, only so long as labour produced something physical, was it productive; the labour of 'churchmen, lawyers, physicians, men of letter of all kinds' was unproductive precisely because the work of all of them perished as it was performed.[11] For Marx, every bit the nineteenth century political economist, productive labour that created value was 'variable capital' to be contrasted with the 'constant capital' of machines; it was because the proportion of variable capital decreased in the production process as the role of machines increased, that market prices declined, threatening the very existence of capitalism. For Mill, consumption always used up resources, depleting the value created by entrepreneurs; for him, value originated only in production.

The marginal revolution in economics in the 1870s was an early stage in a transformation by which consumption practices would come to be thought of by economists as productive. The point of exchange was no longer a moment representing the equivalence of commodities but one of difference in which the two parties to the exchange could each increase their stock of utility. And in time, once the consumer was imagined as having a sense of existence and being, neoliberal economics came to see consumption practices as productive: both of the consumer and of assets (physical or otherwise) that would provide some kind of future revenue stream. The march of what counts as productive passed from the objective to the subjective, from production to consumption, from physical to ethereal, never putting into question the central epistemological figure, the living human being as value-creator. Rather than problematizing the central actor, the point if anything was to marvel at how clever we had become, recognizing the inherent productivity of everything we do, enhancing human capital all the time.

Is it time to call a retreat? Might not the recent past, as outlined in this book, have falsified the idea that all that is consumed is productive, that consumers maybe do things for reasons that are not connected to their supposed aspirations, that do not involve maximizing revenue over their lifetime, and do not lead to the construction of an appropriate portfolio? Perhaps people borrow because the money is there to be borrowed, or because banks have made more money available through an overdraft facility or by offering a customer a credit card? Perhaps, rather like the way Frank Knight characterized savers, people also spend for no particular reason; consuming, as Keynes said, is a habit, and we can get into the habit of consuming all the monetary resources available to us. If so, can consumption always be called productive? Is it ever wasteful?

That consumption is wasteful is the position adopted by the environmentalist movement that, in many ways, offers itself as a new form of governmentality: governing for the planet and sustainability. Those that see themselves as environmentalists might also be viewed as progressive liberals; but for the former, the citizen-consumer is imagined as active and politicized, making use of their individual and collective power as consumers to advance specific ethical causes. This is different from Keynes' habitual consumer or Galbraith's consumer, answering to the beck and call of persuasive corporations. Moreover, environmentalists are unlikely to favour Keynesian policies of increased production as a way to solve economic problems. Nonetheless, whatever the distinctions between environmentalists and progressive liberals, the former, like the latter, have been on the receiving end of criticism from many neoliberals. For instance, one of the Thatcherites, Nigel Lawson, has argued passionately against the environmental movement. His argument is that the potential damage being done to the environment is far less costly than the lost consumption possibilities that environmentalists want to impose on current populations and future generations. For him, quite simply, an environmental perspective represents a direct attack on the consumer.[12]

Environmentalism might therefore represent a new battleground between competing political rationalities and their conceptions of the consumer as a key economic agent. If so, it represents something new and distinct. Environmentalism both replays pre-modern Physiocratic ideas about the role of nature in the creation of value, while at the same time, arguing that the resources that nature has to offer are not the endless gifts of God, but ultimately limited and scarce. Rather than calling for more production and consumption as a way to provide economic security for all, the movement elicits individual consumers to act ethically and to recognize a common global community, which, once empowered, can pressure governments into action. Perhaps environmentalism foreshadows a new form of capitalism in which negative externalities related to production and consumption habits are accounted for on the basis that these resources are not common property, but represent property rights that need to be paid for.

It should not be assumed that future attempts to govern for the environment will necessarily represent the demise of capitalism, rather than just its reconfiguration. In the future, capitalism could find itself subject to the process of creative destruction, as it has done before. As discussed, the classical laissez-faire nineteenth century regime was undone by its own dehumanizing effects, and in its place emerged a regime in which government would take an active role in, among other things, ensuring that there was employment for all. In Britain, this did not imply socialism but instead a progressive liberalism. If industries failed, the government might choose to nationalize, but during downturns, it would aim to ensure that private companies were funded to the extent needed to keep them in operation. The focus on production, however, required relatively higher levels of saving, and a less consumer-oriented economy. In time, growing affluence and rising consumer impulses made this form of capitalism less attractive to the population. The economic problems of the 1970s provided the backdrop to a transition to a new form of neoliberal capitalism, in which the consumer was lauded as an agent of change and adaptability. To be a consumer now meant having integrity in one's actions, far removed from previous notions that consumption was wasteful and often geared towards extravagant displays of conspicuous wealth.

What the future might bring is of course impossible to predict. All the same, there is no reason to assume that capitalism will not change again, that the neoliberal vision of the economy will endure, and that the consumer-as-entrepreneur represents, to use a well-worn phrase, 'the end of history and the last man'. 'Capitalism' just like other grand signifying labels, such as 'state', 'society' and 'economy' means far less as a stand-alone concept than one would think. For Foucault, the search for a theory of the state was far less important than understanding how the state has been governmentalized.[13] The state, how it operated, how governors treated and directed the governed has always been a function of historically contingent knowledge. Different renditions of 'state' and of 'government' operate in historical eras, disconnected and discontinuous from our own time.

The same can be said of 'capitalism'. More important than the search for an underlying definition or for a mythical trans-historical description of its inner workings, is the way that capitalism has been governmentalized by different ascendant political rationalities, articulating and fostering distinctive spirits of production and consumption. Capitalism, in its neoliberal guise, has imagined everyone, consumers and producers alike, to be both enterprising and entrepreneurial. But there is no reason to assume that neoliberalism is the ultimate and final form of capitalism. Indeed, writing the genealogy of the recent economic crisis is intended to raise the possibility of something different.

Notes

1 Introduction: neoliberalism and governmentality

1 Joseph, K., *Conditions for Fuller Employment*, London: Centre for Policy Studies, 1978, p. 5.
2 Stiglitz, J., *Globalisation and Its Discontents*, New York: W.W. Norton and Co, 2003.
3 Thatcher, M., 'Let me give you my vision', Thatcher, M., *Let Our Children Grow Tall*, London: Centre for Policy Studies, 1977, p. 30.
4 Sources: Bank of England and UK Office of National Statistics.
5 Ibid.
6 Featherstone, M., *Consumer Culture and Postmodernism*, London: Sage, 2007; Giddens, A., *Consequences of Modernity*, Cambridge: Polity, 1990, *Modernity and Self Identity*, Cambridge, Polity, 1991 and *Runaway World*, London: Profile, 1999; Lash, S. and Urry, J., *Economies of Signs and Space*, London: Sage, 1994; Miller, D., *The Dialectics of Shopping*, Chicago: University of Chicago Press, 2001.
7 The genealogy of the consumer identity is a topic that has been written about extensively by Frank Trentmann (Trentmann, F., 'Beyond consumerism', *Journal of Contemporary History* 39, 2004, 373–401, 'Knowing consumers', in Trentmann, F. (ed.) *The Making of the Consumer*, Oxford and New York: Berg, 2006, 'The modern genealogy of the consumer', in Brewer, J. and Trentmann, F. (eds), *Consumer Cultures, Global Perspectives*, Oxford and New York: Berg, 2006). For him the consumer first emerged as a political identity taken up by water users in the late nineteenth century in disputes over the public provision of water supplies in London. See also Matthew Hilton (Hilton, M., *Consumerism in Twentieth Century Britain*, Cambridge: Cambridge University Press, 2003) for a historical account of consumer identity and consumer movements in Britain in the twentieth century.
8 A term first used by David Collard in Fabian Tract 387 (1968) to describe the IEA and similarly minded politicians. (Collard, D. and Fabian Society, *The New Right: a critique*, London: Fabian Society, 1968).
9 Mirowski, P., 'Defining neoliberalism', in Mirowski, P. and Plehwe, D. (eds), *The Road from Mont Pèlerin*, Cambridge: Harvard University Press, 2009, pp. 417–51.
10 Harvey, D. *A Brief History of Neoliberalism*, Oxford: Oxford University Press, 2005.
11 Mirowski, op. cit., pp. 417–51.
12 Dean, M., *Governmentality: Power and rule in modern society*, London: Sage, 1999, pp. 9–17.
13 See Foucault's essay, 'Governmentality', in Burchell, G., Gordon, C. and Miller, P. (eds), *The Foucault Effect: Studies in governmentality*, Chicago: University of Chicago Press, 1991, pp. 87–104. In it he discusses how a particular rationality of rule emerged after the Renaissance that saw sovereigns as immanent to the state. Rule was rationalized in terms of placing people and things in their correct order rather than

simply as trying to maintain control over a parcel of land. This *raison d'état*, of the cameralist or mercantilist state, was the forerunner of other rationalities of rule, such as liberalism. Foucault's point is that liberal modalities of rule are still about active government, they are not about absence of government.

14 Foucault, M., *The Archaeology of Knowledge*, London: Routledge, 2002 [1969], p. 214.
15 Ibid.
16 This phrase is borrowed from Paul Veyne (Veyne, P., 'Foucault revolutionizes history', in Davidson, A., *Foucault and His Interlocutors*, Chicago: University of Chicago Press, 1997, pp. 159–71). Veyne however was not referring to consumers but to the very idea that there is any object that we can call through time 'the governed'.
17 Foucault, M., 'Politics and the study of discourse', in Burchell, G. et al., op. cit., p. 61.
18 Mill, J. S., *Essays on Some Unsettled Questions in Political Economy*, Whitefish: Kessinger Publishing, 2006, pp. 33–51.
19 Foucault, M., *The Birth of Biopolitics*, Houndmills and New York: Palgrave Macmillan, 2008, pp. 31–2, 64–7.
20 Ibid., p. 63.
21 Polanyi, K., *The Great Transformation*, Boston: Beacon Press, 2001 [1944].
22 Schumpeter, J., *Capitalism, Socialism and Democracy*, Abingdon: George Allen and Unwin, 1943, p. 167.
23 Foucault, op. cit., p. 186.
24 Foucault, *Governmentality*, pp. 102–4. Thus Andrew Gamble (*The Free Economy and the Strong State*, Basingstoke: Macmillan Press, 1994) is quite right to argue that Thatcherism mixes a supposedly contradictory impulse of a strong state and a free market. Nonetheless recognizing this in no way implies that one should launch a search for a theory of the state that explains this, as if what is constant is always the state.
25 Foucault, M., *The Birth of Biopolitics*, p. 313.
26 Foucault, M., 'Maurice Florence', in Foucault, M. and Faubion, J., *Aesthetics, method, and Epistemology*, London: Penguin, 2000, p. 463.
27 Dean, op. cit., pp. 27–32.
28 Ibid., p. 40.
29 Michael Freeden's *The New Liberalism*, Oxford: Oxford University Press, 1978, gives a full account of the progressive liberalism of Hobson and Hobhouse, where it came from, how it developed and how some of its ideas transformed the Liberal Party, leading up to and beyond the 1906 Liberal government. Richard Cockett also discusses the collectivism of the 'New Liberals' in *Thinking the Unthinkable*, London: Fontana, 1995, specifically in the chapters on Keynes and the Beveridge Report.
30 Burchell, G., 'Liberal government and techniques of the self', in Barry, A., Osbourne, T. and Rose, N. (eds), *Foucault and Political Reason, London*: UCL Press, 1996; Rose, N., 'Governing advanced liberal democracies', in Barry et al., op. cit.; Rose, N., *Powers of Freedom: Reframing political thought*, Cambridge: Cambridge University Press, 1999, pp. 99–136. French sociologist Émile Durkheim is probably the most famous representative of this organic view of society.
31 Rose, *Powers of Freedom*, pp. 137–47, 156–7.
32 O'Malley, P., *Risk, Uncertainty and Government*, London: GlassHouse, 2004, pp. 57, 71.
33 Burchell, op. cit., pp. 19–36; Cruikshank, B., *Revolutions Within: Self-government and self-esteem*, in Barry et. al, op. cit., pp. 231–9; Ehrenreich, B., *Bright-sided*, New York: Metropolitan books, 2009.
34 Brennan, G. and Buchanan, J., *Monopoly in Money and Inflation*, London: Institute of Economic Affairs, 1981, pp. 19–23.
35 Rose, op. cit., pp. 148–9; Dean, op. cit., p. 6.

36 Miller, P. and Rose, N., *Governing the Present*, Cambridge: Polity Press, 2008, pp. 39–42.
37 Power, M., *The Audit Society*, Oxford: Clarendon Press, 1997.
38 Ordoliberalism is the original name adopted by a group of German liberals who, Foucault argued, can be thought of as practising as far back as the 1930s a distinct neoliberal political rationality. The label 'Ordo' was taken from the name of the academic journal to which members of the group contributed, *ORDO – Yearbook for the Order of Economy and Society*. This group of intellectuals is also referred to as the Freiburg School.
39 Foucault, M., *Birth of Biopolitics*, pp. 117, 147–8, 176.
40 Ibid., pp. 225–6.
41 Interview with CPS co-founder Lord Vinson, May 1991, reported by Cockett, op. cit., p. 237.
42 Cockett, op. cit., pp. 11–2, 101–2, 336–8; Plehwe, D., 'Introduction', in Mirowski and Plehwe, op. cit., pp. 10–7; Harris, R. and Seldon, A., *A Conversation with Harris and Seldon*, London: Institute of Economic Affairs, 2001, p. 34.
43 Friedman, M., 'On the IEA's influence in our times', in Harris, R. and Seldon, A., op. cit., 2001, p. 71.
44 Foucault, op. cit., pp. 80–3, 95.
45 Ibid., pp. 120, 177.

2 Constructing the consumer

1 Friedman, M. and Institute of Economic Affairs, *The Counter-Revolution in Monetary Theory*, London: Institute of Economic Affairs, 1970, p. 7.
2 Freeden, M., *The New Liberalism*, Oxford: Oxford University Press, 1978, pp. 100–1; Winch, D., *Economics and Policy*, London: Hodder and Stoughton, 1969, pp. 51–2.
3 For instance see Veblen, T. (1925) *Economic Theory in the Calculable Future* and Veblen (1894), *The Army of the Commonweal* both published in Veblen, T., *Essays in our Changing Order*, London: Routledge, 1994 [1894]; also it is worth noting Keynes' reference to American institutional economist John Commons in his essay *Am I a Liberal*? (1925), when discussing the need to incorporate social concerns in economic theory (published in Keynes, J., *Essays in Persuasion*, New York: W.W. Norton, 1963).
4 Kalecki, M., 'The essence of the business upswing', in Kalecki, M., *Collected Works of Michal Kalecki, volume 1*, Oxford: Clarendon Press, 1990, pp. 188–94; Frisch, R., 'Circulation planning: proposal for a national organization of a commodity and service exchange', *Econometrica*, 1934, vol. 2, pp. 258–73, 322–9.
5 Marshall, A., *Principles of Economics*, London: Macmillan, 1920, pp. 462–75.
6 Ibid., pp. 41–2, 229–30.
7 Winch, D. 'The problematic status of the consumer in orthodox economic thought', in Trentmann, F. (ed.), *The Making of the Consumer*, Oxford and New York: Berg, 2006, pp. 31–2.
8 Walters, W. *Unemployment and Government*, Cambridge: Cambridge University Press, 2000, pp. 13–37; Winch, *Economics and Policy*, p. 47.
9 Marshall, op. cit., pp. 709–10.
10 Jevons, S., *The Theory of Political Economy*, London: Macmillan, 1924, pp. 202–3.
11 Mill, J., *Essays on Some Unsettled Questions of Political Economy*, Whitefish: Kessinger Publishing, 2006, pp. 110, 33–4.
12 Smith, A., *Wealth of Nations*, Amherst, New York: Prometheus Books, 1991, pp. 19–23.
13 This is not to say that there were not dissenting voices within the classical tradition. Keynes consistently pointed out that he believed that Malthus had come close to his position in the early nineteenth century with a theory of underconsumption. Keynes

noted that Ricardo remained 'stone deaf' to this possibility (Keynes, J., *The General Theory of Employment, Interest and Money*, Cambridge, Macmillan and Cambridge University Press, 1973 [1936], p. 362). And while Malthus remained committed to the doctrines of laissez-faire, Giovanni Proccaci (Procacci, G., 'Social economy and the government of poverty', in Burchell, G., Gordon, C. and Miller, P., *The Foucault Effect: Studies in governmentality*, Chicago: University of Chicago Press, 1991) has argued that in the writings of Malthus (and Sismondi) one can see the early formation of a mentality of rule that referenced the existence of a social realm entirely differently to political economists.

14 Hutt, W., *Politically Impossible?* London: Institute of Economic Affairs, 1971, pp. 1–26.

15 Hutt, op. cit., p. 64; similar arguments were made by Leijunhufvud, A., *Keynes and the Classics: Two lectures on Keynes' contribution*, London: Institute of Economic Affairs, 1969, pp. 8–20; and Hayek, F. and Shenoy, S., *A Tiger by the Tail*, London: Institute of Economic Affairs, 1978, pp. 34, 61, 100.

16 Keynes, J., op. cit., pp. 257–71.

17 Hutt, op. cit., pp. 54–6.

18 Hayek and Shenoy, op. cit., p. 100. The same language is used by Hutt, op. cit., p. 59.

19 Hayek, F., *Full Employment at Any Price*, London: Institute of Economic Affairs, 1975, p. 18.

20 David Laidler has championed the view that all of Keynes' theoretical ideas can be found in classical texts, and that *The General Theory* (1936) owed its rapid success to the intellectual support it provided for an already popular approach to policy. The argument here is that this was precisely Keynes' achievement; that he was able to synthesize different economic ideas in a theory that was able to effectively practise an already extant political rationality (Laidler, D., *Fabricating the Keynesian Revolution*, Cambridge: Cambridge University Press, 1999).

21 Keynes, J., *Essays in Persuasion*, p. 335.

22 Knight, F., *Risk, Uncertainty and Profit*, Boston: Houghton Mifflin, 1921, p. 89.

23 Ibid., pp. 76–8, 89.

24 Morgan, M., 'Economic man as model man: ideal types, idealization and caricatures', *Journal of the History of Economic Thought*, 2006, 28, 1–27. Morgan argues that Knight's depiction of economic man marks a point in the history of modern economics when, rather than being a caricature of an actual human agent, economic man becomes disconnected from the real world and instead only lives inside the economists' maths lab.

25 Mill, J., *Principles of Political Economy*, London: Longmans Green, p. 462.

26 von Böhm-Bawerk, E., *Capital and Interest vol. 2, The Positive Theory of Capital*, South Holland: Lobertarian Press, pp. 268–71, 301; Schumpeter, J., *The Theory of Economic Development*, Cambridge: Harvard University Press, 1959, pp. 66, 135–7.

27 See Frank Knight's essay 'The ethics of competition' in *The Quarterly Journal of Economics*, 1923, 37, 579–614, in which he questions the morality of the competitive ethic in economics. Thorstein Veblen (see *The Engineers of the Price System*, New York: Kelly, 1921) was particularly sceptical of the captains of industry who often, he believed, sought to sabotage productive equipment for their own personal gain.

28 Note that Keynes himself did not actually use the term 'macroeconomics', although Frisch and Tinbergen were using the term in their work in the 1930s.

29 Keynes, J., *The General Theory*, pp. 107–10.

30 Ibid., pp. 96–8.

31 Ibid.

32 Goodwin, C., 'The art of an ethical life: Keynes and Bloomsbury', in Backhouse, R. and Bateman, B. (eds), *The Cambridge Companion to Keynes*. Cambridge: Cambridge University Press, 2006, pp. 230–1.

33 As Hacking would say, it changed the space of possibilities for actually experienced personhood. (Hacking, I., 'Making up people', in Biagoli, M. (ed.), *The Science Studies Reader*, New York and London: Routledge, 2002, pp. 226–30.
34 Harris, R. and Seldon, A. (2001), *A Conversation with Harris and Seldon*. London: Institute of Economic Affairs, 2001, pp. 26–7.
35 Hayek, F. and Institute of Economic Affairs Health and Welfare Unit, *The Intellectuals and Socialism*, London: Institute of Economic Affairs Health and Welfare Unit, 1998 [1949], pp. 25–6.
36 Harris, R. and Seldon, A., *Advertising in a Free Society*, London: Institute of Economic Affairs, 1959, p. 55.
37 Hayek, F., 'The use of knowledge in society', in *American Economic Review*, 1945, 35, 527.
38 Ibid., p. 528.
39 Harris, R. and Seldon, A. *Hire Purchase in a Free Society*, London: Institute of Economic Affairs, 1958, pp. 55–6; Harris and Seldon, *Advertising in a Free Society*, pp. 79–80.
40 'Civilisation is progress and progress is civilisation', (Hayek, F., *The Constitution of Liberty*, London: Routledge, 2006 [1960], p. 36).
41 Schumpeter, J., *Capitalism, Socialism and Democracy*, Abingdon: George Allen and Unwin, 1994 [1943], pp. 87–106.
42 Harris and Seldon, op. cit., pp. 42–3, 62.
43 Ibid., pp. 43–7, 59–61, 68–70.
44 Harris and Seldon, *Hire Purchase in a Free Society*, p. 55.
45 McRae, N. and Institute of Economic Affairs, *To Let?* London: Institute of Economic Affairs, 1960, pp. 20–6, 33.
46 Lees, D. and Institute of Economic Affairs, *Health Through Choice*, London: Institute of Economic Affairs, 1961, pp. 16–18, 22.
47 Robertson, D. and Institute of Economic Affairs, *A Market for Labour*, London: Institute of Economic Affairs, 1961, pp. 10, 18–25.
48 Hallett, G., James, P. and Institute of Economic Affairs, *Farming for Consumers*, London: Institute of Economic Affairs 1963, pp. 10–11, 22–5.
49 Canes, M. and Institute of Economic Affairs, *Telephones – Public or Private?* London: Institute of Economic Affairs 1966, pp. 14–17, 29–33.
50 Harris, R., Seldon, A. et. al, *Choice in Welfare 1965: Second report on an inquiry conducted by Mass-Observation into the extent of knowledge and preference in state and private provision for education, health services and pensions*. London: Institute of Economic Affairs, 1965, pp. 1–2, 7–8, 58–66. The Fabian Tract they refer to is Richard Titmuss' *Choice and the Welfare State*, London: Fabian Society, 1967. Titmuss specifically discussed the Hobart Papers and the IEA, and was not totally dismissive. However he still chose to draw the line between public services, say for example of health and giving blood, and private goods and services, like buying a car, where he was willing to agree that the consumer should be free to choose.
51 Fulop, C., *Consumers in the Market*, London: Institute of Economic Affairs, 1967, pp. 11, 14–79.
52 Gyfor, J. and Haseler, S., *Social Democracy: beyond revisionism*, London: Fabian Society, 1971.
53 Stewart, M., *Consumers' Councils*, London: Fabian Society, 1953, pp. 1–9. The foreword endorsing the research was written by prominent Labour politician Hugh Gaitskill.
54 Munby, D., *Home Ownership*, London: Fabian Society, 1957, pp. 1–33.
55 Crosland, A. and Fabian Society, *Can Labour Win*? London: Fabian Society, 1960, pp. 8–11.
56 Crosland, A. and Fabian Society, *A Social Democratic Britain*, London: Fabian Society, 1971, p. 6.

57 Brittan, S., *Government and the Market Economy: an appraisal of economic policy since the 1970 General Election*. London: Institute of Economic Affairs, 1971, p. 14.
58 Hilton, M., *Consumerism in Twentieth Century Britain*, Cambridge, Cambridge University Press, 2003, pp. 22, 189–99.
59 Friedman, M., 'The quantity theory of money: a restatement', in Friedman, M., *The Optimum Quantity of Money and Other Essays*, Chicago: Aldine, 1969, p. 52.
60 Friedman, *The counter-revolution*, p. 7.
61 Keynes, *The General Theory*, pp. 91–5.
62 Friedman, *The Quantity Theory*, pp. 51–6.
63 Ibid.
64 Friedman, M., *A Theory of the Consumption Function*, Princeton, Princeton University Press, 1957, pp. 3, 7, 21–4, 28, 220.
65 Mill, *Unsettled Questions*, p. 371; von Böhm-Bawerk, op. cit., p. 371.
66 Friedman, *The Quantity Theory*, p. 61.
67 Powell, E. and Institute of Economic Affairs, *Saving in a Free Society*, London: Institute of Economic Affairs, 1960, pp. 19–20, 131.
68 Harris and Seldon, *Hire Purchase in a Free Society*, pp. 5–6, 43–4.
69 Ibid., 54–5.

3 Diagnosing the British economy

1 Harris' own description of what the IEA were doing in this period, Harris, R., 'Now for planning', in Booth, P. and Institute of Economic Affairs (eds), *Towards a Liberal Utopia*, London: Institute of Economic Affairs, 2005, pp. 258–67.
2 Gordon, C., 'Question, ethos, event: Foucault on Kant and Enlightenment', in *Economy and Society*, 1986, 15, 71–85.
3 Buchanan, J. M., Wagner, R. E. and Burton, J., *The Consequences of Mr Keynes*, London: Institute of Economic Affairs, 1978; and Brennan, H. and Buchanan, J. M., *Monopoly in Money and Inflation*, London: Institute of Economic Affairs, 1981.
4 Harris, op. cit., p. 258.
5 Clark, C. and Institute of Economic Affairs, *Growthmanship: a study in the mythology of investment*, London: Barrie and Rockliff, 1961, pp. 11–13.
6 Hutchison, T. and Institute of Economic Affairs, *Keynes Versus the 'Keynesians'?*, London: Institute of Economic Affairs, 1977, pp. 10–31.
7 Hayek, F., *Full Employment at Any Price*? London: Institute of Economic Affairs, 1975, p. 20; and Lachmann, L. and Institute of Economic Affairs, *Macro-economic Thinking and the Market Economy*, London: Institute of Economic Affairs, 1973, p. 18.
8 Hutchison, op. cit., p. 34.
9 Clark, op. cit., pp. 11–22.
10 Ibid., pp. 11, 27–46.
11 Cairncross, A., *The British Economy Since 1945*, Oxford: Blackwell, 1995, pp. 142–79.
12 See Hughes, J. and Fabian Society, *An Economic Strategy for Labour*, London: Fabian Society, 1967, as one such example from the Left, where the argument was made that the planning authority needed to directly intervene in investment, wages, prices and manpower allocation. In other words, the argument was made that for planning to work much more control was needed.
13 Polanyi, G., *Planning in Britain: the experience of the 1960s*, London: Institute of Economic Affairs, 1967, pp. 23–7, 38–8, 76–86, 92–9.
14 Institute of Economic Affairs, *Growth Through Competition: an alternative to the national plan*, London: Institute of Economic Affairs, 1966, pp. 24–6.
15 Polanyi, op. cit., pp. 74–5.
16 Cairncross, op. cit, p. 31.

17 Polanyi, op. cit., p. 19.
18 Wilson, H. and Fabian Society, *Post-war Economic Policies in Britain,* London: Fabian Society, 1957, pp. 11–20.
19 HMSO, *Employment Policy*, Cmnd 5527, 1944, pp. 3, 16, 20–1.
20 The Institute of Economic Affairs, op. cit., pp. 13, 28–46.
21 Cockett, R., *Thinking the Unthinkable*, London: Fontana, 1995, pp. 200–1. The story of the IEA's expectations for Heath and subsequent disappointment is relayed in chapter six of Cockett's book.
22 Brittan, S., *Government and the Market Economy: an appraisal of economic policy since the 1970 General Election.* London: Institute of Economic Affairs, 1971, pp. 17–38.
23 As Brian Sewill, a special economic advisor to the Heath government said, Heath was trying to create a more dynamic, thrusting and go-getting economy. (Sewill, B., 'In place of strikes', in Harris, R., Sewill, B. et al., *British Economic Policy 1970–74: Two views*, London: Institute of Economic Affairs, 1975, p. 30).
24 All these measures represented, for John Burton (an IEA author), writing in a Centre for Policy Studies pamphlet entitled *The Job Support Machine* (1979), a morass and crescendo of subsidies rising since the mid 1960s that included, in addition to direct support, a 'great fiscal unknown of soft loans, advice, and preferential treatment' all bringing down the cost of production. (Burton, J. and Centre for Policy Studies, *The job Support Machine: a critique of the subsidy morass*, London: Centre for Policy Studies, 1979, pp. 1–2).
25 Jewkes, J. and Institute of Economic Affairs, *Delusions of Dominance*, London: Institute of Economic Affairs, 1977, pp. 41–3.
26 Hindley, B., *Industrial Merger and Public Policy*, London: Institute of Economic Affairs, 1970, pp. 8–49.
27 Papps, I., *Government and Enterprise*, London: Institute of Economic Affairs, 1975, pp. 10–25, 64.
28 Jewkes, op. cit., pp. 29–30, 37–8, 41–3, 50.
29 Ibid., p. 59.
30 Dean, M., *Governmentality: Power and rule in modern society*, London: Sage, 1999, p. 32.
31 Seldon, A. and Thorneycroft, P. (eds), *Not Unanimous: a rival verdict to Radcliffe's on money*, London: Institute of Economic Affairs, 1960, pp. 20, 38, 64, 69–70, 95.
32 In a modern financial system, the term 'printing money' is a way of saying that the government is borrowing directly from private banks. Where government spending is in excess of tax revenue, the government has to borrow. If it borrows from the non-bank private sector, i.e. individuals, the national debt is being financed from savings, i.e. pre-existing money. However, if it runs out of this source of funding, then the cheques that it writes to pay for goods and services will be presented to banks, and in accepting those cheques, the banks will both increase their deposits at the Bank of England (an asset) and also be receiving money into the deposit accounts of those that presented the cheques (a liability). As a result, the stock of money in the economy will have increased.
33 Henderson, R., 'Money in practice', in Seldon and Thorneycroft, op. cit., pp. 39, 50–2.
34 Morgan, E. V., 'Money in theory', in Seldon and Thorneycroft, op. cit., pp. 19, 27–31.
35 King, W., 'The banking mechanism', in Seldon and Thorneycroft, op. cit., pp. 68–78.
36 Walters, A. and Institute of Economic Affairs, *Money in Boom and Slump*, London: Institute of Economic Affairs, 1969, pp. 12–18, 50.
37 Leijonhufvud, A., *Keynes and the Classics: Two lectures on Keynes' contribution*, London: Institute of Economic Affairs, 1969, pp. 37–44.
38 Walters, op. cit., pp. 52–3.
39 Gibson, N. and Institute of Economic Affairs, *Financial Intermediaries and Monetary Policy*, London: Institute of Economic Affairs, 1970, p. 17.

40 This is a very important point to note, especially with regard to the historical and genealogical narrative contained in this book. Another way of putting it, as Wicksell, K. did in *Interest and Prices*, New York: Augustus M. Kelley, 1899, would be to say that an entirely elastic monetary system meant that banks could meet all borrowers' (including the government's) demands for money. It was no longer sufficient simply to say (as Fisher had done in his statement of the quantity theory) that deposit money stood in a fixed ratio to notes and coins. Keynes, discussed this as part of the *General Theory of Employment, Interest and Money*, Cambridge: Macmillan and Cambridge University Press, 1973 [1936], pp. 81–5, and its recognition was part of his analysis of the *ex ante ex post* equivalence of aggregate investment and saving. Friedman was making the same point when he argued that because deposits had become a more important part of the circulating medium, concern about them had led to an ever-widening degree of direct control over commercial banks (Friedman, M., *A Program for Monetary Stability*, New York: Fordham University Press, 1965, pp. 36–8). Finally, in *The Constitution of Liberty* (1960), Hayek bemoaned that 'perhaps ... if men had not come extensively to use credit instruments as money ... we might have been able to rely on some self-regulating mechanism. This choice, however, is closed to us. We know of no substantially different alternatives to the credit instruments on which the organisation of modern business has come largely to rely.' (Hayek, F., *The Constitution of Liberty*, London: Routledge, 2006 [1960], p. 282). Friedman's and Hayek's views on money are discussed in detail in Chapter 7.

41 Gibson, op. cit., pp. 18–26, 39–41, 55. See also Griffiths, B. and Institute of Economic Affairs, *Money and Economic Policy*, London: Institute of Economic Affairs, 1972, pp. 6, 22–3 for a description of the British banking system prior to 1971. Very similar arguments relating to the need to break the building society pricing cartel were made by Gough, T. and Taylor, T., *The Building Society Cartel*, London: Institute of Economic Affairs, 1979.

42 Gibson, op. cit., pp. 13, 15, 29–30, 41–6.

43 Griffiths, op. cit., pp. 25–7.

44 O'Brien, L., 'Key Issues in monetary and credit policy', in *Bank of England Quarterly Bulletin*, vol. 11, 1971, 198.

45 Harris, R., Sewill B. et. al., *British Economic Policy 1970–74: Two views*, London: Institute of Economic Affairs, 1975, p. 30.

46 Johnson, H. et al., *Memorial to the Prime Minister*, London: London School of Economics archives, 1972, pp. 1–7.

47 Ibid., p. 5.

48 Richardson, G., Speech by the Governor of the Bank of England, in *Bank of England Quarterly Bulletin*, vol. 13,1973, 477.

49 Bank of England, 'Commentary' in *Bank of England Quarterly Bulletin*, vol. 13, 1973, 416.

50 Harris, R., 'A self-confessed monetarist', in Harris, R., Sewill, B. et al., *The British Disease*, London: Institute of Economic Affairs, 1975, pp. 3–11.

51 Morgan, E. V. and Morgan, A., *Gold or Paper?* London: Institute of Economic Affairs, 1976, pp. 37–8.

52 Pepper, G. and Wood, G., *Too Much Money? An analysis of the machinery of monetary expansion and its control*, London: Institute of Economic Affairs, 1976.

53 Sewill, op. cit., pp. 36–40.

54 Ibid., p. 54.

55 Jay, P., *A General Hypothesis on Employment, Inflation and Politics*, London: Institute of Economic Affairs, 1976, pp. 12, 19–21, 25, 31.

56 Ibid., pp. 27–8.

57 Seldon, A., 'Preface', in Allen, G., *The British Disease*, London: Institute of Economic Affairs, 1976, pp. 5–6.

58 Allen, G. op. cit., pp. 19–20.

59 Ibid., p. 24.
60 Bacon, R. and Eltis, W., *Britain's Economic Problem: Too few producers*, London: Macmillan, 1976, pp. 8–10, 18, 24–6, 27–8, 112–13.
61 Allen, op. cit., pp. 23–6, 63–5.
62 Ibid., pp. 71–3.
63 Ibid., pp. 73–6.
64 Chilpin, B. and Coyne, J., 'Property rights, industrial democracy and the Bullock Report', in Chiplin, B., Coyne, J., Sirc, L. and Institute of Economic Affairs, *Can Workers Manage?* London: Institute of Economic Affairs, 1977, pp. 24–8, 38, 44–8; Wood, J., 'The real lesson of Germany', in Chilpin et al., op. cit., pp. 89–90.
65 Harris, R., 'Bullock's basic blunder', in Chilpin et al., op. cit., pp. 97–100.
66 Ibid., pp. 102–6.
67 Veblen, T. and Hobson, J., *The Theory of the Leisure Class*, London: Routledge and Thoemmes Press, 1899, pp. 188–93.
68 Seldon, op. cit., p. 6.
69 Allen, op. cit., pp. 50, 65.
70 See Veblen's essays, 'Army of the Commonweal' in *Essays in Our Changing Order*, London: Routledge and Thoemmes Press (1994 [1894]) and 'The machine process' in the *Theory of the Business Enterprise,* London: Routledge and Thoemmes Press, 1994.
71 Hayek, op. cit., pp. 22–33.

4 How to govern the economy

1 Thatcher, M. and Harris, K., *Margaret Thatcher talks to the Observer*, 1979, London: London School of Economics Archives.
2 Interview with Lord Vinson, May 1991, reported by Cockett, R., *Thinking the Unthinkable*, London: Fontana, 1995, p. 237.
3 Gilmour, I., *Dancing with Dogma: Britain under Thatcherism*, London: Simon & Schuster, 1992, p. 3; Thatcher, M., *The Downing Street Years*, London: HarperCollins, 1993, p. 14.
4 Joseph, K., *This is not the time to be mealy-mouthed*, Margaret Thatcher foundation. Online. Available at: www.margaretthatcher.org/document/110604 (accessed 9 May 2011), 1974, pp. 1–8.
5 Joseph, K., *Inflation is caused by governments*, Margaret Thatcher Foundation. Online. Available at: www.margaretthatcher.org/document/110607 (accessed 9 May 2011), 1974, pp. 1, 5–15.
6 Joseph, K. and Centre for Policy Studies, *Stranded on the Middle Ground?* London: Centre for Policy Studies, 1976, pp. 15, 22, 28, 32, 38, 43.
7 Joseph, K. and Centre for Policy Studies, *Monetarism Is Not Enough*, London: Centre for Policy Studies, 1976, pp. 7–8.
8 Ibid.
9 Ibid., p. 17.
10 James Callaghan, Conference speech, 28 September 1976, quoted in Howe, G., *Conflict of Loyalty*, London: Macmillan, 1994, p. 96.
11 Joseph, op. cit., pp. 16–19.
12 Conservative Central Office, *The Right Approach*, Margaret Thatcher Foundation. Online. Available at: www.margaretthatcher.org/document/109439 (accessed 9 May 2011), 1976, p. 28.
13 There is no published version of this document; only a handful of key Conservative figures were sent copies of the full document for discussion. The copy cited here was located at the Conservative Party Archive, held at the Bodleian Library in Oxford. A much shorter summary version was distributed to a wider policy-making group and is published online by the Margaret Thatcher Foundation. The longer, rather than the abbreviated version of the report is cited here.

14 Thatcher, op. cit., p. 42; Thatcher, M., *The Path to Power*, London: HarperCollins, 1995, pp. 420–2; Howe, op. cit., pp. 104–5. For historical accounts see Young, H., *One of Us*, London: Macmillan, 1989, pp. 114–23 and Cockett, op. cit., pp. 272–4. For Hoskyns' own account see Hoskyns, J., *Just in Time: Inside the Thatcher revolution*, London: Aurum, 2000, pp. 18–95.
15 Hoskyns, J. and Strauss, N., *Stepping Stones*, Oxford: Conservative Party Archive, Bodleian Library, Box SC 15, 1977, p. S31.
16 Ibid., pp. S6–7.
17 Ibid., pp. S17, S3, S36–7.
18 Ibid., p. S19.
19 Cockett, op. cit., p. 286.
20 Hoskyns and Strauss, op. cit., p. S1.
21 Ibid., p. 36.
22 Ibid., pp. S5, S11–13, S33.
23 Ibid., pp. S14, S21.
24 Hayek, F., *The Constitution of Liberty*, London: Routledge, 2006 [1960], pp. 233–43.
25 Hoskyns and Strauss, op. cit., p. S18.
26 Ibid., S21–3, S25, S30, S39–40.
27 Ibid., S24.
28 Hoskyns, op. cit., pp. 140–209.
29 Howe, op. cit., p. 108.
30 Joseph, K., *Solving the Union Problem Is the Key to Britain's Recovery*, London: Centre for Policy Studies, 1979, pp. 1–2.
31 Ibid., pp. 9–12.
32 Thatcher, M., 'Let me give you my vision', in Thatcher, M., *Let Our Children Grow Tall: Selected speeches, 1975–1977*, London: Centre for Policy Studies, 1977, p. 34.
33 Thatcher, M., 'Dimensions of Conservatism', in Thatcher, M., *Let Our Children Grow Tall: Selected speeches, 1975–1977*, London: Centre for Policy Studies, 1977, p. 106.
34 Thatcher, *The Downing Street Years*, p. 671.
35 Gilmour, op. cit., p. 265 recounts, quoting Norman Tebbitt, that the Greater London Council was abolished in 1986 because it was at odds with the government's view of the world.
36 Ibid., pp. 175–8.
37 Howe, op. cit., pp. 130–1.
38 Lawson, N., *The View from No. 11: Memoirs of a Tory radical*, London: Bantam Press, 1992, pp. 348–54.
39 Thatcher, op. cit., p. 673.
40 Lawson, N. *The British Experiment*, Margaret Thatcher Foundation. Online. Available at: www.margaretthatcher.org/document/109504 (accessed 9 May 2011), 1984, pp. 3–4, 13.
41 Joseph, K., *Conditions for Fuller Employment*, London: Centre for Policy Studies, 1978, pp. 11–12.
42 Ibid., p. 6.
43 Joseph, *This is not the time to be mealy-mouthed*, p. 8.
44 Joseph, *Conditions for Fuller Employment*, pp. 13, 20.
45 Ibid., pp. 4–5, 15.
46 Ibid., p. 18.
47 Thatcher, M., 'The new Renaissance', in Thatcher, M., *Let Our Children Grow Tall: selected speeches, 1975–1977*, London: Centre for Policy Studies, 1977, pp. 94–6.
48 Thatcher, M., 'Dimensions of Conservatism', in Thatcher, op. cit., pp. 107–8.
49 Thatcher, M., 'Let our children grow tall', in Thatcher, op. cit., p. 12.
50 Thatcher, M., 'Let me give you my vision', in Thatcher, op. cit., p. 34.
51 Thatcher, M., 'The healthy society', in Thatcher, op. cit., pp. 81–4.

52 Thatcher, M., 'The path to profitability', in Thatcher, op. cit., p. 53.
53 Thatcher, M., 'Let our children grow tall', in Thatcher, op. cit., p. 11.
54 Conservative Central Office, op. cit., p. 12.
55 Thatcher, M., *There is no such thing as society*, Margaret Thatcher Foundation. Online. Available at: www.margaretthatcher.org/document/106689 (accessed 9 May 2011), 1987, pp. 1–3.
56 Thatcher, M., *The Downing Street Years*, p. 626.
57 Foucault, M. *The Birth of Biopolitics*, Houndmills and New York, Palgrave Macmillan, 2008, p. 63.
58 Smith, A., *Wealth of Nations*, Amherst, New York: Prometheus Books, 1991, p. 174.
59 Joseph, op. cit., p. 5.
60 Thatcher, M. 'Short term expediency: long term ruin?', in M. Thatcher, *Let Our Children Grow Tall: Selected speeches, 1975–1977*, London: Centre for Policy Studies, 1977, p. 68.
61 Conservative Central Office, op. cit., pp. 5, 18.
62 Joseph, K., *Stranded on the Middle Ground?* London: Centre for Policy Studies, 1976, pp. 20, 24.
63 Ian Gilmour, one the fiercest critics of Thatcherism, noted that the equivalent of two million working days were lost to strike action in 1990 compared to thirty million in the 'Winter of Discontent' of 1978/9. (Gilmour, op. cit., p. 101).
64 Lawson, N., *Thatcherism in Practice: a progress report*, Margaret Thatcher Foundation. Online. Available at: www.margaretthatcher.org/document/109506 (accessed 9 May 2011), 1981, pp. 4–5.
65 Lawson, N., *The British Experiment*, p. 13.

5 Governing for the consumer

1 Green, E., *Thatcher*, New York: Oxford University Press, 2006, p. 82.
2 Young, H., *One of Us*, London: Macmillan, (1989); Keegan, W., *Lawson's Gamble*, London: Hodder and Stoughton, 1989. Keegan's argument was that Lawson was doing no more than Heath and Barber; using the consumer and consumer credit to create demand in the economy while at the same time hoping the extra demand would incentivize industry to restructure and invest.
3 See discussion in section 5.2. Pepper, G. and Oliver, M.'s retrospective historical account, *Monetarism under Thatcher*, Northampton, Edward Elgar, 2001, p. 27 argued that Lawson in fact was not a monetarist at all, but rather concerned only to lower the inflationary part of nominal GDP.
4 In response to the Government Green Paper, *Monetary Control* (Bank of England and HM Treasury, *Monetary Control*, Cmnd 7858, London: HMSO, 1980), Friedman wrote, 'I could hardly believe my eyes when I read, in the first paragraph of the summary chapter, "the principal means of controlling the growth of money supply must be fiscal policy … and interest rates." Interpreted literally, this sentence is simply wrong.' (Friedman, M., 'Response to questionnaire on monetary policy', in HM Treasury, *Financial Statement and Budget Report 1980–81*, HC 720, London: HMSO, 1980, p. 57).
5 Lawson, N., *Financial Discipline Restored*, London, Conservative Policy Centre, 1982, p. 7.
6 Joseph, K., *Conditions for Fuller Employment*, London: Centre for Policy Studies, 1978, pp. 11–12; Joseph, K., *Stranded on The Middle Ground? Reflections on circumstances and policies*, London: Centre for Policy Studies, 1976, p. 11.
7 Lawson, N., *The View from No. 11*, London, Bantam Press,1992, p. 55.
8 UK Office of National Statistics; Lawson, op. cit., p. 55.
9 Richardson, G., 'Speech by the Governor of the Bank of England', in *Bank of England Quarterly Bulletin*, vol. 19, 1979, 408.

10 Richardson, G., 'Speech by the Governor of the Bank of England', in *Bank of England Quarterly Bulletin*, vol. 20, 1980, 457.
11 Lawson, N., *Financial Discipline Restored*, pp. 5–7.
12 Keegan, op. cit.; I. Gilmour, *Dancing with Dogma*, London: Simon & Schuster, 1992. The same argument is essentially made by monetarists including even Tim Congdon and Jock Bruce-Gardyne, see section 5.2.
13 Crouch, C., 'Privatised Keynesianism: an unacknowledged policy regime', in *The British Journal of Politics and International Relations*, vol. 11, 2009, 382–99.
14 This is not to say that open market operations would have necessarily worked perfectly. The experience of 'overfunding', considered later in the chapter, highlights the inherent difficulties of operating any regime that seeks to control broad money supply.
15 Bank of England, 'Commentary', in *Bank of England Quarterly Bulletin*, vol. 19, 1979, 372–7.
16 Bank of England and HM Treasury, *Monetary Control*, p. 5.
17 Bank of England, 'The supplementary deposits scheme', in *Bank of England Quarterly Bulletin*, vol. 22, 1982, 83–5; Lawson, N., *The View from No. 11*, p. 38; Howe, G., *Conflict of Loyalty*, London: Macmillan, 1994, p. 141. In his memoirs, Geoffrey Howe refers to the removal of exchange controls as an 'ambition … long cherished … [but which had been] … kept off the agenda for too many years by the forces of ignorance, timidity and inertia'. He went on to say that while controls shackled the spirit of enterprise, there were so few voices to be heard calling for their removal. He cited IEA pamphlet, Miller, R. and Wood, J., *Exchange Control for Ever?* London: Institute of Economic Affairs, 1979, as one of the few advocates that helped break the 'intellectual ice pack.'
18 Walters, A. and American Enterprise Institute, *Britain's Economic Renaissance: Margaret Thatcher's reforms, 1979–1984*, New York and Oxford, Oxford University Press, 1986, p. 139.
19 Hoskyns, J., *Just in Time*, London, Aurum, 2000, pp. 173–85.
20 Lawson, N., *The View from No. 11*, p. 98.
21 Howe, op. cit., pp. 197–210; Thatcher, M., *The Downing Street Years*, London: HarperCollins, 1993, pp. 132–9; Walters, op. cit., pp. 86–90.
22 Walters, op. cit., p. 86.
23 Congdon, T., 'Start of a somersault', in Congdon, T., Minford, P. et al., *Whither Monetarism? The Chancellor's Mansion House speech with comments by three wise men*, London: Centre for Policy Studies, 1985, p. 38; Lawson, op. cit, p. 81.
24 Lawson, op. cit., p. 89.
25 364 Economists, 'Statement on economic policy', in Booth, P. and Institute of Economic Affairs (eds), *Were 364 Economists All Wrong?* 2006, pp. 122–3.
26 Minford, P., 'The letter from 364 economists', in Booth, P. and Institute of Economic Affairs (eds), *Were 364 Economists All Wrong?* 2006, pp. 85–7.
27 Bank of England, 'Commentary', in *Bank of England Quarterly Bulletin*, vol. 21, 1981, 8–9, 20.
28 Richardson, G., 'The banks' role in financing industry', in *Bank of England Quarterly Bulletin*, vol. 21, 1981, pp. 77–8.
29 Mockler, C., *Budget Submission, 3.2.81*, Oxford: Conservative Research Department, Conservative Party Archive, Bodleian Library, 1981.
30 Baldwin, B., *Budget Submission, 12.1.81*, Oxford: Conservative Research Department, Conservative Party Archive, Bodleian Library, 1981.
31 Ibid.
32 Lilley, P., *Budget Submission: Ten policy questions about the medium term financial strategy*, Oxford: Conservative Research Department, Conservative Party Archive, Bodleian Library, 1981.
33 Lawson, op. cit., pp. 447–8.

34 Lawson, N., *Thatcherism in Practice: a progress report*, Margaret Thatcher Foundation. Online. Available at: www.margaretthatcher.org/document/109506 (accessed 9 May 2011), 1981, pp. 20–1.
35 Joseph, K., *Inflation is caused by governments*, Margaret Thatcher Foundation. Online. Available at: www.margaretthatcher.org/document/110607 (accessed 9 May 2011), 1974, p. 22.
36 Thatcher, M. and Harris, K., *Margaret Thatcher talks to the Observer*, 1979, London: London School of Economics Archives.
37 Gamble, A., *The Free Economy and the Strong State: the politics of Thatcherism*, Basingstoke, Macmillan Press, 1994.
38 Lawson, N., *Financial Discipline Restored*, p. 4.
39 Wood, G., 'Can 364 economists be wrong?', in Booth, P. (ed.), *Were 364 Economists All Wrong?* London: Institute of Economic Affairs, 2006, p. 69.
40 Lawson, N., *The View from No. 11*, p. 426.
41 Walters, op, cit., p. 16.
42 Giersch, H., *Liberalisation for Faster Economic Growth: Internal and external measures required*, London: Institute of Economic Affairs, 1986, pp. 26–7.
43 Conservative Research Department, *Enterprise Culture Group Meetings, 10–2–81*, Oxford: Centre for Policy Studies, Conservative Party Archive, Box 4/4/40, Bodleian Library, 1981.
44 Conservative Research Department, *Policy Group on the Promotion of Enterprise, October to December 1982*, Oxford: Conservative Party Archive, Box CRD 4/4/41, 4/4/42, Bodleian Library, 1981–2.
45 Conservative Central Office, *The Right Approach*, Margaret Thatcher Foundation. Online. Available at: www.margaretthatcher.org/document/109439 (accessed 9 May 2011), 1976, pp. 16–17.
46 Parker, D., *The Official History of Privatisation, volume 1*, Abingdon, Routledge, 2009, p. 404.
47 Howe, G., *Privatisation: The Way Ahead*, London: Conservative Policy Centre, 1981, pp. 3–5.
48 Lawson, op. cit, p. 224. It is worth adding that this was the way that Lawson and his colleagues viewed privatization. Many people subscribed to these large initial public offerings simply because in previous offerings share prices had risen very quickly, enabling small subscribers to sell the shares and make a quick profit.
49 Redwood, J., *Equity for Everyman: new ways to widen ownership*, London: Centre for Policy Studies, 1986, pp. 5–6, 8.
50 Ibid., p. 23.
51 Letwin, S. and Letwin, W., *Every Adult a Share-owner: the case for universal share ownership*, London: Centre for Policy Studies, 1986, pp. 5–9.
52 Lawson, op. cit., p. 745.
53 Ibid.
54 Lawson, N., *The British Experiment*, Margaret Thatcher Foundation. Online. Available at: www.margaretthatcher.org/document/109504 (accessed 9 May 2011), 1984, p. 13.
55 Leigh-Pemberton, R., 'Personal credit in perspective', in *Bank of England quarterly bulletin*, vol. 28, 1988, 48.
56 During the same period the Bank of England shifted their understanding of savings, from one in which savings were viewed as the difference between consumption and income, to one in which savings meant the change in wealth. If the latter definition was used, then there was no need to worry about the 'savings rate' (income less consumption) falling to almost zero so long as asset prices were rising. This is an important point not just relevant for the 1980s, but critical to the 2000s as well (see Chapter 6).
57 Lawson, N. and Institute of Economic Affairs, *The State of the Market*, 1988, pp. 17–18.
58 Ibid.

59 Bank of England, 'Mortgage lending and the housing market', in *Bank of England quarterly bulletin*, vol. 22, 1982, 390–2.
60 Bank of England, 'Commentary', in *Bank of England quarterly bulletin*, vol. 23, 1983, 16.
61 Bank of England, 'Commentary', in *Bank of England quarterly bulletin*, vol. 23, 1983, 156.
62 Richardson, G., 'The future of building societies: a central banker's view', in *Bank of England quarterly bulletin*, vol. 23, 1983, 216–17.
63 Bank of England, 'Competition, innovation and regulation in British Banking', in *Bank of England quarterly bulletin*, vol. 23, 1983, 371–4.
64 Bank of England, 'Commentary', in *Bank of England quarterly bulletin*, vol. 23, 1983, 322–3.
65 Bank of England, 'Commentary', in *Bank of England quarterly bulletin*, vol. 23, 1983, 5, 14.
66 Congdon, T., *Monetarism lost: and why it must be regained*, London: Centre for Policy Studies, 1989, p. 17.
67 Lawson, N., 'The Chancellor's speech', in Congdon, T., Minford, P. et al., *Whither Monetarism? The Chancellor's Mansion House speech, with comments by three wise men*, London: Centre for Policy Studies, 1985, pp. 13–17.
68 Bruce-Gardyne, J., 'Chancellor Reagan', in Congdon, T., Minford, P. et al., *Whither Monetarism? The Chancellor's Mansion House speech, with comments by three wise men*, London: Centre for Policy Studies, 1985, pp. 24–32.
69 Congdon, T., 'Start of a somersault', in Congdon, T., Minford, P. et al., *Whither Monetarism? The Chancellor's Mansion House speech, with comments by three wise men*, London: Centre for Policy Studies, 1985, pp. 33–41.
70 Minford, P., 'Consulting the oracle', in Congdon, T., Minford, P. et al., *Whither Monetarism? The Chancellor's Mansion House speech, with comments by three wise men*, London: Centre for Policy Studies, 1985, pp. 42–9.
71 Congdon, T., *Monetarism Lost*, pp. 43, 48–52.
72 Pepper, G., Wood, G. et al., *Money, Credit and Inflation*, London: Institute of Economic Affairs, 1990, pp. 13, 36–7, 49–50.
73 Lawson, op. cit., pp. 13–14.
74 Of course to this extent there are similarities with the gold standard. The difference was that the gold standard regime incorporated a much more profound distinction between the consumer and the entrepreneur. Only the latter had access to the credit creation facilities of banks and discount houses. Monetarism referred to a one-class nation of entrepreneurs, the gold standard to a class-based nation of landlords, capitalists and workers.
75 Lawson, op. cit., p. 21.
76 Leigh-Pemberton, R.,'Problems of monetary policy and change in the City', in *Bank of England quarterly bulletin*, vol. 25, 1985, 535.
77 Ibid.
78 Leigh-Pemberton, R., 'Financial change and broad money', in *Bank of England quarterly bulletin*, vol. 26, 1986, 503–7. According to Nigel Lawson, (Lawson, *The View from No. 11*, p. 635) most of this speech was in fact written by Eddie George, who succeeded Leigh-Pemberton as Governor in 1993.
79 Leigh-Pemberton, R., 'The instruments of monetary policy', in *Bank of England quarterly bulletin*, vol. 27, 1987, 365–8.
80 Bank of England, 'Commentary', in *Bank of England quarterly bulletin*, vol. 26, 1986, 323–5.
81 Bank of England, 'Commentary', in *Bank of England quarterly bulletin*, vol. 26. 1986, 464.
82 Bank of England, 'Commentary', in *Bank of England quarterly bulletin*, vol. 27, 1987, 17–19.

83 Miller, P. and Rose, N., 'Mobilising the consumer: assembling the subject of consumption', in *Theory, Culture and Society* vol. 14, 1997, 1–36.
84 Schumpeter, J., *Capitalism, Socialism and Democracy*, Abingdon, George Allen and Unwin, 1994 [1943], p. 167.
85 Minford, P. and Institute of Economic Affairs, *The Supply-side Revolution in Britain*, Aldershot: Edward Elgar and Institute of Economic Affairs, 1991, pp. 70–1.
86 Ibid.
87 Bank of England, 'Commentary', in *Bank of England quarterly bulletin*, vol. 29, 1989, 15–17, 27.
88 Leigh-Pemberton, R., 'Monetary policy, equity markets and the City's infrastructure', in *Bank of England quarterly bulletin*, vol. 29, 1989, 529.
89 Leigh-Pemberton, R., 'Monetary policy in the second half of the 1980s', in *Bank of England quarterly bulletin*, vol. 30, 1990, 215–16.
90 Ibid., pp, 215–20.
91 Leigh-Pemberton, R., 'Personal saving and borrowing, in *Bank of England quarterly bulletin*, vol. 30, 1990, 362.
92 Lawson, N., *The New Conservatism*, Margaret Thatcher Foundation. Online. Available at: www.margaretthatcher.org/document/109505 (accessed 9 May 2011), 1980, p. 14.
93 Lawson, N., *The View from No. 11*, p. 983.

6 Misidentification and crisis

1 Blair, T. and Fabian Society, *Socialism*, London: Fabian Society, 1994, pp. 3–4.
2 Ibid., p. 2.
3 Minford, P. and Institute of Economic Affairs, *The Supply-side Revolution in Britain*, Aldershot: Edward Elgar and Institute of Economic Affairs, 1991, pp. 241–2.
4 Blair, T. and Fabian Society, *Let Us Face the Future: the 1945 anniversary lecture*, London: Fabian Society, 1995, p. 3.
5 Joseph, K., *Stranded on the Middle Ground? Reflections on circumstances and policies*, London: Centre for Policy Studies, 1976, p. 27.
6 Blair, T., *Socialism*, pp. 1–4.
7 Blair, T., *Let Us Face the Future*, pp. 4, 8, 10–11.
8 Blair, T. and Fabian Society, *The Third Way: New politics for the new century*, London: Fabian Society, 1998, p. 10.
9 Foucault, M., *The Birth of Biopolitics*, Houndmills and New York: Palgrave Macmillan, 2008, p. 63.
10 Blair, T., *Socialism*, p. 7.
11 Thatcher, M., *Let Our Children Grow Tall: Selected speeches, 1975–1977*, London: Centre for Policy Studies, 1977, pp. 12, 34.
12 Blair, T., *Let us Face the Future*, pp. 4, 8, 10.
13 Ibid., p. 4.
14 Ibid., p. 15; Blair, T., *The Third Way*, pp. 7, 15.
15 These are all features of a neoliberal political rationality discussed by governmentality scholars. See Barry, A., Osbourne, T. and Rose, N. (eds), *Foucault and Political Reason,* London: UCL Press, 1996; Rose, N., *Powers of Freedom: Reframing political thought*, Cambridge: Cambridge University Press, 1999; Miller, P. and Rose, N., *Governing the Present*, Cambridge: Polity Press, 2008; Power, M., *The Audit Society*, Oxford: Clarendon Press, 1997; O'Malley, P., *Risk, Uncertainty and Government*, London: GlassHouse, 2004.
16 Butt, R. and Centre for Policy Studies, *The Unfinished Task: the Conservative record in perspective: summer address*, London: Centre for Policy Studies, 1986, pp. 22–6.
17 Lilley, P. and Centre for Policy Studies, *Thatcherism: the next generation*, London: Centre for Policy Studies, 1989, pp. 14–6.

18 Portillo, M. and Centre for Policy Studies, *The Blue Horizon*, London: Centre for Policy Studies, 1993, p. 12.
19 Rifkind, M. and Centre for Policy Studies, *Conservative Britain in the 21st Century*, London: Centre for Policy Studies, 1996, pp. 16, 23. According to Portillo, Europe in the 1990s showed many of the characteristics of Britain in the 1970s with overmanned and protected nationalized industries (Portillo, M. and Institute of Economic Affairs, *Democratic Values and the Currency*, London: Institute of Economic Affairs, 1998, pp. 22–3).
20 Novak, M. and Centre for Policy Studies, *The Crisis of the Welfare State: Ethics and economics*, London: Centre for Policy Studies, 1993, pp. 6, 9–11.
21 Thatcher, M., *There is no such thing as society*, Margaret Thatcher Foundation. Online. Available at: www.margaretthatcher.org/document/106689 (accessed 9 May 2011), 1987, pp. 1–3.
22 Portillo, M., *The Blue Horizon*, p. 9.
23 Blair, T., *The Third Way*, p. 3. In fact for most individuals to succeed Blair believed society must be strong. Society was strong in turn because individuals could take responsibility for themselves and succeed.
24 Novak, M., Giddens, A. et al., *Is there a Third Way? Essays on the changing direction of socialist thought*, London: IEA Health and Welfare Unit, 1998, pp. 13–7.
25 See in particular Thaler, R. and Sunstein, A., *Nudge*, New Haven: Yale University Press, 2008. The British edition of this book specifically singles out the current Conservative Party Prime Minister, David Cameron, for the interest he has shown in 'libertarian paternalism'.
26 Novak, op. cit., p. 2.
27 King, M., *Monetary policy: Practice ahead of theory*. Online. Available at: www.bankofengland.co.uk/publications/speeches/2005/speech245.pdf (accessed 10 May), 2005, p. 2.
28 Taken from a transcript of Blair's 1995 Mais Lecture published by the *Financial Times*: Blair, T., *Blair sets out framework to cure economic ills*, London: *Financial Times*, 23 May 1995.
29 Lawson, N., *The British Experiment*, Margaret Thatcher Foundation. Online. Available at: www.margaretthatcher.org/document/109504 (accessed 9 May 2011), 1984, pp. 3–4.
30 Blair, op. cit, p. 1.
31 Leigh-Pemberton, R., 'The case for price stability', in *Bank of England quarterly bulletin*, vol. 32, 1992, 447.
32 Balls, E. and Fabian Society, *Euro-monetarism: Why Britain was ensnared and how it should escape*, London: Fabian Society, 1992, p. 7.
33 Brown, G., *Speech by the Chancellor of the Exchequer, Mansion House*, London: HM Treasury. Online. Available at, http://archive.treasury.gov.uk/press/1998/p102_98.html (accessed 10 May 2011), 1998, p. 5.
34 Leigh-Pemberton, op. cit., p. 446.
35 Brown, op. cit., p. 2.
36 Bank of England, 'Inflation report', *Bank of England quarterly bulletin*, vol. 33, 1993, 34.
37 Brown, op. cit., p. 3.
38 Balls, op. cit., pp. 4, 16; Balls, E., 'Open macroeconomics in an open economy', in *Scottish Journal of Political Economy*, vol. 45, 1998, 119–21, 127–8.
39 In September 2003, the government instructed the Bank of England to move to a different inflation index, the harmonized index of consumer prices, the 'CPI', with a central target (and 1 per cent symmetrical range) of 2 per cent. This new index removed all possible links to house prices, as the previous index, RPIX, had included housing stock depreciation, local government tax and home insurance.
40 King, M., 'Credit and economic policy', in *Bank of England quarterly bulletin*, vol. 34, 1994, p. 170.

41 George, E., 'The prospects for monetary stability', in *Bank of England quarterly bulletin*, vol. 34, 1994, p. 260.

42 Additionally it should be added that interest rate targeting was not just a UK phenomenon, but became the standard feature of developed world monetary policy.

43 To be precise the Bank of England could have followed to the letter the 'Taylor rule' in setting interest rates. While the Bank did accept the notion that, 'in response to inflation pressures, a central bank that wishes to maintain control over inflation needs to raise the nominal rate of interest enough to generate a positive real return' (Besley, T., 'Inflation and the Global Economy', in *Bank of England quarterly bulletin*, vol. 48, 2008, 210), it, and the Federal Reserve did not follow Taylor's specific guidelines on how much interest rates should be changed by, or how to monitor inflation on an ongoing basis. Even so the Bank and the Taylor rule were both entirely endorsing of the view that inflation policy should remain focused on high street prices and not asset prices of any sort.

44 King, M., 'The inflation target five years on', in *Bank of England quarterly bulletin*, vol. 37, 1997, 434–7; Balls, op. cit., pp. 117–20.

45 Brown, G., *The conditions for full employment, Mais Lecture*, London: HM Treasury. Online. Available at: http://archive.treasury.gov.uk/press/1999/p168_99.html (accessed 10 May 2011), 1999, p. 7.; Brown, G., 'The conditions for high and stable growth and employment', in *The Economic Journal*, vol. 111 (471, Conference Papers), C30-C44, 2001, p. C34. Additionally, the ongoing deflationary problems with which Japan was (and continues to be) beset gave another impetus towards a symmetrical target of around 2.5 per cent.

46 King, M., 'Governor speech', in *Bank of England quarterly bulletin*, vol. 43, 2003, p. 477.

47 George, E., 'The New Lady of Threadneedle Street', in *Bank of England quarterly bulletin*, vol. 38, 1998, 176.

48 Benston, G. and Institute of Economic Affairs, *Regulating financial markets: a critique and some proposals*, London: Institute of Economic Affairs, 1998, pp. 32–3, 53–63, 99. See discussion in section 7.4.

49 Goodhart, C. and Seldon, A. et al., *Financial Regulation – or Over-regulation?* London: Institute of Economic Affairs, 1988, pp. 18–25.

50 Benston, op. cit., pp. 13–5.

51 Lodge, O., Williams, S. et al., *A Review of the UK Banking Industry: a case study*, London: Centre for Policy Studies, 2002, pp. 1–5.

52 King, M., 'Credit and economic policy', p. 170.

53 Goodhart, C., 'The constitutional position of the Central Bank', in Friedman, M., Goodhart, C., Wood, G. and Institute of Economic Affairs, *Money, Inflation and the Constitutional Position of the Central Bank*, London: Institute of Economic Affairs, 2003, pp. 104–6.

54 See Friedman, M. and Schwartz, A., *A Monetary History of the United States 1867–1960*. Princeton: Princeton University Press, 1963, pp. 300–411 for their famous analysis of the 'Great Contraction' in money supply between 1929 and 1933. Their argument was that the downturn from a 'normal' business investment cycle was massively accentuated by the Federal Reserve's insistence of raising interest rates and requiring banks to immediately build capital reserves. The tumultuous collapse in the economy that followed (36 per cent decline in real income, 25 per cent unemployment) reflected, they argued, not the investment cycle per se but a fall in the stock of money (33 per cent) over the same period that was entirely unnecessary and caused by the Federal Reserve.

55 Bank of England, 'Commentary', in *Bank of England quarterly bulletin*, vol. 27, 1987, 473.

56 George, E., *Speech*. Online. Available at: www.bankofengland.co.uk/publications/speeches/1999/speech45.htm (accessed 9 May 2011), 1999, p. 1.

57 George, E., *Speech*. Online. Available at: www.bankofengland.co.uk/publications/speeches/1999/speech32.htm, (accessed 9 May 2011), 1999, p. 5.
58 Large, A., *Puzzles in today's economy – the build up of household debt*. Online. Available at: www.bankofengland.co.uk/publications/speeches/2004/speech217.pdf (accessed 9 May 2011), 2004, pp. 4, 9–14.
59 Nickel, S., *Household debt, house prices and consumption growth*. Online. Available at: www.bankofengland.co.uk/publications/speeches/2004/speech227.pdf (accessed 9 May 2011), 2004, pp. 3–6.
60 Tucker, P., *Credit conditions and monetary policy*. Online. Available at: www.bankofengland.co.uk/publications/speeches/2003/speech201.pdf (accessed 9 May 2011), 2003, p. 11.
61 King, M., 'No money, no inflation – the role of money in the economy' in *Bank of England quarterly bulletin*, vol. 42, 2002, 174; Gieve, J., 'Speech' in *Bank of England quarterly bulletin*, vol. 47, 2007, 434.
62 King, M., *Governor speech*. Online. Available at: www.bankofengland.co.uk/publications/speeches/2006/speech263.pdf (accessed 9 May 2011), 2006, pp. 2–7.
63 Benito, A. et al., 'The role of household debt and balance sheets in the monetary transmission mechanism', in *Bank of England quarterly bulletin*, vol. 47, 2007, 70–6.
64 Goodhart, C., and Hofmann, B., *House Prices and the Macroeconomy: Implications for banking and price stability*, Oxford: Oxford University Press, 2007, Chapters 7 and 8, which demonstrate statistically the connection between the economic cycle, asset prices, and the scale of bank lending against property. See also Fernandez-Corugedo, E. and Muellbauer, J., *Consumer Credit Conditions in the United Kingdom*. Online. Available at: www.bankofengland.co.uk/publications/workingpapers/wp314.pdf (accessed 9 May 2011), 2006, which purports to show a causal relation between the availability of credit and increases in consumer debt.
65 Gieve, J., 'Speech', in *Bank of England quarterly bulletin*, vol. 47, 2007, 434.
66 King, M., 'No money, no inflation – the role of money in the economy', in *Bank of England quarterly bulletin*, vol. 42, 2002, 174.
67 Schwartz, A., 'Origins of the financial market crisis of 2008', in Booth, P., Alexander, P. et al., *Verdict on the Crash: Causes and policy implications*, London, Institute of Economic Affairs, 2009, p. 49.
68 Greenspan, A., *The Crisis*. Online, Available at: www.brookings.edu/~/media/files/programs/es/bpea/2010_spring_bpea_papers/spring2010_greenspan.pdf2010 (accessed 9 May 2011), 2010, pp. 38–9.
69 Lawrence White, writing for the Cato Institute, a Washington, DC-based think tank with strong links to the IEA, has suggested that adjustable rate mortgages went from being 20 per cent of new mortgages in 2001 to over 40 per cent in 2004. White, L., *How did we get into this financial mess*? Online. Available at: www.cato.org/pubs/bp/bp110.pdf (accessed 9 May 2011), 2008, p. 4.
70 Bernanke, B., *Monetary policy and the housing bubble*. Online. Available at: www.federalreserve.gov/newsevents/speech/bernanke20100103a.htm (accessed 9 May 2011), 2010, p. 6.
71 Greenspan, op. cit., p. 45.
72 In addition to Anna Schwartz cited above see also Lawrence White, op. cit., and Taylor, J., *Getting Off Track*, Stanford: Hoover Institution, 2009. The same argument is made by John Greenwood in his essay, 'The successes and failures of UK monetary policy, 2000–8', in Booth, P., Alexander, P. et al., *Verdict on the Crash: Causes and policy implications*, London, Institute of Economic Affairs, 2009.
73 Bernanke, B., *The global saving glut and the U.S. current account deficit*. Online. Available at: www.federalreserve.gov/boarddocs/speeches/2005/200503102/ (accessed 8 September 2011), 2005, pp. 2–13.
74 Dean, M., *Governmentality: Power and rule in modern society*, London: Sage Publications, 1999, pp. 198–207.

75 Foucault, op. cit., p. 187.
76 Foucault, M., 'What is Enlightenment?' in Foucault, M. and Rabinow, P., *The Foucault Reader*, Harmondsworth: Penguin, 1986, p. 42.
77 Veyne, P., 'Foucault revolutionises history', in Davidson, I., (ed.), *Foucault and His Interlocutors*, Chicago: University of Chicago Press, 1997, pp. 147–81.
78 Keynes, J., *The General Theory of Employment, Interest and Money*, Cambridge: Macmillan and Cambridge University Press, 1973 [1936], p. xxvi.
79 Foucault, *The Birth of Biopolitics*, pp. 68–9.
80 Ibid.

7 The sub-prime American homeowner consumer

1 Blair, T. and Fabian Society, *Socialism*, London: Fabian Society, 1994, pp. 4–7.
2 Brown, G., *Beyond the Crash*, New York: Free Press, 2010, pp. 3, 8, 38.
3 Clift, B. and Tomlinson, J., 'Credible Keynesianism? New Labour macroeconomic policy and the political economy of coarse tuning', in *British Journal of Political Science*, vol. 37, 2007: 47–69; and Tomlinson, J., 'Tale of a death exaggerated: how Keynesian policies survived the 1970s', in *Contemporary British History*, vol. 21, 2007, 429–48.
4 Brown, op. cit., p. 10.
5 Down Payment Assistance resources, *A home of your own: expanding opportunities for all Americans*. Online. Available at: www.americandreamdownpaymentassistance.com/whdoc06012002.cfm (accessed 20 March 2011), 2002, p. 5.
6 Bush, G., *President hosts conference on minority homeownership*. Online. Available at: http://georgewbush-whitehouse.archives.gov/news/releases/2002/10/20021015-7.html (accessed 9 September 2011), 2002, p. 1.
7 Bush, G., (2004), *Remarks by the President to the National Association of Home Builders*. Online. Available at: www.americandreamdownpaymentassistance.com/whsp10022004.cfm (accessed 20 March 2011), 2004, p. 1.
8 Weiss, M., 'Marketing and financing home ownership: mortgage lending and public policy in the United States, 1918–1989', in *Business and Economic History*, vol. 18, 1989, 109–15.
9 Joseph Rowntree Foundation. Online. Available at: www.jrf.org.uk/publications/home-ownership-and-poverty-britain (accessed 3 April 2011).
10 Frogner, M., 'Housing tenure and the labour market', in *Labour Market Trends,* vol. 523, 2002, p. 525.
11 From 1968 on, Fannie Mae was a private, publicly traded, for-profit company. Freddie Mac was given the same status in 1989.
12 Weiss, op. cit., p. 114; Snowden, K., 'Mortgage securitisation in the United States: twentieth century developments in historical perspective', in Bordo, M. and Sylla, R. (eds), *Anglo-American Financial Systems: Institutions and markets in the twentieth century*, 1995, pp. 267–9.
13 Bernanke, B., *Housing, housing finance, and monetary policy*. Online. Available HTTP: www.federalreserve.gov/newsevents/speech/bernanke20070831a.htm (accessed 2 April 2011), 2007, pp. 6–7.
14 Reagan, R., *Remarks on signing the Garn-St Germain Depository Institutions Act of 1982*. Online. Available at: www.reagan.utexas.edu/archives/speeches/1982/101582b.htm (accessed 2 February 2011), 1992.
15 Ibid.
16 Hanc, G., 'The banking crises of the 1980s and early 1990s: summary and implications', in *FDIC Banking Review*, vol. 11, 1998, pp. 5, 8.
17 Clinton, W., *Speech by President at realtors conference*. Online. Available at: http://archives.clintonpresidentialcenter.org/index.php?u=110594-speech-by-president-at-realtors-conference.htm (accessed 20 March 2011), 1995, p. 4.

18 Clinton's policies were in many ways connected to the 1977 Community Reinvestment Act (CRA), which enabled regulators to check whether banks were servicing the borrowing (business and household) needs of local communities in which they were based. The CRA offered no specific targets. Clinton's concern was specifically with home ownership, whatever the source of funding.
19 Levitin, A. and Wachter, S., *Explaining the housing bubble*, pp. 43–4. Online. Available at: http://ssrn.com/abstract=1669401 (accessed 19 March 2011), 2010, pp. 43–4.
20 Clinton, W., *Speech by President at HUD home ownership event*. Online. Available at: http://archives.clintonpresidentialcenter.org/index.php?u=060595-speech-by-president-at-hud-home-ownership-event.htm (accessed 20 March 2011), 1995, p. 3.
21 Clinton, W., *Presidential radio address on homeownership*. Online. Available at: http://archives.clintonpresidentialcenter.org/index.php?u=122300-presidential-radio-address-on-homeownership.htm (accessed 20 March 2011), 1995, p. 1.
22 Department of Housing and Urban Development, *Homeownership and its benefits, Urban Policy Brief, Number 2*. Online. Available at: www.huduser.org/publications/txt.hdbrf2.txt (accessed 20 March 2011), 1995.
23 Clinton, W., *Speech by President at realtors conference*, p. 4.
24 Clinton, W., *Speech by President at HUD home ownership event*, p. 3.
25 Ibid.
26 Clinton, W., *Speech by President at realtors conference*, p. 5.
27 Ibid.
28 Ibid.
29 Clinton, W., *Speech by President at HUD home ownership event*, p. 3.
30 Clinton, W., *Speech by President at realtors conference*, p. 5.
31 Ibid., p. 3.
32 Clinton, W., *Speech by President at Empowerment Zone Reception*. Online. Available at: http://archives.clintonpresidentialcenter.org/index.php?u=071598-speech-by-president-at-empowerment-zone-reception.htm (accessed 20 March 2011), 1998, p. 1.
33 Blair, T. *Tony Blair: a journey*, London, Hutchinson, 2010.
34 Bush, G., *President calls for expanding opportunities to home ownership*. Online. Available at: http://georgewbush-whitehouse.archives.gov/news/releases/2002/06/20020617-2.html (accessed 9 September 2011), 2002, pp. 1–2.
35 Down Payment Assistance resources, op. cit., p. 1.
36 Ibid., pp. 1–3, 6.
37 Levitin and Wachter, op. cit., pp. 43–4.
38 Bush, G., *President discusses strong economy, homeownership in radio address*. Online. Available at: www.americandreamdownpaymentassistance.com/whsp03272004.cfm (accessed 20 March 2011), 2004, p. 1.
39 Bush, G., *President hosts conference on minority homeownership*, pp. 1, 2, 4.
40 Ibid., p. 2.
41 Bush, G., *President Bush meets with first-time homebuyers in NM and AZ*. Online. Available at: www.americandreamdownpaymentassistance.com/whsp03262004.cfm (accessed 20 March 2011), 2004, p. 5.
42 Bernanke, B., *GSE portfolios, systemic risk, and affordable housing*. Online. Available at: www.federalreserve.gov/newsevents/speech/bernanke20070306a.htm (accessed 2 April 2011), 2007, p. 3.
43 Felsenheimer, J. and Gisdakis, P. *Credit Crises*, Weinheim: Wiley-VCH, 2008, pp. 53–204; G. Gorton and A. Metrick, *Securitized banking and the run on repo*. Online. Available at: www.moodys.com/microsites/crc2010/pres/day1/gorton_run_on_repo_may_2010.pdf (accessed 13 March 2011), 2009; G. Gorton and A. Metrick, *Regulating the shadow banking system*. Online. Available at: www.brookings.edu/~/media/Files/Programs/ES/BPEA/2010_fall_bpea_papers/2010fall_gorton.pdf (accessed 9 September 2011), 2010.

44 Gramlich, E., (2001), *Promoting and sustaining home ownership*, Online. Available at: www.federalreserve.gov/boarddocs/speeches/2001/200111082/default.htm (accessed 1 April 2011), 2001, p. 1.
45 Ibid., pp. 1–2.
46 Olson, M., *Revisiting traditional paths to ownership*. Online. Available at: www.federalreserve.gov/boarddocs/speeches/2005/20050623/default.htm (accessed 9 September 2011), 2005, pp. 1–2.
47 Financial Crisis Inquiry Commission, *Final report of the national commission on the causes of the financial and economic crisis in the United States*, New York: PublicAffairs, 2010, pp. 217–9.
48 Levitin and Wachter, op. cit., p. 24.
49 Bush, G., *President Bush signs American Dream Downpayment Act of 2003*. Online. Available at: www.americandreamdownpaymentassistance.com/whsp12162003.cfm (accessed 20 March 2011), 2003, p. 2; G. Bush, *President discusses strong economy, homeownership in radio address*, p. 1.
50 Gramlich, E., *Subprime lending, predatory lending*. Online. Available at: www.federalreserve.gov/boarddocs/speeches/2000/20001206.htm (accessed 2 April 2011), 2000, p. 1.
51 Gramlich, E., *Lending to lower income households*. Online. Available at: www.federalreserve.gov/boarddocs/speeches/2002/20020301/default.htm (accessed 2 April 2011), 2002.
52 Olson, M., op. cit., p. 5.
53 Gramlich, E., *Promoting and sustaining home ownership*, p. 3.
54 Gramlich, E., *Subprime lending, predatory lending*, p. 4.
55 Greenspan, A., *Banking evolution*. Online. Available at: www.federalreserve.gov/boarddocs/speeches/2000/20000504.htm (accessed 2 April 2011), 2000, p. 1.
56 Greenspan, A., *The mortgage market and consumer debt*. Online. Available at: www.federalreserve.gov/boarddocs/speeches/2004/20041019/default.htm (accessed 2 April 2011), 2004, p. 2.
57 Bernanke, B., *Balance sheets and the recovery*. Online. Available at: www.federalreserve.gov/boarddocs/speeches/2003/20030221/default.htm (accessed 2 April 2011), 2003, p. 5.
58 Ibid., pp. 3–4.
59 Ibid., p. 5.
60 Greenspan, A., *Home mortgage market*. Online. Available at: www.federalreserve.gov/boarddocs/speeches/2003/20030304/default.htm (accessed 2 April 2011), 2003, pp. 3–5.
61 Ibid., p. 5.
62 Greenspan, A., *Mortgage banking*. Online. Available at: www.federalreserve.gov/boarddocs/speeches/2005/200509262/default.htm (accessed 9 September 2011), 2005, pp. 2–3.
63 Greenspan, A., *The mortgage market and consumer debt*, 2004, pp. 2–3.
64 Greenspan, A., *Understanding household debt obligations*. Online. Available at: www.federalreserve.gov/boarddocs/speeches/2004/20040223/default.htm (accessed 2 April 2011), 2004, pp. 2–4.
65 Gramlich, E., *Consumption and the wealth effect: the United States and the United Kingdom*. Online. Available at: www.federalreserve.gov/boarddocs/speeches/2002/20020220/default.htm (accessed 3 April 2011), 2002, p. 1.
66 Clift and Tomlinson, op. cit.; Tomlinson, op. cit.
67 Bernanke, B., *Deflation: making sure 'it' doesn't happen here*. Online. Available at: www.federalreserve.gov/boarddocs/speeches/2002/20021121/default.htm (accessed 2 April 2011), 2002, pp. 5–7.
68 Bernanke, B., *What the Fed did and why: supporting the recovery and sustaining price stability*. Online. Available at: www.washingtonpost.com/wp-dyn/content/article/2010/11/03/AR2010110307372.html?hpid=topnews (accessed 16 April 2011), 2010.

69 Greenspan, A., *The Crisis*. Online, Available at: www.brookings.edu/~/media/files/programs/es/bpea/2010_spring_bpea_papers/spring2010_greenspan.pdf2010 (accessed 2 April 2011), 2010, pp. 4–5.
70 Brown, op. cit., pp. 156–9.
71 Friedman, M. and Schwartz, A., *A Monetary History of the United States 1867–1960*. Princeton: Princeton University Press, 1963.
72 White, L., *Federal Reserve policy and the housing bubble*. Online. Available at: www.cato.org/pubs/journal/cj29n1/cj29n1–9.pdf (accessed 2 April 2011), 2009, pp. 121–4.
73 White, L., *How did we get into this financial mess*? Online. Available at: www.cato.org/pubs/bp/bp110.pdf (accessed 2 April 2011), 2008, p. 7.
74 Ibid., pp. 4–6.
75 Wallison, P., *Cause and effect: government policies and the financial crisis*. Online. Available at: www.aei.org/outlook/29015 (accessed 2 April 2011), 2008, p. 1.
76 Levitin and Wachter, op. cit., pp. 30–3.
77 Financial Crisis Inquiry Commission, op. cit., pp. 102, 104.
78 Bernanke, *GSE portfolios, systemic risk, and affordable housing*, pp. 1–2.
79 Levitin and Wachter, op. cit., p. 45.
80 Wallison, op. cit., pp. 2–4.
81 In addition to White and Wallison, see also Pinto, E., *Acorn and the housing bubble*. Online. Available at: http://online.wsj.com/article/SB10001424052748703298004574459763052141456.html (accessed 2 April 2011), 2009; and Sowell, T., *Housing boom and bust*. Online. Available at: www.nationalreview.com/articles/227468/housing-boom-and-bust/thomas-sowell (accessed 2 April 2011), 2009.
82 Hayek, F. and Institute of Economic Affairs, *Denationalisation of Money: an analysis of the theory and practice of concurrent currencies*, London: Institute of Economic Affairs, 1976, p. 80.
83 Friedman, M., *A Program for Monetary Stability*, New York: Fordham University Press, 1965, p. 68.
84 Ibid., p. 66.
85 Veblen, T., *Essays in Our Changing Order*, London: Routledge, 1994 [1894], p. 103.

8 Conclusion: problematizing the consumer

1 Knight, F., *Risk, Uncertainty and Profit*, Boston: Houghton Mifflin, 1921.
2 See for example the critiques of economics often made by economic sociologists such as Granovetter, M., 'Economic action and social structure: the problem of embeddedness', *American Journal of Sociology*, vol. 91, 1985, 481–510 and Zukin, S. and Dimaggio, P., 'Introduction'. in Zukin, S. and Dimaggio, P. (ed.), *Structures of Capital: the social organization of the economy*, Cambridge: Cambridge University Press, 1990.
3 Max Weber, for instance, certainly took this to be true as far back as 1908 when he wrote, 'under today's conditions of existence the approximation of reality to the theoretical propositions of economics has been a constantly increasing one.' (Weber, M., 'Marginal utility theory and the fundamental law of psychophysics', in *Social Science Quarterly*, 56, 1975, p. 33.)
4 Hacking, I., 'Making up people', in Biagoli, M. (ed.), *The Science Studies Reader*, New York and London: Routledge, 1999, pp. 165–6.
5 Hilton, M., *Consumerism in Twentieth Century Britain*, Cambridge, Cambridge University Press, 2003, pp. 22, 189–99.
6 Galbraith, J., *The Affluent Society*, London: Penguin, 1998.
7 Offer, A., *The Challenge of Affluence*, Oxford: Oxford University Press, 2006, pp. 1–11, 357–9.
8 Polanyi, K., *The Great Transformation*, Boston: Beacon Press, 2001 [1944], p. 80.

9 Veblen, T., *Essays in Our Changing Order*, London: Routledge, 1994 [1894], pp. 97–100.

10 'Before the end of the eighteenth century, man did not exist – any more than the potency of life, the fecundity of labour. … He is quite a recent creature, which the demiurge of knowledge fabricated with its own hands less than two hundred years ago' (Foucault, M., *The Order of Things*. London: Routledge, 2002 [1966], p. 336).

11 Smith, A., *Wealth of Nations*, Amherst: Prometheus Books, 1991, pp. 36, 271.

12 Lawson, N., *Appeal to Reason*, London: Duckworth Overlook, 2008.

13 Foucault, M., 'Governmentality', in Burchell, G., Gordon, C. and Miller P. (eds), *The Foucault Effect: Studies in governmentality*, Chicago: University of Chicago Press, 1991, pp. 102–4.

Bibliography

Allen, G., *The British Disease: a short essay on the nature and causes of the nation's lagging wealth*, London: Institute of Economic Affairs, 1976.

Bacon, R. and Eltis, W., *Britain's Economic Problem: Too few producers*, London: Macmillan, 1976.

Balls, E., 'Open macroeconomics in an open economy', in *Scottish Journal of Political Economy*, vol. 45, 1998, 113–32.

Balls, E. and Fabian Society, *Euro-monetarism: Why Britain was ensnared and how it should escape*, London: Fabian Society, 1992.

Bank of England, 'Competition and credit control', in *Bank of England quarterly bulletin*, vol. 11, 1971, 189–93.

Bank of England, 'Commentary', in *Bank of England quarterly bulletin*, vol. 13, 1973, 401–18.

Bank of England, 'Commentary', in *Bank of England quarterly bulletin*, vol. 19, 1979, 359–78.

Bank of England, 'Commentary', in *Bank of England quarterly bulletin*, vol. 21, 1981, 3–17.

Bank of England, 'The supplementary deposits scheme', in *Bank of England quarterly bulletin*, vol. 22, 1982, 74–85.

Bank of England, 'Mortgage lending and the housing market', in *Bank of England quarterly bulletin*, vol. 22, 1982, 390–8.

Bank of England, 'Commentary', in *Bank of England quarterly bulletin*, vol. 23, 1983, 3–18.

Bank of England, 'Commentary', in *Bank of England quarterly bulletin*, vol. 23, 1983, 153–70.

Bank of England, 'Commentary', in *Bank of England quarterly bulletin*, vol. 23, 1983, 321–36.

Bank of England, 'Competition, innovation, and regulation in British banking', in *Bank of England quarterly bulletin*, vol. 23, 1983, 363–76.

Bank of England, 'Commentary', in *Bank of England quarterly bulletin*, vol. 26, 1986, 309–32.

Bank of England, 'Commentary', in *Bank of England quarterly bulletin*, vol. 26, 1986, 449–71.

Bank of England, 'Commentary', in *Bank of England quarterly bulletin*, vol. 27, 1987, 3–25.

Bank of England, 'Commentary', in *Bank of England quarterly bulletin*, vol. 27, 1987, 473–95.

Bank of England, 'Commentary', in *Bank of England quarterly bulletin*, vol. 29, 1989, 3–26.

Bank of England, 'Inflation report', in *Bank of England quarterly bulletin*, vol. 33, 1993.

Bank of England and HM Treasury, *Monetary Control*, Cmnd 7858, London: HMSO, 1980.

Barry, A., Osbourne, T. and Rose, N. (eds), Foucault and Political Reason, London: UCL Press, 1996.

Benito, A. et al., 'The role of household debt and balance sheets in the monetary transmission mechanism', in *Bank of England quarterly bulletin*, vol. 47, 2007.

Benston, G. and Institute of Economic Affairs, *Regulating Financial Markets: a critique and some proposals*, London: Institute of Economic Affairs, 1998.

Berlin, I., *Liberty: Incorporating four essays on liberty*, Oxford: Oxford University Press, 2002.

Bernanke, B., *Deflation: making sure 'it' doesn't happen here*. Online. Available at: www.federalreserve.gov/boarddocs/speeches/2002/20021121/default.htm (accessed 2 April 2011), 2002.

Bernanke, B., *Balance sheets and the recovery*. Online. Available at: www.federalreserve.gov/boarddocs/speeches/2003/20030221/default.htm (accessed 2 April 2011), 2003.

Bernanke, B., *The global saving glut and the U.S. current account deficit*. Online. Available at: www.federalreserve.gov/boarddocs/speeches/2005/200503102/ (accessed 8 September 2011), 2005.

Bernanke, B., *Housing, housing finance, and monetary policy*. Online. Available at: www.federalreserve.gov/newsevents/speech/bernanke20070831a.htm (accessed 2 April 2011), 2007.

Bernanke, B., *GSE portfolios, systemic risk, and affordable housing*. Online. Available at: www.federalreserve.gov/newsevents/speech/bernanke20070306a.htm (accessed 2 April 2011), 2007.

Bernanke, B., *What the Fed did and why: supporting the recovery and sustaining price stability*. Online. Available at: www.washingtonpost.com/wp-dyn/content/article/2010/11/03/AR2010110307372.html?hpid=topnews (accessed 2 April 2011), 2010.

Bernanke, B., *Monetary policy and the housing bubble*. Online. Available at: www.federalreserve.gov/newsevents/speech/bernanke20100103a.htm (accessed 9 May 2011), 2010.

Besley, T., 'Inflation and the global economy', in *Bank of England quarterly bulletin*, vol. 48, 2008.

Blair, T., *Blair sets out framework to cure economic ills*, London: Financial Times, 23 May 1995.

Blair, T., *Tony Blair: a journey*, London, Hutchinson, 2010.

Blair, T. and Fabian Society, *Socialism*, London: Fabian Society, 1994.

Blair, T. and Fabian Society, *Let Us Face the Future: the 1945 anniversary lecture*, London: Fabian Society, 1995.

Blair, T. and Fabian Society, *The Third Way: New politics for the new century*, London: Fabian Society, 1998.

von Böhm-Bawerk, E., *The Positive Theory of Capital*, South Holland, Ill.: Libertarian Press, 1959.

Booth, P., Alexander, P. et al., *Verdict on the Crash: Causes and policy implications*, London, Institute of Economic Affairs, 2009.

Booth, P. and Institute of Economic Affairs (eds), (2006) *Were 364 Economists All Wrong?* London: Institute of Economic Affairs, 2006.

Brennan, G. and Buchanan, J., *Monopoly in Money and Inflation: the case for a constitution to discipline government*, London: Institute of Economic Affairs, 1981.

Brittan, S., *Government and the Market Economy: an appraisal of economic policy since the 1970 General Election*, London: Institute of Economic Affairs, 1971.

Brown, G., *Speech by the Chancellor of the Exchequer, Mansion House*, London: HM Treasury. Online. Available at: http://archive.treasury.gov.uk/press/1998/p102_98.html (accessed 10 May 2011), 1998.

Brown, G., *The conditions for full employment, Mais Lecture*, London: HM Treasury. Online. Available at: http://archive.treasury.gov.uk/press/1999/p168_99.html (accessed 10 May 2011), 1999.

Brown, G., 'The conditions for high and stable growth and employment', in *The Economic Journal*, vol. 111 (471, Conference Papers), C30–C44, 2001.

Brown, G., *Beyond the Crash*, New York: Free Press, 2010.

Bruce-Gardyne, J., 'Chancellor Reagan', in Congdon, T., Minford, P. et al., *Whither Monetarism? The Chancellor's Mansion House speech, with comments by three wise men*, London: Centre for Policy Studies, 1985.

Buchanan, J., Wagner, R. et al., *The Consequences of Mr Keynes: an analysis of the misuse of economic theory for political profiteering, with proposals for constitutional disciplines*. London: Institute of Economic Affairs, 1978.

Burchell, G., 'Liberal government and techniques of the self', in Barry, A., Osbourne, T. and Rose, N. (eds), *Foucault and Political Reason*, London: UCL Press, 1996.

Burchell, G., Gordon, C., Miller, P. and Foucault, M., *The Foucault Effect: Studies in governmentality; with two lectures by and an interview with Michel Foucault*, London: Chicago: University of Chicago Press, 1991.

Burton, J. and Centre for Policy Studies, *The Job Support Machine: a critique of the subsidy morass*, London: Centre for Policy Studies, 1979.

Bush, G., *President hosts conference on minority homeownership*. Online. Available at: http://georgewbush-whitehouse.archives.gov/news/releases/2002/10/20021015-7.html (accessed 9 September 2011), 2002.

Bush, G., *President calls for expanding opportunities to home ownership*. Online. Available at: http://georgewbush-whitehouse.archives.gov/news/releases/2002/06/20020617-2.html (accessed 9 September 2011), 2002.

Bush, G., *President Bush signs American Dream Downpayment Act of 2003*. Online. Available at: www.americandreamdownpaymentassistance.com/whsp12162003.cfm (accessed 20 March 2011), 2003.

Bush, G., *President discusses strong economy, homeownership in radio address*. Online. Available at: www.americandreamdownpaymentassistance.com/whsp03272004.cfm (accessed 20 March 2011), 2004.

Bush, G., *President Bush meets with first-time homebuyers in NM and AZ*. Online. Available at: www.americandreamdownpaymentassistance.com/whsp03262004.cfm (accessed 20 March 2011), 2004.

Bush, G., (2004), *Remarks by the President to the National Association of Home Builders*. Online. Available at: www.americandreamdownpaymentassistance.com/whsp10022004.cfm (accessed 20 March 2011), 2004.

Butt, R. and Centre for Policy Studies, *The Unfinished Task: the Conservative record in perspective: summer address*, London: Centre for Policy Studies, 1986.

Caldwell, B., *Hayek's Challenge: an intellectual biography of F. A. Hayek*, Chicago: University of Chicago Press, 2004.

Cairncross, A., *The British Economy Since 1945*, Oxford: Blackwell, 1995.

Canes, M. and Institute of Economic Affairs, *Telephones – Public or Private? A comparative study of the British and American systems*, London: Institute of Economic Affairs, 1966.

Chiplin, B. and Coyne, J., 'Property rights, industrial democracy and the Bullock Report', in Chiplin, B., Coyne, J., Sirc, L. and Institute of Economic Affairs, *Can Workers Manage?* London: Institute of Economic Affairs, 1977.

Clark, C. and Institute of Economic Affairs, (1961), *Growthmanship: a study in the mythology of investment*. London: Barrie and Rockliff, 1961.

Clift, B. and Tomlinson, J., 'Credible Keynesianism? New Labour macroeconomic policy and the political economy of coarse tuning', in *British Journal of Political Science*, vol. 37, 2007: 47–69.

Clinton, W., *Speech by President at realtors conference*. Online. Available at: http://archives.clintonpresidentialcenter.org/index.php?u=110594-speech-by-president-at-realtors-conference.htm (accessed 20 March 2011), 1995.

Clinton, W., *Speech by President at HUD home ownership event*. Online. Available at: http://archives.clintonpresidentialcenter.org/index.php?u=060595-speech-by-president-at-hud-home-ownership-event.htm (accessed 20 March 2011), 1995.

Clinton, W., *Presidential radio address on homeownership*. Online. Available at: http://archives.clintonpresidentialcenter.org/index.php?u=122300-presidential-radio-address-on-homeownership.htm (accessed 20 March 2011), 1995.

Clinton, W., *Speech by President at Empowerment Zone Reception*. Online. Available at: http://archives.clintonpresidentialcenter.org/index.php?u=071598-speech-by-president-at-empowerment-zone-reception.htm (accessed 20 March 2011), 1998.

Cockett, R., *Thinking the Unthinkable*, London: Fontana, 1995.

Collard, D. and Fabian Society, *The New Right: a critique*, London: Fabian Society, 1968.

Congdon, T. 'Start of a somersault', in Congdon, T., Minford, P. et al., *Whither Monetarism? The Chancellor's Mansion House speech, with comments by three wise men*, London: Centre for Policy Studies, 1985.

Congdon, T., *Monetarism Lost: and why it must be regained*, London: Centre for Policy Studies, 1989.

Conservative Central Office, *The Right Approach*, Margaret Thatcher Foundation. Online. Available at: www.margaretthatcher.org/document/109439 (accessed 9 May 2011), 1976.

Conservative Research Department, *Enterprise Culture Group Meetings*, Conservative Party Archive, Centre for Policy Studies Box 4/4/40, Oxford: Bodleian Library, Oxford University, 1980–81.

Conservative Research Department, *Budget Submissions*, Conservative Party Archive, Box 4/4/11, Oxford: Bodleian Library, Oxford University, 1981.

Conservative Research Department, *Policy Group on the Promotion of Enterprise*, Conservative Party Archive Box 4/4/41, Oxford: Bodleian Library, Oxford University, 1982–3.

Crouch, C., 'Privatised Keynesianism: an unacknowledged policy regime', in *The British Journal of Politics and International Relations*, vol. 11, 2009, 382–99.

Crosland, A. and Fabian Society, *Can Labour Win?* London: Fabian Society, 1960.

Crosland, A. and Fabian Society, *A Social Democratic Britain*, London: Fabian Society, 1971.

Cruikshank, B., 'Revolutions within: self-government and self-esteem', in Barry, A., Osbourne, T. and Rose, N. (eds), *Foucault and Political Reason*, London: UCL Press, 1996.

Dean, M., *Governmentality: Power and rule in modern society*, London: Sage Publications, 1999.

Department of Housing and Urban Development, *Homeownership and its benefits, Urban Policy Brief, Number 2*. Online. Available at: www.huduser.org/publications/txt.hdbrf2.txt (accessed 20 March 2011), 1995.

Down Payment Assistance resources, *A Home of your own: expanding opportunities for all Americans*. Online. Available at: www.americandreamdownpaymentassistance.com/whdoc06012002.cfm (accessed 20 March 2011), 2002.

Felsenheimer, J. and Gisdakis, P., *Credit Crises*, Weinheim: Wiley-VCH, 2008.

Fernandez-Corugedo, E. and Muellbauer, J., *Consumer Credit Conditions in the United Kingdom*. Online. Available at: www.bankofengland.co.uk/publications/workingpapers/wp314.pdf (accessed 9 May 2011), 2006.

Financial Crisis Inquiry Commission, *Final report of the national commission on the causes of the financial and economic crisis in the United States*, New York: PublicAffairs, 2010.

Foucault, M., 'What is Enlightenment?' in Foucault, M. and Rabinow, P., *The Foucault Reader*, Harmondsworth: Penguin, 1986.

Foucault, M., 'Governmentality', in Burchell, G., Gordon, C. and Miller, P. (eds), *The Foucault Effect: Studies in governmentality*, Chicago: University of Chicago Press, 1991.

Foucault, M., 'Maurice Florence', in Foucault, M. and Faubion, J., *Aesthetics, Method, and Epistemology*, London: Penguin, 2000.

Foucault, M., *The Archaeology of Knowledge*, London: Routledge, 2002 [1969].

Foucault, M., *The Order of Things*. London: Routledge, 2002 [1966].

Foucault, M., *The Birth of Biopolitics*, Houndmills and New York: Palgrave Macmillan, 2008.

Freeden, M., *The New Liberalism*, Oxford: Oxford University Press, 1978.

Friedman, M., *A Theory of the Consumption Function*, Princeton: Princeton University Press, 1957.

Friedman, M., *A Program for Monetary Stability*, New York: Fordham University Press, 1965.

Friedman, M., 'The quantity theory of money: a restatement', in Friedman, M., *The Optimum Quantity of Money and Other Essays*, Chicago: Aldine, 1969.

Friedman, M., 'Response to questionnaire on monetary policy', in HM Treasury, *Financial Statement and Budget Report 1980–81*, HC 720, London: HMSO, 1980.

Friedman, M., 'On the IEA's influence in our times', in Harris, R. and Seldon, A., *A Conversation with Harris and Seldon*. London: Institute of Economic Affairs, 2001.

Friedman, M., *Capitalism and Freedom*, Chicago and London: University of Chicago Press, 2002.

Friedman, M. and Institute of Economic Affairs, *The Counter-revolution in Monetary Theory*, London: Institute of Economic Affairs, 1970.

Friedman, M. and Schwartz, A., *A Monetary History of the United States 1867–1960*. Princeton: Princeton University Press, 1963.

Frisch, R., 'Circulation planning: proposal for a national organisation of a commodity and service exchange', in *Econometrica*, vol. 2, 1934.

Frogner, M., 'Housing tenure and the labour market', in *Labour Market Trends,* vol. 523, 2002, 525–32.

Fulop, C., *Consumers In the Market: a study in choice, competition and sovereignty*, London: Institute of Economic Affairs, 1967.

Galbraith, J., *The Affluent Society*, London: Penguin, 1998.

Gamble, A., *The Free Economy and the Strong State: the politics of Thatcherism*, Basingstoke: Macmillan Press, 1994.

George, E., 'The prospects for monetary stability', in *Bank of England quarterly bulletin*, vol. 34, 1994.

George, E., 'The New Lady of Threadneedle Street', in *Bank of England quarterly bulletin*, vol. 38, 1998.

George, E., *Governor speech*. Online, Available at: www.bankofengland.co.uk/publications/speeches/1999/speech32.htm (accessed 10 May 2011), 1999.

George, E., *Governor speech*. Online, Available at: www.bankofengland.co.uk/publications/speeches/1999/speech45.htm (accessed 10 May 2011), 1999.

Gibson, N. and Institute of Economic Affairs, *Financial Intermediaries and Monetary Policy*, London: Institute of Economic Affairs, 1970.

Giddens, A., *Consequences of Modernity*, Cambridge: Polity Press, 1990.

Giddens, A., *Modernity and Self Identity: Self and society in the late modern age*, Cambridge, Polity Press, 1991.

Giddens, A., *Runaway World*. London: Profile, 1999.

Giersch, H., *Liberalisation for Faster Economic Growth: Internal and external measures required*, London: Institute of Economic Affairs, 1986.

Gieve, J., 'Speech', in *Bank of England quarterly bulletin*, vol. 47, 2007.

Gilmour, I., *Dancing with Dogma: Britain under Thatcherism*, London: Simon & Schuster, 1992.

Goodhart, C., 'The constitutional position of the Central Bank', in Friedman, M., Goodhart, C., Wood, G. and Institute of Economic Affairs, *Money, Inflation and the Constitutional Position of the Central Bank*, London: Institute of Economic Affairs, 2003.

Goodhart, C., and Hofmann, B., *House Prices and the Macroeconomy: Implications for banking and price stability*, Oxford: Oxford University Press, 2007.

Goodhart, C., Seldon, A. et al., *Financial Regulation – or Over-regulation?* London: Institute of Economic Affairs, 1988.

Goodwin, C., 'The art of an ethical life: Keynes and Bloomsbury', in Backhouse, R. and Bateman, B. (eds), *The Cambridge Companion to Keynes*, Cambridge: Cambridge University Press, 2006.

Gordon, C., 'Question, ethos, event: Foucault on Kant and Enlightenment', in *Economy and Society*, vol. 15, pp. 71–85, 1986.

Gorton, G. and Metrick, A., *Securitized banking and the run on repo*. Online. Available at: www.moodys.com/microsites/crc2010/pres/day1/gorton_run_on_repo_may_2010.pdf (accessed 13 March 2011), 2009.

Gorton, G. and Metrick, A., *Regulating the shadow banking system*. Online. Available at: www.brookings.edu/~/media/Files/Programs/ES/BPEA/2010_fall_bpea_papers/2010fall_gorton.pdf (accessed 9 September 2011), 2010.

Gough, T. and Taylor, T., *The Building Society Price Cartel*, London: Institute of Economic Affairs, 1979.

Gramlich, E., *Subprime lending, predatory lending*. Online. Available at: www.federalreserve.gov/boarddocs/speeches/2000/20001206.htm (accessed 2 April 2011), 2000.

Gramlich, E., *Promoting and sustaining home ownership*. Online. Available at: www.federalreserve.gov/boarddocs/speeches/2001/200111082/default.htm (accessed 2 April 2011), 2001.

Gramlich, E., *Consumption and the wealth effect: the United States and the United Kingdom*. Online. Available at: www.federalreserve.gov/boarddocs/speeches/2002/20020220/default.htm (accessed 3 April 2011), 2002.

Gramlich, E., *Lending to lower income households*. Online. Available at: www.federalreserve.gov/boarddocs/speeches/2002/20020301/default.htm (accessed 2 April 2011), 2002.

Granovetter, M., 'Economic action and social structure: the problem of embeddedness', *American Journal of Sociology*, vol. 91, 1985, 481–510.

Green, E., *Thatcher*, New York: Oxford University Press, 2006.

Greenspan, A., *Banking evolution*. Online. Available at: www.federalreserve.gov/boarddocs/speeches/2000/20000504.htm (accessed 2 April 2011), 2000.

Greenspan, A., *Home mortgage market*. Online. Available at: www.federalreserve.gov/boarddocs/speeches/2003/20030304/default.htm (accessed 2 April 2011), 2003.

Greenspan, A., *The mortgage market and consumer debt*, Online. Available at: www.federalreserve.gov/boarddocs/speeches/2004/20041019/default.htm (accessed 2 April 2011), 2004.

Greenspan, A., *Understanding household debt obligations*. Online. Available at: www.federalreserve.gov/boarddocs/speeches/2004/20040223/default.htm (accessed 2 April 2011), 2004.

Greenspan, A., *Mortgage banking*, pp. 2–3. Online. Available at: www.federalreserve.gov/boarddocs/speeches/2005/200509262/default.htm (accessed 2 April 2011), 2005.

Greenspan, A., *The crisis*. Online, Available at: www.brookings.edu/~/media/files/programs/es/bpea/2010_spring_bpea_papers/spring2010_greenspan.pdf2010 (accessed 2 April 2011), 2010.

Greenwood, J., 'The successes and failures of UK monetary policy, 2000–8', in Booth, P., Alexander, P. et al., *Verdict on the Crash: Causes and policy implications*, London, Institute of Economic Affairs, 2009.

Griffiths, B. and Institute of Economic Affairs, *Money and Economic Policy*, London: Institute of Economic Affairs, 1972.

Gyford, J. and Haseler, S., *Social Democracy: beyond revisionism*, London, Fabian Society, 1971.

Hacking, I., 'Making up people', in Biagoli, M. (ed.), *The Science Studies Reader*, New York and London: Routledge, 1999.

Hallett, G., James P. et al. *Farming for Consumers*, London: Institute of Economic Affairs, 1963.

Hanc, G., 'The banking crises of the 1980s and early 1990s: summary and implications', in *FDIC Banking Review*, vol. 11, 1998, 1–55.

Harris, R., 'A self-confessed monetarist'. in Harris, R., Sewill, B. et al., *British Economic Policy 1970–74: Two views*, London: Institute of Economic Affairs, 1975.

Harris, R., 'Bullock's basic blunder', in Chiplin, B., Coyne, J., Sirc, L. and Institute of Economic Affairs, *Can Workers Manage?* London: Institute of Economic Affairs, 1977.

Harris, R., 'Now for planning', in Booth, P. and Institute of Economic Affairs (eds), *Towards a Liberal Utopia*, London: Institute of Economic Affairs, 2005.

Harris, R., Seldon, A. et al., *Hire Purchase in a Free Society*, London: Institute of Economic Affairs, 1958.

Harris, R., Seldon, A. et al., *Advertising in a Free Society*, London: Institute of Economic Affairs, 1959.

Harris, R., Seldon, A. et al., *Choice in Welfare 1965: Second report on an inquiry conducted by Mass-Observation into the extent of knowledge and preference in state and private provision for education, health services and pensions*, London: Institute of Economic Affairs, 1965.

Harris, R., Seldon, A. et al., *A Conversation with Harris and Seldon*, London: Institute of Economic Affairs, 2001.

Harris, R., Sewill, B. et al., *British economic policy 1970–74: Two views*, London: Institute of Economic Affairs, 1975.

Harvey, D., *A Brief History of Neoliberalism*, Oxford: Oxford University Press, 2005.

Hayek, F., *Prices and Production*, New York: Macmillan, 1932.

Hayek, F., 'The use of knowledge in society', in *American Economic Review*, vol. 35, 1945.

Hayek, F., *The Pure Theory of Capital*, London: Routledge & Keegan Paul, 1950 [1941].

Hayek, F., *Full Employment At Any Price?* London: Institute of Economic Affairs, 1975.

Hayek, F., *The Road to Serfdom*, New York: Routledge, 2001.

Hayek, F., *The Constitution of Liberty*, London: Routledge, 2006.

Hayek, F. and Institute of Economic Affairs, *Denationalisation of Money: an analysis of the theory and practice of concurrent currencies*, London: Institute of Economic Affairs, 1976.

Hayek, F. and Institute of Economic Affairs Health and Welfare Unit, *The Intellectuals and Socialism*, London: Institute of Economic Affairs Health and Welfare Unit, 1998 [1949].

Hayek, F. and Shenoy, S., *A Tiger by the Tail: a 40-years' running commentary on Keynesianism by Hayek*, London: Institute of Economic Affairs, 1978.

Henderson, R., 'Money in practice', in Seldon, A. (ed.), *Not Unanimous; a rival verdict to Radcliffe's on money*, London: Institute of Economic Affairs, 1960.

Hilton, M., *Consumerism in Twentieth Century Britain*, Cambridge, Cambridge University Press, 2003.

Hindess, B., 'Liberalism, socialism and democracy', in Barry, A., Osbourne, T. and Rose, N. (eds), *Foucault and Political Reason: Liberalism, neo-liberalism and rationalities of government*, London: UCL Press, 1996.

Hindley, B., *Industrial Merger and Public Policy*, London: Institute of Economic Affairs, 1970.

HM Treasury, *Employment Policy*, Cmnd 5527, HMSO, 1944,

Hoskyns, J., *Just in Time: Inside the Thatcher revolution*, London: Aurum, 2000.

Hoskyns, J. and Strauss, N., *Stepping Stones*, Oxford: Conservative Party Archive Bodleian Library, Box SC 15, 1977.

Howe, G., *Privatisation: the way ahead*, London: Conservative Political Centre, 1981.

Howe, G., *Conflict of Loyalty*, London: Macmillan, 1994.

Hughes, J. and Fabian Society, *An Economic Strategy for Labour*, London: Fabian Society, 1967.

Hutchison, T. and Institute of Economic Affairs, *Keynes Versus the 'Keynesians'?* London: Institute of Economic Affairs, 1977.

Hutt, W., *Politically Impossible? An essay on the supposed electoral obstacles impeding the translation of economic analysis into policy; or, why politicians do not take economic advice*, London: Institute of Economic Affairs, 1971.

Institute of Economic Affairs, *Growth Through Competition: an alternative to the national plan*. London: Institute of Economic Affairs, 1966.

Jay, P., *A General Hypothesis of Employment, Inflation and Politics*, London: Institute of Economic Affairs, 1976.

Jevons, W., *The Theory of Political Economy*, London: Macmillan, 1924.

Jewkes, J. and Institute of Economic Affairs, *Delusions of Dominance: a critique of the theory of large-scale industrial dominance and of the pretence of government to 'restructure' British industry*, London: Institute of Economic Affairs, 1977.

Johnson, H. et. al., *Memorial to the Prime Minister*. London: London School of Economics archive, 1972.

Joseph, K., *This is not the time to be mealy-mouthed: intervention is destroying us*, Margaret Thatcher Foundation. Online. Available at: www.margaretthatcher.org/document/110604 (accessed 9 May 2011), 1974.

Joseph, K., *Inflation is caused by governments*, Margaret Thatcher Foundation. Online. Available at: www.margaretthatcher.org/document/110607 (accessed 9 May 2011), 1974.

Joseph, K., *Monetarism is Not Enough*, London: Centre for Policy Studies, 1976.

Joseph, K., *Stranded On the Middle Ground? Reflections on circumstances and policies*, London: Centre for Policy Studies, 1976.

Joseph, K., *Conditions for Fuller Employment*, London: Centre for Policy Studies, 1978.

Joseph, K., *Solving the Union Problem Is the Key to Britain's Recovery*, London: Centre for Policy Studies, 1979.

Kalecki, M., 'The essence of the business upswing', in Kalecki, M., *Collected Works of Michal Kalecki, volume 1*. Oxford: Clarendon Press, 1990.

Keegan, W., *Mrs Thatcher's Economic Experiment*, Harmondsworth: Penguin, 1984.

Keegan, W., *Mr Lawson's Gamble*, London: Hodder and Stoughton, 1989.

Keynes, J., *Economic Consequences of the Peace*, London: Macmillan, 1919.

Keynes, J., *Essays in Persuasion*, New York: W.W. Norton, 1963.

Keynes, J., *The General Theory of Employment, Interest and Money*, Cambridge: Macmillan and Cambridge University Press, 1973 [1936].

King, M., 'Credit and economic policy', in *Bank of England quarterly bulletin*, vol. 34, 1994.

King, M., 'The inflation target five years on', in *Bank of England quarterly bulletin*, vol. 37, 1997, 434–7.

King, M., 'No money, no inflation – the role of money in the economy' in *Bank of England quarterly bulletin*, vol. 42, 2002.

King, M., 'Governor speech', in *Bank of England quarterly bulletin*, vol. 43, 2003.

King, M., *Monetary policy: practice ahead of theory*. Online. Available at: http://ww.bankofengland.co.uk/publications/speeches/2005/speech245.pdf (accessed 10 May), 2005.

King, M., *Governor speech*. Online. Available at: www.bankofengland.co.uk/publications/speeches/2006/speech263.pdf (accessed 9 May 2011), 2006.

King, W., 'The banking mechanism', in Seldon, A. (ed.), *Not Unanimous: a rival verdict to Radcliffe's on money*, London: Institute of Economic Affairs, 1960.

Knight, F., *Risk, Uncertainty and Profit*, Boston: Houghton Mifflin, 1921.

Knight, F., 'The ethics of competition', in *The Quarterly Journal of Economics*, vol. 37, 1923, 579–614.

Lachmann, L. and Institute of Economic Affairs, *Macro-economic Thinking and the Market economy: an essay on the neglect of the micro-foundations and its consequences*. London: Institute of Economic Affairs, 1973.

Laidler, D., *Fabricating the Keynesian Revolution*, Cambridge: Cambridge University Press, 1999.

Large, A., *Puzzles in Today's Economy – the build up of household debt*. Online. Available at: www.bankofengland.co.uk/publications/speeches/2004/speech217.pdf (accessed 9 May 2011), 2004.

Lash, S. and Urry, J., *Economies of Signs and Space*, London: Sage Publications, 1993.

Lawson, N., *The New Conservatism*, Margaret Thatcher Foundation. Online. Available at: www.margaretthatcher.org/document/109505 (accessed 9 May 2011), 1980.

Lawson, N., *Thatcherism in Practice: a progress report*, Margaret Thatcher Foundation. Online. Available at: www.margaretthatcher.org/document/109506 (accessed 9 May 2011), 1981.

Lawson, N., *Financial Discipline Restored*, London, Conservative Policy Centre, 1982.

Lawson, N., *The British Experiment*, Margaret Thatcher Foundation. Online. Available at: www.margaretthatcher.org/document/109504 (accessed 9 May 2011), 1984.

Lawson, N., 'The Chancellor's Speech', in Congdon, T., Minford, P. et al., *Whither Monetarism? The Chancellor's Mansion House speech, with comments by three wise men*, London: Centre for Policy Studies, 1985.

Lawson, N. and Institute of Economic Affairs, *The state of the Market*, 1988.

Lawson, N., *The View from No. 11: Memoirs of a Tory radical*, London: Bantam Press, 1992.

Lawson, N., *Appeal to Reason*, London: Duckworth Overlook, 2008.

Lees, D. and Institute of Economic Affairs, *Health Through Choice: an economic study of the British National Health Service*, London: Institute of Economic Affairs, 1961.

Leigh-Pemberton, R., 'Problems of monetary policy and change in the City', in *Bank of England quarterly bulletin*, vol. 25, 1985, 534–6.

Leigh-Pemberton, R., 'Financial change and broad money', in *Bank of England quarterly bulletin*, vol. 26, 1986, 499–507.

Leigh-Pemberton, R., 'The instruments of monetary policy', in *Bank of England quarterly bulletin*, vol. 27, 1987, 365–70.

Leigh-Pemberton, R., 'Personal credit in perspective', in *Bank of England quarterly bulletin*, vol. 28, 1988.

Leigh-Pemberton, R., 'Monetary policy, equity markets and the City's infrastructure', in *Bank of England quarterly bulletin*, vol. 29, 1989, 529–30.

Leigh-Pemberton, R., 'Monetary policy in the second half of the 1980s', in *Bank of England quarterly bulletin*, vol. 30, 1990, 215–20.

Leigh-Pemberton, R., 'Personal saving and borrowing, in *Bank of England quarterly bulletin*, vol. 30, 1990, 362–3.

Leigh-Pemberton, R., 'The Case for Price Stability', in *Bank of England quarterly bulletin*, vol. 32, 1992.

Leijonhufvud, A., *Keynes and the Classics: Two lectures on Keynes' contribution*, London: Institute of Economic Affairs, 1969.

Letwin, S. and Letwin, W., *Every Adult a Share-owner: the case for universal share ownership*, London: Centre for Policy Studies, 1986.

Levitin, A. and Wachter, S., *Explaining the Housing Bubble*, pp. 43–4. Online. Available at: http://ssrn.com/abstract=1669401 (accessed 19 March 2011), 2010.

Lilley, P. and Centre for Policy Studies, *Thatcherism: the next generation*, London: Centre for Policy Studies, 1989.

Lodge, O., Williams, S. et al., *A Review of the UK Banking Industry: a case study*, London: Centre for Policy Studies, 2002.

MacRae, N. and Institute of Economic Affairs, *To Let? A study of the expedient pledge on rents included in the Conservative election manifesto in October 1959*. London: Institute of Economic Affairs, 1960.

Marshall, A., *Principles of Economics*, London: Macmillan, 1920.

Mill, J., *Principles of Political Economy: with some of their applications to social philosophy*, London: Longmans, 1909.

Mill, J., *Essays on Some Unsettled Questions of Political Economy*, Whitefish: Kessinger Publishing, 2006.

Miller, D., *The Dialectics of Shopping*, Chicago: University of Chicago Press, 2001.

Miller, P. and Rose, N., 'Mobilising the consumer: assembling the subject of consumption' in *Theory, Culture and Society*, vol. 14, 1997, 1–36.

Miller, P. and Rose, N., *Governing the Present*, Cambridge: Polity Press, 2008.

Miller, R., Wood, J. et al., *Exchange Control for Ever?* London: Institute of Economic Affairs, 1979.

Minford, P., 'Consulting the oracle', in Congdon, T., Minford, P. et al., *Whither Monetarism? The Chancellor's Mansion House speech, with comments by three wise men*, London: Centre for Policy Studies, 1985.

Minford, P., 'The letter from 364 economists', in Booth, P. and Institute of Economic Affairs (eds), *Were 364 Economists All Wrong?* 2006.

Minford, P. and Institute of Economic Affairs, *The Supply-side Revolution in Britain*, Aldershot: Edward Elgar and Institute of Economic Affairs, 1991.

Mirowski, P., 'Twelve theses concerning the history of post war neoclassical price theory', in Mirowski, P. and Hands, D. (eds), *Agreement on Demand: Consumer theory in the Twentieth Century*, Durham: Duke University Press, 2006.

Mirowski, P., 'Defining neoliberalism', in Mirowski, P. and Plehwe, D. (eds), *The Road from Mont Pèlerin*, Cambridge: Harvard University Press, 2009.

Morgan, E. V., 'Money in theory', in Seldon, A. and Thorneycroft, P. (eds), *Not Unanimous: a rival verdict to Radcliffe's on money*, London: Institute of Economic Affairs, 1960.

Morgan, E. V. and Morgan, A., *Gold or paper? An essay on governments' attempts to manage the post-war monetary system, and the case for and against restoring a link with gold*, London: Institute of Economic Affairs, 1976.

Morgan, M., 'Economic man as model man: ideal types, idealization and caricatures', in *Journal of the History of Economic Thought*, vol. 28, 2006, 1–27.

Munby, D., *Home Ownership*. London: Fabian Society, 1957.

Nickel, S., *Household debt, house prices and consumption growth.* Online. Available at: www.bankofengland.co.uk/publications/speeches/2004/speech227.pdf (accessed 9 May 2011), 2004.

Novak, M. and Centre for Policy Studies, *The Crisis of the Welfare State: Ethics and economics*, London: Centre for Policy Studies, 1993.

Novak, M, Giddens, A. et al., *Is There a Third Way? Essays on the changing direction of socialist thought*, London: IEA Health and Welfare Unit, 1998.

O'Brien, L., 'Key issues in monetary and credit policy', in *Bank of England quarterly bulletin*, vol. 11, 1971.

O'Malley, P., *Risk, Uncertainty and Government*, London: GlassHouse, 2004.

Offer, A., *The Challenge of Affluence*, Oxford: Oxford University Press, 2006.

Olson, M., *Revisiting traditional paths to ownership*. Online. Available at: www.federalreserve.gov/boarddocs/speeches/2005/20050623/default.htm (accessed 9 September 2011), 1995.

Papps, I., *Government and Enterprise: an analysis of the economics of governmental regulation or control of industry*, London: Institute of Economic Affairs, 1975.

Parker, D., *The Official History of Privatisation, volume 1*, Abingdon: Routledge, 2009.

Pepper, G. and Oliver, M., *Monetarism Under Thatcher: Lessons for the future*, Northampton: Edward Elgar, 2001.

Pepper, G. and Wood, G., *Too Much Money? An analysis of the machinery of monetary expansion and its control*, London: Institute of Economic Affairs, 1976.

Pepper, G., Wood, G. et al., *Money, Credit and Inflation: an historical indictment of UK monetary policy and a proposal for change*, London: Institute of Economic Affairs, 1990.

Pinto, E., *Acorn and the housing bubble*. Online. Available at: http://online.wsj.com/article/SB10001424052748703298004574459763052141456.html (accessed 2 April 2011), 2009.

Plehwe, D., 'Introduction', in Mirowski, P. and Plehwe, D. (eds), *The Road from Mont Pèlerin*. Cambridge: Harvard University Press, 2009.

Polanyi, G., *Planning in Britain: the experience of the 1960s: a study of the theory and practice of planning in Britain and of the lessons of failure*, London: Institute of Economic Affairs, 1967.

Polanyi, K., *The Great Transformation*, Boston: Beacon Press, 2001 [1944].

Portillo, M. and Centre for Policy Studies, *The Blue Horizon*, London: Centre for Policy Studies, 1993.

Portillo, M. and Institute of Economic Affairs, *Democratic Values and the Currency*. London: Institute of Economic Affairs, 1998.

Powell, E. and Institute of Economic Affairs, *Saving in a Free Society*, London: Institute of Economic Affairs and Hutchinson, 1960.

Power, M., *The Audit Society*, Oxford: Clarendon Press, 1977.

Procacci, G., 'Social economy and the government of poverty', in Burchell, G., Gordon, C. and Miller, P. (eds), *The Foucault Effect: Studies in governmentality*, Chicago: University of Chicago Press, 1991.

Reagan, R., *Remarks on signing the Garn-St Germain Depository Institutions Act of 1982*. Online. Available at: www.reagan.utexas.edu/archives/speeches/1982/101582b.htm (accessed 2 February 2011), 1992.

Redwood, J., *Equity for Everyman: New ways to widen ownership*, London: Centre for Policy Studies, 1986.

Richardson, G., 'Speech by the Governor of the Bank of England', in *Bank of England quarterly bulletin*, vol. 13, 1973, 476–9.

Richardson, G., 'Speech by the Governor of the Bank of England', in *Bank of England quarterly bulletin*, vol. 19, 1979, 407–8.

Richardson, G., 'Speech by the Governor of the Bank of England', in *Bank of England quarterly bulletin*, vol. 20, 1980, 457–9.

Richardson, G., 'The banks' role in financing industry', in *Bank of England quarterly bulletin*, vol. 21, 1981, 77–8.

Richardson, G., 'The future of building societies', in *Bank of England quarterly bulletin*, vol. 23, 1983, 216–20.

Rifkind, M. and Centre for Policy Studies, *Conservative Britain in the 21st Century*, London: Centre for Policy Studies, 1996.

Robertson, D. and Institute of Economic Affairs, *A Market for Labour*, London: Barrie and Rockliff, 1961.

Rose, N., 'Governing "advanced" liberal democracies', in Barry, A., Osbourne, T. and Rose, N. (eds), *Foucault and Political Reason*, London: UCL Press, 1996.

Rose, N., *Powers of Freedom: Reframing political thought*, Cambridge: Cambridge University Press, 1999.

Schumpeter, J., *The Theory of Economic Development*, Cambridge: Harvard University Press, 1959.

Schumpeter, J., *Capitalism, Socialism and Democracy*, Abingdon: George Allen and Unwin, 1994 [1943].

Schwartz, A., 'Origins of the financial market crisis of 2008', in Booth, P., Alexander, P. et al., *Verdict on the Crash: Causes and policy implications*, London, Institute of Economic Affairs, 2009.

Seldon, A., 'Preface', in Allen, G., *The British Disease: a short essay on the nature and causes of the nation's lagging wealth*, London: Institute of Economic Affairs, 1976.

Seldon, A. and Thorneycroft, P. (eds), *Not Unanimous: a rival verdict to Radcliffe's on money*, London: Institute of Economic Affairs, 1960.

Sewill, B., 'In place of strikes', in Harris, R., Sewill, B. et al., *British Economic Policy 1970–74: Two views*, London: Institute of Economic Affairs, 1975.

Sirc, L., 'Worker's management under public and private ownership', in Chiplin, B., Coyne, J., Sirc, L. and Institute of Economic Affairs, *Can Workers Manage?* London: Institute of Economic Affairs, 1977.

Sowell, T., *Housing boom and bust*. Online. Available at: www.nationalreview.com/articles/227468/housing-boom-and-bust/thomas-sowell (accessed 2 April 2011), 2009.

Smith, A., *Wealth of Nations*, Amherst: Prometheus Books, 1991.

Snowden, K., 'Mortgage securitisation in the United States: twentieth century developments in historical perspective', in Bordo, M. and Sylla, R. (eds), *Anglo-American Financial Systems: Institutions and markets in the twentieth century*, 1995.

Stiglitz, J., *Globalisation and Its Discontents*, New York: W.W. Norton and Co, 2003.

Stewart, M., *Consumers' Councils: Based on investigations by local Fabian societies*, London: Fabian Society, 1953.

Taylor, J., *Getting Off Track*, Stanford: Hoover Institution, 2009.

Thaler, R. and Sunstein, A., *Nudge*, New Haven: Yale University Press, 2008.

Thatcher, M., 'Short term expediency: long term ruin?' in Thatcher, M., *Let Our Children Grow Tall: Selected speeches, 1975–1977*, London: Centre for Policy Studies, 1977.

Thatcher, M., 'The new Renaissance', in Thatcher, M., *Let Our Children Grow Tall: Selected speeches, 1975–1977*, London: Centre for Policy Studies, 1977.

Thatcher, M., 'Dimensions of Conservatism', in Thatcher, M., *Let Our Children Grow Tall: Selected speeches, 1975–1977*, London: Centre for Policy Studies, 1977.

Thatcher, M., 'Let our children grow tall', in Thatcher, M., *Let Our Children Grow Tall: Selected speeches, 1975–1977*, London: Centre for Policy Studies, 1977.

Thatcher, M., 'Let me give you my vision', in Thatcher, M., *Let Our Children Grow Tall: Selected speeches, 1975–1977*, London: Centre for Policy Studies, 1977.

Thatcher, M., 'The healthy society', in Thatcher, M., *Let Our Children Grow Tall: Selected speeches, 1975–1977*, London: Centre for Policy Studies, 1977.

Thatcher, M., 'The path to profitability', in Thatcher, M., *Let Our Children Grow Tall: Selected speeches, 1975–1977*, London: Centre for Policy Studies, 1977.

Thatcher, M., *There is no such thing as society*, Margaret Thatcher Foundation. Online. Available at: www.margaretthatcher.org/document/106689 (accessed 9 May 2011), 1987.

Thatcher, M., *The Downing Street Years*, London: HarperCollins, 1993.

Thatcher, M., *The Path to Power*, London: HarperCollins, 1995.

Thatcher, M. and Harris, K., *Margaret Thatcher talks to the Observer*, 1979, London: London School of Economics Archives.

364 Economists, 'Statement on economic policy', in Booth, P. and Institute of Economic Affairs (eds), *Were 364 Economists All Wrong?* 2006.

Titmuss, R. and Fabian Society, *Choice and 'the Welfare State'*, London: Fabian Society, 1967.

Tomlinson, J., 'Tale of a death exaggerated: how Keynesian policies survived the 1970s', in *Contemporary British History*, vol. 21, 2007, 429–48.

Trentmann, F., 'Beyond consumerism: new historical on consumption', *Journal of Contemporary History*, vol. 39, 2004, 373–401.

Trentmann, F., 'Knowing consumers – histories, identities, practices', in Trentmann, F., *The Making of the Consumer*, Oxford: Berg, 2006.

Trentmann, F., 'The modern genealogy of the consumer', in Brewer, J. and Trentmann, F. (eds), *Consuming Cultures, Global Perspectives: Historical trajectories, transnational exchanges*, Oxford: Berg, 2006.

Tucker, P., *Credit conditions and monetary policy*. Online. Available at: www.bankofengland.co.uk/publications/speeches/2003/speech201.pdf (accessed 9 May 2011), 2003.

Veblen, T., *The Engineers and the Price System*, New York: Kelley, 1965.

Veblen, T., *Essays in Our Changing Order*, London: Routledge, 1994 [1894].

Veblen, T., *The Theory of Business Enterprise*, London: Routledge, 1994.

Veblen, T. and Hobson, J., *The Theory of the Leisure Class: an economic study of institutions*, London: Routledge, 1899.

Veyne, P., 'Foucault revolutionises history', in Davidson, I. (ed.), *Foucault and His Interlocutors*, Chicago: University of Chicago Press, 1997.

Wallison, P., *Cause and effect: government policies and the financial crisis*. Online. Available at: www.aei.org/outlook/29015 (accessed 2 April 2011), 2008.

Walters, A., *Britain's Economic Renaissance: Margaret Thatcher's reforms, 1979–1984*, New York and Oxford: Oxford University Press, 1986.

Walters, A. and Institute of Economic Affairs, *Money in Boom and Slump: an empirical inquiry into British experience since the 1880s*, London: Institute of Economic Affairs, 1969.

Walters, W., *Unemployment and Government: Genealogies of the social*, Cambridge: Cambridge University Press, 2000.

Weber, M., 'Science as vocation', in Gerth, H. and Mills, C. (eds), *From Max Weber: Essays in sociology*, London: Routledge Kegan Paul, 1948.

Weber, M., 'Marginal utility theory and the fundamental law of psychophysics', in *Social Science Quarterly*, 56, 1975.

Weiss, M., 'Marketing and financing home ownership: mortgage lending and public policy in the United States, 1918–1989', in *Business and Economic History*, vol. 18, 1989, 109–15.

White, L., *How did we get into this financial mess*? Online. Available at: www.cato.org/pubs/bp/bp110.pdf (accessed 2 April 2011), 2008.

White, L., *Federal Reserve policy and the housing bubble*. Online. Available at: www.cato.org/pubs/journal/cj29n1/cj29n1–9.pdf (accessed 2 April 2011), 2009.

Wicksell, K., *Interest and Prices: a study of the causes regulating the value of money and the article, enigma of business cycles*, New York: Augustus M. Kelley, 1965 [1899].

Winch, D., *Economics and Policy*, London: Hodder and Stoughton, 1969.

Winch, D., 'The problematic status of the consumer in orthodox economic thought', in Trentmann, F. (ed.), *The Making of the Consumer*, Oxford: Berg, 2006.

Wilson, H. and Fabian Society, *Post-war Economic Policies in Britain*, London: Fabian Society, 1957.

Wood, G., 'Can 364 economists be wrong?' in Booth, P. (ed.), *Were 364 Economists All Wrong?* London: Institute of Economic Affairs, 2006.

Wood, J., 'The real lesson of Germany', in Chiplin, B., Coyne, J., Sirc, L. and Institute of Economic Affairs, *Can Workers Manage?* London: Institute of Economic Affairs, 1977.

Young, H., *One of Us: a biography of Margaret Thatcher*, London: Macmillan, 1989.

Zukin, S. and Dimaggio, P., 'Introduction'. in Zukin, S. and Dimaggio, P., (ed.), *Structures of Capital: the social organisation of the economy*, Cambridge: Cambridge University Press, 1990.

Index